BECOMING A
JEWISH
PARENT

ALSO BY DANIEL GORDIS

God Was Not in the Fire:
The Search for a Spiritual Judaism

Does the World Need the Jews?
Rethinking Chosenness and American Jewish Identity

BECOMING A
JEWISH
PARENT

HOW TO EXPLORE
SPIRITUALITY AND TRADITION
WITH YOUR CHILDREN

DANIEL GORDIS

 THREE RIVERS PRESS • NEW YORK

Published by Three Rivers Press, New York, New York.
Member of the Crown Publishing Group.

Random House, Inc. New York, Toronto, London, Sydney, Auckland
www.randomhouse.com

Three Rivers Press is a registered trademark and the Three Rivers Press
colophon is a trademark of Random House, Inc.

Originally published in hardcover by Harmony Books in 1999.

Printed in the United States of America
Design by Bonni Leon-Berman
Library of Congress Cataloging-in-Publication Data
Gordis, Daniel.
    Becoming a Jewish parent : how to explore spirituality and
    tradition with your children / by Daniel Gordis.
        Includes index.
        1. Child rearing—Religious aspects—Judaism.   2. Parenting—
    Religious aspects—Judaism.   3. Jewish religious education of
    children.   4. Jewish families—Religious life.   5. Fasts and feasts—
    Judaism.   I. Title.
    HQ769.3.G67   1999
    296.7′4—dc21   99-22784

ISBN 0-609-80526-6

10 9 8 7 6 5 4 3 2 1

First Paperback Edition

FOR OUR CHILDREN

טליה בת-שבע
אביאל מאיר
מיכה ראובן

יהי רצון שכל נטיעות
שנוטעים מכם יהיו כמוכם
(תענית ה:)

CONTENTS

IV
CONCLUSION
355

A FEW WORDS OF THANKS

This will be brief. Not because there aren't many thanks to offer, but because no words would really be adequate to express my gratitude to these people. Given that I can't thank them sufficiently, I'll thank them succinctly.

To Morton L. Mandel, Seymour Fox, Annette Hochstein, Alan Hoffmann, and Daniel Marom, my thanks for making my Mandel Fellowship, during which I wrote this book, both possible and as fulfilling as it has been. It's a gift for which I'll always be grateful.

Richard Pine is a phenomenal literary agent. He believed in this project from the outset, and offered ideas that made it a much better book than it would otherwise have been. I hope we work together for many years to come. Jessica Schulte is a superb editor. An absolute pleasure to work with, she's one of those people who have developed the perfect balance between being both critic and cheerleader. Jessica's ear for language and her sensitivity to the world of contemporary Jews and their struggles helped me find a voice for these pages when I began to go astray. Here's to future projects!

Jeni Friedman has been a partner in previous books, and I am very fortunate that she happened to be living in Jerusalem at the same time I was on sabbatical writing this book. For her reading the manuscript, her work on the glossary, and her great attention to detail, my thanks.

Shawn and Tom Fields-Meyer have read the manuscript of every book I've written. With three kids of their own and two professions to boot, it's never been clear to me how they make the time for all this. But they're terrific writers, thoughtful Jews, and great parents, so their ideas added much to what follows. More than anything, they're wonderful friends. To David and Ellen Chaikof, my thanks for a careful reading and many wonderful suggestions.

To the BDJ Boyz' in the Row—Albi, Bob, Josh, Jeff, Peter—my thanks for years of sharing war stories of agony and victory. Wouldn't it be great if we'd known everything we've learned the hard way when we first got started?

I started learning about Jewish parenting at a very early age—I had (and still have) great Jewish parents! My parents raised us in a home filled with love and books, in which Jewish life coexisted comfortably with the rest of the world, in which the big questions were always on the front burner, in which passion for things Jewish was always obvious. You can't ask for more.

It sounds self-evident to say that this book wouldn't have been possible without Beth, but it's true in ways that aren't obvious. Beth is not only the mother of my kids (in addition to being my wife), but she's the one who taught me that parenting is about looking at the big picture. I fell in love with her all over again as I "met" the mother in her when our daughter was born; I got another chance to see afresh what a thoughtful, intuitive, and caring human being she is and how fortunate I was to have met her that fateful Friday afternoon just about twenty years ago.

I've dedicated this book to our children—to Talia, Aviel, and Micha—because they're the ones who've taught us the most about parenting. They've been the victims of our mistakes, but also our partners in building a Jewish home. To our kids: I hope that someday you'll read this, say to yourselves "So *that's* what they were doing!" and decide that you'll continue the chain with your own children when the time comes. Ema and I marvel at the people you're already becoming, and more than you'll probably ever know, we love you.

January 1999
Rosh Chodesh Shevat 5758

I

SOME
INTRODUCTIONS

1

YES, YOU CAN DO THIS!

A couple of days after the Los Angeles riots of the early 1990s were over, my wife, Beth, and I decided to take our kids downtown to participate in the cleanup. Our children had been watching the riots on television for days, and I was worried by the fact that they seemed pretty detached from the scenes of buildings going up in flames, police officers having to protect firefighters, and National Guard troops patrolling a city that had basically gone mad. We felt they needed to see that these were real buildings that had been destroyed and real people who had been hurt. We wanted them to see for themselves the senseless destruction that hatred and poverty can cause.

So with a few other families we piled a whole bunch of brooms into our cars and drove to a section of the city our kids had never seen before. As we searched for a place to park and to join the thousands of others who'd come to help, my daughter (who was just learning to read) saw some words spray-painted on many of the doors. "What does 'Black Owned' mean?" she asked. Rather uncomfortable with what she was about to learn about the world, I took a deep breath and explained that the African-American owners of those stores had painted these words on the doors of their businesses so that the arsonists wouldn't burn their buildings down.

Tali was quiet for a minute or two. Then, seemingly out of nowhere, she said, "That's just like what the Jewish people did when they were getting ready to leave Egypt! Remember how God told us to put blood on the doorposts of our doors, so that the angel of death wouldn't hurt anyone in the Jewish people's houses?"

I have no recollection of what I said to Talia then, but I do remember being stunned. *I* hadn't made any such association! Surveying the devastation of the city in which I lived, Bible stories were the farthest thing from my mind. But a story Tali had learned in nursery school or kindergarten had suddenly come alive for her and had given her a way to understand the horror and sadness of what she was seeing. Faced with something she couldn't explain, she had reached deep into her collection of Jewish myth and knowledge for a way to make some sense of the burnt wreckage surrounding her.

And I thought to myself, "Something's working." This was a child whose Jewish self was not just a separate and detached part of who she was; this wasn't a girl for whom being Jewish was only about certain "stuff" that she did. Rather, this was a little girl for whom being Jewish touched everything; it gave perspective to much of what she saw and a way to reflect even on those things that didn't make sense. Even at the age of five or six, this was a kid for whom being Jewish was simply who she was.

I remember feeling grateful at that moment. Grateful that I'd married a woman who was such a fantastic mother and terrific Jewish role model, grateful that we'd found a school that could make these stories come alive for our daughter, grateful that we lived in a supportive community of friends who shared many of our values and who were raising their kids in much the same way we were, grateful that my own parents had taught my siblings and me a great deal about how to make Judaism rich and vibrant for little kids, grateful that we were lucky to have a child who responded to the "music" of Jewish life, for whom these stories and this way of living spoke in such a powerful and even intimate way.

And beyond being grateful, I remember realizing at that moment—perhaps for the first time—what a gift all of us can give our kids when we show them and teach them that being Jewish is *about* something, that it's more than just a bunch of holidays or quaint ethnic practices. Living a rich Jewish life, filled with meaning and substance, is something many people of our generation didn't grow up with, but often, that is exactly what we want for our kids. Making Jewish life compelling, rich, meaningful, and close to the center of who our children are is what Jewish parenting is all about. It's also what this book is all about.

JEWISH PARENTING— NOT AS SCARY AS IT SOUNDS

"Jewish parenting." Sound difficult, overwhelming, a little scary? If these feelings are familiar as you contemplate the prospect of being a Jewish parent, rest assured you're not alone. Lots of us feel the same way. We have the sense that we're very competent when it comes to raising kids in general, teaching them and creating safe, warm, and nurturing homes for them. We know that we've got what it takes to do a good job.

Yet when we turn our attention to the Jewish side of parenting, our self-confidence begins to evaporate. We're flooded with questions and doubts—not just about our kids, but about ourselves and our own feelings about being Jewish. What's being Jewish really all about? we ask ourselves. What does it mean to be a Jew? And while many of us have thought about these questions at various times throughout our lives, we didn't have to *really* find an answer before. Now that we're parents, we know someone else is going to ask *us* and expect us to have the answers.

And there are other questions: How can I raise my children to care about being Jewish and to understand what it has to offer if I didn't get that when I was growing up? What do I do if I've had no real models for Jewish parenting? Can I raise my kids with pride in their Jewishness if I'm still ambivalent about my own Jewish feelings? I'm a single parent—can I really pull this off without a mom *and* a dad in the same house? I don't speak or read Hebrew, and the holidays basically confuse me—can I still be a decent Jewish parent if I don't know all that much? I'm not the parent; I'm the grandparent. Is there any way *I* can have a positive impact on my grandkids' Jewish lives?

These are all understandable doubts. Lots of people have them. But yes, not only can you do a good job of Jewish parenting (or Jewish grandparenting), but you can do a great job. You can be a great Jewish parent regardless of how you grew up. You don't have to be an expert about Judaism to help your kids come to love being Jewish. And no, you don't have to have all your ambivalence about Jewish life worked out before you get started. Nor is there one way or style that is "right." As in all sorts of parenting issues, each of us has to find the way that works for us, that feels right, that speaks to us, to our partners, and to our children. The purpose of this book is to help you do that.

JEWISH PARENTING IS JUST LIKE PARENTING!

Jewish parenting, no matter what your background, is nothing to fear. That's because Jewish parenting is not any different from other forms of parenting. It is not terribly difficult, yet doing it well takes thought, planning, and care. So, to begin our journey into the world of Jewish parents, it's probably worthwhile remembering what it was that we did—or are still doing—to become good parents in general.

Do you remember that moment when you first found out that you were going to be a parent? It might have been at the doctor's office, or it might have been in a phone call from the doctor. More and more these days, it's the results from a home pregnancy test. But no matter how you first found out, you probably did lots of the same things other people did. You may have gone to a bookstore and started collecting books about pregnancy, delivery, child care, and other related subjects. You probably talked with friends who'd already had children, making mental notes of the things they told you that worked and those that didn't. You started looking out for the kinds of equipment you thought you'd need. You probably also began to relive your own childhood, remembering those aspects of your parents' parenting style that you wanted to emulate, and those you wanted to avoid at virtually all cost. In all, your entire being began to focus on being a prepared parent. Even before your child was born, you were parenting.

What this book is going to help you do, is to begin that same process for the realm of *Jewish* parenting. Jewish parenting is a lot like parenting in general. There's advice to collect, "stuff" to get, books to begin to gather. There's a lifetime of memories—pleasant and not—to recall and to sift through. Did we like the way our parents taught us about being Jews? Did we learn enough? Was being Jewish a source of joy? And if we're Jews by choice, does the way we were raised in our former faith have anything to tell us about how we'd like to raise our own kids?

Like parenting in general, Jewish parenting can be fun, exhilarating, and, of course, even a little trying at times. Just as being a decent parent in general means thinking through who and what we want our children to be, to be good Jewish parents we have to begin to imagine what kind of Jews we'd like our kids to be. If we're to be good parents in general, we need to know what's important to us—ethics, art, literature, fun, sports, family, politics—and we've got to figure out how to transmit that to our children (and grandchildren). It's the same in the world of Jewish parenting. We can't just assume that our kids will figure this out on their own. We need a pretty clear vision of what's important to *us* about Jewish parenting, so we will know what we want to transmit.

And that's the focus of this book: the "big ideas" that make Judaism what it's all about. Of course, we're going to talk about specific things to do for holidays, life cycle events, and the like. But we're going to look carefully at how to figure out for ourselves what being Jewish is all about, so we can plan our Jewish parenting (or grandparenting) carefully and thoughtfully.

JEWISH PARENTING IS ALSO ABOUT OUR OWN JOURNEY

As is true with all big issues in parenting, thinking about being a Jewish parent will get us to think about being Jewish ourselves. As we teach our children, we, too, will grow. This isn't just their journey, but ours as well. If we do this right, it can be a journey that we travel with our children, bringing us close in ways we can only begin to imagine now. With this book, we'll figure out this journey together and transform it from a frightening dimension of parenting to one filled with excitement, wonder, mystery, and joy.

Some of the excitement, wonder, and joy will come from exploring what being Jewish is all about. "What is Judaism?" is a question Jews have wrestled with for centuries. Is it a religion? A culture? A people? A "tribe"? A nation? Truth is, of course, it's all of those, and more. This is one of those rare cases where the sum of the parts is not greater than the whole. For even if we were to label all of the "parts," the "whole" would still be greater. There would still be something magical about being Jewish that would be beyond explanation. That's why some of us feel connected to

Jews in other parts of the world even though they are completely different from us. They may speak different languages than we do, the Jewish customs they observe might be totally foreign to us, and they may even believe things that trouble us. Nonetheless, we feel connected. That's why some people, often completely disconnected from Jewish life, get to Israel and are overwhelmed by a feeling of belonging that they've never felt anywhere else. It's why as angry as some Jews get with their tradition, it's very hard to walk away.

We get nervous when we hear that things like Jewish life can have a power we can't describe. There's a hocus-pocus quality to the claim that our rational, thinking minds just can't tolerate. But let's remember, most of the things that make life really wonderful can't be easily explained. Why is being at the edge of Niagara Falls such an unbelievably powerful experience? Why is the beach so mesmerizing? Why can we just stare at the water for hours on end, never getting tired of watching it?

Or love. Why can falling in love with someone change everything when we can't even explain why we love them, or what love is? Why does having a lover—if we're lucky enough to find somebody to share our life with—make life so much fuller? Why do we love our kids so selflessly and passionately when we don't even know what kinds of people they're going to be? And why do we love them so intensely even when they disappoint us?

The parts of our lives that are often the most powerful and meaningful often defy explanation, but that doesn't make them any less important or real. And the same is true of being Jewish. For many of us, it's a part of who we are that just won't disappear, no matter what. It's about lots of things. It's about sharing a history, a sense of purpose, a unique place to belong in a vast and shifting world. For some of us, it's about the Jewish idea that people, even if not numerous or powerful, can make a difference and can survive against incredible odds. It's about hope, about possibility. It might be about pride—in the Jewish state, in our traditions, in the ethics by which we try to live.

It's really like love. We know it's real even if we can't define it. And we can't run away from it. What we need to do is to cherish it and to make it a joyful and passionate part of our lives.

That's why our children are such a wonderful gift. In giving us occasion to "figure out" the Jewish part of our lives, they give us the chance to fall in love all over again.

THE CHALLENGES WE'LL FACE
THAT OUR PARENTS DIDN'T

But at the same time, we can't parent well if we're not going to be honest. If we're not willing to confront the reality of the world our children are going to encounter, we can't prepare them for it. They're going to have to make serious choices about friends, relationships, sex, drugs, schools, and interests; our job as parents is to prepare them for it. The same is true of Jewish life. We can't prepare our kids for a meaningful Jewish life unless we're willing to be honest about the world in which they're going to grow up as Jews.

So let's be honest. It's a lot tougher today to ensure that our kids will grow up to be committed Jews in the United States, Canada, and elsewhere than it was just a generation or two ago. Ironically, that's because the world our children (or our grandchildren) will confront is no longer hostile to Jewish people, Jewish ideas, or Jewish tradition. In the "old days," when we could rely on the secular world harboring some negative feelings about Jews, Jewish parents could assume that their children's Jewish identities would be reinforced by a hostile outside world. But today, no one is going to remind our kids that they're Jewish. They'll be able to work in virtually any law firm, business, professional office; join almost any social organization; live in any neighborhood; choose any way of life—regardless of their Jewish heritage. This attitude is both good news and bad.

It's good news, of course, because that kind of openness is exactly the kind of freedom and tolerance Jews just a generation or two ago didn't dare believe could ever be possible. But it's also the bad news because it means that it's going to be harder to ensure that our children remember they're Jewish. The outside world isn't going to remind them, so we have to raise them in a way that will teach them to love being Jewish. Being Jewish isn't something that will be forced on them; we have to make sure that it's something they'll want to choose.

That's going to take a lot more thought and investment than many of our parents devoted to Jewish parenting. Our parents, or certainly our grandparents, could count on distinctly Jewish neighborhoods, in which Jewish language, holidays, mannerisms, and even neuroses created an automatic sense of Jewishness among the people who lived together. In that generation, it wasn't uncommon for multiple generations of families to live in close proximity; kids would grow up near their grandparents, whose kitchens were filled with the scents of Jewish cooking, whose accents made clear where they had come from, and whose entire beings were palpably Jewish. Even if the parents were somewhat disconnected from or ambivalent about Jewish life, the grandparents were enough to let the children know who and what they were.

But those disconnected, ambivalent parents are today's grandparents. The sounds and scents of Eastern Europe, or Morocco, no longer pervade the kitchens and homes of the new generation of grandparents. And most kids today don't even live as close to their grandparents as kids once did. So "live and let live" isn't going to work. Today, Jewish parenting requires a conscious decision, a determination to help our children learn and love the tradition that is theirs.

Our honesty about Jewish parenting has to extend to another area as well. We know something that our parents' generation may not have understood as clearly: Home is the place our kids will learn to love being Jewish. Many of our parents believed that if they sent us to Hebrew school (religious school, afternoon school—call it what you will, it was all basically the same!), we'd come out Jewish "enough." The school was to be the substitute. Our parents themselves didn't feel the need to actually live the traditions we learned about in school; nor did they feel hypocritical about dealing with our Jewish upbringing that way. It was what everyone was doing, and no one at that point had any real reason to believe it wasn't going to work.

But today we know a lot more. We know, first of all, that lots of Jewish schools aren't that great at instilling a positive view of Jewish life in our kids. (That's why I devote some time later in this book to picking Jewish schools, and what to look for.) And we know that there has to be at least some continuity between what gets taught in school and what happens at home. We know, too, that we can't "outsource" our kids' Jewish development.

Outsourcing, though no one ever called it that, is precisely what a whole generation of parents did with their children's Jewish education and development. They believed that a little schooling, an occasional visit to a synagogue, and, in a very few cases, a trip to Israel would "take care of" their kids' Jewish identification. But think about it for a second. Is that what we do with any other part of our kids' lives?

If we want them to love music, are we content to simply send them to a music lesson once or twice a week? No. Those lessons might be part of the picture, but we certainly don't leave it to lessons alone. We carefully choose our children's music teachers, and we make sure they practice. If our kids' loving music is important to us, then we probably make sure music is heard at home on a regular basis; we'll play music in the car as a matter of principle, and we'll probably take them to concerts. We want our children to see how important music is to us, so we integrate it into the fabric of our lives, hoping that some of that love will be instilled in them.

Or take our children's moral and ethical development. Would it ever occur to us that we should outsource *that*? Would twice-weekly "morality" classes do it? Obviously not! We know that if we want our children to grow up to be decent, moral people, the brunt of the work needs to be done at home. They'll learn lots more from watching us interact with our friends, our coworkers, people who call on the phone, than from any lectures we give them. And in fact, it's precisely *because* our children's moral fiber is so important to us that we are hesitant to let anyone else have that sort of influence on them. When we really care about something that relates to our children, we want to do it ourselves.

The same has to be true of their Jewish selves. So it's up to us to make the difference, and the purpose of this book is to show you how.

WE'RE ALL IN THIS TOGETHER

When we start a new project, especially something that might make us a bit nervous, it's nice to have partners, to know that we're not alone. That's why it's important to realize that no matter how much we do or don't know, no matter what kind of Jew we might call ourselves, we're really partners with all other Jewish parents. There are no easy answers here, and none of the Jewish denominations (or "movements") have it all figured out. Thus, this is not a book for Reform Jews, Reconstructionist Jews, Conservatives or Orthodox. This is a book for Jewish parents—all of us. You'll note that throughout this book I try very hard to avoid using terms like Orthodox, Conservative, Reconstructionist, and Reform.

The reason is simple: Labels like those give us excuses to ignore the commitments of people who are different from us, and labels are often excuses for focusing on our differences instead of what we have in common. All Jewish parents today face similar challenges, even though the specifics of their communities create variations. In the hope that Jews of all stripes will learn to work as partners in raising a generation of children who care deeply about being Jewish, our conversation will stay away from denominational names except when some description absolutely requires them.

So, forget the titles, forget the labels. We're all in this together. And if we're fortunate, we'll discover that there's no one right way to do this. The goal is to learn—from our tradition, from our partners, from our kids, and from each other.

2

HOW TO USE THIS BOOK

Chances are, no matter why you wanted to read this book, no matter what first prompted you to pull it off the shelf, you don't have lots of extra time on your hands. So it's important for you to know that there are several ways to use this book. Very quickly, let's outline a few of the major possibilities.

THE FIRST POSSIBILITY:
READ THE WHOLE BOOK

Obviously, it's your book. If you want to read the whole thing, why, that's perfectly fine! In the book you'll find two kinds of chapters. The first major section of the book, the "Big Ideas" section, approaches Jewish parenting from a theoretical perspective. Though there are practical suggestions throughout, these chapters talk about ideas like creating memories, helping to shape our children's identity, rethinking the role of God in their lives, and many more.

After the "Big Ideas" section comes a kind of "Reference Guide" section that addresses the major Jewish holidays, the life cycle events, and Jewish history.

If you've got the time, and are interested in the broadest possible picture of Jewish parenting, then just start at the beginning and read through. Hit a section that seems to cover stuff you already know, or aren't interested in? Skip it. Each chapter is written so that it should make sense whether or not you've read what came immediately before.

A BETTER IDEA?
DON'T READ THE WHOLE BOOK!

The fact that each chapter is written so that it could stand on its own means that you have another important option: Don't read the whole book! Sound strange? Admittedly, most books don't begin by telling you that you don't have to read the whole thing. Those books assume that unless you read the whole thing, they simply won't make sense. And so we are expected to read them from beginning to end.

But there are exceptions to that—dictionaries and encyclopedias, for example. This book, of course, is neither. A better analogy for this book is one of those third-party books on how to use a piece of computer software. If you're brand new to the program, and really want to know how to use it well, you might decide to read the whole thing, page by page, skimming perhaps those sections that are less relevant to what you want to learn. But if you know the program a little already, you probably won't read the entire book. Instead, you'll check out the contents and index to find the information you need at a particular moment. Over the course of time, you might actually end up reading most of the book, but you'll do it as you need each piece of information.

This book can work for you in much the same way. You can read it from beginning to end, but you don't have to.

Some of you reading this book are new to Jewish life. You may have bought this book just before one of the holidays, and want to get to that material right away. It might be Hanukkah, and you're interested in a more sophisticated explanation of the holiday than what you've been able to give your kids thus far. No problem, just go to the holiday chapter and look it up, or find all the references to Hanukkah in the index. Or you and your kids may have been invited to what you know is going to be a reasonably traditional Jewish wedding and you want to learn a bit about weddings so you'll know what to expect. No problem, you can simply look up the section on weddings and go right to the basics.

On the other hand, you may have grown up with a rich Jewish background. The holidays are pretty familiar to you, so you don't feel you need much of the background material provided in that section. Instead, you're interested in a broader discussion of why holidays matter in Jewish life, perhaps so you can talk about these issues with your friends and family—or even your children. Or your daughter is growing up, and suddenly issues of gender are more important to you than they were before. On each of these issues, and for lots of others, there is a chapter that raises the major issues to begin thinking about.

TREAT THIS BOOK AS YAHOO.COM

Now that the Internet has made its way into most of our lives, many of us are accustomed to using a search engine like Yahoo. A search engine is where you go in order to find places that can provide information you need. The same is true with this book. There's a big section at the end called "Suggestions for Further Exploration." That section is organized according to the chapters in this book. If you're interested in more information on a certain subject, just look at that chapter's section in "Suggestions for Further Exploration." Here you'll find suggestions of books, software for kids and adults, Web sites to check out, and much more.

Not sure where something is covered in this book? No problem, there's a pretty detailed table of contents at the beginning, and a long index at the back. Either one should help you find what you want quickly and easily.

THERE'S A MINI-DICTIONARY, TOO

One of the things that is often overwhelming in Jewish life is the number of terms that seem so unfamiliar. Judaism's a pretty complex business, and since Jews have conducted their business in Hebrew, Aramaic, Yiddish, and lots of other languages, there can be many strange terms. Don't let that overwhelm you. Many words that may be new to you appear in **bold.** If you find one and want to know what it means, turn to the Glossary at the back.

Months from now, if you're reading something about Jewish life and you don't know what it means, try the Glossary in this book. It won't have everything you'll ever want to know, but it'll be a start.

NO READER HAS TO BE AN ISLAND

Another point. When we read a book, we do it alone. Sure, we might read a paragraph we particularly liked to someone who happens to be around at the moment, but generally, we think of reading as a solitary process.

Try something different here. One of the most comforting things about beginning our journey into Jewish parenting is learning that there are other parents struggling with exactly the same issues we are. So why not organize a "Jewish parents' book club," and work through the book together. Before Hanukkah, read the Hanukkah section and share ideas for what you're each going to do. During the "dry seasons," when there are no Jewish holidays, try the theoretical chapters.

Sometimes you'll be talking about the book. At other times you might never get to it. Just having a group of people who are thinking about similar things will give you support, ideas, and energy—and the group will have served its purpose.

SOME CONCLUDING THOUGHTS

Remember that this book is here to help you. Use it as you see fit. You are the person who is going to make a difference in the Jewish lives of the children you touch. Don't forget that you're a competent person, good at what you do. The same is going to be true of your Jewish parenting style—you just have to give yourself a chance to think about what it is you're trying to accomplish and how you're going to get there.

Too often, when we think about Judaism, we imagine that there's stuff we're "supposed" to do. When it comes to this book, forget all that! This is your book; it's your tool to help you on your journey.

II

THE BIG IDEAS

3

"JEWISH PARENTING 101"
Immersion, Memories, and Identity

What does it mean to be a Jewish parent? What is a Jewish parent really supposed to do? Are we supposed to celebrate the holidays with our children? Send them to Hebrew school? Find a Jewish summer camp for them? Teach them about Israel? Maybe even take them to Israel?

These are tough questions; probably unanswerable for many of us. But even when we know a question doesn't have easy or clear answers, we sometimes can't help trying to find one. In this chapter we offer a very quick (but not so simple) answer to the question of what Jewish parenting is.

Simply put, Jewish parenting is about immersion, memories, and identity. In other words, the job of Jewish parents is to create a Jewish home where there are enough ongoing Jewish moments (immersion) so that our children will remember their childhood years as deeply Jewish (memory) and will ultimately come to see being Jewish as an integral part of who they are (identity).

Now, this may sound very theoretical. And you may be wondering or saying to yourself, "I didn't want all this theoretical stuff! I just want someone to tell me—in simple language—what are the things I or we can do to raise our kids to care about being Jewish."

But being told "what to do when" is not enough. Understanding why we do what we do gives us an extremely rich, limitless entry into our traditions, our history, and our future. Jewish parenting will be much less enjoyable—and probably much less effective—if we simply lurch from decision to decision, holiday to holiday, moment to moment, deciding each time what to do and what not to do. If we're to make this journey a successful and meaningful one, we need to have a theoretical basis for what it is we're doing and why.

JUDAISM AT THE CORE

Our goal as Jewish parents is to make being Jewish central to our kids' identities. Effective Jewish parenting means raising our children in such a way that they come to see being Jewish as "who they are," as "the kind of people they were raised to be." If we're effective as Jewish parents, our children's Jewishness will be as important to them as their gender, their nationality, and their most basic moral commitments. But getting them to that place is going to take a lot of work. And that work is what we're calling "immersion."

To get a sense of the kind of investment this is going to require of us, let's consider for a moment how our children develop values and identities in other areas. As they grow, our children come to see themselves as having certain traits that are simply so obvious that they don't require thought. They will be either girls or boys, women or men; there will be no way for them to think of themselves without their gender being a natural and central part of how they think about themselves. As they grow up and learn more about the community in which they live, they will come to see themselves as members of some national group. Their political views, their beliefs about the world, and their cultural interests will often derive from their sense of the national community to which they belong.

Our children will also develop moral sensibilities as they grow up. They will come to understand that certain things are fundamentally right or wrong, and when asked why, their beliefs will be so much a part of who they are that they'll think the question is silly. (That's the "identity" part of our "big picture.") "Why do I give to United Way? I don't know; it's just something I can't imagine not doing. The only thing I don't understand is why anyone would *not* give to the United Way!" "Why would I never mistreat another person just because of the color of his skin? What kind of question is that? That's just not who I am, the kind of person I was raised to be."

We have to raise our children to feel and believe that being Jewish is about being the kind of person they were raised to be, and the kind of person they want to be.

THE CHALLENGE
OF CONTEMPORARY AMERICA

There's another reason why it's important to have a very clear idea of the overall "game plan": Jewish parenting is probably more difficult today than it's ever been; there is so much else in the world that competes for our kids' time, attention, allegiance, loyalty. All kids grow up trying to fit in, wanting to be part of the larger group, a certain style of living. They learn about these choices from TV, radio, magazines, movies, billboards, and the other kids at school. Access to the Internet means our kids can learn about virtually anything, anytime, anywhere. There is no dimension of life that is off-limits to them. In their own quest for identity, what might seem to us like a crazy fad or a dangerous trend sounds to them like a good way to carve out something to stand for, someone to be.

The culture of America is so pervasive and so powerful that it seems to crowd out everything else. Music, clothes, jewelry, language styles, sexual behavior, choices of friends—these are the things that become important to our kids as they decide what group they want to be part of. In the midst of all this, will being Jewish feel very important?

The answer is that being Jewish will be important to them only if we communicate the sense that Judaism isn't just something that we *do,* it's something that we *are.* Jewish life isn't simply a set of activities; if it were, our kids would only have to choose whether to do those things or not. What constitutes Judaism has to be part of the very core of our being—what we feel a part of, the ethical tradition that speaks to us, the history that gives us pride, the state that seems so miraculous only a few decades after the Nazi smokestacks were still smoking, the intellectual tradition that excites and challenges us, the community that comforts and engages us.

Of course, our children will inevitably choose to do many things differently from how we did them, and what *we* like about Jewish life might not be what speaks to them. That's part of their growing up and becoming an individual. Indeed, it's what we want. But our job in the meantime is to immerse them in Jewish life, and by so doing, to create memories of meaningful Jewish moments. Still, this is not easy. Pop culture and each new fad seems to overwhelm our efforts in the not-so-subtle competition for our kids' attention. So, if America is so inviting, and being Jewish means being a bit different, our children have every reason to want to fit into the pop culture, which they will perceive as being "less Jewish." That's what we're up against. Can we create real Jewish identity in our kids without having them reject the world around them? If we could—and I believe that we can—we can win the battle to create for our kids both serious engagement with the world around us and passionate Jewish commitment and identity. It's a tall order perhaps, but it's definitely possible.

FORGING IDENTITY—THE ROLE OF IMMERSION

Yes, we can win, but we have to figure out how to wage the battle. As Jewish parents, we need to forge a plan to counteract the forces that seek to pull our kids away from Jewish life. That's why "immersion" is so important.

Over the course of time, our kids come to think of themselves as boy/girl, American/Canadian, part of a family, a citizen of a city, etc. How does this happen? Society immersed them in experiences that reminded them of and reinforced those aspects of their identity. Our challenge is to do the same with Jewish life.

How do we do that? The answer, as we've said, is "Jewish immersion." Our goal as Jewish parents has to be to surround our children with Jewish life, to have Jewish symbols, music, books, ideas, words, people, and much more so pervade their lives that they cannot imagine living without that Jewishness as part of their world.

Does that seem a little overwhelming? Does it make you wonder if you're going to so smother your children with Jewish life that they'll be too shielded from the rest of the world, or come to resent being Jewish? Every Jewish parent who thinks that the non-Jewish world is also valuable, wonderful, and worth learning from inevitably worries that giving our children a deep sense of their Jewishness might pull them away from the world around them. But that is not what we want; we want our children to have both.

Before we tackle the problem of how to keep our Jewish immersion in balance with our openness to the rest of the world, let's make sure we understand why immersion is important in the first place. To do that, let's look briefly at some of the other forms of immersion present in our children's lives.

Immersion and Our Children's Gender

Take gender, for example. How do our children come to know and express what it means to be a girl or a boy? The answer is immersion. Virtually every clothing store, TV show, and magazine shows how Americans think boys and girls ought to speak, behave, dress.

In many ways, our society is much less comfortable with this idea than it used to be. Many of us try hard to get beyond the notion of which toys are for girls and which are for boys; we're glad that our culture has begun to shatter the notion that dolls are only for girls and trucks are only for boys. We're trying to teach our daughters to have concepts of what they can accomplish as adults that are even more radical than we had as children, and we're asking boys to see both themselves and girls differently than was the case even a generation ago.

But our discomfort with classic gender roles notwithstanding, the simple and undeniable truth is that children's gender is critical to who they are and to how they see themselves, and that in a myriad of subtle ways, society communicates to our kids what it means to be a girl or a boy.

Every time a little girl goes to nursery school, she sees how the other girls are dressed, and she notices the differences between the girls and the boys. She sees how girls play and interact with each other and the kinds of relationships they form. Boys see the same thing in the world of boys. Boys and girls also watch their fathers and mothers; they see how their parents talk to each other, how they each speak with their friends. Children see what their parents do during the day. They see what they do to relax. And throughout all this, these daughters and sons begin to intuit what it means to be a girl, and what it means to be a boy. What might we call this process of children learning what it means to be male and female? Immersion.

Now, you might say: "Of course her gender is critical to who my daughter is. But Judaism is not nearly as clear. You can't deny your gender, but we certainly can move away from Jewish life!"

On one level that's completely true. But it doesn't undermine the importance of immersion as much as we might suspect. Let's take another example: our children's coming to know that they are Americans. How do our kids come to sense that their being American is central to who they are? Again, the answer is immersion.

Immersion and Citizenship

Children come to see themselves as American because they are inundated with the symbols and content of American life from their very earliest memories. The flags around the neighborhood at Memorial Day, the Fourth of July, or other holidays remind children where they live. The stamps pasted on the letters they send and receive do the same. So, too, do the tiny flags painted on their toy space shuttles, rockets, and planes. The post office has flags. Official mail from the state or city often has some symbol.

As kids get older, they often accompany their parents to the voting booth. They learn the pledge of allegiance, and they hear, at every baseball game—at almost every sport played in the United States—the national anthem. Almost all the people they know are Americans. Most of the holidays they celebrate are American. They have a Thanksgiving dinner, a Fourth of July barbecue, a family trip on Presidents' Day.

As they watch international sports competitions, the broadcast they see is for Americans. The games shown are the ones American are the most interested in. Profiles of American athletes are highlighted. The American total of medals is a constant focus as the Olympic tallies are computed each day. It's clear who the audience is, and our kids learn from that, too.

And, of course, our children learn to read and to understand the world. The newspapers they look at, the television news they watch, the radio shows the listen to—all these see the world from the perspective of the United States. Our children's language may be English, but it's not the English spoken in Britain. It's our own, and our children hear the difference. Even the English spoken in Canada is just different enough, both in accent and spelling, to alert our children to the distinction.

The point is that what makes a child feel American is not one lesson in school or one particular custom or practice at home. It's a veritable flood of images, ceremonies, attitudes, and experiences that together create a sense of loyalty and identity.

Politics and Sports—The Immersion Continues

Let's look at a few examples that are a bit less far-reaching than citizenship. Take political activism, for example. There are parents for whom it is terribly important that their children become politically aware. Such parents create a home in which the children are immersed in politics. The magazines that came to the house. The television shows they watch. The conversation around the dinner table. Many of these children have very early memories (we'll come back to memory very soon) of working on campaigns as kids. They gave out bumper stickers; perhaps, as they grew older, they answered phones or canvassed neighborhoods.

The same could be said of sports. Homes in which parents are rabid sports fans are easy to spot. They have cable with a zillion sports channels. A game is always on the screen. The magazines that come in the mail are about sports, the part of the newspaper that gets grabbed first is the sports section, the conversation around the house is about one team or another. The garage is filled with paraphernalia of this game or that, and the trunk of the car is probably no different.

This is, quite simply, immersion. A huge portion of what the kids in the house see and hear expresses the parents' love of that subject, whether it be politics, sports, or whatever. A child growing up in either of these homes gets a very clear message, very early on, about what is ultimately important and worthy of their time.

～

Jewish parenting also has to be a matter of "flooding" our children's lives with ceremonies, celebrations, books, ideas, memories, and such, all of which will create a sense of Jewish pride, Jewish loyalty, and Jewish identity.

Jewish Parenting as Immersion

Immersion communicates passion, love, and devotion. And as we'll see down the road, it doesn't have to crowd out everything else. After all, those homes in which politics is a virtual religion don't necessarily crowd everything out. And people who are crazy about sports aren't necessarily people who don't care about other things. They might also like music, love travel, be well read. Passion for one part of life does not have to mean disregarding others. Quite often, in fact, people who are passionate about one thing tend to carry that passion into other areas. Immersion does not mean "tunnel vision," but it is one of the keys to serious Jewish parenting, for it's immersion that communicates to our children a sense that this subject (being American, caring about politics, loving sports) is critical, important, worthy of their time.

Now think about how many American Jewish parents raise their kids as committed Jews. Would you call it immersion?! Hardly. In fact, it seems to be precisely the opposite. In too many Jewish homes, there's no passion about Jewish life. Parents outsource their kids' Jewish upbringing, communicating a sense (often unintentionally) that they themselves don't really care about it all that much. Why should children enjoy Hebrew school or think being Jewish is important if they never sees their parents express any passion for things Jewish? Would it make any sense to take your kids to a ball game but not go in yourself because you don't enjoy going? It might be okay, of course, but the chances are they'll pick up on your disinterest and lose theirs. Could you teach your kids to love music if you sent them to music lessons, bought them tickets to concerts, but never once showed them that you enjoyed music, that you share the love you want them to develop?

Again, it's not out of the question that such children would come to love music, but it's certainly a long shot.

The same is true of Jewish life. There are hundreds, perhaps thousands, of young Jewish adults who have found Judaism on their own. Perhaps it was a trip to Israel. Or some program at a university's Hillel. Or a course at college with a professor who excited them about Jewish life in a way no one else ever had. Or even a boyfriend or girlfriend. It definitely can happen.

But for each one of these young people, there are dozens more who grew up in homes that gave them very little and who never find their way back. The "success" stories of the kids who did it on their own are the high-profile cases we hear about. But they're still relatively rare, and the odds are not good. Immersion is one of the things we can do to make the odds better.

There's more to immersion, by the way, than parents showing their children a passion and enthusiasm for Jewish life. Those are important, but an equally significant part of immersion is the consistency of the children's exposure to Jewish life, ritual, and culture. All too often, it's not only that parents do not express enthusiasm and passion for Jewish life, but that they expose their kids to it in a very sporadic, unpredictable way. A holiday here, a service there—that, too, is hardly immersion. Kids learn from consistency. If parents proclaim an interest in something, but months go by in which that "something" is not part of the parents' lives, then kids quickly figure out that it's really not all that important.

Gender, citizenship, politics, music, sports—the lives of the people who really care about these things are colored by them consistently, constantly. As we think about how we're going to teach our kids about Jewish life, about how we're going to give our lives Jewish content, we have to ask ourselves if our kids will sense that we love being Jewish. If we're really exposing our children to Jewish "stuff" consistently, we have a reasonable chance that it will genuinely become part of the core of who they are.

JEWISH PARENTS AS CREATORS OF MEMORIES

Why is immersion important? Not because we want to overwhelm our kids or ourselves, and not because we want to shut out the rest of the world. Immersion is important because of a very simple idea: The more time we transform into "Jewish time," the more events we turn into "Jewish events," the more memories of Jewish moments our kids will have as they grow up.

These memories are a large part of what will "fuel" their Jewish interests and desires as adults. These memories are an important step on the road to creating identity. Immersion, therefore, is simply another word for the work we'll do to ensure that as we raise our children, we also create powerful memories of Jewish life that will be buried deep inside their souls.

Childhood memories are powerful. Some of them are deeply painful, and some are filled with joy, love, and a deep sense of security. Other memories fall somewhere in between. We might remember simple things, like where we sat at the dinner table as kids, or what our houses looked like, whom we carpooled with, which teachers we liked best. Even those memories that don't strike us a necessarily joyous or painful are still important parts of the reservoir of images that make us who we are. The more those images have a Jewish quality to them, the more we (and our kids, when they grow up) are likely to feel Jewish at our core.

No Ordinary Time, Doris Kearns Goodwin's wonderful biography of Franklin and Eleanor Roosevelt, tells how, for FDR, the return to the home of his youth was a constant source of inspiration and reinvigoration when the pressures of leading the Western world during World War II became simply overwhelming. The house, filled for FDR with memories of his mother, the world in happier times and his marriage in simpler times, was a soothing balm that in a matter of days could give him the strength to face Washington for months on end. We may not have grown up like

President Roosevelt, but most of us have images of our childhoods to which we can retreat and imagine ourselves once again in simpler, perhaps more comforting times.

Imagine how powerful a connection to Jewish life we would give our children if their warm, comforting, and nurturing memories of youth were also Jewish memories, including Friday nights with everyone sitting down at the family table in a room filled with singing, love, happiness, and a sense of spirituality. The mere image of Friday night is a connection to deep primal feelings and belongings. Even after those "kids" grow up and move away, the likelihood is that the comfort and warmth of those evenings will be so deeply etched in their hearts and souls that it will be almost impossible to really leave it all behind. Indeed, as they themselves become parents, they'll probably want to give their own children those very same memorable experiences.

Many of the Jewish memories we create for our children will be memories of ritual moments: Friday evening Shabbat dinners, family gatherings at the High Holidays, the warmth of Hanukkah in the darkness of winter, or the various life cycle events—births, bar and bat mitzvah celebrations, weddings. But such ritualized moments are not the only things that can burrow deep into our souls.

THE MEMORIES WE CAN'T PLAN

I was about eight years old at the time of the 1967 Six-Day War. Though I was too young to understand much about the day-to-day events of the war, or to really understand what Israel was or how fragile the young state appeared to be, I still have vivid memories of it. One of the memories is of a Jewish community rally at the Baltimore National Guard Armory to which our parents took us. I don't know how many people were there, but as an eight-year-old, it seemed that the entire world had convened on the huge lawn in front of the building. I remember feeling that everyone we knew was there; and for the first time, I had a sense that we were connected by something deeper than the day-to-day stuff that normally brought us together (school, car pools, Cub Scouts, whatever). More than thirty years later, I remember the night. I probably don't remember it exactly the way it happened, but the truth is that by simply taking us to that rally, my parents taught us something about Jewish belonging that no words would ever have communicated as powerfully.

My other memory of the Six-Day War is even more powerful. I can still picture our kitchen in that house, and I remember that at dinnertime during those days my parents didn't sit at the table with us. They stayed in the kitchen. They fed us, but when we asked why they weren't also sitting at the table, they simply told us they weren't hungry. My younger brothers and I sat eating dinner, while my parents stood in the kitchen, watching the evening news with a concern I'd never seen before etched on their faces. My parents' places at the dinner table remained empty. Even as we ate dinner, there was a void in our lives.

Again, nothing they could have said could ever have communicated to us how connected they were to Israel. When I wonder, now, when the love that I feel for Israel began to develop, I often find myself returning to the images of that kitchen, that war, and the sense that if Israel was in danger, then even the fabric of my own family wasn't quite the way it should be.

It's also important to realize something else about memory: We create memories even when we don't intend to. John Dewey, the famous educator and American philosopher, said that every moment is a teaching moment. Some are positive, some are not. But students and kids learn from everything in their lives, not just the moments that a parent or a teacher plan as a "teaching moment." That's a really important lesson to remember in our parenting.

I'm certain my parents did not make a conscious decision not to eat dinner with us because they thought it would teach us something important. They didn't eat because they weren't hungry; they were too upset. The memory I have of those days is a product not of what they wanted me to learn but simply of who they were. So we teach our kids not only in moments we've "programmed" for them, but in the countless and subtle ways in which our loves and fears and concerns and values get expressed.

Our kids overhear our conversations. They see what kinds of books we read. They notice which programs on television bore us so that we simply change the channel. They know when we're really worried; they can tell when we don't care. We teach them every minute of the day, for better and for worse. No matter what we tell children about the importance of speaking nicely, they'll learn the most from how they see us speak to our spouses, our friends, our colleagues.

No matter what we say about the appropriate use of money, our kids will ultimately derive their most lasting images from what they see us do. (When we send on-line checks to charities that are important to us, I often ask my kids to use the mouse and to click on Send; I want our decisions about giving **tzedakah** [the Hebrew word for charity, more appropriately translated as "justice"] to be something they see and understand.)

Ultimately, it matters much less what we tell our children about caring for the poor than what they see us do. We live in Los Angeles, and at the bottom of virtually every freeway ramp is a homeless person with a sign that says "will work for food." Each time we drive by and ignore the person we communicate something to our children; similarly, each time we stop and hand the person a granola bar (they don't spoil, so they're great for keeping in the car), we communicate something much more powerful than any lecture could.

Even the rules in our homes create memories. When I was a kid, my parents had a rule that we couldn't watch the TV show *Bridget Loves Bernie*. That show was one of the first that celebrated the marriage of a Jewish and non-Jewish person, and to my parents, who were deeply opposed to intermarriage, it did not make sense to let us kids watch it. Did they think they could hide from us the fact that Jewish people can marry anyone they wish? Hardly. But I guess they decided that at our young ages, that simply wasn't what they wanted us to watch. We still knew what people did, but the rule also made it very clear what our parents thought.

We had some cousins in town who had a different rule in *their* house. Their parents didn't mind if the kids watched *Bridgett Loves Bernie,* but those kids weren't allowed to watch *Hogan's Heroes.* Part of that family had come from Germany and had narrowly escaped Hitler and the Nazi regime. To their father, any TV show that made light of Nazism or cast the Nazis as jovial, lovable heroes simply wasn't going to be part of his kids' youth. My parents didn't care if we watched *Hogan's Heroes.*

Does that mean my parents had no strong feelings about the Shoah?* Of course not. Does it mean that my cousins had no feelings one way or the other about whom their kids married? No. What it does mean is that each family has its own priorities. No parent can be ultimately concerned with every issue. No two families raise the same children, and even within the same family, no two parents are the same and no two children are the same. Again, what we have to strive to be is not perfect Jewish parents, because we're not perfect parents in any regard. We just have to be thoughtful Jewish parents

---

* "Shoah" is the Hebrew word for "Holocaust." Throughout this book I will use Shoah rather than the more commonly used English word. "Shoah" in Hebrew actually means "calamity." "Holocaust" is an English word that means "burnt offering" or "sacrifice to God." The Jews of Europe in the 1930s and 1940s were not sacrificed; they were murdered. There is a tremendous difference. This book uses "Shoah" in order to take that difference seriously. Even the words we use as we speak to our children can teach them a great deal. That is why the choice of language in matters as horrific as the Shoah is particularly important.

who understand that each step we take or don't take will either immerse our kids in Jewish life or it won't. Every moment of our kids' childhood is a building block of memory. It's up to us whether those building blocks are Jewish.

AND FINALLY, IDENTITY

Immersion and memory are the keys to raising children who will love being Jewish, who will feel Jewish at their core. That's what we mean by "identity." When we use the word "identity," we're talking about raising kids who might say things like "I could never not have Jewish things as part of my life. That's just who I am." Or kids who, when asked to pick one word to describe themselves, might choose the word "Jewish." When we use the word "identity," we're talking about using immersion to create memory, and memory to create the sense that deep down, being Jewish is just who we are. If we can do that, our children's questions will be not whether to be Jewish but how to express their Jewishness.

Gone are the days when we could delude ourselves into thinking that we would be able to "guilt" our kids into being Jewish. (It never worked, of course, but we pretended that it did.) The Shoah and the legacy of its victims is a powerful call to people who already feel deep commitments to the Jewish people, but neither the Shoah nor Israel will create the emotional attachment to Jewish life we want our kids to have.

There are no magical solutions to raising Jewish children in the complex world of the almost-twenty-first century. Like raising kind children, confident children, children who feel good about themselves, raising Jewish children is something that we do bit by bit, day by day, memory by memory.

What does it mean to be an effective Jewish parent? It means to recognize that we communicate our own values to our children at each and every moment, and that for Jewish life to compete with all the other social and cultural forces our kids are exposed to, we have to help Jewish "stuff" burrow to the core of who they are. To paraphrase what the talmudic sage Hillel said to the man who asked Hillel to teach him the entire Torah while the man stood on one foot: "Those are the basics; the rest is the details."

Now is the time to go and learn.

4

USING JEWISH LIFE
AND HOLIDAYS TO CREATE
A RHYTHM FOR TIME

Most of us don't think of being Jewish as being part of a system of time. If our kids or our friends were to ask us "What does it mean to be Jewish?," it probably wouldn't occur to us that the word "time" should be part of the answer.

But it should. Time is what life is all about. It's the fact that time passes that makes it valuable; it's the knowledge that we're not going to live forever that pushes us to be productive, to be good, to try to live life fully. If we had limitless time there'd be no urgency. Not as much would be important.

This is where Jewish life has the capacity to be extremely helpful. One way to think about Jewish life is to see living as a Jew as a way of living that provides moments of closeness and transcendence. It's a way to remind us that even in the drudgery there can be joy, and that even though the years seem to fly by, there is a pattern and a comforting predictability to life.

So there are really two related reasons why being Jewish has to create something important out of time. The first is because it's the passing of time that ultimately shapes everything we do. The knowledge that eventually we will die frightens us, but it also gives us drive and purpose.

The second, more mundane, reason is that Judaism itself marks the passage of time. By creating markers and ceremonies along the way, Jewish tradition helps us either to slow things down or to keep a better grip on the wondrous stages of our own lives and the lives of our children.

Remember Tevye, the father in *Fiddler on the Roof*? As he contemplates the upcoming marriage of his daughter in the famous song "Sunrise, Sunset," he wonders, "Is this the little girl I carried, is this the little boy at play . . . I don't remember getting older, when did they?" Deep down, we're all Tevyes. Every one of us knows (or if we're just expecting, *will* know) how Tevye feels. Where does all that time go? How did we suddenly end up twice as old as we were when we graduated college? How's it possible that we've really been at this job for a whole decade?

Those are the questions and the feelings that make us human, and that's why Judaism, a tradition that wants to touch and deepen our humanity, takes time so seriously.

JEWISH LIFE AS MARKING TIME

Why don't we realize that Judaism is partly about time? Usually, it's because we don't allow Jewish life enough space on the canvas of our lives for the hues of its palate to add any real color to our days. But that's a mistake. Especially as parents, a large part of our task involves creating meaningful and comforting patterns for our kids. That's why we often have morning routines for when our children wake up and have breakfast, special "rituals" for going to sleep, for leaving for school, and the like. Since Jewish life has to be about marking time and making it meaningful, and since Jewish parenting has to take immersion and the creation of Jewish memories seriously, understanding the ways that Judaism creates very similar cycles is a critically important part of thinking deeply about Jewish parenting.

Remember, it's not that every parent has to do exactly the same thing, or that the only way to be a good or thoughtful Jewish parent is to take on every suggestion here; nothing could be farther from the truth. This book is not an argument for living Jewish life in any particular way; it's a conversation about the "big ideas" in Jewish parenting. Don't think of the section that follows as a checklist of "stuff" that you have to do to be a good Jewish parent. Instead, ask yourself what this tradition was trying to do when it created this way of living. If I choose not to follow the tradition exactly as it is taught, is there any idea or concept that might still be worth trying—somehow—to make a part of my child's life?

THE CYCLES OF JEWISH LIFE

Students who come upon Judaism's classic legal code, the **Shulchan Arukh,** for the first time are often amazed at the way it is organized. First published in 1565, the Shulchan Arukh is probably the single most important legal work in all of Jewish life, and how it is organized has something very important to teach about being Jewish.

The first of its four major sections begins with a discussion of morning rituals, and succeeding paragraphs discuss the order of the Jewish day: the process of waking up, getting dressed, praying, eating, and the like. Next, it goes on to describe the structure of the Jewish week, then the Jewish month. Finally, of course, it gets to the Jewish yearly cycle and a discussion of the various holidays.

The very structure of this text tells us something important: To make Jewish life as compelling and fulfilling as it can possibly be, we need to try to fill all these cycles—daily, weekly, monthly, yearly—with Jewish content and passion. What better guide could we possibly have as we strive to create Jewish memories for our children, to immerse them in their Jewishness?

Morning Rituals with a Jewish Twist

Think about how you wake your child up in the morning. In all probability, especially when your child is young (few parents relish waking their teenagers!), you follow some ritual or pattern. You might play some music, sing a song, sit in a rocking chair as the baby gets his first bottle. As your kids get older, the pattern probably involves getting them to brush their teeth and wash their faces, getting them dressed (maybe searching for the ever-missing shoes) and ready for school.

And in the hustle and bustle of morning, we often miss what matters most. Sleep is a miracle. When we go into our kids' rooms in the morning to wake them up, we often marvel at the serene look on their faces and their easy, constant breathing. We wonder what is going on in their minds—are they dreaming of something they love, or someone they cherish? As they get older there is a visible change as they come out of that slumber. Slowly they realize where they are, and remember that it's off to school they go, that they have to face the stresses of the day, and before long, the serenity and peace that only minutes before had been all over their faces is but a faint memory.

Isn't there some way to hold on to that calm, that peace, that sense of wonder? Does the morning rush have to ruin all of that? Jewish tradition says no. It says that part of being Jewish is about sanctifying even crazy times, making even the morning rush into something meaningful, connective, peaceful.

Jewish tradition capitalizes on the fact that most families have this pattern by injecting into the morning rush powerful Jewish elements of bonding and memory for parents and children.

One of these elements is the prayer called **Modeh Ani** that is said upon waking up. It's very short, only twelve words in Hebrew, and it says: "I give thanks to You, living and enduring Ruler, that

You have restored my soul to me, with mercy. Your steadfastness is great." This prayer makes the act of waking up a Jewish act; it makes those first waking moments of the day distinctly spiritual. We can say it with our young kids as they wake up. We can begin the day with a Jewish song; we can begin the day by sitting at the side of their bed saying, essentially, "Before the day gets away from us, let's just grab this minute to be together, to be Jewish, to remind ourselves that we're part of something big and beautiful." Remember the saying "Don't sweat the small stuff—and it's almost all small stuff"? Isn't that what the Modeh Ani really tries to do? Isn't it saying that whatever tests are coming up, whatever homework didn't get finished, whatever meeting is worrying us, if we've got people we love to sit with us as we wake up, to sing, or to muse—and to be Jewish at the same time—things are really more than just OK? What better way to begin a day of Jewish immersion?!

But saying the Modeh Ani isn't the only way Jewish tradition tries to sanctify the beginnings of our days. There's also a blessing that's recited upon going to the bathroom. Known as **Asher Yatzar**, it is a bit longer, but in English it would go as follows (somewhat loosely translated):

Praised are You, Lord our God, Ruler of the Universe, who created human beings with many openings and passageways. It is revealed and known to You that if one of them should open [when it is not supposed to] or if one of them should close [when it is not supposed to], it would not be possible to survive and to stand before You. Praised are You, God, who heals all flesh and does wonders.

As we get older, the wisdom of this blessing becomes more apparent. We are too aware of what happens when arteries become clogged, we know that as we age, a variety of maladies can close important openings, that valves can be too open. What this blessing says to adults is that the body is a miracle, albeit one that we often take too lightly. The blessing says that even going to the bathroom can be a spiritually enriched moment if we only take the time to think about the amazing miracle that is the human body.

That message about spirituality is important, and is a critical part of being Jewish. But though we don't usually think about it this way, the blessing is also about time. As strange as it might seem to utter a blessing each time we leave the bathroom, the function of this blessing is similar to that of the Modeh Ani: It takes a daily part of life and makes it into a Jewish moment.

The big question now: Is this something we should teach our children? The answer depends on your religious outlook (Jews who consider Jewish law, or *halakhah,* to be binding would obviously say that they have an obligation to recite this blessing, while more liberal Jews might not) and such factors as your Jewish educational background (parents for whom Hebrew is daunting might feel less comfortable than parents who have rudimentary Hebrew) and general attitudes about privacy. But again, for our purposes at this moment, the point isn't the blessing itself but the idea that the secret for creating profound Jewish life and deep Jewish commitments (what we've been calling "identity") is to touch as many of the waking moments of our lives with rituals to remind us of our Jewishness—without denying the legitimacy and importance of the world around us.

Jewish Uniforms?

At this point in most people's morning routine, it's time to get dressed. And amazingly, Jewish tradition says that even this can be made into a Jewish moment.

In traditional communities it's pretty easy. Many of us are familiar with *tzitzit,* the traditional fringes worn by Jewish men on the four corners of a (usually) white garment. We've seen them on paintings, in photographs, or when visiting traditional Jewish communities. In the eyes of most of the liberal Jewish community, these garments are essentially the sign of "those" Jews, the ones who are different, cloistered, not part of the "modern" world.

But rather than be so judgmental, let's try to understand what the custom is all about. Again, the point here is not that we have to do all these things, but that we should try to *understand* the tradition so that even if we choose to do things differently, we can do things to achieve the same ends.

In many segments of the modern religious community boys and men (and in a very few cases, women) wear *tzitzit,* first as a fulfillment of the biblical command to wear these fringes, but also as a means of Jewish identification. As these Jewish people get dressed in the morning, and each time they change or adjust their clothing throughout the day, the presence of these *tzitzit* serves as a reminder that they are Jewish, that their actions and words should reflect Jewish values, and that the ultimate goal of much of their Jewish day is to "clothe" their life in Jewish meaning.

Again, in today's world, the mere idea of *tzitzit* seems thoroughly extreme to most contemporary Jewish parents. The point here is not to combat this, but to force us to ask ourselves, "Is there, perhaps, some value to the idea of a 'Jewish uniform'—after all, Muslims and Sikhs have theirs, even lawyers, doctors, and athletes have them?" If dress is a means of identification (with a certain socioeconomic class, a particular generation, or a given social movement), why shouldn't Jews have a "uniform" that will give our kids a sense of who they are?

And if *tzitzit* aren't for us (perhaps, because they're not common in our community, wearing them would make us or our children feel very uncomfortable), what about other possibilities? Do we want to think about a necklace for our daughter with her name in Hebrew, or a Jewish star for boys or girls? People have very different reactions to these symbols, and that's fine. Our agenda here is simply to look at what is traditional, to ask what wisdom is contained in that tradition, and then to begin to think honestly and openly about what of it we will incorporate, what we won't, and why. Our job as parents is to make decisions not on the basis of what we're used to or what we grew up with (though that is all certainly important), but on the basis of what rituals we think might help us instill Jewish "identity" and "immersion."

An incident with one of my kids taught me how powerfully these simple rituals had impacted him. When he was about five or six years old, my middle child occasionally decided to run away from home when he was angry. He didn't get very far—he was too afraid to go much beyond the driveway, but occasionally he'd make it to our neighbor's lawn—but he was definitely serious about going. He would go up to his room, take the suitcase with his name on it, "pack," and walk out the front door.

One day I came home from work late, after the kids had already gone to bed. When I walked into the house and saw Avi's suitcase just inside the doorway, I knew that he'd "run away" again. I was quickly assured that he was long since home and fast asleep in his bed. At the end of the evening, I carried his suitcase back to his room to unpack it. In it were the three items he wanted with him as he prepared to leave home forever: his stuffed tiger, a set of pajamas, and his *tzitzit*. And I immediately understood why.

He'd run away from home toward the end of the afternoon, when it was clear that he'd soon have to go to bed. If he was going to go to sleep, he must have reasoned, he'd need his stuffed tiger and his pj's. But after he went to sleep, of course, he'd also have to wake up. And waking up meant getting dressed, and it seems that as mad as he was at the moment, he couldn't conceive of the idea of getting dressed without his *tzitzit*. Getting dressed was a distinctly Jewish moment for him; as he planned for the next day, he couldn't imagine that it could be any other way.

Thankfully, Avi has stopped running away from home. But he taught me, that day, that the little rituals we use to make our children's days into Jewish days can be profound and can have deep impact. The little steps we take to make our children's time into "Jewish time," and the rituals with which we fill their days, can say more about the beauty and power of Jewish life than words.

HOW TO PUT A JEWISH KID TO BED

Bedtime is one of the most ritualized parts of our children's day. It's the rare parent who hasn't read Margaret Wise Brown's *Goodnight Moon* at bedtime. Like stuffed animals, night-lights, and tattered old blankets, that book has become a fixture in many kids' bedrooms. Even without a story line, *Goodnight Moon*'s gentle cadence and simple whispers create a space for feeling, for quiet, for wonder. Read it slowly and softly, and a child's whole world is transformed, setting the stage for dark, for night, for separation from parents and for dreams.

Goodnight Moon is not a religious book. It is just a sweet story that invites kids—and their parents—to say good night to kittens, to mittens, and to an old lady whispering "Hush." But thousands of parents across the world know it virtually by heart; it has become liturgy. Like the words of any prayer, it has become the text we "recite" to feel something beyond us, to turn a bedroom into sacred space, to transform bedtime into time for feeling.

But while not everyone reads *Goodnight Moon*, or even knows about it, all parents and children have bedtime rituals and "rules": how far the door must be open, where the night-light is, which stuffed animals get to stay on the bed and which get relegated to the floor, how that special blanket (long past its days of real use-fulness) needs to be placed in the crib or on the bed, what songs are sung to say good-bye until tomorrow. These rituals are reas-suring to our children. They make the world predictable and safe. They communicate what we often can't say as effectively in words. At a moment of saying good-bye, of greeting the dark, of drifting off to dreams, those predictable patterns comfort our children, reassure them that we're part of their world and that we love them, that we want their world to be a safe and gentle place and that we will protect them.

The next logical step is to offer our children a sense of spiritu-ality, and so the question we as Jewish parents should ask ourselves is: "If we're creating such a powerful moment for concluding the day, shouldn't we also make it a distinctly Jewish one?"

And the answer is yes. Though different Jewish communities have different bedtime rituals, the feature they all have in com-mon is the saying of the **Shema** (a Hebrew word that means "lis-ten" or "hear") at bedtime. The basic phrase of the Shema couldn't be more simple. Six Hebrew words that mean: "Listen, O Israel, God is ours, and God is one." It's a simple melody, easy to learn. It's also a timeless phrase, one that's been uttered by Jews for thou-sands of years. Added to the stuffed animals, storybooks, and lul-labies that are a part of all bedtimes, the Shema quickly brings a Jewish dimension to one of the most intimate and treasured parts of the day. It says to our children, as they drift off to sleep, that being Jewish is a central theme of their lives. In an unmistakable yet gentle and loving way, it is a reminder that being Jewish is inseparable from who they are.

As was true with morning-time, we've got many options here. We can make bedtime into Jewish time with traditional elements or we can create our own. Some parents have their children drift off to sleep with Jewish music playing softly in the background; for others, the way to make the last minutes of the day meaningfully Jewish is to make sure that the bedtime story they read to their children is a Jewish one.

As children get older and start to read on their own, we can encourage them to include in their bedtime reading books with some sort of Jewish content—whether by famous Israeli authors, about well-known Jewish sports figures, or anecdotes from Jewish history. Then, as they tire of the childish Jewish songs they grew up with, there is plenty to substitute in its place. There's Israeli rock, there's **klezmer** (a kind of traditional Jewish bohemian beat) that features Andy Statman with David Grisman (Grisman often teamed with Jerry Garcia of the Grateful Dead). Not all kids will go for it, and to be sure, Statman and Grisman may not be the end-all and be-all of Jewish content, but they surely serve these purposes better than most top-ten hits. The trick is to find what speaks to our kids and to do whatever we can to infuse some Jewish content into those critical moments.

NEW TRADITIONS?

What about those parents who may want to make morning-time Jewish without using the traditions we've discussed, or who like the idea of making bedtime Jewish but don't feel that the rituals we're mentioning are a good fit. Some parents may not be sure they believe in God and be opposed in principle to invoking His name. Others may be concerned that their children will not understand Hebrew, or that *tzitzit* reminds them of Jews whose lives they don't want to emulate. There can be a myriad of issues.

But to make mornings or bedtimes Jewish, you don't have to pick one from Column A and one from Column B. Jewish life is not a Chinese menu. Each family can certainly devise its own ways of creating Jewish time. It can be the singing of Jewish songs—in English. It can be talking about Judaism or Israel at the breakfast table, or it can be the wearing of *kippot* at mealtimes (many liberal communities have adopted this practice for girls as well). It can be the way parents say good-bye to their children before sending them off to school, the notes they tuck into the lunchboxes, the books they encourage them to read before they go to bed.

What is important is that parents shouldn't look only at the traditions, decide they're not for them, and then conclude that the whole idea of using "time" as a tool for a powerful Jewish life can't fit into their lives. We simply have got to be more flexible and creative than that. As with many other dimensions of parenting in general, it's important to seriously consider traditions and ideas that have worked for centuries before deciding that they're not for you. Before you conclude that "this ritual just isn't one of the things that our family does," it's important to ask why. There are lots of things our family didn't do until our kids got to be a certain age, but we responded to changing ages by changing our behavior.

Are New Traditions Really Traditions?

As we consider the possibility of "new traditions," we should also recognize that we face a huge challenge. Simply by virtue of their age and the fact that they are recognized by Jews throughout the world, traditional Jewish rituals have a power that newly created rituals can't possibly replicate. If our kids say the Shema at night, as they grow older, they will likely be moved—maybe even awed—by the realization that across the globe, literally hundreds of thousands, if not millions, of Jews are going to sleep saying the very same words. Just as one can usher in the Shabbat with something other than candles, part of the power of the candles is the series of horizontal and vertical connections it makes; it makes horizontal connections to Jews across the world who usher in Shabbat the same way, whether in Jerusalem, Nepal, or Paris, and it creates vertical connections through the knowledge that our great-great-great-grandparents ushered in Shabbat in the same way.* The power to be found in participating in ancient customs and making them part of our modern lives is profound.

But again, using traditional rituals and ceremonies just because they're ancient and powerful won't work for everyone. If that's the case, then the next step isn't to drop the whole idea but to ask ourselves what traditions try to accomplish and, if we're not going to participate in them, what new way can be found to create the same effect or impact in our homes. That's the "creative" part.

MOVING BEYOND THE "DAY"

While our discussion of "time" in the Jewish tradition has focused on daily rituals, they're only one example of how the tradition tries to mark time. After the tradition thinks in terms of days, it moves to weeks, and in that Shabbat becomes very important. And after weeks come months, and there's a celebration called **Rosh Chodesh** to usher in new months. And after months come holidays, which are also important elements in the creation of the kind of Jewish home we're talking about.

How to celebrate each holiday will be discussed later. For our purposes now, the issue is that even though some Jewish people often see holidays as a burden or as meaningless occasions, and therefore choose not to observe, the genius of the "system" is that

* We should acknowledge, however, that many Jews by choice cannot say this. They are not continuing the chain, they are joining it. Jews born into the tradition should thus be awed by the courage of those who are Jewish by choice, who have adopted a tradition in which they have no roots.

holidays afford numerous opportunities to fill our children's lives with joy and Jewish content. That process—immersion and memory creation—is key to making their Jewishness a central part of their being; the holidays are a critical element in our "toolbox" for making that happen.

Rather than ask ourselves if we really have to observe *that* holiday, we can begin to ask a more productive question: If I want to create a home and a way of living that is powerfully and joyfully Jewish, how could I use this moment to its fullest? The question isn't how much we have to do, but how much can we do if we really want to make our children's lives as palpably Jewish as possible. When the themes our kids might hear about in Jewish youth groups or in synagogue are reflected in our homes, their Jewish life begins to grow into a seamless Jewish universe that might, if we're fortunate, touch the very core of their souls, to make this something that matters to them for the rest of their lives.

As parents, especially if we didn't grow up with these traditions, cycles, and holidays as part of our own lives, we need to ask questions and seek answers. Now is the time to be honest about how we'd like our kids to grow up, and forthright about what it will take to do it. If we're serious about immersion, identity formation, and memory creation, there's nothing more helpful than Judaism's clock and its cycle of daily, weekly, monthly, and yearly holidays and traditions, each of which adds to the depth and power of the Jewish feelings, memories, and associations our kids can have.

THE SPACE WE MAKE
FOR FEELINGS
Why Ritual Really *Matters*

Many of the Jewish people we know who have balked at Jewish life, who have walked away, did so not so much out of anger or disgust as out of sheer disinterest. It wasn't that they found something in Jewish life so revolting or objectionable that they turned and walked away. It was just that nothing about Jewish life touched them enough to make it worth investing in, worthy of learning more about.

THE SPIRITUAL EMPTINESS
JEWS TOO OFTEN FEEL

Most of us have Jewish friends who have found real religious or spiritual satisfaction in another tradition. For some, Christianity provided a place of meaning and comfort. Increasingly in America, Eastern religious are fulfilling that need. Some estimates suggest that close to 30 percent of all Buddhists in the United States were born Jewish. Ashrams in Nepal and India are filled with young Jewish people, mostly American and Israeli. And in a much more pernicious and sadder phenomenon, a huge percentage (some say as high as 40 percent) of cult members in America are Jewish—yet American Jews comprise only 3 to 5 percent of the total population of the United States.

What's the reason for this seeming mass exodus from Jewish life? There are many reasons, but one important element must be mentioned if we're to think honestly and openly about the work that confronts us as Jewish parents. To put it simply: Many of the people who leave Jewish life do so because nothing about Jewish life ever touched the core of their souls; they may have participated in services, or been involved in a youth group, but they just never felt anything.

We all know the story. Who hasn't lived through synagogue services that were just a matter of following along as the page numbers were announced, listening to the rabbi pontificate about some political issue we could just as easily have read about on the op-ed page of the *New York Times,* followed perhaps by the singing of a song we scarcely understood. Who hasn't had the experience of walking out of a service wondering what the point of it all was.

Or maybe it was the proverbial family **Passover Seder,** conducted "religiously" each year, but with no religious content. The old quip that contemporary Jews summarize Jewish history and the meaning of each holiday by saying "They tried to kill us but failed; let's eat!" isn't so far off the mark. Thousands of Jewish households gather each year for Passover, but the person who dares to suggest that they actually study the **Haggadah,** or reflect seriously about the issues that Passover raises, risks being ignored at best, ridiculed at worst. Is it any wonder that, as kids, we sometimes wondered what the fuss was all about?

The reason why so many of us laugh at depictions of the inanity of suburban American Jewish life in books like Philip Roth's *Portnoy's Complaint* is that we recognize ourselves in his caricatures. Woody Allen is also a keen observer of Jewish life in America. Yet no matter how harsh, and sometimes even mean, these artists can be, we sense that the real reason they're sometimes so vicious is that they feel let down; something deep inside them knows that there's more to Jewish life, and they're bitter that they never were allowed to experience it. Our challenge is to ask ourselves: What are we going to do to make things different—and better—for our own children?

One of the keys when trying to instill in our children a sense that being Jewish is important is to help them learn that being Jewish is also about touching the innermost reaches of their souls. It's not just about following along, page after page, at synagogue services, and it's not just about a command appearance at the annual Passover gathering. Nor can it be about rote avowals of support for Israel, or mentioning the Shoah as some sort of mantra. The Judaism we show and teach our kids has to be deeper, more profound, more meaningful. We have to show our children that being Jewish is about confronting and expressing our wonder about the world, our fear of being alone, our vulnerabilities. It has to be about our yearning to sense that our lives have purpose, and it has to give us a place to express the unadulterated joy that we're sometimes privileged to feel. Being Jewish is to feel part of a community beyond ourselves and, at pivotal moments, to reach out to realities beyond those we can see and touch. Being Jewish, in other words, has to be about living spiritually.

The question, of course, is how do we do that?

RITUAL AS THE KEY
TO JUDAISM'S SPIRITUALITY

Ritual once again enters the picture. Ritual is important in Jewish life not only because it helps transform "regular time" into "Jewish time," but also because ritual is the forum for expressing all the sentiments and moments that make up spiritual living. Ritual is the space that we make for feelings.

The problem many of us have with ritual is that it often seems artificial. The clothes we have to wear, the places we are told to be, the words we are expected to utter—they all make Jewish ritual feel contrived, forced, and we understandably rebel against that.

Yet there's no reason to be more judgmental or critical of Jewish culture than we are of the larger culture in which we live. Ritual is, in fact, omnipresent, and very often we find it compelling.

Before we proclaim that we're simply uninterested in "contrived" ritual, we need to look at some events of recent years. Did you watch any of Princess Diana's funeral in 1997? If you did, you were probably moved by some of the ritual. You may have been moved by Elton John's rewritten "Candle in the Wind," or by the two boys following their mother's coffin through the streets of London, Prince Charles's stoicism, the thousands of mourners along the streets, the presence of dignitaries from around the world. We might have been cynical in our analysis after the fact, but for many of us, the moment was very touching.

Closer to Jewish life, many of us remember the funeral of Israeli's prime minister Yitzhak Rabin. The simplicity of the coffin, the poignancy of the non-Jewish American president saying good-bye to Rabin in Hebrew (with the now famous *shalom chaver*), the presence of Arab leaders on Mount Herzl—it all added up to images that for some of us are unforgettable. And faced with the unspeakable horror that a Jew had killed Rabin, the grief in the ritual somehow gave expression to feelings for which we simply couldn't find the words.

A friend of mine, in his fifties, newly involved in Jewish life after not being all that connected for a long time, is a television journalist. He was sent by his network to Jerusalem to cover the Rabin funeral, and as the funeral procession made its way to Mount Herzl, he found himself on his hotel balcony watching it pass by.

Suddenly (and unexpectedly to him, as this was his first time in Israel) the air-raid sirens throughout the city began to sound. Israeli citizens knew exactly what this meant on that day and immediately stopped in their tracks and stood in silence. Buses didn't move; cars on the road stopped in the middle of the street, and drivers got out to stand quietly. Radio stations went silent. In stores, all activity came to a complete halt. Even little children knew to stop playing. For what seemed an eternity, but was actually only a minute or so, an entire modern city froze. My friend told me later that it was the most profound moment of his life; he had never, ever experienced anything so powerful. Words, he said, could never convey what he felt at that moment.

And that's precisely the importance of ritual. At times, even things that might seem contrived have the power to convey feelings that words never could. And those feelings don't always have to be sad; the same is true at happy moments. No matter how many weddings we've been to, our eyes still brim with tears. Why? Because of ritual—for in moments of ritual, we experience feelings that would otherwise never bubble to the surface. The mere sight of the bride and groom under the wedding canopy brings to mind our own relationships, our own loves, our triumphs and disappointments, and our hopes for the future. In a world that so often seems to overflow with hopelessness, the image of these two people pledging to spend the rest of their lives together sometimes overwhelms us with hope, and even with gratitude. It's nothing that we could articulate very well, but the lump in our throats and the tears welling in our eyes tell us that the feelings are real. And those are feelings we probably wouldn't be able to access if it weren't for the ritual we were a part of.

To teach our children that Jewish life is not only important but also powerful, compelling, and profound, we have to ensure that our Jewish parenting gives them as many opportunities as possible to experience this side of Jewish life—the side that bring us joy, that makes us cry, that moves us deep in our souls.

RITUAL AS A WAY OF
ELEVATING THE MUNDANE

You might be saying to yourself: "Well, sure. Obviously, moments like funerals for people like Princess Diana or Yitzhak Rabin are going to be powerful. And yes, weddings are moving, too. But those are special moments. How could we possibly make that sort of intensity part of our children's regular life?"

The truth, of course, is that we can't always provide that sort of intensity. But that doesn't mean we can't fill Jewish life with profound, sensitive, intimate, touching, transcendent moments. And that's where the rituals that comprise so much of Jewish life come in—it is through them that Judaism tries to help us create those moments.

Bedtime Again—Ritualizing Closeness and Wonder

Now we can understand better why Judaism has its bedtime rituals, and why they are so important and powerful. What makes going to bed such an important moment for parents and children is that in a few short moments we communicate more love and devotion than we often can during the rest of the day. And our children respond. Even if they've been quiet all afternoon and evening, at bedtime children seem to burst with questions, with reflections, with the need for connection to us.

They ask the craziest things at bedtime, and they talk about things that would seem to be farthest from their minds. They ask about a homeless person they saw on the street days earlier, about people, places, or events that we'd assumed they'd long since forgotten. Lots of times, kids use the quiet moments of bedtime to list a whole series of maladies and aches that they hadn't mentioned earlier. So why do kids insist on mentioning them right before they go to sleep? Because in the quiet moments of bedtime, they know they have our attention. There's something about the dark, the quiet, the intimacy that makes them feel safe and secure; once they have us, they feel free to tell us about all the things they'd like us to fix.

Our children sense the different pace of bedtime, and they respond to it. With questions about the world, about life, about meaning. That's why fairy tales are such common fare for bedtime reading. They are ultimately about good triumphing over evil, about the possibility of hope and fairness, about dreams that people really can live "happily ever after." Even if our kids are older, they still sense that this is the time of day when they can be more open; this is the time when security, intimacy, and closeness are close at hand.

Now we can understand even better why Jewish life pays such close attention to bedtime rituals: They give us a way to express feelings for which we don't ordinarily have words. Just as the "frozen" modern Jerusalem expressed the feelings of loss, of hurt, of humiliation, of devastation that many Jews could not articulate after the murder of Yitzhak Rabin, so, too, the intimacy that rituals create at night enables parents and children to express feelings for which there really are no words. The kiss on a child's forehead as they drift off to sleep says more than words ever could. When that kiss follows a Jewish moment, then we've told our kids that being Jewish is also about warmth, comfort, security, and love.

OTHER JEWISH RITUALS
AND EXPRESSIONS OF CLOSENESS

As we learn more about the Jewish holiday cycle and Judaism's life cycle, we will encounter other rituals that create similar moments, that express similar feelings. But rather than leave all of those other examples until later, we should mention a few here to make the point even clearer.

There are many other moments in which Jewish ritual is about much more than the cynical "they tried to kill us but failed; let's eat." Jewish life is about something much deeper, more intimate, more nurturing and beautiful. If the moments of drifting off to sleep are one example, rituals attached to the entry of Shabbat on Friday night are another. Let's look at two examples very briefly.

One of the things ritual often does is give us a chance to talk about those things we don't often express. When we're at funerals, we sometimes find ourselves speaking to people with an honesty that is usually hard for us. These may be people from whom we usually shy away; yet at moments like this we find ourselves try-ing to be more considerate. We have more patience for those who usually annoy us. In part, that's because funerals remind us of what's really important in life, but it's also because something about these ritualized moments gives us "permission" to step out-side our normal behaviors and to say what is sometimes hard to say. The same is true of birth celebrations, weddings, and other moments, like graduations—the power of ritual somehow liber-ates us, frees us to say the things we wish we could say more often.

Do Spouses Still Sing to Each Other?

In traditional Jewish households, as families gather around the Friday evening Sabbath table, fathers actually sing a song—an ode—to their wives. Usually, this song is sung before the meal, as everyone is standing around the table. In some homes, the chil-dren join in and sing to their mother as well.

The words to this ode are taken from the end of the book of Proverbs, from a section called **Eishet Chayil,** commonly trans-lated as "A Woman of Valor." Here's a brief excerpt:

What a rare find is a capable wife!
Her worth is far beyond that of rubies.
Her husband puts his confidence in her,
And lacks no good thing.
She is good to him, never bad,
All the days of her life.

She gives generously to the poor;
Her hands are stretched out to the needy.

She is clothed with strength and splendor;
She looks to the future cheerfully.
Her mouth is full of wisdom,
Her tongue with kindly teaching.
She oversees the activities of her household
And never eats the bread of idleness.
Her children declare her happy;
Her husband praises her,
"Many women have done well,
But you surpass them all."
Grace is deceptive,
Beauty is illusory;
It is for her fear of the Lord
That a woman is to be praised.
Extol her for the fruit of her hand,
And let her works praise her in the gates.

To summarize quickly: The poem is an ode of praise to the woman, and it thanks her for her role in creating the family home. Many people today object to this song because of the way it describes the woman's role in the family; this is, after all, an old poem, taken from the Hebrew Bible. As such, the language of this passage certainly doesn't reflect the division of labor or the shared responsibilities that most of us try to create in our homes. For that reason, some people don't sing it at all; others sing only sections, and still others substitute something entirely different. But still, in traditional households, even in households committed to a very different conception of women than the one found in the poem, this song is one of the pivotal moments that mark the beginning of Shabbat.

Now, imagine that you went to a local high school and did a quick poll of the kids leaving school for the day. You go up to each one and ask: When was the last time your father stood up in front of the whole family, sang a song to your mother, and in front of you and your brothers or sisters, thanked her for everything that she does and is?

The looks of disbelief you would elicit from those high school kids! The looks they would give you would say: What are you talking about? For most American kids these days, the idea that their father would stand up at the dinner table and sing to their mother is either laughable or horrifying. That kind of public behavior is just not part of what kids expect from their parents. Most kids can remember seeing their parents hug, and they can certainly remember their parents arguing. But singing to each other? It's just not part of reality for them.

Unless, that is, you happen upon a teenager who comes from a traditional Jewish family. If you asked that person when was the last time he saw his father sing to his mother, he'd probably just shrug and say: "Last Friday night. Why do you ask?" To kids who grow up in such homes, seeing their parents sing to each other, watching their father publicly thank their mother at the end of the week for everything that she does and is, simply isn't an unusual thing.

How does the world of Jewish tradition make this happen? By ritualizing it. If the tradition simply said that at the beginning of the Friday evening meal, fathers should stand and compose a poem of praise to their wives, very few people would bother. We wouldn't find the words; we'd be self-conscious. And if the tradition didn't say anything at all about it, the idea wouldn't even cross our minds. It's just too different from the culture in which we live.

What the ritualized poem does, then, is free us from all that, and makes it "safe" for us to do something that we know is valuable. We know it's great for our kids to see us singing to each other; we know it's healthy for them to see that kind of expression of affection as a balance to what they're inundated with from television, billboards, magazines, and the like. And the fact that it's ritual removes the self-consciousness. Even if we've got friends coming over, it's not hard to sing the Eishet Chayil poem. If our friends are traditional, they sing it, too. And if this is not part of the way they celebrate the Sabbath, then they're likely to appreciate that it's part of *our* Sabbath ritual, and to treat it respectfully.

Telling Our Kids We Love Them, Publicly

On Friday night, mothers and wives are not the only ones to receive public demonstrations of love. The children in the family do as well. Imagine yourself back at the local high school conducting another poll, but this time the question is: When was the last time, as your family gathered at the table for dinner, your parents gently touched your head, blessed you, told you that they loved you and kissed you? Again, the looks of incredulity you'd get from most kids would defy description. Parents, their faces would tell you, just don't do that. And if they did, they imply, I'd be mortified!

But again, not if you happened upon a kid from a home with traditional Shabbat rituals. For in traditional settings, after the father finishes singing to the mother, he (or, more and more commonly these days, he *and* she) approaches each child, places his hands on the child's head, and blesses him or her. When the child is a boy, they say:

May God make you like Ephraim and Manasseh
May God bless you and keep you
May God shine His countenance upon you and be gracious to you
Make God lift His face to you and grant you peace.

If the child is a girl, the first line of the blessing would be "May God make you like Sarah, Rebecca, Rachel, and Leah." Usually, the parents work their way "down the list," beginning with the oldest child, moving to the next youngest, and so on, each time reciting this brief blessing, usually whispering something special in each child's ear as their hands are still on the child's head. It's a quiet moment, a moment of intimacy that our hectic lives don't often allow us. It's a wonderful moment with little kids, and many parents can remember the first time that, instead of their having to walk to their child to bless them, the child anticipated the moment and actually walked to the parent and bowed his or her head.

This moment of blessing at the Friday night Shabbat table is also an especially powerful moment with older children, since we no longer have other moments like bedtime with them, and because children at that age are very resistant to public displays of affection from their parents. The tradition of having parents bless their children, even when their children are themselves married and have children of their own, makes this a moment of closeness, of intimacy, of love.

Again, what makes this possible? The fact that this is a ritual regularizes these moments and makes them "safe." The ritual is also predictable, so that, in this instance, as the children gather around the Shabbat evening table, they come to know in advance that their father will sing to their mother, that their parents will bless them, and that the family's dinner will be palpably different from what it normally is.

I remember when our daughter, our eldest child, was about ten years old, we told her that we were going out for the evening and that a baby-sitter was coming to watch her and her brothers. She asked who the baby-sitter was, and when we told her, she seemed disappointed. So (reflecting every parent's worry about baby-sitters who may not be what they seem) I asked her, "Don't you like this baby-sitter?" Talia responded, "Oh, she's nice. But next time, do you think you could get a baby-sitter who knows the Shema?"

A little surprised, I told her that of course we could, but I asked why it mattered. She replied, "Well, every night when you're not here to sing the Shema to us, I go to each of the boys' rooms and sing it to them as they fall asleep, but then there's no one to sing it to me."

I was immediately struck by two things. First, it made me realize that even on the cusp of preadolescence, she still liked that quiet moment with her parents more than she could actually let on. And second, I was touched by what this story told us about her relationship with her brothers. After all, our kids fight and argue like all kids do; it had never occurred to us that Tali was singing the Shema to them. We had surely never asked her to do it. Yet the tradition that our kids had become used to, this custom that someone they loved sang to them before they went to bed, got our daughter to sing to her brothers. The memories of those evenings were deeply embedded in our children's minds; down the road, I'd like to believe, when our kids are adults, memories like those will add much to the friendship they'll have and the love they'll feel for each other.

Ritual can change everything. Suddenly, bedtime is not just

bedtime. It's something much more powerful. And dinner on Friday night is very different from dinner on any other night of the week. The ritual of Jewish life helps us step into a world in which people tell each other that they love them. It helps us enter a world in which parents bless their children, in which spouses sing to each other. It sounds kind of hokey, of course, but that's precisely the point. Jewish tradition gives us the tools to get beyond our concern with what everyone else does. It creates a mini-universe in which we can tell people how we genuinely feel about them.

RITUAL IS NOT ONLY ABOUT PEOPLE . . .

The rituals we've described—bedtime rituals, Friday evening rituals—and many more that we could have mentioned create moments that draw people closer to one another. And yes, creating connections between people should be part of the role of any religious experience. But at the same time, we should not forget that, in most cases, religion is not just about drawing people together. Religion is about something else: God.

As soon as we say the word "God," we begin to raise issues with which many adults are very uncomfortable. Children, however, are much more open to the idea of God. Most of us can remember our kids asking about God. They may have asked where God is, or what God does, what God looks like. Children, unlike us, are not embarrassed about their spiritual lives. They are willing to believe in angels. They know that miracles really can happen.

Then, as they grow up, children lose some of this openness and this innocence. Now, to be honest, we may not be sorry that they'll no longer believe in angels, and our overly rational side may also hope that they won't believe in miracles. But let's be honest— some of the changes that our kids will go through as they get older are losses, not improvements.

Most parents can remember a time when their child had absolutely no worries in the world. Most two- and three-year-olds never go to bed at night anxious about the next day. (Tragically, some, like those who are ill or abused, have this period of innocence and security stolen from them much too early.) Many of us watch our kids fall asleep at night and marvel at the miracle of a life virtually without stress. They play, they have fun, they learn and grow, and at the end of the day, they seem to drift off without too much worry about what the next day will bring.

But then something begins to change. As we put our kids to bed we begin to realize that they're worried. There is something about the next day that is on their minds, and they can't let go of it. It could be school and the responsibilities it can bring; it may be a performance or a sports event in which they'll be competing. At the moment we see that look of anxiety, we know that they've forever left behind a life without stress and without worry. Is that part of growing up? Of course it is. Can we honestly say that we're happy for them? No, we can't.

The truth is, not every part of growing up is good. It's not good that we have to begin to deal with stress, it's not good that we gradually learn that we can't trust everyone, and quite frankly, it's not good that it eventually gets harder for us to talk about God. This is not a book of philosophy, and as such, it's not the place to argue either for or against God's existence. So let's put the matter as simply as we possibly can: Throughout human history, there have been profoundly intelligent people who have believed in God, and equally wise people who have been convinced that God does not exist. The bottom line is that we ultimately don't know with certainty if God exists. Both the believer and the denier, ultimately, are guessing. What we have to decide is whether we want to make it possible for our kids to seriously try on the "believing" side, as well as the questioning side.

Unfortunately, we live in a world that treats religious belief as silliness, as something to be hidden if it must be part of our lives. Think about it. The United States was founded by people who fled Europe not so they could be free from religion but so they could be free *for* religion. Their objection was not to a religious Europe but to a Europe that would not let them express religion the way *they* wanted to.

All that has changed. In today's society, too many of us think about religion as the domain of the fanatical religious right. Religious people, we've come to believe, are the ones who burn down abortion clinics, who die in flames, like the Branch Davidians in Waco, Texas. Religious people, we tend to think, are the crazed Muslims who blow up American buildings in the Middle East and devout Jews who machine-gun Arab worshipers without warning. And even if religious people aren't complete fanatics, we worry. They might just be the Promise Keepers renewing their religious faith, but at what cost to the individuality and autonomy of the women with whom they share their lives and homes.

That view of religion, like the entrance of stress into our lives, is a true loss. Belief in a transcendent being who created the world as a meaningful place is deeply comforting to a great many people. And it's no surprise that twelve-step recovery programs place God at the center of the work they do. For often it's the serious belief in the God who created mankind that gives people the strength to hold themselves accountable to serious and adult standards of behavior and conduct.

Since we don't know with certainty that God exists, and since we have to guess, we might find life more meaningfully lived if we assume "yes" as opposed to "no." The challenge for us as parents, if we want to help our kids hold on to the religious openness that is part of their youth, is to make "God-talk" an ongoing part of their lives.

These rituals that we've been discussing are critical in making God a part of our children's vocabulary. And making God a comfortable part of our children's speech is crucial—for if we hope to preserve our children's openness to God as an idea, we have to preserve their comfort with God in language and in their experiences. Ritual, once again, is the key.

Let's go back to bedtime. If we recite the Shema with our kids at night, we are creating a uniquely Jewish moment for them and for us together. But we're also bringing a "third party"—God—into the picture. After all, the Shema mentions God, and thus creates a setting in which, as our child drifts off to sleep, he or she is conscious not only of our presence but of God's as well.

Why is God present at those moments? Obviously, the "idea" of God is present because the Shema actually mentions God. But God is also present as a source of comfort in an often scary and lonely world.

Let's not trivialize God by imagining that "really" religious people see God as a big old man with a long white beard on a huge throne. Instead, we should remember that for many deeply religious people, there is a word for "wonder, security, intimacy, and closeness"—and that word is God. Childish images like that proverbial old man are sometimes our defense against having to take the possibility of God seriously; God can be understood as our tradition's way of describing the world as caring, as warm, as filled with meaning. In creating a moment like none other at the end of the day, as we create warmth, comfort, and trust, we actually make a space for God.

In mentioning God at moments like bedtime, we, as Jews, are really reminding our children that there is a Presence whose closeness means they're not alone; it means that the world can be wonderful. Let's remember what we want. We want our kids to connect to Jewish life not out of guilt or a sense of obligation. We want them to love being Jewish because it touches them, transforms their life, opens their soul.

As we look back on our own Jewish upbringing, many of us wish that Judaism had been about more than Hebrew school, perfunctory trips to the synagogue, and family holiday celebrations that were too often devoid of any transcendent meaning. Some of us didn't have even that! Either way, we often wish that being Jewish had touched our hearts and nurtured our spirits.

This, therefore, is the other reason that ritual is important. It's God. Ritual helps to bring God to bedtime. It's ritual that gives us Friday night candles, the delicate, fragile lights that remind us to consciously rekindle our lives and our spirits lest they become extinguished. Ritual is what enables us to bless our children and, at the same time, to ask God to watch over them and, if we're fortunate, experience a fleeting moment in which both we and our children can feel God's presence.

Jewish Bedtime—One Last Time

The Jewish bedtime rituals we've been discussing have one component that we have yet to mention. There's another passage that is commonly recited at bedtime: "The Angel who has redeemed me from all harm—Bless the children." It's a prayer that was recited by Jacob shortly before his death, his last blessing to his children (Gen. 48:16). Interestingly, as Jacob blesses his own children, he is keenly aware of his own mortality. His prayer is actually a bit longer: "The Angel who has redeemed me from all harm—Bless the children. In them, may my name be recalled. . . ."

We might think that to ask for our own name to be remembered as we bless our kids doesn't make sense. After all, aren't we supposed to be caring for our children? Why ask for something for ourselves? But it does make sense.

As we watch our little children fall asleep, don't we sometimes wonder who will take care of them when we're no longer around? As we watch their tiny chests rise and fall with each breath, aren't we often struck by the fragility of their bodies, the frailty of life, and, in turn, our own mortality? As we bless our children, we're also asking for something for ourselves. More than anything, we don't want to be forgotten. And they are the key to our being remembered, and loved.

As day descends into night, as we look back on what's been and gaze ahead to tomorrow with hope and perhaps a bit of fear, this ritualized moment gives us a chance to express thoughts we normally repress, what we usually ignore, what we all too commonly pretend we don't really feel.

For us as parents, then, this is a perfect prayer, for not only are we asking God to take care of our children, we are asking that we, too, be taken care of.

Ritual is what gives us the opportunity to create these special moments with our children. What we now have to do is to learn how to talk to them about God, and to create a home that gives them the space to believe in the ideas that the rituals bring into their lives.

6

MAKING SPACE FOR GOD, OR HOW WE STEAL WONDER FROM OUR KIDS

One day, when my daughter was about five years old, she and I were sitting together on the sofa in the family room. I was absentmindedly reading a newspaper or a magazine, and she was watching the video of *Bambi* for the umpteenth time. Suddenly, completely out of the blue, she turned to me and asked, "What was God doing when she was a little girl?"

Although I remember the moment very clearly, I have absolutely no recollection of what I said to my daughter. But I do remember how her question took my breath away.

There were many things about Talia's question that struck me as genuinely profound. Some had to do with her assumption that God was a girl, just like her. She assumed that just as she was a girl, so, too, was God. I loved the idea that she didn't assume, as so many do, that God is male. She taught me something very important about what it's like to be a girl, an issue to which we'll return when we discuss the role of girls in the Jewish tradition.

I was also struck by the fact that my little girl assumed that God had once been a child—just like her—and had since grown up. But most of all, I was struck by how real God seemed to Tali. This wasn't one of those "where is God" questions, or some inquiry about whether God was really out there. Of that my daughter seemed to have no doubt. To her, God was so real that God must have once been young. God was so much like us that God must also have grown up.

As much as I was surprised and even struck by Talia's question, I was also delighted by it. I was delighted because her question told me that something we had done from the very start of her young life was beginning to pay off. That "something" was talking about God.

THE IMPORTANCE OF "GOD-TALK"

If we want our children to have a good chance of finding a spiritual home in Jewish life, if we want being Jewish to be something that touches not only their minds but their hearts and souls as well, then God-talk is important. That doesn't mean that we should have conversations with our five-year-old about why an all-powerful and kind God would allow bad things to happen in the world, or about what God did or didn't say at Sinai—or anywhere else, for that matter. God-talk isn't a matter of "teaching" our children anything in particular. Nor is it about convincing them to "believe" that something about God is true or not. Rather, God-talk is about making our children comfortable with the word "God" as part of their regular vocabulary.

Kids become comfortable with what they see and what they hear. If they observe their parents occasionally hugging or kissing each other, they learn that that's a healthy and appropriate way to show affection. If they never see this, they never learn that a simple hug is part of the vocabulary of healthy relationships, that it's a nice and important way for people to show they love each other. If our children never hear us say "I love you" to each other, they miss the chance to learn that telling people we love them is an important part of making a relationship continue to grow. The things children see and hear us do, they learn to do and say themselves. What they don't see becomes foreign to them, and the older they get, the harder it is to add that missing piece to either their actions or their words.

That's why God-talk is so important for our kids at an early age. As they get older, the world they live in will virtually conspire to make talking about God socially awkward. Think about it; if, at a party, you ask someone where their money is invested, he or she will probably tell you something even though it's a fairly personal question. Our salaries, our sexual attitudes (and behaviors), our political positions—these are all legitimate topics of conversation at a party. But walk up to a group of people and talk about your inner need to feel God's presence or closeness, or your discomfort at not being able to prove God's existence, and people will immediately begin to move away.

So, if we're going to help our kids become comfortable talking about God, we're going to have to create that comfort before the world teaches them that it's somehow weird or wrong. Doing exactly that was something my wife and I were committed to even before we had children. I had grown up in a deeply committed Jewish home. My parents are very learned Jews, having themselves grown up in traditional homes. We observed the traditions of *kashrut* (the Jewish dietary laws), we went to synagogue, we spent a considerable amount of time in Israel, and on and on. But we never talked about God. Strange as it might seem, we lived a very rich Jewish life without reference to the very reason most people think being religious (in any religion) is important.

When I was older, I came to understand that my parents had been deeply influenced by the Reconstructionist movement in Judaism and the ideas of its leader, Rabbi Mordecai Kaplan. Kaplan felt that Judaism should be "reconstructed" so that people could identify Jewishly without believing in a supernatural God.

So, consciously or not, my parents shied away from any mention of God as I was growing up.

When I got to college, though, I felt something was missing. I was committed to many of the practices I'd grown up with but I was also eighteen years old, trying to figure out the world, trying to build a sense of myself in the larger universe. All of a sudden, questions about God began to become more important than they'd been before. In school I was reading lots of philosophy, and I came to realize that I had no idea what I actually believed. Most of my committed Jewish friends had grown up in communities where God was a part of their daily vocabulary, and while part of me wanted to be able to talk about God, I simply couldn't.

In retrospect, there were lots of reasons for this. Speaking about God meant being vulnerable to other people's judgments. But also, I had grown up in a world in which "truth" was defined as things about which we could be certain. My dad is a scientist; while I was in high school, my mom was working on a Ph.D. in history. We lived in a home in which reason reigned supreme; God-talk, it seemed, just didn't fit. Taking God seriously meant basing our lives on postulates we couldn't prove, opening ourselves to questions we'd never really be able to answer.

In the many years that have passed since then, my being part of many wonderful Jewish communities has taught me to become much more comfortable with the idea of God and with speaking of God. I've learned that we all base ourselves on postulates that we can't prove; after all, the atheist, the agnostic, and the believer are all guessing. We all have to choose some basic premise that we can't prove, and move from there. And I've also learned that though we're too commonly taught that what's "true" is what's demonstrable, life isn't that simple.

Our love for our spouses, our kids, our family is real, but it can neither be proven nor completely explained. Some of the most wonderful things in life are those that touch us in nonrational ways. And the fact that they're not rational doesn't mean that they're wrong, or silly, or anti-intellectual. Both the denier and the believer have problems accounting for their world. The believer must account for a world in which terrible evil can exist—both the evil caused by mankind as well as the destruction caused by nature. The denier has to explain how the random development of our species could yield beings that can love, have consciences, and make lifelong commitments. If the believer has to explain the Shoah, the denier has to explain the miracles of birth and love.

We need to learn to think differently. If we're to be the best parents we can be, we need to develop a different set of tools and a broadened vocabulary to take the nonrational parts of our experience seriously.

Slowly, then, I inched toward being able to talk about God, to wonder about God, and to accept the idea that I could have lots of unanswered questions and still try to take God seriously. But it wasn't easy, and I recall many moments when I really wanted to be able to talk about God, believe in God's presence, or pray to God, when I just couldn't. I didn't want the same thing to happen to our kids; so as our children were born and became verbal, my wife and I made sure that they would grow up in a home in which God was a "part of the family" or at least part of their regular vocabulary.

That's why I was so thrilled with Talia's question about God. It wasn't because I had a great answer, and it wasn't because I wanted my daughter to grow up and continue to believe that God was once a little girl (or a little boy). It was just that God was real to her, that she was comfortable talking and asking about God, and that as she began to make sense of the universe, she had no doubt that God was part of the larger picture. That, it seemed to me, was a wonderful gift to have as she started to take note of what the world was all about.

WHAT ARE KIDS ASKING WHEN
THEY ASK ABOUT GOD?

That story about Talia and God's life as a little girl was important for another reason. And it had to do not with what she said but with why she said it. Remember, the question came up while I was reading and she was watching *Bambi*. Though we think of *Bambi* as a sweet kids' movie, it's actually quite upsetting at the beginning. Not long after the movie begins, Bambi's mother is killed by hunters. The rest of the movie is about how Bambi learns to get along in the world when he is all alone, completely by himself.

Talia's question came not long after Bambi's mother had been shot. And that made perfectly good sense, because every child feels for Bambi, and many probably wonder on some level what the world would be like for them if their mother were taken away. Though Talia never told me why she asked her question, I suspect that somewhere deep inside she was wondering what would happen to her if her parents were taken away, and that led her to think about God. The combination of thinking about God and the place of little girls in the world led her to ask what God was doing when she was a little girl.

In that light, her question was not only cute, but it was important as well. She was trying to make sense of her world, wondering what would happen to her if she were all alone. Was there anyone, anything, any Being that would take care of her? Who took care of God when "she" was little? When our kids ask about God, they're often not asking about God. They're really trying to make sense of the world; their use of God is part of their way of constructing a world that makes sense, a world that is loving, a world that is not random or cruel.

Benjamin, the four-year-old son of some friends, asked his father where God was. Very appropriately, his father told Benjamin that God is everywhere. "Wherever you go," he told his son, "God will be there to take care of you." Benjamin paused for a second and then said, "So God lives everywhere? Well, then, does he just have his office in Israel?"

Again, it's an incredibly cute story, but it's also more than cute. Benjamin was trying to make sense of two very different things that he'd been taught or told. One was that God is everywhere, and the other was that Israel is a very special and holy place. Benjamin was obviously trying to figure out how both could be true. Benjamin made sense of this by deciding that God's office was in Israel. Why? Because he knows that his father is present in all parts of his life, but he also knows that his father spends lots of time at the office. Dad is everywhere, but Dad is especially at the office. The same with God.

When my son Avi was told in school that many Jews believe that in the end of time God will bring everyone back to life, he was confused. For we had never discussed that issue with him. We *had* told him that there are very bad people in the world, and that when they do very bad things, it makes God very sad. I think the subject we were discussing was what happened to the Jews of Europe during the Shoah, and we told him that we doubted that God would forgive the Germans who had murdered so many innocent people.

But now, school was confusing him. How could God be angry at those people forever, and then bring them back to life? Does that mean that God wasn't angry at them anymore? Did that mean that God no longer thought that what they did was so terrible? Is it OK not to apologize (grown-ups might say repent) in your lifetime, because you can always have that taken care of later? Does that mean that nothing is so bad that it can't be undone?

It's really a great question, when you think about it. And I didn't have an easy answer. But I was glad that like his sister and his friend Benjamin, he was secure enough in his sense of God's presence that his questions about right and wrong, the permanence of guilt, and God's forgiveness could be expressed so openly and unselfconsciously.

There's really no end to the questions about the world that our kids will frame in terms of God. I was impressed when a colleague of mine told me that a child in his congregation asked him: If God loves all the animals in the world, why did he let the dinosaurs die? What a great question! This child had been taught that God loves all the animals on the earth. After all, didn't God make them all (in children's minds)? And don't we often tell our kids that part of the reason they have to be nice to animals is that God made *them,* too, and that God wants us to be kind to all creatures? Well, if that's true, then why did God let all the dinosaurs die? And if God didn't do anything to save them, how can we be sure that God will save us?

Those Jews lucky enough to walk out of the Nazi murder camps asked exactly the same question. How can we believe in God's promise to make the Jewish people into a great nation, they wondered, if God could let Hitler and his armies kill six million Jews in the space of a few short years? That question sounds more adult, more mature, and more sophisticated, but it's the very same question. There may be no good answers, no easy answers, perhaps no answers at all to such questions, but no thoughtful human being can avoid asking them at some point. Our job as parents is to begin to create for our kids a Jewish and religious world in which they can frame those questions early, in which we understand that those queries are not just "cute," in which a sense of God and a belief in the predictability and kindness of the world can survive all the "reality" that our children will gradually begin to perceive.

WHAT IS "HONEST" PARENTING?

As simple as it may sound, helping our children continue to be comfortable talking about God isn't easy. In fact, without actually intending to, we not only avoid talking to our kids about God, we actually undermine their attempts to make sense of a world with God at the core. And the reason that we make this mistake is that we become too preoccupied with telling our kids the truth.

Now, that certainly sounds like a strange thing to say! After all, how can anyone become too concerned with telling their kids the truth? Isn't telling the truth important, and isn't it something we want to model for our children? Can we reasonably expect the next generation to become committed to the truth if we don't model it for them from the earliest moments of their lives?

The answers to all these questions are obvious. Yes, telling the truth is important, and yes, we want to model that for our children. And yes, it's important that our children see us modeling truth telling in many different areas, perhaps especially when it's uncomfortable for us, such as when we've made a mistake, or hurt someone, or forgotten something important. Yes, the truth matters. It matters a lot.

But saying that the truth matters is not the same as saying that what we owe our children is the complete and whole truth at every moment, or that when it comes to God, it's imperative that we tell them all the things we're not sure about and all the things that make us uncomfortable and angry at God. At least not at the beginning.

Deep down we know this from other realms of our parenting. When a four-year-old asks where babies come from, we don't necessarily have to respond with a detailed physiological explanation of how people make love. Indeed, most of us would think an answer that included the mechanics of sex would be inappropriate—*even though it would be the truth.*

When it comes to sex, we understand that there are different kinds of truth. Part of our job as parents is to figure out what it is that our kids are really asking, and what they're old enough to hear and understand. Not to tell them the technicalities of sexuality when they're ready certainly isn't good parenting, but then again, neither is telling them when they're too young, or when that information would be more confusing or upsetting than helpful.

It's not only with sexuality that honesty is not always the best policy, at least if honesty means telling our kids exactly what we think. Or to put it differently, honesty *is* the best policy as long as we understand that there are many roads to honesty, depending on the subject, on the listener, and what's appropriate.

When very young children ask what police officers do, most of us probably say something along the lines of the job of the police is to protect us, to make sure that everyone is safe, to ensure that, if someone does something bad, he or she will be caught so that no one else will get hurt. We know there are rogue cops, that there are policemen who are on the take, who commit crimes themselves, who are hardly role models. If honesty meant telling our child *everything* when they ask what police officers do, we'd have to tell them all that. But that would be bad parenting, because that kind of answer, though it provides a great deal more information, makes the child's world less secure, less predictable, less nurturing. Will our children eventually learn about that part of the world? Of course. But if we tell them about it before they're ready, we aren't helping them. We are actually stealing from them something very precious, and once that's gone, it can never be restored.

One last example will move us close to the subject of God. When our children ask how we know when we're in love with someone, or how we know that a certain person is the "right" person to marry, there are many different answers we can give. We can tell them that it's hard to explain, but when they're ready to spend their life with someone, they'll know. When they get older, we can tell them how we think someone who loves them will make them feel—secure, cared for, listened to, respected. Or, if we were fully intent on being honest, we could say that there's really no way to

know if a person is right, that even the best relationships sometimes don't make it, that falling in love can actually make you vulnerable and subject to hurt, particularly from the person you love.
Is all that true? Yes. Is it wise parenting? No.

When our adult children fall in love, we'll be thrilled—and
we'll be worried. We'll be thrilled because we will recall how wondrous it was to love somebody, how full of hope and possibility
our lives felt in those ecstatic days. We'll be delighted that someone out there understood what is so terrific about our child and
chose him or her from all the other people they could have chosen. All that will make us feel great.

But we'll also be worried, because unlike our kids, we'll have
been around the block a couple of times, and we'll know that
nothing we say could possibly prepare them for the complicated
world of relationships. We know that there will be bruises and
hurts even under the best of circumstances. There will be betray-
als and disappointments along with the joy and trust. That's just
the way it is.

Should we therefore raise our children with this more realistic
and more mature idea of marriage and relationships? Or do we
want to raise them to believe that with work, and some luck, two
people can build a wonderful life together? We'll let them watch
fairy tales like *Sleeping Beauty, Snow White,* and *Beauty and the
Beast* because, when they're kids, there's nothing wrong with
teaching them that it is possible for people to live "happily ever
after." Bruno Bettelheim, in his famous book *The Uses of
Enchantment,* actually argued that it's important for kids to grow
up believing in happy endings, knowing that goodness, joy, and
trust are possible. That's what being a kid is about, and as parents
we should not steal it from them.

None of this changes when our kids become teenagers. We
imagine sometimes that when our children hit their teens, they're

ready for us to be completely honest with them about everything, all our doubts, all our misgivings. But they're still not ready. To be sure, as our children get older, our conversations with them do need to change; we do need to talk to them about things we would not have discussed when they were younger. But they are still children, and our job is still to protect them. We need not saddle them with all our doubts and misgivings. We need not tell them about our financial concerns, about the complexities of our marriages, or the details of why we got divorced or what it is about life that scares us. Those are things they are just not ready to absorb.

With God, too, there are questions that our children are not yet ready to absorb. As adults, we've seen things and asked questions that may be too difficult for our children to handle. Our job as parents is not to share our misgivings with them, but to make faith possible for them. We know this about other areas of parenting; now we have to extend that to our children's faith, as well.

NOW FOR GOD—
HOW "HONEST" SHOULD WE BE?

If being a good parent means having a subtle, sophisticated, and appropriate sense of what is "honest" when it comes to love, sex, police, the government, or other complicated issues, the same is clearly true with God. We could, when our children ask about God, tell them about all the things we're not sure about, all the reasons we could come up with to doubt that God is "out there."

But before we do that, we ought to ask ourselves what we're trying to accomplish when we answer their question. What are our kids really asking? Is our job at such moments to give our kids information, or is it to build a safe, secure, nurturing sense of the world, one in which they can begin to make Jewish life a core part of who they are? Different parents will answer differently, but I would suggest that we should consider very seriously a second option: When we talk to our kids about God, we're not "information providers." Rather, we're "world builders," the people who are most responsible for the outlook on life our children will develop and carry with them for a lifetime.

For many of us, the Judaism on which we were raised seemed hollow; it never seemed to touch the spiritual side of our lives. Because of that, many of us have trouble imagining our role in building a Jewish world for our children in which God-talk does happen, in which being Jewish means being part of something sacred, intimate, touching—something that makes life warm and nurturing, comforting and reassuring, spiritual in the very best sense of the word. It's hard for us.

But our job is not to reproduce our own childhood for our children in every single way. Hopefully, there were many things about our own childhoods that we would like to re-create for our children. Yet there are also things we specifically don't want our children to experience. And part of what helps us raise our children is our desire for our children not to go through those things.

The point that matters most here is that we shouldn't assume that our job as parents is to duplicate our spiritual or nonspiritual upbringing. Perhaps our children can have something richer, something deeper, something that touches them in ways that our own Jewish upbringing didn't. If that's to happen, we have to answer their questions and talk to them about God in ways that encourage that, not in ways that make it impossible.

Effective Jewish parenting, then, is not just a matter of telling our kids what we genuinely believe about God, any more than it's about telling our kids all that we know about how the people whom we love the most can also hurt us the most. When it comes to love and relationships, our job is to raise children who can trust other people, who can grow close to them. When it comes to God, our job is to raise Jewish children for whom God is a reality, so that faith can be a possibility when they are adults.

Very few adults are entirely certain about God. Outside the traditional community (and often even within it), people have serious doubts and, among close friends, would have no trouble admitting or discussing that. It's not only inevitable, it's part of what being Jewish is all about. The Jews in the Torah are called the "Children of Israel," not the children of Abraham, Isaac, Moses, or anyone else. But why "Israel"? Because the Hebrew word for "Israel" is *yisrael*, which means "to wrestle with God." We're named for the patriarch (Jacob) who's name was changed to "the one who wrestled with God." That's who we are; Jews are God-wrestlers. Our doubts don't make us inauthentic or incomplete; they just mean we're human.

But as legitimate as our doubts are, our kids aren't necessarily ready for them. When our kids ask us questions about God, they're not really asking for information. All they are probably seeking is confirmation that it's OK with us if they talk about God, believe that there's a God, wonder about the ultimate meaning of the larger world.

When a child asks if God is going to bring all the bad people back to life, just as God will bring all the good people back, we could say: "Well, I'm not really sure that God is going to bring anyone back to life. I think that when we die, we die, and there's nothing else after that. That's why it's so very important to live our lives as fully as we can now."

There's nothing wrong with that view. It might well be "correct." Lots of committed Jews, in fact, have this belief. But that's not the point. The real issue is what happens to a child when he or she hears that answer. Does it make the world seem more secure or less secure? Does the answer create a sense of faith in the ultimate goodness of the world, or does it steal it away? We know the answer to that question. It's not dishonest to tell our children that policemen are here to help us, that people can love each other and live happily ever after; it's also not dishonest to help our children grow up to believe that the world is guided by a loving and caring God who values and treasures each and every human being, including them.

BRINGING GOD INTO OUR HOMES

Answering our children's questions about the world and about God without undermining the possibility of their developing a faith that can carry them into adulthood is part of our task, but it's not the whole task. For even if we answer all their questions in a way that does not undermine their sense of God, or even bolsters it, they will still grow up in a world in which God-talk is simply not part of the environment. Eventually, their curiosity about the world, and their tendency to make God part of the way they make sense of things, will give way to the overwhelming "Godless" vocabulary of the world in which they grow up.

Thus, we should probably think seriously about doing more than simply answering their questions in a nondestructive way. Perhaps we ought to try to actually "bring God into" our homes. We could do that by talking about God more openly than we might be used to. We might do something (either a traditional blessing or something we create) to thank God for our food, before and/or after we eat it. On family trips, when we visit particularly beautiful places, we might bring God into the picture. There's a beautiful phrase from the traditional *siddur* (the Hebrew world for prayer book) that says *mah rabbu ma'asekha*, which we can loosely translate "how great and wondrous are Your creations." With our kids at Niagara Falls, at the side of the Grand Canyon, standing on a snowcapped mountain peak in the middle of summer, riding down a white-water rapid in the midst of a powerful river, or even at much more mundane moments, a simple phrase like that or a brief mention of the godliness of the place would help make God an ongoing part of our kids' lives. Remember, even if we're not sure that God's "out there," we probably also can't be sure He's not. So wouldn't those conversations also add something to *our* lives, as well?

Many of the rituals discussed earlier can help us bring God into our children's lives and our homes. But even having our children come with us on Thursday or Friday as we shop for challah will give us the opportunity to explain Friday night's special meal. Sharing with them the excitement of the preparation, together with all the wonderful rituals of the meal, will, if "all the pieces fall together" and the mood is just right, usher in the feeling that God has entered the house. Doing so might create a memory and a sense of God as real that no lecture or intricate ritual could begin to match. However we do it, the idea is to make God part of our kids' world, to understand that being Jewish is about having God as part of their lives, about having a place to grow intellectually, religiously, and spiritually.

BUT IS GOD REALLY THAT IMPORTANT?

One of the most common questions parents ponder is: How important *is* God to this whole Jewish thing? After all, haven't lots of Jews grown up in the United States, very committed to Jewish life, and not too concerned with all that God-talk?

That's a very fair question, and an important one. Some people would add that it's exactly on the mark, and that all our emphasis on God is misplaced and unnecessary. That may be true, and some people I know, very committed Jews and deeply thoughtful people, believe exactly that. But I disagree, particularly if we're talking about raising our Jewish kids in places like the United States.

America Isn't Kind to Ethnicity

To put matters very simply, Judaism without God is a history, a people, an ethnicity. And as important as those are, and as central as they are to any thoughtful construction of what Judaism is, there's a very serious question as to whether they can survive in America without some religious component as well. I'm very dubious that an ethnic, nonreligious, variety of Judaism has much of a future in the United States (the situation in Israel is more complicated, but we'll talk about that in our Israel discussion).

If we're honest, we have to admit that America is not generally kind to ethnic groups. That doesn't mean that America is mean to them, or tries to harm them. Precisely the opposite. America has been so welcoming to so many people from around the world that, except for those who appear different because of skin color, facial characteristics, and so on, groups tend to blend in much more rapidly than most immigrants would ever have imagined. Yes, there are still Polish, Italian, and German neighborhoods in many U.S. cities, but more and more, the affluent and younger members of those communities don't live there. They don't dress the way their grandparents did, they don't eat the same foods (except, perhaps, on holidays and traditional festivals), their English is fully American and bears no trace of their ancestors' homelands, and their familiarity with their own cultural traditions pales when compared to what their ancestors had just a generation or two ago.

It's not that these people tried not to be Polish, or Italian, or German. The point is that they didn't have to. American society is so fluid, and on the whole, so welcoming and so upwardly mobile that people do not have to try to leave their ethnic group. There's a virtual magnet in our culture that pulls them away.

Being Jewish in America, if you view being Jewish as an ethnic issue, is not very different from being Polish, Italian, or German.

Some of the traditions and associations of the past will survive, but over the course of time, there will be fewer and fewer. What we will be bequeathing to our kids will be some sort of anemic tradition, not the vital, profound, and constantly renewed tradition that we hope Jewish life can continue to be.

A GODLESS JUDAISM MAKES
THE TRADITION A STRANGER

The next logical questions are: But why does it have to be that way? After all, Judaism has a host of rituals, books, and traditions that can be the reservoir of insight and meaning that enrich our lives. Couldn't that strengthen and renew our Jewish connection even without God, perhaps in a way that might be different from the Polish, Italian, or German American experiences? And the answer is possibly. But here, too, I doubt it. There are several reasons why, as parents, we should take seriously the possibility that a Judaism that has God as part of its vocabulary is more likely to be a powerful and provocative (in the very best sense of that word) home for our children. But at this point, we will focus on only one.

The point here is simple: So much of the Jewish tradition (and prior to the modern period, virtually all of the Jewish tradition) speaks of God as a given, that to raise our kids in a world in which God is not present, or silly, or fantasy, or something not to be taken seriously, creates a huge chasm between our children and the traditions and texts we'd like them to enjoy later in life. If God is not at least a plausible possibility for our kids, then any encounter with the Bible becomes difficult. If we don't take God seriously, then the Passover **Haggadah** reads more like a fairy tale than the profound statement of faith that it is. If God is just an ancient idea not suited to modern people, then the liturgy of the wedding is quaint and ethnic but not terribly powerful, and the words of the **Kaddish** (the Jewish memorial prayer) have much less power to comfort.

Even if what we want our children to get from Jewish life is a rich encounter with its intellectual tradition, and not necessarily its religious dimension, that will be hard if God is somehow out of bounds. For the richest parts of the Jewish intellectual tradition are the Bible, the **Mishnah,** the **Talmud,** the works of the medieval philosophers. And all of these works assume that God is real and central, not just some interesting metaphor for "the stuff we don't understand about the world."

If we raise our kids so that God isn't even a possibility for them, then each time they encounter one of the great works of the Jewish tradition, they encounter something that is fundamentally different from them, something "other." Their meeting with that book, that idea, that personality, that tradition ends up feeling not like something that is comfortable, validating, and nurturing, but instead it becomes an encounter that at every turn reminds them that there is a huge difference between them and the tradition they are trying to study. More often than not, our kids won't hang around for many more such encounters. They may go to Hebrew school, but they'll quickly come to the conclusion that as soon as we stop forcing them, usually immediately after their bar or bat mitzvah, they're not going to do this anymore.

That's why it's important for parents to try to make God a part of their children's lives as they grow up. We should remember that, sometimes, brutal honesty when we're parents is just a bit selfish. It's easier for us to be honest than to stretch, to make something possible for our kids even if it wasn't or isn't possible for us. Effective Jewish parenting may require setting aside our own doubts about God in order to make space for our children's faith to grow and take root without our own insecurities undermining it. Even if we are not certain about God, let's be careful not to rob our children of having the opportunity for Judaism to nourish their spiritual lives.

BUT WHAT IF WE'RE *SURE* WE DON'T BELIEVE?

For all of these reasons, I believe that Jewish parents, to paraphrase John Lennon and Yoko Ono, should at least "give God a chance." That doesn't mean we have to be sure about God, or that having our doubts makes us bad or incompetent Jewish parents. Hardly. But it does mean that some of our doubts and some of our difficulties with God may be the result of how we were raised; we should give our kids the chance to believe and to feel things that still may be hard for us.

Our job as parents is to create a world in which it's safe for our children to wonder, to imagine God, to believe in a world with ultimate values and a transcendent Creator. Sure, it sounds weird to us, but that doesn't mean we should steal it from our children. Working with our children as they grow up Jewishly may be the point when we come to understand that we, too, will have to work at believing—and that concept may be foreign to you. Work at believing? But why not? If love is sustained only if we work at it, then why, especially in a world in which God-talk isn't common, is it strange to have to work and make a conscious effort to learn to be comfortable with God? If having children and learning about their needs causes us to realize that we've been the poorer for not having a place for God in our lives, our roles as parents might be the impetus for us to begin to work on our own spiritual lives.

Yet at the same time, that may not work for all of us. There will undoubtedly be some of us who are completely convinced that God should not—must not—be a part of our kids' Jewish world. For whatever reason, some of us may not agree with the idea that both the deeply religious person and the absolute atheist are both "guessing," basing their lives on an idea that they can't ultimately prove. Does everything we've said in this chapter mean that those parents shouldn't even bother trying to give their kids a serious Jewish education?

No, of course it doesn't mean that. What the Jewish world needs more than anything these days is to learn how to take people seriously, even if we disagree with them. We need to learn to see their views not as ideas to be "defeated" but as positions from which we might learn, even if we see the world differently. *I* may think God is an important part of the Jewish world for my kids, but that's only my view. Ultimately, my Jewish world will be enriched, not depleted, by listening to someone else explain to me why he doesn't want God to be a focus of his child's life, how he believes that he can make Judaism make sense even without a central "role" for God. Just as is true in marriage and in other meaningful relationships, being challenged doesn't always feel great, but it's the place that we really begin to change, to grow, to see the world more broadly. If our kids just get to witness us having these conversations, disagreeing but hearing each other, we'll have taught them both an incredibly important lesson about learning and growing in general, as well as about what Jewish life at its best can be.

I believe that all human beings have a spiritual side. Some of us use that language and others don't. Some of us think about that part of our lives a lot and others put it aside. Some of us do our "spiritual journey" through religion while others find music, nature, or art more compelling. But deep down, I believe that almost all people wonder about the world, think about what happens after they die, and desperately want to believe that their lives have meaning.

Because we are all on a search for meaning, many of us will find a religious tradition that will fuel that search, that will offer a community of people who are interested in similar things. If our kids grow up with a Judaism that has a major place for God, then I think there's a good chance that they may take part in that search—as teenagers, young adults, or even as they approach middle age—as Jews, within the Jewish tradition. But if the Judaism my kids grow up with sees God only as some kind of ornament, nothing particularly serious, or doesn't have a place for God at all, then I suspect the chances are much greater that they will do their "spiritual searching" somewhere else. It might be music; it could be Buddhism. It might be poetry; it might be Christianity.

All too commonly, parents are willing to discuss politics, morality, sex, and virtually everything under the sun with their kids, but not God. For many children, this creates a sense that Judaism is ultimately not the place to do their spiritual wondering and wandering. As they grow older, this becomes one of the major obstacles to continued Jewish connection. That's not what we want for our children; we want Judaism to be their base, so we need to try to raise them with a Jewish world that can meet as many of their spiritual needs as possible as they grow, mature, and change.

7

THE WONDER OF SHABBAT

A had Ha-Am, one of the most important early Zionist thinkers, once remarked that "more than Israel has kept the Shabbat, the Shabbat has kept Israel." In his mind, the survival of the Jewish people, perhaps more than almost anything else, depended upon Shabbat. While Ahad Ha-Am might have taken a bit of poetic license in making that claim, he was probably much more on target than we might imagine. Whether Shabbat (the Hebrew word for "Sabbath") is really at the core of Jewish survival is hard to say. But some things we do know, and one of them is that Shabbat is perhaps the most important element of a home in which our kids are growing up with a sense of Judaism's power, beauty, and depth.

Of course, some of us had no semblance of Shabbat in our homes as we were growing up. For others, Shabbat was a day of restriction or of seemingly capricious limitation, a day of "command performances" at family meals or synagogue services. Whatever it was, it didn't seem like the stuff of which holiness and transcendence are made. The Shabbat of our youth hardly seemed like a tradition that could preserve the Jewish people.

Few of us grew up with Shabbat as a source of wonder and joy. Few of us grew up with Shabbat as sanctified, spiritual time. Few of us grew up with Shabbat as a special part of our week.

But what if Shabbat had not been absent? What if Shabbat had been shown to be the Jews' unique way of creating powerful spiritual moments? What if Shabbat had been a time in which we touched that part of our souls that time, work, and school almost never let us encounter? Could we have experienced something beautiful, intimate, compelling? Maybe. And though we didn't have that experience ourselves, we can still create it for our children. And that, quite simply, is a thumbnail definition of our jobs as parents. If we want this "Jewish parenting thing" to work, we have to do something very different; we have to give our kids much more than we had.

Shabbat, perhaps even more than most Jewish celebrations and rituals, is complex, subtle, and rich in meaning. There's no way we could ever begin to summarize even a reasonable portion of the traditions, rituals, and laws of Shabbat in a chapter like this. So let's approach it differently. Let's focus on the meaning of Shabbat and some of the most salient rituals that communicate that meaning.

SHABBAT—A PALACE IN TIME

Probably no one has described Shabbat better than the theologian Abraham Joshua Heschel (1907–1972), who wrote that Shabbat is a "palace in time." Heschel articulated better than anyone else why we so desperately need Shabbat. In his own inimitable way, he suggested that a world without Shabbat threatens to snuff out our souls:

> *The seventh day is the exodus from tension, the liberation of man from his own muddiness, the installation of man as a sovereign in the world of time. In the tempestuous ocean of time and toil there are islands of stillness where he may enter a harbor and reclaim his dignity. The island is the seventh day, the Sabbath, a day of detachment from things, instruments and practical affairs as well of attachment to the spirit.**

* Abraham Joshua Heschel, *The Sabbath* (New York: Farrar, Straus and Giroux, 1951), p. 29.

It's a strange idea, this notion that Shabbat can somehow save our souls. But it's also a powerful one, and if we work hard to make it a regular part of our lives and the lives of our kids, both we and they can experience what Heschel called the "island" of Shabbat.

Why do we need an island? Because we're drowning in a sea of work, obligations, commitments, responsibilities. It's really that simple. When our kids are born, we promise that we'll never forget that they are miracles. We pledge ourselves to being completely giving, constantly attentive, sensitive to their most subtle nuance. Watching our children emerge into the world, or gently stroking their tiny fingers as they lie in the hospital "warmer" just minutes after birth, it seems absolutely inconceivable to us that anything would ever be more important than they, that anything could ever distract us from their needs, wants, and hopes. Watching them being born, we suddenly feel that now we truly know what is important, and we promise ourselves that we won't forget.

But we do forget. We forget because the world in which we live doesn't take parenting as seriously as it should. If our "baby beeper" goes off, everyone understands that we have to hurry off to the labor and delivery ward, even if it means missing an important meeting. If tragedy strikes and our child becomes seriously ill, people understand. But if our kid is in a school play, or has a Little League game, or just has a cold and doesn't want to be left home with the housekeeper, the world suddenly isn't so understanding. Sure, kids are nice, and parenting is important. But right now there's a deadline to meet, a deal to close, a client to appease. The kids can wait.

And our kids do wait. Too long, and often for a mommy or daddy who just doesn't make it home in time. Deep down, we know it. No matter what we promised ourselves in those first moments of their lives in the hospital weeks, months, or years ago, most of us find it really difficult to keep our priorities straight. "Just one more e-mail" we tell ourselves, and then we'll go home. But what should have taken fifteen minutes takes a bit longer, we take one more call, and by the time we get home, our kid is asleep. Another day when we weren't there to kiss them on the forehead and whisper "good night" as they drift off to a place of dreams and calm.

We know something is amiss. We know that if our child were in the hospital, we'd be there regardless of whether their illness was serious or not. Many of us have received one of "those" phone calls—a child who fell and needs stitches or who broke her leg—and most of us remember rushing to the emergency room. We knew that at that moment, even if our spouse was already "taking care of it," we needed to be there. And we dropped whatever we were doing because we knew what mattered.

But why does it have to take an emergency to wake us up? That's a question many of us ask but few can truly answer. Jewish tradition has decided not to wait for the answer; it's decided just to fix the problem. Our "fix" is Shabbat.

Shabbat, by imposing a period of twenty-five hours per week that shuts out the rest of the world, reminds us what's really important. It reminds us, and it reassures our kids.

Like many kids, mine have learned that just because I'm home from work doesn't necessarily mean I'm not at work anymore. Even if I've walked in the door, put down the briefcase, and started to unwind, the world seems to conspire to take me away from them. The phone can still ring. Faxes come to the house, the e-mail seems to beckon even at home, and there are home chores to do that somehow steal me from them even when I'm in the same room.

That's why our kids love Shabbat so much. For when Shabbat comes, they know that the deadline to get home is real and non-negotiable. When the sun sets, I simply have got to be home. No more excuses, no "just one more phone call." Because we don't answer the phone on Shabbat, the phone has long since stopped ringing. Faxes might come in, but we don't look at them. The computer doesn't get used, the beepers get put away, the cell phones are left to recharge. Work is loyal—it won't go away just because we're spending an evening just with our kids. Shabbat is our way of reminding ourselves that almost nothing in our lives is truly urgent. No more FedExes. No more distractions. All of a sudden, all those contraptions that allegedly make us more efficient get put away, and our kids move back into the center of our consciousness. That, of course, is where they belong, and it's where we promised ourselves so long ago that they'd always be. Shabbat is our way of keeping the promise.

In all the years that I've been a rabbi, and have sat with people in their last conscious moments, no one has ever told me that they wished they'd worked harder or made more money. They've cried about time they wished they had spent with their kids, about grandchildren they wanted to watch grow up, about wrongs they never had the time to right. But never about wishing that they'd done more, or earned more, or worked harder. Never. Shabbat is our way of learning that lesson, long before we have no time left.

RITUAL AND THE MAGIC OF SHABBAT

If we can teach ourselves and our children to think of Shabbat as a protective harbor that will shield us from the storm of modern technological life, we'll probably never ask ourselves "Who says we have to do this?" The question will instead be "How could we ever live without this?"

But to let this happen, we have to take the rituals of Shabbat seriously. For most of us, Shabbat starts with the lighting of a simple set of candles on Friday evening. Some families light a single pair of candles; other families light two candles plus one for each child in the household. In some families, the daughters light along with the mother; in other families, only the mom lights. In some homes, boys also light Shabbat candles. But no matter who kindles the flames, we start Shabbat with light.

It's pretty simple. As the sun sets, you light the candles, cover your eyes, and you recite the blessing:

Praised are You, Lord our God, Ruler of the Universe, who has sanctified us by the commandment that we light the Shabbat candle.

Then, perhaps, after musing about dreams we once had but forget, or about something our children did or said during the week that brought a smile to our faces, we slowly open our eyes . . . to the magic of the flame that burns gently but powerfully. To the look of wonder in our children's eyes as, cradled in our arms or holding our hand, they watch the flame. To the miracle of our ability to create time anew, to reprioritize, to dream of a world at peace and at play.

Though the Shabbat candle lighting blessing is familiar to many, there's a less well known paragraph that some traditional women recite that adds a very special moment to the beginning of Shabbat. After the mother recites the lighting prayer, she quietly says the following:

May it be Your will, our God and God of our ancestors, that You show favor to our family, that You grant us and all Israel a good and long life, that You recall us with beneficent memory and with blessing, that You make our households complete and that You cause Your presence to dwell among us. Privilege me to raise children and grandchildren who are wise and understanding, who love and fear God, who are people of truth . . . and who illumine the world with Torah and good deeds. Please, hear my supplication at this time, in the merit of Sarah, Rebecca, Rachel, and

Leah, our mothers, and cause our light to burn brightly that it not be extinguished forever. . . . Amen.

If we're fortunate, and if we work at it, we can make sure that a calm and a beauty descend upon our home at that moment. The outside world is shut out. Suddenly we've reconnected with our children the way we promised ourselves we would. Our kids are in our arms or holding our hands, and the delicate, flickering flames brighten the darkness that's descending outside, and we are reminded what being Jewish is all about: closeness, family, love. All that can be conveyed by two simple candles.

Candles are not the only ritual that makes up the world of Shabbat. There are many others; each has its own meaning (and very often, more than one clear meaning). Instead of looking at each one separately, let's try to understand the general themes these rituals try to communicate.

SHABBAT AS A COSMIC WEDDING

When our kids learn about Shabbat in Hebrew school, they are probably taught that we observe Shabbat in order to "imitate" what God did when the world was created. Just as God "created" for six days and then rested, the argument goes, so, too, do we "labor" for six days and then rest. And that explanation is quite correct. But it's not the whole story.

Given that Shabbat is such a central part of Jewish life, it's not surprising that over the course of time different Jewish communities have given it different meanings and explanations. The earliest traditions see Shabbat as a reliving of how God created the world. But later in Jewish life, particularly in the sixteenth century, in a town called Safed in the Galilee, mystical Jews began to describe Shabbat not only in terms of creation but also in terms of a cosmic wedding.

According to some of these Jewish mystics, none of the previous explanations for evil in God's world worked. They refused to accept the idea that their suffering was a result of their sinfulness; even if they had not been perfect, they reasoned, nothing they could have done justified their mistreatment during the Inquisition and at other periods of their history. So over the course of time, these mystics began to argue that the world was fundamentally fractured, broken. Our job, they said, was *tikkun olam*—the repair of the world. In a repaired world, they reasoned, God's goodness would once again flow freely into our lives and suffering would gradually end.

How these mystics, commonly known as Kabbalists, proposed to repair the world is actually very complicated. But one element of their program that is quite important for us is the cosmic wedding. They saw Shabbat as a grand ceremony in which God and the Jewish people would be reunited, and God's distance from our lives would be erased. When we celebrate Shabbat, they argued, we're actually participating in that wedding.

Think about it. There are lots of similarities between the rituals of Friday night and the typical Jewish wedding. White is the color of choice. In the traditional Jewish wedding, the bride wears a white gown, and the groom wears a *kittel*—a white robe that looks a bit like a kimono. On Shabbat, the tablecloth is typically white, it's customary for men to wear a white shirt, and in traditional communities, men typically put aside their colored *kippah* in favor of a Shabbat *kippah,* which is usually mostly white.

One of the most prominent features of a Jewish wedding is the two cups of wine; the Shabbat meals (both dinner on Friday night and lunch on Saturday) begin with the recitation of **Kiddush,** or a sanctification of the day that is usually made over wine. Weddings are typically followed by festive meals with singing and dancing; on Shabbat, too, we typically have a meal that's a bit more lavish than during the week. It's customary to sing special Shabbat songs called *zemirot,* and to this day, in some Hassidic households the men still dance around the dining room table.

Even if we don't share with our kids the Kabbalistic theology of a cosmic wedding between God, Israel, and Shabbat (yes, three partners in this wedding; it's a long story!), they can certainly begin to appreciate and look forward to the special feeling that all this festivity creates. Eventually, if we try to get away without doing it, they're likely to let us know they miss it.

My wife and I learned this very clearly one Friday night. Our kids were getting bathed and dressed for Shabbat, and we were setting the table in the dining room. Since this was one of those rare Friday nights when we weren't having company, we decided to "cheat" and not use the china. The china, after all, is a pain. It has to be washed by hand instead of in the dishwasher, it has to be put back in the special padded cases with liners between each plate, and on and on. It takes time, and we were exhausted. So we decided to use the regular plates. No big deal, we figured.

Wrong. When our kids came and saw the table, they were upset! Our middle child asked, "What happened to those pretty plates?" When we explained what was up, he said, "But it's Shabbat! I don't like the table this way!" So we changed the plates. If Shabbat has become so special that not having china on the table offends our kids' sensibilities, something has clearly gotten through. It seemed silly to squander that just because we were tired and too lazy to wash dishes by hand. We learned that night never to underestimate how much our kids get attached to rituals and the things that make them special.

And kids can very quickly get used to the other elements of the cosmic wedding that make Shabbat special. Even if they don't like cleaning up, they like how the house looks when it's neater and cleaner than usual. And even if they don't always appreciate the subtlety of fancy food, they know it's special, and they often like it.

I have a friend, a nationally known Jewish educator, who often tries to convince parents that a great way to give their kids a Jewish upbringing is to make a Friday night dinner. When parents tell her how tired they are, and how a nice meal on Friday night sounds like yet another chore, she responds, "So serve pizza!" As long as it's a Friday dinner, she argues, the food doesn't matter that much. What matters, she reminds her students, is setting aside Friday night as a time for connection, for intimacy, and for a sense that we're participating in something cosmic along with Jewish families around the world.

But when we're trying to create something as glorious as Shabbat, the details do matter. What we wear might matter, and I think what we eat might also matter. Part of what makes an evening special is the food. We wouldn't serve pizza at a wedding, and we wouldn't serve pizza at a **bar mitzvah**. If Shabbat is going to be special, the food should communicate that. If we want the wedding image to come through, then the food, songs, festive dress, and a nicely set table all come into play. Can we "get away" without one or more of these? Of course we can. But like everything else, the more we pour into the ritual, the more it will give back—to us and to our kids.

SHABBAT AS A GLIMPSE OF A PERFECTED WORLD

Beyond creation, and beyond the image of a cosmic wedding, Shabbat is also a day in which we try to create a reality that is a foretaste of the "world to come," the era in which many religions believe reality will be perfected. Our kids won't use that language, but they can certainly understand the idea. Shabbat, they can come to understand, is the day when everything is as it should be.

On Tuesday or Wednesday or Thursday nights, we don't usually "dine." We eat. There's a big difference. We prepare some food, or pop something into the microwave, rush through dinner, and then move on to homework, bath time, bedtime, and whatever it takes to get ready for another day. And our kids sense the rush. They know there's not lots of extra time for talking; they know that some nights mom or dad will be out at a meeting or a book club or grocery shopping; they know that even if their parents are home, we're not always completely available to them.

But Friday night and the rest of Shabbat are supposed to change all that. How many times during the week do we pause before dinner, place our hands on our kids' heads, bless them, kiss them, and tell them that we love them? How often do husbands sing to their wives at the dinner table, thanking them for making their lives so full and so rich with meaning and love? How often do kids really see their parents tell each other they love one another? And how often do our kids know that there's simply nothing that can take us away from them that night?

On Friday night, lots of Jewish families "dine" instead of eat. And they sit around the table for hours, catching up on the week, hearing what's really going on in their kids' lives. They sing with their kids; kids sit on their parents' laps and, as in our house, sometimes even fall asleep in their arms as everyone just hangs out around the table enjoying each other's company. It's Shabbat, and they know that there's nothing that matters to us more than they.

There are other Shabbat rituals that help to create this sense of Shabbat as a glimpse of a perfected world. All too often our kids learn of Shabbat as a day on which traditional Jews "are not allowed" to go shopping, a day on which religious Jews "can't" cook. Technically, that's all true, but it misses the point.

The idea that traditional Jews don't shop on Shabbat is not meant to randomly or capriciously restrict their autonomy, to stop them from doing things they enjoy. Rather, it is a tradition that's meant to remind us of the difference between "needing" and "wanting," and to create time for us to reflect on the fact that most of us have everything we "need." We are fortunate to live in a country where our lives are filled with abundance. Getting away from the shopping frenzy for one day is a way of reminding ourselves that it's perfectly possible to live, and live well, with what we already have; there's really not that much we truly need.

Similarly, while it's true that traditional Jews don't cook on Shabbat because of restrictions in Jewish law, we ought to concentrate not on the "don't"s of Shabbat but rather on what "reality" the custom of not cooking creates. Here, too, my kids have taught me what Shabbat really means.

During the week, it's not uncommon for our kids to go into the kitchen, open the refrigerator, and just stand in front of it silently for minutes on end. The fact that the food is going to spoil, or that the fridge's compressor is going to burn up, or that this little ritual of theirs costs a fortune in electricity doesn't seem to bother them. They just amble up to the refrigerator, open the door, and seemingly stare into space. That is, until I interrupt them and ask, "What are you doing?" To which their response is always, "I'm looking for something to eat." My final retort is say something like, "Well, if you don't see it in there, it's not going to appear out of nowhere, so how about if you close the refrigerator door?" Typically, they grunt, shrug in exasperation, and make some comment about how "there's never anything to eat in this house."

Now, my kids are hardly malnourished, but the truth is that they're not entirely wrong. There are lots of days when there's nothing particularly appealing to eat. They don't want fruit or salad or yogurt; they want something "fun." And it isn't there.

Except for Shabbat. On Shabbat, because we usually have guests, and because we can't cook on Shabbat, Thursday night and Friday are spent preparing food, buying food, storing food—all for the celebration of Shabbat. But what it means to our kids is that when they open the refrigerator right before Shabbat, it's full. Again, just as the no-shopping rule basically says that we already have what we need, and that we're better off spending time with each other than running around a mall, the no-cooking tradition creates a new reality in which there's plenty of food; in which, to use more adult language, our kids experience their world as full, as complete, and whole—a little glimpse of what an ideal world might be like.

That's how we have to understand and explain the restrictions that our kids too often think of as meaningless rules. We have to introduce them to Shabbat as our way of creating one day a week when they can taste the world as a place perfected. Where we can talk about the week that has just passed, and the week to come, because there's no job, no errands. A time to dine, rather than eat. Even our young children feel the difference—we *know* they do.

When the rules of Shabbat aren't simply a litany of "don't"s, but are part of a larger whole, one that makes sense, that touches us, that envelops us in time we otherwise simply wouldn't have, the rules suddenly make sense.

SHABBAT'S RITUAL AS A "SUBVERSIVE" SOCIAL CRITIQUE

Shabbat is likely to become most difficult during our children's teenage years. That's when it's most important for kids to be the masters of their own time, and as we can easily see, Shabbat conflicts with that a bit. Adolescence is also the time when children are in the process of differentiating themselves from their parents, and in order to do that, they need to be different from the rest of the family. Shabbat thus becomes even more difficult.

Is there anything we can do? An enormous help in getting through the teenage years would be a social network for our kids. If they have friends who do the same things, who care about the same issues, and who are as committed to Jewish involvement as they are, then being Jewish will be much less of a problem and their resistance will drop. It won't disappear, but it will be more limited.

It would also be helpful to speak to your children about Jewish life in terms that have meaning to them. The teen years are a period of cynicism, of (hopefully moderate) rebellion, of seeing everything that's wrong with the world. Wouldn't it be wonderful if we could show our kids that Judaism and Shabbat *share* their sentiments and values? We can.

Many people, Jews among them and our teenage kids prime among *them,* fault religion for being insufficiently critical of society and its priorities. There's plenty that's wrong with the world, and Jewish kids, like many others, feel that religion doesn't do enough or say enough about this. In his famous critique of religion, Karl Marx claimed that religion was an "opiate for the masses." He said that religion fostered an unthinking sense of obedience and undermined people's ability to be critical of a system that took advantage of them. Religion, he said, had inadvertently become society's accomplice in denying their humanity, in repressing their soul.

But Marx did not understand Shabbat. He did not appreciate that beyond "imitating" God and creating a connection to other Jews, Shabbat also has a deeply subversive quality. Throughout Jewish history, as poverty and oppression threatened to erode Jews' sense of dignity, Shabbat intervened. Virtually every detail of their Shabbat experience has assured Jews throughout the ages that repair of the world was possible, and that in the interim, they did matter. As the sun sets, Jews walk off to the local **shul,** where, as Shabbat begins, they recite the Sabbath psalm (Psalm 92), evoking a vision of a more just universe:

> though the wicked sprout like grass,
> though all evil doers blossom,
> it is only that they may be destroyed forever.

. . .

The righteous shall blossom like a date-palm,
they will thrive like a cedar in Lebanon;
planted in the house of the Lord,
they will flourish in the courts of our God.

Shabbat is our way of living the dream of a way of life we dare believe the world could one day become. It's our way of reminding ourselves that the world's oppressors are not God, and that their power will someday diminish.

Throughout our history, we have to remind our occasionally cynical children, on Shabbat even the most impoverished Jews gathered around their tables, dressed in their finest clothes. Poor as they were, their food was more festive on Shabbat. Overworked and exhausted (infinitely more exhausted than anything we can begin to imagine, no matter what we may think), they dined and they sang. In Hasidic communities, to this day in some, they literally danced their way out of the synagogue. At home, gathered around the table, they danced again, and sang. But these special Shabbat songs weren't just songs. They were subversive songs, which they sang to remind themselves that the reality in which they lived was unfair—and also impermanent. As such, they said, their reality wasn't the ultimate reality.

One of the songs they commonly sang (and which traditional Jews still sing) was called Menuchah ve-Simchah, "Contentment and Joy." Written by an unknown poet in the mid-1500s, it begins with a standard description of Shabbat. The first verse, for example, reads:

Contentment and joy, light for the Jewish people,
It is a day of rest, a day of delight.
Those who observe it act as witnesses
That in six days, all was created and still endures.

The next three verses continue in much the same vane. By the fifth and final verse, however, the tone changes dramatically. Even as the song continues to enumerate the customs of Shabbat, it suggests that Jews who celebrate Shabbat are doing more than fulfilling a biblical command. They are living a "taste of the world to come":

With an additional loaf of challah and the majestic Kiddush;
with delicacies aplenty and a spirit of generosity,
those who revel in it will merit infinite blessing:
the arrival of the Messiah, life in the world to come.

This song and dozens of others just like it assert that Shabbat is not only about creation, nor is it only about connection to other people. It is about something even more cosmic. Shabbat, as we said before, is about a different world. It is the opportunity to experience the world repaired, humanity healed. Even more, it's a demand that we remember that reality as it looks today is ultimately unacceptable.

As traditional Jews conclude their Shabbat meal, they begin the Grace after Meals with a special addition, reserved primarily for Shabbat. They add Psalm 126 to their prayer, heightening their conviction that their present reality is not what God has in mind for them:

When the Lord restores the fortunes of Zion
—we see it as in a dream—
our mouths shall be filled with laughter,
our tongues, with songs of joy.
. . .
They who sow in tears
shall reap with songs of joy.
Though he goes along weeping,

carrying the seed bag,
he shall come back with songs of joy
carrying his sheaves.

What we as parents have to explain to our kids is that the myriad
rituals and texts of Shabbat are all about something really important. They're not just "nice" or "quaint" or "ethnic." They come not
only to mimic God's rest on the seventh day, but to cry out against
the injustices of the world as we see it, and to insist that something
better is possible. Shabbat is subversive, in its own strange way,
because it is meant to so enthrall us with the vision of a world perfected that we become committed to going out and making that
dream a reality.

We ought to remind our kids that it's no accident that many of
the great socialists of the early part of the twentieth century were
Jews, usually the descendants of traditional Jewish families. It's no
accident that the Workers Circles of New York and other American
cities in the early 1900s were composed largely of Jews as well. These
people had internalized the message of Shabbat, and had the
courage to try to make the dream of Shabbat a reality in America
and Europe.

That's what we're doing when we celebrate Shabbat. And that, we
ought to tell our kids, is why we think it's important that they participate with us. For the Jew who observes Shabbat and understands
the sacred drama it creates, the message is clear. Jewish tradition is
afraid that we will despair of the possibility of that perfected world
ever coming to be, so it creates a day on which we can actually live it.
By allowing Jews to taste a bit of a redeemed world, Jewish life forces
them to ask powerful questions about their priorities, their dreams,
their willingness to make sacrifice in order to change reality. Shabbat
comes not to say that everything is fine, but to remind Jews that it is
not and to demand that they change it.

BUT DOES SHABBAT "WORK"?

The next questions our kids may ask are: Does the ritual "work"? Does it really make a difference to anyone, or is this all some theoretical poetry that actually changes nothing? A fair question. But we can answer it. We can point to the socialists mentioned above. For them, the message of Shabbat clearly did strike home. That's why they devoted their lives to causes that were often unpopular and occasionally dangerous. But they were not the only ones to whom Shabbat spoke so powerfully.

Consider the testimonies of those Jews who survived the Nazi death machine and who told of Shabbat in the camps. They spoke of inmates who violated the Nazis' law, risking immediate death by hoarding Thursday's bread so they could have two pieces on Friday (symbolic of the two loaves of challah that tradition requires on Friday evening and Shabbat afternoon). Why would people on the verge of starvation, in which Shabbat could scarcely be celebrated, take this risk? What was to be gained?

What they stood to gain was a chance to reassert their denial of Nazi Europe as an ultimate reality. Honoring Shabbat, even in a murder camp, was their way of saying, "I believe in the possibility of a better world. I deny that you are the real ruler. Despite you, I insist that I am human, that I am created in God's image, and that one day a world will arise when good will triumph over evil, when God will triumph over you."

Is this Marx's "opiate of the masses"? Hardly. On this level, Shabbat is about rebellion, about dissatisfaction with the world, about retaining hope in the face of adversity, about making Jewish life about joy and beauty, but also about impatience with what we need to fix, to change, to improve.

To Jews today, thankfully no longer in the clutches of Nazis,

Shabbat comes as a challenge. It's a challenge to triumph over the world that seems to steal us from our families, from our selves, from our souls. It's a challenge to us to "fight back," to rebuild the relationships that work and pressure often cause us to abandon or neglect. On those occasions when speaking or teaching takes me away from home for Shabbat, I make a point of calling my kids before Shabbat. I doesn't matter whether I'm in New York or London or Jerusalem—I call, and I recite over the phone the same blessing that I say to them at the table. Thousands of mile away, the call allows a brief moment of calm and of love before the speech, the dinner, the class. It reminds me of what's really important, of who really matters.

I actually got the idea of blessing my kids over the phone from a friend who, at a conference, excused himself, saying he'd be right back—he had to call his kids to bless them. I was surprised; he'd never struck me as the type who was into "new-fangled" Jewish ritual. But in learning that he was going to bless his kids, he taught me something important: He showed me that if calling my kids made me uncomfortable because I really shouldn't have been out of town lecturing, but should instead be at home with them, then by calling them, and being reminded of what really matters, I was being blessed no less than they were.

That's what Shabbat does. It is more than a taste of the world to come; it is a challenging, demanding taste designed to recommit us in the battle to make that dream a reality. We have to learn and then show our kids that through the unique combination of food, song, dress, and study, the fragrance of wine and the magic of fire, Jewish tradition takes a simple day and makes it profoundly spiritual. It is in ritual that Judaism's cerebral seriousness begins to give way to passion, to dreams, to a sense of the possibility of a world transformed. It's in the world of Shabbat that Jewish life is often at its most powerful.

SHABBAT AS THE ANCHOR
OF THE JEWISH WEEK

So far we've been focusing on the impact that a committed celebration of Shabbat has on the day of Shabbat itself. And while that
is surely the most important part of Shabbat, there is another side:
Shabbat helps to make the entire week a Jewish week. By giving all
seven days of the week a Jewish focus, Shabbat serves as one of the
most important tools Jewish parents have for creating the immersion that we've talked about throughout this book.

To get an idea of how central Shabbat has always been to Jews
and their conception of time, it helps to remind ourselves that
Hebrew doesn't even have names for the days of the week. Unlike
most other languages, Hebrew names the days of the week by
counting them and noting their place relative to Shabbat. Since
the Hebrew word "Shabbat" can mean either "Sabbath" or "week,"
there's a kind of double entendre in the way we describe these
days. Thus, Sunday is Yom Rishon be-Shabbat, or the first day of
this Shabbat week. Monday is Yom Sheni be-Shabbat, or the second day of this Shabbat week. Each day's place is determined by
its distance from Shabbat. And "Saturday"? There isn't even a
Hebrew word for Saturday, and no one says "the Seventh Day."
Even completely secular Israelis can't say "Saturday"—there is no
word to use! There is only one word for that day: Shabbat. It's the
only word that exists: Shabbat.

Why does all this matter? It matters because it's one small indication of how, in traditional Jewish communities, the entire week
is somehow focused on Shabbat. At the beginning of the week
families are often inviting people over for Shabbat meals or
accepting invitations to go to the homes of others. Typically, the
middle of the week is when menus are planned and shopping lists
compiled. Wednesday and Thursdays are often for cooking. In
some homes, children help with the making of challah a day or

two before Shabbat, and by Fridays, the house is being scrubbed, children and adults are getting ready for the climactic beginning of Shabbat. Shabbat thus becomes a focus for the entire week.

It's not only in the preparation for Shabbat that this day can add distinctly powerful Jewish moments and memories to the lives of our children. If our kids know that when Saturday night comes their family will "make *havdalah*" (the ceremony that ends Shabbat with a cup of wine, a candle, and a spice box),* sing songs, and exchange wishes for a good and healthy week, the cycle of their lives becomes a Jewish one. Those families that are uncomfortable with overtly religious rituals have found other practices for making the end of Shabbat a memorable moment. Some gather together to exchange brief wishes for the upcoming week, others make a point of calling relatives who live out of town either right as Shabbat begins or as it ends. The specifics, ultimately, may not matter; our job as parents is to find *something* we can do to make Shabbat a highlight of the week, something we can all do together, something that will provide our children with a lifetime of warm and nurturing memories.

The rituals of Shabbat, like so many other rituals in Jewish life, give a richness, a wonder, and a tenderness to our children's lives in ways we can't even begin to anticipate. I still remember one Saturday evening, as the sun was setting and Shabbat was ending, when I suddenly realized that I had no idea where my kids were. They're not normally the quietest of kids, and it's unusual for all three to be in the house not making a sound. Sensing that trouble

* In the *havdalah* ceremony, we use wine just as we do at most ceremonies that mark the passage of time. The spice box is meant to prolong the sweet scent of Shabbat, and the candle, which must have more than one wick, is no longer the frail light with which we began Shabbat, but a "torch" with which we will venture out during the next six days and make the dream that we lived on Shabbat a reality.

was afoot, I began to look for them. When it was pretty clear they weren't in the house, I went out to the backyard to see if I could find them. And there, lying on their backs, one next to the other, I found the kids staring up at the sky. They knew they weren't going to be able to watch the video they had just gotten while it was still Shabbat. So, as much as they like Shabbat, they were anxious to know when it was going to be over. Knowing that one of the Jewish traditions about the end of Shabbat is that it is over when we can see three stars close together in the sky, they'd gone out to look. When they got tired of craning their necks upward, waiting for the stars to appear, they figured out that it would be easier to lie on the ground and wait. And that's how I found them; close together, lying in the backyard, quietly gazing at the heavens, filled with wonder as they watched the stars slowly begin to appear in the cloudless sky.

What else in their lives could have prompted that kind of an encounter, that sort of peace and transcendence? That brief moment, I told myself, was reason enough for all the time and energy we'd invested in Shabbat. Whether they remember that particular day or not, I don't know. Will the feelings that Shabbat evokes for them remain with them for a lifetime? That's our hope; that's our goal.

HOW MUCH OF THIS TO DO?

Where do we go from here? Does all this mean that in order to communicate this "perfected time" we have to do the whole nine yards of Friday night ritual? Probably not. What's true in other cases is also true here; the more we invest in it, the more we'll get out of it. And the more we participate in the traditional way of making Shabbat, the more we'll also create and feel connections to other Jews throughout the world who are also making Shabbat. But here, too, different families will do things differently.

One of the big challenges we'll have to face on Shabbat is that of Shabbat afternoon, and all the competing activities that our kids are going to want to do—soccer, Little League, and the like. This can be a tough decision. If we live in the kind of community in which people typically spend all day together on Shabbat, our kids will have a support network for staying busy and happy all day. But if our community tends to celebrate Friday night but not Shabbat day, or the morning of Shabbat but not much after lunch, it is going to be difficult for us to create for our kids the sort of reality that will make a full day of Shabbat fun and meaningful. There are balances to be struck here, based on what we believe, what we think will work for our kids, and what sort of community support we've been able to provide them. Nothing easy about that, at all.

Clearly, not all Jewish families are going to celebrate Shabbat in the same way. Some will adhere to all the traditional modes of observance, while others will be more innovative and less concerned with the details of what Jewish law requires. But everyone *could* make Shabbat a focus of the week. Those families that observe a traditional Shabbat will follow much of the usual routine; they'll light candles, make Kiddush, say the blessing over the challah, perhaps attend synagogue services, maybe abstain from work and even try to focus on the holy in life. But even those families who will choose something very different can still make Shabbat a critical Jewish moment. Let's do here what we've talked about before; if we're not going to follow the traditional patterns, let's ask ourselves what the purpose or effect of those customs or traditions might have been, and how we might create our own rituals to accomplish the same goal, even if in a slightly different manner.

Some liberal Jewish families with teenagers have a rule: The kids can do whatever they want to do after Friday night's Shabbat dinner, but they must be home for the family meal. If they want to be with friends later that night, that's fine, but the friends have to come over for the Shabbat meal. These families have chosen not to restrict their kids' Shabbat activities to those permitted in the traditional community, but they still want to make sure Shabbat is a pivotal part of their children's lives.

Other parents we know have imposed a rule not on their kids but on themselves: They won't go out on Friday night to anything that doesn't involve their kids. If their friends want to have an "adult only" evening out, it has to be a different night. If they want to get together on Friday, it has to be at their home, or their kids have to be welcome. Their rule: If Shabbat is about time perfected, about getting our priorities straight, then we're with our kids. No matter what.

Interestingly, in the Sephardic community, both in Israel and beyond, it's not at all unusual to see young people come to synagogue on a Friday evening completely "decked out" for a Friday night on the town. These young people are coming to synagogue because, after all, it's Shabbat; on Shabbat, they'd tell you, Jews go to shul. But they're also clearly dressed for going out. So after services, they're off to the city with friends.

Some people might say that coming to synagogue on a Friday night when you're about to go out and party doesn't make sense; it's completely hypocritical. While that may seem to be the case for people who are committed to the standards of Jewish law, it might be a critique that misses the point for many Jews. Those people would say, "Sure, it's not *your* style of Shabbat, but it's our way of making even Friday evening a distinctly Jewish time. It's something that the rest of our week is focused on." We're with the Jewish community, we're with people we care about. That's what Shabbat is.

Is that mode of Shabbat "good enough"? I think that's the wrong question. The question isn't what's "good enough," or what makes someone else think what we're doing is OK. The question is: Are we investing enough in making Friday night unique and special to communicate to our kids the beauty and passion of Jewish life? If we're honest with ourselves, we'll be able to see from their reactions how good a job we're doing. Do they look forward to Shabbat? Or do they resist it? Have we succeeded in getting them to feel the special time we're trying to create? Is our reality really transformed?

For some Jews the traditional modes of Shabbat observance are going to be the most effective ways of doing this. But for others, a different sort of "celebration" speaks more powerfully. Consider the phenomenon on the Upper West Side of New York City known as Bnai Jeshurun—BJ to its adherents. At this liberal synagogue, so many people come to sing, dance, and welcome Shabbat as the start of their weekend that the congregation now holds two services. Hundreds of people attend each one, lining up around the block long before the service actually begins. Many of these worshipers will clearly go out to a restaurant or to a club afterward, but what their being at BJ on Friday night proves is that even those who are not committed to traditional Shabbat observance in every way can find meaning in making the end of the workweek and the beginning of the weekend a distinctly Jewish moment, one that seems somewhat holier and more in touch with what our souls really need.

The challenge is to figure out how to do that with our children, regardless of their age, in synch with their interests and personalities. That's why Shabbat is such a critical part of the Jewish tradition: When kids know that they have to clean their rooms on Friday afternoon because Shabbat is coming, when they know that Friday night is the night that the whole family showers and bathes before dinner, when we all dress up a bit before coming to the table, when they come to associate Friday night dinner with the good china or with eating in the dining room rather than in the kitchen, their lives revolve around a rhythm that is distinctly Jewish and, hopefully, filled with joy. If they know that Shabbat is the day on which their parents are simply around, that there's time for idle chatting, for board games, for walks around the neighborhood with nowhere in particular to go, they'll get the point. The "immersion" into Jewish life that we talked about earlier simply can't be done any better than that.

So where do we start? How do we create this if we've never done it before? Jewish tradition can feel strange, daunting. It seems that there's so much to master, and we fear appearing foolish. That's what the resources listed at the end of this volume are all about. We're tempted to wait, to put it off just a bit more. But we need to be honest; if we wait, our kids will grow up before we make Shabbat a compelling Jewish memory, a haven from a world that is too fast and too harsh.

THE MOST IMPORTANT THING IS TO BEGIN

With time, we'll figure out how our families can create those magical moments. Perhaps we'll decide to stay home each Friday night, keeping our family together for a few treasured hours. After all, if people really need to be with us, they can be guests in our home, in our perfected world. We can let our children know that on that one night, nothing—not work, not friends—will take us away from them. Later, we can even extend a night into a full day of rest, of walks, of reading, of reconnecting. We might even extend it to some of the more traditional behaviors of Shabbat— not writing, not working, maybe not traveling to anyplace other than the synagogue, or, perhaps, eventually not using the car for anything at all on Shabbat. All of these are possibilities. But for now, the issue is to start. Or if we've already started, we can think about whether we'd like to add more, to invest more, to give our kids the gift of the one Jewish institution that's always been the cornerstone of meaningful Jewish life.

Is this all new to you and your family? Don't worry, Friday night's candles are the perfect place to begin. Let the quiet surround you. Don't hurry. Watch the candles. Burning candles seem to dance, beckoning us to join a people who, for centuries, have used Shabbat as a time to focus on what really matters, to escape from the "real world" that threatens to extinguish our dreams and our souls. That is what Shabbat and its candles are about. For some, Shabbat will grow into Saturday. Some of us will suffice with Friday night. But we all need those moments when we hold our children, shut out the racket, and make space for a beauty and spirit that we can have regularly, every Friday night, just by lighting candles and creating sacred time.

It's time to listen to our children. They love those moments of quiet and tenderness. They shudder to that power. Let's become their partners by letting Shabbat help us evoke that power, sense that wonder, feel that awe. That's what life so often lacks, and that's what Shabbat has to offer. It's time to accept the offer, and to begin the journey.

8

~

"WHY DO WE HAVE TO?"
Getting Over Our Fear of Rules

A couple of years ago, when my son Avi was about seven years old, he and I were taking a walk through our neighborhood. It was a quiet Shabbat afternoon, and everyone else in the house had fallen asleep. So out we went, just enjoying a nice afternoon and a few quiet moments to talk.

As we were walking up our street, Avi pointed to the house of one of our neighbors and said, "That's Allison's house." Then he said, "You know, she's Jewish, but she's not religious." "That's true," I said, dreading the conversation I suspected was about to follow. I explained that Allison's family was Jewish, but that they lived their Jewish lives very differently from us. And hoping to avoid a conversation about why we did some things they didn't do, I told him how nice Allison's parents are, and how lucky we were to have them as neighbors.

But Avi was not to be distracted. "But I don't get it," he said. I was sure I knew what was coming. After all, this was a Shabbat afternoon, a day of the week on which our kids don't watch TV, don't play their CDs, don't go shopping. But while my wife and I understand the special and intimate environment that all these "rules" try to create on Shabbat, I was afraid that Avi was too young to understand all that, and that Allison's freedom was something he'd be jealous of. But he asked, so I had to respond.

"What don't you get?" I asked him back. To which he said, "I don't get why her family would be Jewish but not be religious. After all, why be Jewish if you're not going to do all the things that make it so much fun?"

For a moment I was just relieved that I didn't have to have that "why do we have to when they don't have to" conversation. But after that momentary relief I realized that I had learned something very important from Avi: Even little kids can respond to limits as positive elements in their lives if they're part of a larger picture that makes sense. Are there never moments that my kids wish that they could turn on the VCR on Shabbat? Of course there are. Aren't they sometimes anxious for Shabbat to conclude so they can get on the computer and check their e-mail? Obviously. But what Avi taught me is that if rules are part of a larger whole, a deeper and more meaningful reality than the VCR or his e-mail, the reaction will be not "why do we have to do this" but rather (to use Avi's inimitable phrase), "why would anyone be Jewish and not want to do the things that make it so much fun?"

THEY'RE NOT THE TEN SUGGESTIONS

It's inevitable that, as Jewish parents, we're going to come up against the issue of rules. After all, parenting in general has rules. There are clothes our kids can't wear, words we don't allow them to say, magazines and movies that are off-limits, behaviors we don't allow, and on and on. Are those rules a matter of being mean? Are we trying to be capricious? Obviously not. It's just that good parenting means setting limits and enforcing moral and ethical standards. And the same is true of good Jewish parenting. In the Torah, rules are part of the creation story (don't eat from the Tree of Knowledge), the story of the flood (God gives Noah and his sons a whole variety of commandments when they leave the ark), the Exodus from Egypt (the giving of the Torah at Mount Sinai), and much more. And what did we get at Mount Sinai? Not the Ten Suggestions. The word our tradition uses is "commandments"—rules are simply part of this culture we call "Judaism."

We would never imagine that we could raise our kids to be thoughtful and caring human beings without rules. Raising thoughtful, caring, and committed *Jewish* kids also requires rules. And if they're part of something larger and wonderful and magical and joyful, the rules won't chase them away. One of the most interesting phenomena in contemporary American Jewish life is the large number of young people, usually in their twenties and thirties, who grew up in the liberal Jewish community but who later adopted a much more traditional way of life, one filled with all the restrictions we commonly think will chase our kids away. Why do these young people—well-educated, professionally successful, fully integrated into American life—choose something so different and seemingly so restrictive? Why would they consciously choose a more traditional way of life, with all the limitations it imposes? Because they don't experience rules as oppressive.

People who love playing an instrument, who are dedicated to getting better and better at it, make rules for themselves about how often they'll practice, how hard they'll work. They will sometimes give up doing other things because of the rules, but they choose to be restricted; the restrictions make space for something that to them is meaningful, magical, beautiful.

Being a spouse also has its rules; it's the rare marriage that doesn't have *some*. Being a lover has its rules. Being a parent restricts us. Taking care of our parents as we get older means that there are some things we must do, and other things we can't do. But we do—and don't do—these things because those relationships are all part of a larger world that means a great deal to us. If we didn't love our wife or our husband, or if we didn't care about our parents, we might drop the rules. But because we usually do love and care about these people, the rules are acceptable, even welcomed. They show that this "relationship stuff" is serious business.

The truth is that the standards also reinforce the relationships. We don't talk to our spouses in hurtful ways just because we love them. Knowing there are expectations of certain behaviors and courtesies makes it easier to be open with one another, to allow ourselves to experience the vulnerability that love is sometimes about.

In a world that threatens to pull us away from our parents, our sense of obligation to them (even when we don't "feel" the desire at that very moment) pulls us back and often creates moments in which we're reminded what we love about them. Rules express relationships, but rules also preserve relationships. We've got to make the same point to our kids about rules in Jewish life.

The important thing for us as we begin our journey into Jewish parenting is to understand what the rules do and why they matter. Once we understand that, we'll feel more comfortable with these standards ourselves, and we'll be able to explain them more clearly to our kids.

So why do rules matter? And does good Jewish parenting really have to involve rules?

RULES SHOW WE'RE SERIOUS

Do we want our kids to hate us? Do we want them to resent being part of our family? Obviously not. So why the rules? Because ultimately the rules show that we're serious. If we tell our kids not to hit other kids, but we don't enforce it, we let them know that we really don't care. If we don't want our kids to talk to people harshly or meanly, but then don't stop them when it happens, we let them know that this is just advice; ultimately, though, it's not really that important. The point is simple: What's important has rules. Being part of a family means accepting that there are limits, standards, expectations. It's just part of the territory.

The same with our Jewish lives. If we want to create a tradition of everyone being home for a Friday night Shabbat dinner together, then that's the rule. For if it's the general idea, but we decide that we're not going to push it, two things will happen. The first will be that our kids will intuit that it's not really all that important to us. After that, we'll find that their frequency of being at home for Shabbat will decrease as they have more and more things (often nice and positive things, by the way) to lure them away. If Friday night is a night at home, then that's the limit.

A colleague of mine told me that he and his wife try to get their kids not to do certain things at home on Shabbat. But they don't like adversarial interactions with their kids (who does?), so when the kids push and resist the limits they've imposed, he tends to back down a little. But he has an uncle, he told me, who's very religious and very strict about his observance of Shabbat. So David, my friend, told me that he was very clear with his kids: At the uncle's house, they had to be extremely careful not to do anything that would make the uncle uncomfortable. And the kids responded; they were great.

Months later, when David got a tiny bit annoyed that his kids weren't taking Shabbat at home as seriously as he would have liked, he asked them rather cynically, "How come you guys are so cooperative when we go to my uncle's house, but you just ignore your mom and me?" Without thinking, he told me, one of the kids looked up from his board game and nonchalantly said, "Because your uncle's serious about it."

Out of the mouths of babes! Our kids can read us like an open book. They know when we're serious, and they know when we're not. If we're serious about standards in Jewish life, then Jewish life has to have rules. If we want to let our kids know that lighting Hanukkah candles is an important part of our family's life together, then we probably need a rule that they've got to be home for that. No matter what. If we want them home for the seder, then we've got to set that limit. If we're trying to teach them the value of *tzedakah* (a word commonly translated as "charity" but which actually means something closer to "righteousness"), then when they're young, we probably have to insist that part of their allowance goes right to the *tzedakah* box. It's the regularity of the practice that makes it serious. And it's seriousness that will ultimately communicate that we want this to be part of their core selves. Rules create regularity.

How do we get our kids to practice the piano? By letting them do it whenever they want to? That rarely works. How do we get them to do their homework? By suggesting that they not watch TV before they finish? We know better. If we want to be helpful and realistic Jewish parents, we need to transfer our lessons from parenting in general to the world of Jewish life.

FROM NON-NEGOTIABILITY TO CONSTANCY

One of the ways in which having serious standards is important relates back to a concept we talked about at the beginning of the book: immersion. We've suggested a few times that if we're going to be successful in raising our kids as committed and joyous Jews, we need to move "being Jewish" into the core of who they are as human beings. The goal, we suggested, would be to have them think of their Jewishness as being as central and as critical to their sense of who they are as is their gender or their family. And in order to do that, we've suggested, we've got to immerse them in Jewish life.

One of the contributions that rules make to this goal is that they create what we might call "constancy" in Jewish life. When we see something as a rule or a standard, and not just as a behavior that we can choose to do or not do, that "thing" ends up being a much more regular feature of our life. Let's take a few examples.

One of the central features of Jewish life that we have not addressed yet is *kashrut,* or the system of Jewish dietary laws. Very simply, *kashrut* involves two basic principles: not eating certain foods (products of animals that are considered nonkosher), and not mixing milk and meat products. Needless to say, the details are infinitely more complex than that (see the sources listed in the "Suggestions for Further Exploration"), but that's the gist.

Why is *kashrut* important? Why would anyone think of making this a part of their life? Clearly, for Jews who are committed to the authority and sanctity of *halakhah,* or "Jewish law," there's not much to discuss. These Jews believe that God gave us the Torah; since the Torah commands the rules of *kashrut,* and the Torah is Divine, the authority of *kashrut* is obvious.

What's interesting, however, is that *kashrut* is one of those areas of Jewish practice that's taken very seriously even by Jews who do not follow all the details of *halakhah.* Why would they do that?

One of the many reasons *kashrut* speaks to contemporary Jews is that it's a way of sanctifying a part of our lives that all too often becomes debased. We live in a world that takes food for granted. While we know that millions of people go hungry every day, we are oblivious to the fact that we have so much. We eat on the run without a thought. We cavalierly throw out enough food at the end of a big meal to feed another family. Judaism's tradition of pausing to say blessings before and after eating, and its dietary laws that virtually require that we think about what we're consuming, are designed to counteract the callousness that sometimes overwhelms us.

This idea struck home for me most clearly during my first visit to a Burger King. As a kid growing up in a kosher home, fast-food burger places were always a part of the American culture that were off-limits to me. So when a kosher Burger King opened in Jerusalem, even though I was already in my thirties, I was as excited as any kid. During my next trip to Israel, a friend picked me up at the airport and asked, "Where do you want to go for dinner?" No question, I told him. And off to Burger King we went.

We walked into the restaurant, and I was in seventh heaven. Finally, I was going to have my very own Whopper! I looked at the menu above the counter, found the biggest burger they had, saw the fries, the hot, wrapped hamburgers already waiting (they call it fast food for a reason!), got my tray, paid, and went to find a table.

We sat down at the table, burgers, fries, Coke, and ketchup at the ready, but suddenly, my classic American experience came to an end. For before eating bread, traditional Jews perform a ritual of washing their hands. Before I could bite into the burger, I had to pour water over each of my hands and recite a very quick blessing. Now, the advantage of being in Jerusalem was that there was a "washing stand" (a place with a large cup and a sink for exactly this purpose) just a few feet away. But then, I realized, the rules of washing our hands, which are effectively part of the dietary tradition, mean that there really is no Jewish fast food. Not even in Jerusalem. Not even at a kosher Burger King. Fast food is food we don't think about, food we just consume and then forget. That, says the tradition, is not what food is all about. And the rules, or the standards, are the way our tradition tries to make that point.

There's another part to *kashrut*. As citizens of the modern world, we also ignore the fact that for those of us who are not veg-etarians, the food we eat comes at the expense of another animal's life. Judaism says that taking an animal's life for human food is permissible, but only if we prepare and eat the food in a way that reminds us that a life was, after all, taken to provide us with food.

But while there are many other reasons that Jews across the globe commit themselves in varying degrees to *kashrut,* one of the primary ones has to do with constancy. A kosher home is a home in which children are given Jewish immersion; a kosher kitchen is a laboratory for Jewish identification.

Sound strange? When you think about it, it's not that hard to figure out. The kitchen is one of the most used rooms in our homes. Days go by in which our family does not use our living room. And if we're not entertaining and it's not Shabbat, we hardly ever use the dining room. My kids don't commonly have occasion to hang out in my study, and in the winter months, even the backyard gets neglected. But not the kitchen. Each of us is in the kitchen dozens of times a day; it's the hub of family activity. And that means that when a kitchen is filled with symbols of Jewish life (by having separate cabinets for milk and meat dishes, different drawers for the two sets of silverware, two different-color dish towels hanging side by side, and much more), our kids are given constant reminders that being Jewish is simply part of what this home is about. Being Jewish is simply who they are.

I understood this more clearly once my kids got old enough to take their own snacks from the fridge. Sitting at the kitchen table, sipping a cup of tea and reading the paper, I'd occasionally see one of my kids open the refrigerator door, take a chocolate pudding off the shelf, and then come back into the main part of the kitchen. There they would pause for a moment and try to remember which drawer they should open as they went to get a spoon. I wasn't involved; I had said nothing. But somehow, even at an early age, they had learned that certain spoons were for some foods, and other spoons were for other foods. As I watched my kids try to remember which drawer to open, I realized that even eating a chocolate pudding had become a Jewish act. Getting a snack was part of their immersion.

The same is true of going to the market. As they were growing up, they'd sit in the supermarket wagon as their mom or I pushed them down the aisle and collected the foods we needed. But my kids always saw something more than our simply seeing the food, grabbing it, and placing it in the cart. They saw that in addition to all that, we paused for a split second to make sure that the food had a *hechsher,* a mark that showed it was kosher. All of a sudden, even going food shopping was a "Jewish" expedition.

Sometimes, of course, the way our kids understand these rules can be rather amusing. One Sunday of Thanksgiving weekend, we were driving home to Los Angeles after a few days in San Diego. The traffic was horrendous, and we were creeping along at five or seven miles an hour. Suddenly my daughter (probably about five or six at the time) announced that she had to go to the bathroom—*now.* While I wondered why it was that kids always seem to wait until things are an emergency before telling us they have to go, I realized that this was not the time for a philosophic conversation. We clearly didn't have much room for negotiation. Thankfully, we just happened to be a few yards from an exit ramp, at the bottom of which I saw the golden arches of a McDonald's. I got off the freeway, hightailed it into the McDonald's parking lot, and said to my obviously uncomfortable daughter, "OK, here's a bathroom. Let's go." Tali looked outside, saw the arches, and said, "You know I can't go in there."

Now, obviously, we could go into McDonald's to use the bathroom! (And she did.) But I was struck by her reaction: that wasn't a place she could go. It seemed silly, almost ludicrous, at the moment. But in thinking about it, I was glad that even in the midst of her "bathroom crisis" she had a sense of who she was. And I realized that the simple and constant rules of *kashrut* had played an important role in that.

Examples abound, but the point is simple: Though we often have a sense that the rules of Jewish life are negatives, our kids won't necessarily feel that way. Rules can simply be part of defining who we are, of communicating what's important to us, what we stand for, how we live.

CONSTANCY LEADS TO INTENSITY

Constancy, or immersion, is an important part of what rules provide, as is the general idea of showing what we think is important. But there's another aspect to the constancy that rules create, and we call it intensity.

Do you remember learning how to dance? Ballroom dancing, Israeli folk dancing, or whatever—the kind in which it actually matters what you do, where you put your feet, how you move.

Try to remember what it was like to learn the dance. First you tried to get a sense of what the dance was. Then you started to learn the steps. Gradually you began to get a bit more comfortable with the steps, but you still had to concentrate. And while the process might have been fun, it wasn't the kind of experience in which you could lose yourself, in which your feet moved virtually on their own, so that your thoughts and imagination could be in a completely different place.

But eventually, if you practiced enough, you got good enough at the dance that you really could stop thinking about it, that you really could be transported to some "place" far away as you and your partner danced. *That's* when the dance is really dance; *that's* when your feet give freedom to your spirit, when what your body does somehow takes you completely outside of your physical self. And that, of course, came only with lots of practice. It was the "constancy" of your practice that eventually let you experience the genuine "transcendence" of the dance.

Music works in much the same way. It's one thing to practice the piano; it's a completely different experience to be able to come home at the end of a long and frustrating day at work, sit down at the piano, place your hands on the keyboard, close your eyes, and let your fingers make the music while your soul floats to a new place. Jazz, a Mozart sonata—it makes no difference. When you are really making music, you're no longer thinking about what your fingers are doing; you've gone way beyond the notes. You're experiencing something very different, the transcendent side of music making, the point where the notes are going directly to the innermost reaches of your soul.

That's music, and it comes only after hours and hours of practice, of learning how to position your hands, of playing scales and finger exercises virtually without thinking about them, of training your fingers to remember the composition. Once we've worked on that, usually for hundreds and hundreds of hours, we're able to experience the magic that playing music can create. Again, it's the "constancy" of the practice that eventually yields the "intensity" of the ultimate musical experience.

The same is true with Jewish life. There's nothing easy about prayer, for example. We're troubled or intrigued by lots of questions; we wonder whether God hears our prayers, whether praying really does any good, why our prayers sometimes seem to go unanswered.

But like in dance or in music, it takes practice to get to the point that prayer becomes comforting. If we're still concentrating on how to pronounce the words, or if we're not certain when to stand, when to sit, what to do, or if we're still trying to get the melody completely right—that is all part of the process, but it gets in the way of having an "out of body" experience. It's the beginning of prayer, but it's not prayer at its best. Prayer at its most profound and most moving happens when we're not worried about the details anymore. It happens when we feel so very comfortable with the mechanics that the words on the page transform themselves into virtual springboards, lifting us high into the air, setting us free to imagine, to dream, to wonder, to ask, to implore, and to feel.

The Jewish tradition's "rule" that we pray three times a day might well have been developed because the sages understood that with repetition and practice comes comfort. At three times a day, prayer becomes a skill that we hone, practice, try hard to perfect. It doesn't matter if we're not part of the Jewish community that prays three times a day for this point to ring true: The more we do something, the more power we'll feel in it. The better we get at something, the more it can move us, take us somewhere our bodies alone could never bring us.

That, too, is the "magic" of rules. That, too, is the "intensity" that comes from the "constancy." As we bless our kids on Friday night, we'll be moved, and our kids transfixed, once we've gotten past the point of self-consciousness, wondering if we're doing it right. If we're going to make Kiddush on Friday night, we may at first feel rather artificial, awkward, as if we're trying to figure out what to do. But eventually, when we're used to it, when we know what we're doing is basically correct, when we've stopped worrying about it enough to actually experience it, we'll be able to revel in the experience of being surrounded by our spouse, our kids, our friends, and the tranquillity of Shabbat. Then we can raise a glass of wine and sing about—and feel—the miracle of the day about to begin, the transcendent experience of the alternate reality, the palace in time that Jews call Shabbat.

FROM RULES TO INTERMARRIAGE

A non-negotiable Jewish life doesn't come easily to us modern Westerners. We've been raised on the notion that being an American, a Canadian, a Westerner of any sort, is all about not having to do what we don't want to do. We live in a society of infinite choice. There are more brands of toothpaste, cereal, diapers, and salad dressing in our markets than most people in the world could ever dream of or use.

That's part of the greatness of American life, but it's also part of its sickness. Because that attitude convinces us that anything worth having ought to come easily, when, in fact, the opposite is true. Much of what's worth having actually takes lots of work. Marriages and kids are a classic example. Our relationships with our spouses and our children take tremendous investment but, ultimately, they define our lives and bring us joy and satisfaction in ways that nothing else could. Judaism could play a similar role in our lives. It's not easy, and it takes a lot of investment. But the rewards can be great, indeed. That's the message of the "rules" part of Jewish life.

Each of us has to make choices about which rules are going to be part of our lives. And as we make those decisions, we need to remember why rules matter: They create constancy and immersion. They create intensity. They build a path toward transcendence. And they show our kids what we think really matters.

~

When our family packs up the van for our Thanksgiving vacations to San Diego, our kids know pretty well what has to get tossed into the back. There's clothing, beach toys, bicycles (with helmets, pumps, gloves, and the works), CDs for the car ride down, junky paperback books, Scrabble and Monopoly—the works. But they also know that we're going to pack two white tablecloths (for Shabbat dinner and lunch), Shabbat candles, wine, challah, a *havdalah* set. Why? Because Shabbat happens wherever we happen to be. At home, or in San Diego, or in Hawaii for that matter.

And the message to our kids, we hope, is clear. San Diego is fun, but it doesn't trump Shabbat. Vacations are wonderful, but Shabbat matters more.

I wonder what the opposite message would be. I fear that if San Diego trumped Shabbat, the message would be that "Jewish stuff" is nice as long as it's not inconvenient. But that's wrong; nothing that's *really* important is important only as long as it's easy to do. It's when things are inconvenient that we test whether they're really important or not.

If something is important only when it is convenient, what will we say to our children when they're old enough to fall in love? After all, not being able to marry someone you love is more than a little inconvenient! What we as parents have to teach our children is that the issue isn't always convenience; it's commitment, consistency, principle, tradition. And if we want our kids to take those ideas seriously, we have to model them—early, often, and consistently.

My wife and I very much want our children to marry other Jews when the time comes. There are lots of reasons for that, but mostly, I think, it's because we want them to love the kind of intensive Jewish life they can only live with someone who shares that love. But I also know that our kids will have to rebel, and they'll look for things that will "press our buttons." That's part of the process of growing up.

When they do that, I want to be able to tell them how important it is to us that they marry someone who shares their values. In order to ensure that, we have to make sure that these values are central to who they are.

Regardless of what our children ultimately do as adults, I don't want them to ever think that our expectations of them were somehow out of synch with how we lived as they were growing up. I want them to know that we imposed limits on ourselves just as we did on them. I can only hope that they'll understand that these limits were not about needlessly curtailing their freedom, but about carving out space for the things that would otherwise have been left by the wayside, about creating a way of life that put Jewish concerns at the core, and about reminding ourselves of what we really stand for.

ROSH CHODESH AND THE "JEWISH MOON"
The Challenge of Girls in a Male Tradition

Like most parents, I imagine, I still remember the birth of our first child pretty vividly. Some details have naturally gotten fuzzy; there are names and faces of doctors I no longer recall. But I remember most of it: the ride to the hospital, the labor, the delivery room, my wife's first words to our first child, the drive home from the hospital with the baby. But more than anything else, I remember the miracle. The miracle that two cells and nine months created this incredible creature. The miracle that a child could be born so incredibly small, so perfect, and so filled with potential.

I remember Talia in her first moments. She'd been cleaned up, brought back to us, and placed in the little warmer hospitals use these days. She seemed so fragile. I remember touching her but not daring to pick her up, terrified that if I moved her she would break. And I remember looking at her and promising she would want for nothing, that she would grow up in a world in which she could do anything, be anything, experience everything. In those next moments, with our daughter cradled in my wife's arms and me sitting on the edge of the bed, the future was just beginning.

Within hours, we were home from the hospital, and friends began to come by. People brought food, clothes, mobiles for the crib. We felt enveloped in a world of support and love. Later that day, though, as the crowd begin to wane, one of my closest friends sat down to chat. He perfunctorily said all the right things—how beautiful she was, how perfect her tiny fingers were, how she looked just like her mother. Then he reflected on the birth of his own first child, and remarked on the blessing it was to have a *bekhor,* the Hebrew word for a firstborn male. I still recall the sting.

No, Tali wasn't my *bekhor.* She was my baby daughter, and I wanted her to have a world with limitless possibilities. Yet from the moment of my friend's comment, I realized that it wouldn't be as simple as we'd imagined in that hospital room only hours earlier. With a child only a few hours old, I'd had my initial chance to witness firsthand how challenging it can be to be a girl in the world we call Judaism. I quickly learned—the hard way—that having a daughter was going to take me on an unexpected journey of challenge, triumph, and, mostly, learning.

And I'm not alone. Anyone trying to raise daughters will have to go on a similar journey, and it is a different one for moms and for dads. What makes the journey even harder is that like many of life's most important odysseys, the destination is still pretty much uncharted.

So let's start at the beginning.

In the section on Jewish holidays that follows later in this book, I have omitted one that occurs more frequently than any other—except for Shabbat. That holiday is **Rosh Chodesh,** the beginning of the Jewish month. To people familiar with the Jewish holidays, calling Rosh Chodesh a holiday sounds strange. After all, except for some minor changes in the liturgy for that day (the daily worship services, the Grace after Meals, etc.), there are simply no rituals attached to it. It's a major nonevent, so much so that many books on Jewish holidays ignore it altogether.

Why, then, would we devote a special section to it in a book like this? Because Rosh Chodesh, which has lately become predominantly a "woman's holiday," gives us a chance to discuss one of the great challenges of Jewish parenting today: finding a place for our daughters in a tradition in which men and the male perspective have usually been seen as central.

In many communities, women—and often "women only"—have chosen to "reclaim" Rosh Chodesh as their own since it is based on a lunar, monthly cycle, evoking for many women a parallel to their own menstrual cycles. Observed perfunctorily by men in the synagogue, Rosh Chodesh is more genuinely celebrated by those women who see it as a way of celebrating their womanhood, their femininity, and the miracle of their bodies.

Why is any of this important for Jewish parents? Why would the issue of gender roles be important today, now that we live in an era in which there are women rabbis and women cantors, now that there are dozens of books about Judaism and feminism, now that synagogue roles are, in many communities, as open to women as they are to men? In fact, though, "equality" isn't the issue. Yes, women have much more access than used to be the case (though even that paternalistic language is problematic), but that doesn't change the fact that if we're successful in getting our children to take Judaism seriously, to love Jewish life and to invest time in studying their tradition, our daughters in particular are going to discover elements that are more problematic than any "mere" equality in public roles can repair.

IS GOD A GIRL?

Earlier I related the time my daughter asked me, "What was God doing when she was a little girl?" And I said that her question taught me many things. It taught be that little children have an incredible capacity for healthy naïveté and wonder, that they're willing to talk about things even adults find too embarrassing, and that they are very open to believing in and wondering about God. But Talia's question also taught me that when we nonchalantly call God "He," we steal something from our little girls. Until our girls hear us use masculine pronouns when referring to God, they have a chance to grow up believing that God could be just like them. My daughter, growing up in a house in which we were careful never to say "He" or "Him," simply assumed that God must be like her—a girl.

As much as we loved Talia's question, my wife and I also found that it made us sad. It saddened us because it forced us to admit and to realize that one day Tali would go off to school. She would start to read books and she would talk with people very different from us. And in all these contexts, she was likely to hear God called "He"; little by little, the outside world would rob her of the luxury of imagining her God as being just like her.

She continued to grow up, of course, seemingly content in her Jewish life. A few years later, though, the first major "bump" in the road hit home. It, too, was in the form of a question, one I distinctly remember.

It happened on a Friday night. Tali and I were at synagogue, attending Friday evening services, and she was sitting next to me. We were somewhere in the middle of the service, and I was in a great mood. Our whole family was together, we'd managed to get our kids out of the house with a minimum of fuss, we were surrounded by our friends and community in a congregation that we love, and Shabbat was beginning. What could be better?

Suddenly, as I was *davenning* (the Yiddish word for "praying"), Tali turned to me and asked: "Do you really say *that*?" I had no idea what she was talking about, and was even momentarily annoyed that she'd interrupted me. But I looked to see what she was pointing at, and where her finger met the page I saw the following passage: "For these three things, do women die in child-birth—because they are not careful with the laws of menstrual purity, the laws of challah, and the lighting of Sabbath candles."

That passage is part of a section called **Ba-meh Madlikin,** an ancient passage from the **Mishnah** (about seventeen hundred years old) that mostly discusses what sorts of things can be used for Sabbath candles—that's why it's read on Friday night. But in the middle of this innocuous passage about lighting candles comes this extraordinary suggestion that women die in childbirth because they deserve it; and amazingly, of all the many words on the dozens of pages of the service, my daughter, about ten years old at the time, found that!

Luckily, I was able to answer her completely and truthfully that I don't say it. I see it every Friday night, but when I get to it, I skip it. I skip it not only because it strikes me as wrong (I don't believe that's why women die in childbirth), but because I also find it incredibly offensive. So I simply choose not to say it when I'm praying.

But that personal preference on my part was only a small bit of help. For my daughter wasn't accusing *me* as much as she was accusing her tradition. How, she wanted to know, could she feel part of something that could make such a mean-spirited comment about women—about her?

My heart broke when she asked me that question, because it was one of those moments that I'd hoped would never happen, even though deep down I knew it would. All parents have those moments—it may come when our kids ask why we were married to someone else before we married their father or mother, or it may come when they become aware of our serious faults, or when they come to understand that the world we've tried to create for them isn't as perfect as we wish it were.

I had no really good explanation for what she'd found. It's hurtful, but it's also part of the tradition I want her to love. I don't want her to love *that* line, but I do want her to love the book from which it comes. Can that happen? Can parents really pull that off? It's a hard challenge at best, but whether it's Mishnah we're talking about or simply the Jewish tradition in general, we should recognize that our daughters will all face this.

But the problems run even deeper.

CAN A WOMAN BE A JEW?

Let's be honest. If you ask your kids to close their eyes and conjure up the image of a "Jew," are they going to think of a man or a woman? Most will probably think of a man. Whenever I've tried this little experiment with groups, most people have imagined the Rembrandt-like traditional bearded Jewish man, sitting at a table, hunched over a book. Others thought of a Jewish man wearing *tallis* and *tefillin*—a prayer shawl and the leather phylacteries that Jewish men wear in morning prayer. For still others, the picture that came to mind was that of an Israeli soldier, dressed in green and armed, defending the Jewish state.

What was even more interesting was that except for a few here and there, women, too, "saw" a man. And what that means is that when Jewish women are asked to think of a Jew, they imagine someone not like themselves. And that's a huge problem. The degree to which that alienates many of our daughters is probably indescribable.

The Role Model Problem

Even the fact that some Jewish communities have women rabbis and cantors isn't really enough, because there aren't yet enough of them and they haven't been around long enough to counter basic assumptions. Think of the role models our daughters will have. Take synagogues. Most of our daughters will know that there are women rabbis, but still, for the foreseeable future, when they see a rabbi they'll see a man. The same will often be true of their image of the cantor—though this is less true in the Reform movement. And what about outside the synagogue? What about the Federation, one of the most important Jewish institutions in most American Jewish communities. Who runs it? The reality in the Jewish world is just like the reality in much of the rest of the world. In virtually all cases, the top executives are men. There are lots of women on the staff, but they're not the top execs.

So role models are part of the problem. Yet the problem extends even deeper, reaching from the people who teach the tradition to the tradition they actually teach.

Images of Girls and Women in Jewish Texts

The text my daughter pointed to is only one of many problematic portions that our daughters will encounter. There's also the famous exhortation in **Ethics of the Fathers** not to engage in excessive conversation with women (Avot 1:5), or the comment in the **Palestinian Talmud** that it would be preferable for the Torah to be burned than to be taught to women (Sotah 19a). Those are a mere sampling.

Shortly before Moses receives the Torah atop Mount Sinai (Exod. 19), God instructs him to tell the Israelites to prepare for the giving of the Torah (Exod. 10–15). But note the difference between what God tells Moses to say and what Moses actually says:

and the Lord said to Moses, "Go to the people and warn them to stay pure today and tomorrow. Let them wash their clothes. Let them be ready for the third day; for on the third day the

*Lord will come down, in the sight of all the people, on Mount
Sinai. You shall set bounds for the people round about, saying,
'Beware of going up the mountain or touching the border of it.
Whoever touches the mountain shall be put to death: no hand
shall touch him, but he shall be either stoned or shot; beast or
man, he shall not live.' When the ram's horn sounds a long
blast, they may go up on the mountain."*

*Moses came down from the mountain to the people and
warned the people to stay pure, and they washed their clothes.
And he said to the people, "Be ready for the third day: do not
go near a woman."*

Notice that God said nothing about staying away from women.
All God said to do was to "stay pure." That, in Moses' mind, seems
to have meant staying away from women! Not only is the idea that
purity requires staying away from women extremely problematic
and hurtful, we also have to ask an even more important question.
When God says to Moses, "Go to the *people,*" to whom does Moses
believe God wants him to speak? It would seem that as far as
Moses is concerned, "the people" doesn't include women! What
will we say to our daughters about *that?* How are we going to
bring our daughters "in," teach them that there is a place for them
in our tradition, despite the male-centeredness of much that
they'll encounter?

Where Texts and Role Models Meet

Occasionally, the problems of role models and texts even
merge, for when our daughters begin to study Jewish texts, they
will discover that just as there are still too few places where women
have a chance to be seen, they are also absent from many of the

texts. Women notice—and some are bothered by the fact—that at the beginning of the **Amidah** (the Silent Devotion, one of the main elements of all Jewish prayer), the traditional prayer book mentions the Patriarchs (Abraham, Isaac, and Jacob) but not the matriarchs (Sarah, Rebecca, Rachel, and Leah). The traditional prayer book also contains a blessing at the beginning of the morning service in which men thank God for not having made them women, but in which women thank God for making them "as He wished"; why don't women thank God for not having made them men?!

As our daughters study the Talmud, they'll find that they can go for many pages—sometimes even for entire volumes—without encountering a woman's voice, without learning what women might have said about the same subject. I see this even in the faces of the graduate students to whom I teach Talmud—the men encounter the Talmud as a conversation in which they're the next link; the women invariably see it as a conversation that they need to be invited to join.

~

For all these reasons, raising daughters in the Jewish tradition is much more problematic and difficult than it might seem at first blush. "Equality" of roles isn't the issue—many communities have already begun to address that, and it's really the easy part. The hard part comes when we recognize how deeply male the tradition is, how women are too often made to feel "other." There are too many bright, committed, and searching young Jewish women who have turned away from Jewish life to one degree or another because of this alienation. No parent can make everything "right" in this regard, but if we're to do our work well, we need to admit the challenge, and then we need to begin to think clearly about how to address it.

WHERE DO WE GO FROM HERE?

Those of us for whom this is an important issue have a few choices. Some of the Jewish community's most vocal feminists are committed to abandoning the male-centered Jewish tradition, its texts and rituals, and trying to create something entirely new. But most Jews, and most Jewish feminists, believe that this step would so radically and completely disconnect us from our past that it's not realistically going to work. If we get rid of everything in the tradition that is male-centered, they ask, what will remain that will have us feel that we're the "next link in the chain"?

Other people believe that we simply ought not to pay too much attention to these problems. The Jewish tradition is so beautiful and rich, they say, we should be mature enough to look beyond these "minor bumps" and pay attention to the beauty of the overall composition. There's something to that. Indeed, the issue of feminism and the role of women in the Jewish tradition has become such a "hot topic" that many Jewish girls and women learn about the problems of the tradition before they learn about its beauty. So many adults studies classes, so many of the books on the Jewish shelves at Borders or Barnes & Noble, and so many weekend retreats focus on this issue that we sometimes rob our daughters of the chance to see the parts of the tradition that could call to them and attract them, even if the Jewish world is not perfect.

But that's not a reason to pretend that these challenges aren't real. If we don't want our daughters to be among those who walked away from Jewish life because it seemed insensitive to gender issues, we're going to have to do better than merely glossing over these inequalities. We need to have something more substantial to say than "yes, it's a problem, but look at how wonderful the other parts of Jewish life are." We owe them better, and if we care about their love for Jewish life, we even owe ourselves better.

Which means that we have to find a middle path. And we do that by, I believe, showing our kids that these issues matter to us, and that we're trying to create new role models, to invite women into the conversation, to create a *renewed* tradition. That involves, first and foremost, creating a whole variety of new role models for our children, sons and daughters alike.

THE IMPORTANCE OF ROLE MODELS, AGAIN

My son Avi asked me one day what I teach when I go to work. I told him that I teach a bunch of things, but mostly Talmud. He said to me, "*You* can't teach Talmud! Talmud is for girls!"

I was perplexed. What on earth would make him say that?! And then I realized. Until that moment, the only person he'd ever heard talk about studying Talmud was his mother. He knew that every Monday night, rain or shine, his mother went to a Talmud class. It was something she loved to do but didn't have to. Monday night, he knew, were nights that I was home for bath time, story time, and bedtime. Why? Because his mom was studying Talmud.

Because of my wife's class, my kids assumed that Talmud was not a man's domain. Because of the many different sorts of graduate students who are always at our home, they don't assume that only men can be rabbis. Because my daughter's school provides her with incredibly charismatic and powerful women role models, I suspect that as she grows up, she'll just as easily imagine a Jew as a woman as she would a man.

That doesn't mean there won't be a tension for her. There will. But I hope that as she grows and studies these classic Jewish books, her discomfort at what she'll occasionally find will be mitigated by having been raised by parents who were obviously committed to finding a "better" way, a more open tradition, a more equal reading of the roles of men and women in the Jewish world. Will we make all the problems disappear? Of course not. But hopefully, we can provide her with a model of two people who care deeply about the issues of women in Judaism but who are also deeply committed to Judaism's traditions, and don't see a conflict between the two.

What this points to is the importance of providing our daughters and our sons with powerful new role models, new examples of how women interact with the tradition and make it their own. Moms who go to Talmud classes are one example, women rabbis and cantors are another.

And then there's music. Music is important to most kids. It's surely important in the culture that surrounds us, but it's also important in the Jewish community. Fortunately, many of the Jewish community's most important musical artists these days are women. In America, there's Debbie Friedman, whose CDs and tapes are available all over (and from a few Web sites, as well). Not only have Friedman's songs come to define this generation of Jewish music, but they have also made their way into the liturgy of the Reform movement, and some of the Conservative movement as well. She's a frequent performer, often on tour—and her concerts are a perfect way to show our kids how one woman has used music as her entrée into Jewish tradition, as her way of speaking out about women's place in the community.

And there are dozens of Israeli singers and performers, several of whom have achieved worldwide fame. Yehudit Ravitz, Chava Alberstein, and Achinoam Nini (Noa, as she's known by her fans) are some examples. No concert in the near future in your community? The CDs and tapes are widely available, and have a lot to teach our kids.

And then there are the Jewish feminist thinkers who lecture frequently across Israel, the United States, Canada, and beyond. And here, there is something else that both adults and children can learn: There is no one "right" way to be a Jewish feminist. In many communities, in the space of just a few months, we can expose our older kids to many different models. There's Blu Greenberg, an Orthodox feminist who is passionately committed to change and publicly frustrated with the slow pace of that change in the Orthodox community, who adamantly refuses to leave Orthodoxy because it's her community. It's the community in which she grew up, the community in which she raised her children, the community in which she wants to remain despite her frustration and occasional anger.

Then there's Alice Shalvi, a Shakespeare scholar and one of Israel's most important voices in Jewish feminism, who at the end of the 1990s gave up waiting for Orthodoxy to make sufficient progress. She left Orthodoxy to become one of the leaders of Conservative Judaism in Israel (it's called Masorti Judaism there). Next is Rachel Adler, a very important feminist theologian who also grew up in the Orthodox community. Adler now teaches mostly in the Reform movement, but has a deep love for Jewish traditions of all sorts. She's also well known for changing many of her public and published positions during her own lifetime— another important lesson for our kids.

And let's not forget that as important as living role models are, our tradition also takes seriously the idea that people from long ago can be valuable models, too. There is **Ushpizin**—the ritual of "inviting" to our *sukkah* famous personalities from the Jewish past. Typically, prayer books have us invite Abraham, Isaac, Jacob, Moses, Aaron, Joseph, and David. But lately, Jewish feminists have been asking why women aren't invited. Lots of families now add a woman to each evening. Among those they choose are people like Sarah, Rebecca, Rachel, Leah, Deborah, and Esther. Vendors who sell decorations for the *sukkah* now make decorations that include female "guests" as well as male "guests."

Which brings us back to the subject of ritual, which is no less important than role models, as we re-create for our daughters a world that is both old and new, sacred and innovative, traditional and creative. Let's look at the role of ritual in opening new possibilities for our daughters.

THE IMPORTANCE OF RITUAL, AGAIN

Given the centrality of ritual in powerful and meaningful Jewish life, it stands to reason that we're not going to make much headway in creating these "brave new worlds" for our daughters if we don't see ritual as a serious and important part of the process. Many women are doing just that, and our challenge is to figure out how to tap into those options. (Here especially, never underestimate the importance of the Internet in finding out what's going on. Use a search engine to find some interesting Web sites or discussion groups. If you're on AOL, its section called the "Jewish Community" can get you started. Or put out a question on a message board, and wait—you'd be amazed at the response you'll get!)

Women's groups now exist in all walks of Jewish life. In Reform, Reconstructionist, Conservative, and Orthodox communities, women meet to create women's rituals, to talk about Jewish women's issues, to dance on Rosh Chodesh, to sing in the company of women, and to study Jewish texts from a distinctly female perspective. Interestingly, these groups are more common in traditional Jewish communities, where women are still not included in the public sphere and therefore experience a greater need for this kind of support. So, here's the first idea:

• Women's prayer groups, sometimes on Rosh Chodesh, sometimes during Shabbat mornings or afternoon, exist in many communities. Try them out. See if they work for you or for your daughter.

There are very different models of what will help our daughters feel included. Just because something isn't equal doesn't mean that everyone finds it oppressive. Arna, a good friend of mine who lives in a very traditional Orthodox community in Canada, told me that she raised her daughters to experience praying on the women's side of the *mechitzah* (the "wall" separating the men's and women's section) as liberating, as their "private" place to connect with God without the presence of men. Will this concept work for everyone? No, but it works for some. People don't have to agree with us, or rebel against the same things we might rebel against, in order to be committed Jewish feminists.

- Create ritual moments that are reserved for girls. If the boys in your family make **Kiddush** at the Sabbath table, then let candle lighting be reserved for the girls.
- Create ritual moments that are unique to girls. Most of the women with whom I've discussed the problem of women's place in Judaism have told me that they wish there had been some ritualized way to mark the onset of their menstruating. The old pinch (or slap) on the cheek, many of them said, simply didn't work for them.

Lots of these rituals are beginning to be developed. The most common theme in these new rituals is the use of the *mikvah,* the ritual bath that traditional women use before they get married and before they resume sexual relations with their spouses after their periods. But the *mikvah* doesn't have to be used only at those times. In very traditional communities, men go to the men's *mikvah* before festivals, sometimes even before Shabbat. Women have started to use their *mikvah* as a symbol of renewal after divorce, when taking steps to extricate themselves from an abusive relationship, after rape, and so on. There's a primal quality to the soothing, warm waters of the *mikvah* that many find very powerful.

Since any ritual for the onset of menstruation should be private, women argue, the *mikvah* is a perfect place. A mother can take her daughter, and the two can create any sort of moment they see fit. It's private, it's primal, it's powerful, and it's Jewish. Not a bad start, given the fact that, until recently, there's been absolutely no ritual to mark this important transition.

But not all rituals about menstruation involve the *mikvah*. Alana, a student of mine, an incredibly bright woman and a very committed feminist, told me:

> *My mother did to me what hers did to her, which is to pinch my cheeks so that "they would always be red and healthy," but I've read some really phenomenal things that have been done. My personal favorite was a Mizrachi [Eastern] custom where the mother went and melted butter, called the girl over and told her that charity and wisdom will flow from [the daughter's] hands like butter.*

Regardless of the ritual we choose, there's something nice about using the magic and the power of ritual to make the onset of menstruation a celebrated moment, a time to mark the miracle of the body, a way to establish a close bond between mother and daughter, and an opportunity to make all of this a distinctly Jewish process.

• While it's probably important to find ritual moments that are reserved specially for women and for girls, it may also be useful to find rituals that emphasize the fact that though different, boys and girls can also be treated equally in Jewish life.

Jodi, a woman I've watched grow up since she was in elementary school, is now a teacher in a day school. Discussing this issue,

she said to me, "Lighting Shabbat and Yom Tov candles is important to me; it's a very feminine empowered moment. But I wish
my parents had done the Shabbat blessings for the children when
we were younger. It would have given us each 'equal time.' They
returned from a retreat a few years ago wanting to do it, but we
missed it when we were younger."

Jodi's point is important; it says to kids that even though boys
and girls might have different roles in Jewish life, when it comes
to Friday night and to receiving their parents' blessing, they get
blessed together—not boys first or girls first, but all children in
the order in which they were born.

• There can also be value in using similar rituals for boys and
girls, to let your daughter know that she's part of the larger Jewish
experience, not just a group of women trying to find their way in
a woman's tradition.

Take the wearing of a *tallis* (prayer shawl) and *tefillin* (phylacteries), for example. In some traditional communities, of course,
women are strongly discouraged (or even forbidden) from adopt-
ing these traditionally male practices. But in all Reform communities, most Conservative congregations, and even a few Orthodox
settings, women are welcome to try this. Will it work for them? It
depends. Some women derive a great deal of satisfaction from
participating in a ritual of prayer that is distinctly Jewish but had
never been open to them. Other women find *tefillin* very male,
even when they see other women doing it. For some, there's something about the association of this ritual with men that makes it
uncomfortable; for others, it's the binding of leather straps to their
arm that feels very unfeminine. How will your daughter respond?
You'll never know until you give her a chance to learn, or at least
let her know the option is available should she want it.

DANGER ZONE—BEWARE OF MIXED MESSAGES

Now we have to put in a warning. There's also a risk in inviting girls into these rituals; for unless the ritual is required of girls as it is of boys, girls will see the "double standard" very quickly. Jodi spoke to me about that, too. She said:

> I was always aware of how the boys "had" to wear **kippot** [yarmulkes, or traditional head coverings] and the girls didn't have to but could—and never did. It was usually a good thing because it was one less thing I got sent to the office about! And besides, the boys had to pay for a kippah if they forgot one, and I didn't. Still, it seemed inconsistent. So, as a teacher, I wear one and encourage the girls to. I tell them that if we want to say we are equal in other areas, then we girls and women owe the same kavod [sign of respect and reverence] to our studies.

But while Jodi tried to make things better by choosing to do things differently as a classroom teacher, not everyone does. Sometimes the damage is more permanent. Alana told me, "A friend of mine just had a big problem with her daughter refusing to wear a *tallit* or a head covering in shul, even to get an *aliyah* [the Hebrew word for the ceremony of being 'called up' to the Torah in synagogue services], because none of her peers would do it." Here was a girl whose parents were trying to give her more options, but she experienced what they did as making her different from everyone else, and she resented it. Especially in those formative teenage years, standing out and seeming different is the very last thing kids want.

And there's another mixed message that we too often communicate to our kids. We need to remind ourselves that it's important to teach our children tolerance of those more traditional than we might be, even as we teach them to think creatively and openly about the roles they'd like to have in Jewish life. Just because some parents don't push their daughters to try all the things we might want our kids to try doesn't mean those parents are Neanderthals. Different families have different religious communities that are important to them, different emotional attachments to the way things are done, and different theological beliefs about the way that things ought to be done. This is the perfect time for us to teach our kids that if we don't want others to judge our religious choices, both about the things we do as well as the things we don't do, we need to develop the same openness when it comes to families who may see girls' roles differently than we do.

CONCLUDING THOUGHTS

One thing ought to be clear: There's nothing simple about raising children in the Jewish tradition. But the issue of girls and their role in the tradition raises special and important challenges.

What's true in American life is also true of Jewish life: It's much easier to change outward "roles" and "privileges" than to effect more subtle attitudes. As Americans and Canadians, we live in societies with women's suffrage, where all professions are open to women, where many of the dreams of the women's movement of the sixties and seventies are now reality.

But we've barely scratched the surface. In "allowing" women to work and pursue careers, men have simply come to expect women to run households, raise children, *and* work. And to be happy! And beautiful. It's just not possible. A real change in our culture would involve a change in men's roles, too, and though that is starting, it's slow to develop. We live in a culture in which a focus on girls' bodies still erodes the self-esteem of many of the kids we're raising, where girls are given Barbie dolls that propose an image of the ideal female physique not one of them could ever acquire. American culture has shown that it's much easier to change roles than to change attitudes.

The same is true with Jewish life. While many Jewish communities have opened synagogue roles, the rabbinate, the cantorate, and many other public positions to women, it's the more basic and less "changeable" elements that are really important. That's a huge challenge.

And there's the danger, as well. As important as this issue is, if we make it the whole of being Jewish, we set our daughters up for serious internal conflict and grave disappointment. This book is filled with ideas about holidays, life cycle rituals, searches for community and meaning that are open equally to girls and boys. The gender issue is important, but it's not all that Judaism is about. Let's not let our appropriate convictions about gender equality get in the way of our children loving what Judaism can be. In the words of my friend Gil, a nationally known Jewish educator, "If my daughter is interested in seeking out [new frameworks for Jewish women's involvement], fine; if she is not so inclined, also fine. What I hope is that throughout it all, she'll still find a way to appreciate the many dimensions of her tradition."

That's not always easy. As a man, I've never had to wrestle with the tradition this way. I've watched my wife and my daughter "work their way in," but I've also seen lots of other intelligent and sophisticated women who could never get beyond their sense of exclusion. Our job as parents, I think, is to try to help our daughters find their way "in," without denying the complicated feelings they're likely to encounter along the way.

∾

There's a reason why this chapter has included the voices and ideas of different people. It's because the challenges of raising girls in the Jewish tradition are enormous, and we're just beginning to realize what they are. Solutions are a long way off. Which means that in the meantime, we and our kids will be best served if we're open to learning from lots of different people, and if we're committed to teaching our families that this is an important issue, but only part of Jewish life. Ultimately, if we model for our kids a commitment to Jewish life at the same time that we model a commitment to taking seriously the talents, contributions, and needs of girls and women, we'll teach them a lot. And when there are conflicts, as there may sometimes be, we should be honest about that. After all, one of the most important things we can teach our kids is that it's possible to love many different people, even if they don't all get along all the time. It's possible to be committed to lots of different principles and ideals, even if they sometimes conflict. Life, we know, is most interesting and most richly lived in the moments when we struggle, for it's then that we grow.

What do we say when our daughters ask us what God was doing when she was a little girl? What matters is that we raise them feeling they can ask the question, loving the fact that they are little girls (and then bigger girls, and then women) and knowing that their gender doesn't mean that God, or Judaism, cares about them any less than if they were male. What is true for our kids is probably true for us. The questions matter more than the answers. The questions are where we stretch. They are where the journey begins. And that, of course, is what Jewish life is all about.

10

~

"DON'T TRY THIS ALONE"
It (Usually) Takes a Village

I never would have thought that working in a Jewish summer camp for college students would mean being in staff meetings with disciples of the Dalai Lama. Yet in the early 1990s, the Dalai Lama sent several of his disciples to camp to watch us teach. He told them, "American Jews are experts at surviving in exile. They've developed communities rich with effective institutions from which we can learn." It was ironic: As Jewish educators, we saw ourselves as doing our work largely because so much had gone wrong with American Jewish life. We saw our contact with the students we were teaching as perhaps the last chance we had to get them invested in Jewish life; it seemed to us that we were working with a whole population in immediate danger of falling into the abyss of assimilation. But at the same time, the Dalai Lama sent his assistants to study us because they felt so much was going well!

We're both right, of course. There is much about American Jewish life that needs rethinking, but we've also been incredibly successful at building a whole variety of institutions that are the backbone of our communities. We probably wouldn't have survived without them, and an important part of Jewish parenting is learning how and why to make the most use of them.

There are many reasons why good Jewish parenting is harder today than in the past. Part of the challenge, as we mentioned earlier, is that the culture in which we're raising our kids is much more invasive than it used to be. Another is that we're the first generation that's really doing it alone. It wasn't all that long ago that Jewish parents in America had a vast and complex support network on which to rely. Members of extended families lived in close proximity, maybe even in thick and culturally rich Jewish neighborhoods; many in the community spoke the language that binds us together, and of course, an often "hostile" outside world forced us to depend on one another.

Those days are gone. It's wonderful, obviously, that the outside world is no longer hostile. That's why many of our ancestors came here in the first place. But it's not as clear that we're better off with the other support systems gone. True, it's wonderfully liberating to be able to live in any neighborhood we choose, but we've lost the closeness, intimacy, and support that came with living so close together. As parents today, part of our job is to consciously re-create that network, to make sure that our kids grow up not only in a nurturing and inquisitive Jewish family, but in a richly textured and supportive Jewish community as well.

COMMUNITIES IN JEWISH LIFE

But isn't the idea of "creating community" silly? Isn't community something much larger than us, something we join, not create?

We're not accustomed to thinking about creating communities. Yet when we join a country club, or a health club, or a book club, in a sense that's what we're doing. Our regular Sunday morning pickup softball or basketball game is part of the same thing. We do it because we like companionship, because we enjoy being around people who are interested in the things that interest us, who are dedicated to the causes we think are important.

Again, if it's true in general life, it's probably true in Jewish life, too. If we want being Jewish to feel natural, we have to at least partially surround ourselves with people who have similar feelings. If we want our kids to have even some of the immersion we spoke about earlier, then we know that we need to be part of a community.

Kids who fear being different will take comfort in knowing that there are other people more or less like them. If we worry that there may be something important or basic about Jewish life that we don't know, it's important to know there are people we can turn to for answers. When holidays are celebrated, it's much more fun and meaningful to have a community in which we can celebrate. As we come to live farther and farther from our families, we need to create surrogate structures. When tragedy strikes, as it inevitably will, it's critical to know that we will not be alone, that we will have a support system.

Judaism is a culture that has always believed that meaningful life is supported by groups and organizations that lend help wherever it is needed. That's what the Dalai Lama wanted to learn how to re-create.

JEWS IN COMMUNITY—
A TRADITION THAT GOES WAY BACK

To many of us, talk of the need for "community" sounds very contemporary. We hear about the "breakdown" of community in America, the need for "community patrols" or "community schooling." And while it sounds like a contemporary American buzzword, the truth is that Jews have seen community as central from the very beginning of our history.

Almost two thousand years ago, the Talmud listed the elements a given location needed for us to live there (Shabbat 17a). It said that we should only live in a place that has a court for dispensing justice, a charity fund, a synagogue, public baths, a rest room, a *mohel* (a person who performs circumcisions), a notary, a slaughterer, and a schoolmaster.

Today's list would, of course, be very different—we don't need to worry about public baths or rest rooms! But amazingly, some of the items are the same two thousand years later, and what's definitely still true is that we need to be sure that the place we choose to raise our families can provide a full and deeply textured Jewish life. Communal institutions are still an important part of what we do and how we live; they can be a very important resource for us as parents—as long as we know how to use them.

Compare the stories the Jewish and American traditions tell about their travels through the wilderness; you'll notice some significant differences. According to the American myth, the wilderness was conquered by individuals or small groups of people. Daniel Boone. Davey Crocket. A single family that crossed from east to west with its animals and covered wagons. Little by little, pocket by pocket, these people created the communities that we now call the western United States.

In contrast, the Jewish myth recounts that we were 600,000 people at Mount Sinai (according to other versions, 600,000 men— more than 2 million people when women and children were counted), crossing the desert en masse. The Jewish story isn't one of individuals or small families but of a massive migration toward the Promised Land, a suggestion that only in the company of many others can we reach our ultimate destination.

The stories we tell our kids about our families reflect the way we want them to think about family in general, and themselves. The image of our trek through the desert tells us one thing in particular: We're a people who need community.

YOUR SYNAGOGUE—WHAT IS IT?

A long time ago, in graduate school, I was in a seminar with a variety of Christian clergy, some Catholic nuns among them. Over the course of the seminar, we'd gotten to know each other a bit, and one day one of the nuns struck up a conversation with me. Searching for something she imagined we had in common, she said, "Tell me about your faith community."

I was stunned. I was a rabbi, but I'd never thought of myself as having a "faith community"! Within a moment or two I realized she was asking about my synagogue. But I was struck by the fact that until her question, I would never have referred to my synagogue as a faith community. And then I wondered how *would* I describe my synagogue.

When people ask me to describe my synagogue, I assume they want me to describe the rabbi, where it's located, the yearly membership cost, the size of the congregation. I had never thought of the **shul** (the Yiddish word for "synagogue") as a "faith community."

The nun's question made me realize that it's important to ask ourselves what our synagogue really is, what do we want to get out of it, and what do we get?

Even for those who may not be sure about God, or prayer, or even organized religion, the synagogue matters. It matters because for better or worse, it's still the main place where Jews in America come together. And for committed American Jews, it's the foundation of Jewish community.

We may be a pretty sophisticated community, but many of us tend to handle synagogue life in an incredibly unsophisticated way. The first mistake we make is that we assume that just because we don't like one, we won't like any. If we don't like one dentist, we don't usually decide that dentists in general are not for us. If our experience with a baby-sitter isn't great, the conclusion isn't that we should never go out again. We find a different baby-sitter. With dentists and with baby-sitters, real estate agents and physicians, attorneys and housepainters—we know what we want, and we shop around until we find it.

For some reason, though, with synagogues we behave differently. We try one out, don't like it, and all too often decide to forget the whole thing. Or we stick it out but give up on getting anything particularly meaningful out of it. We belong because we think we should, but we never assert ourselves, never say to anyone that there's something we want out of this experience that we're not getting.

But why? Why not determine what it is that we want out of a synagogue, and then find the best place to satisfy that need? Are we looking for a faith community, a place to do our spiritual searching? Are we looking for friends our age and from our part of town? Are we looking for a synagogue that's particularly focused on social action, fusing Judaism and a concern for the causes that mean most to us? Are the aesthetics of prayer important? Do we want a well-known cantor? A rabbi known for her or his oratory skill? Do we need a really beautiful place, or does that not matter as much? How important is the early childhood program? The youth groups? The Hebrew school? The day school? Location? Cost?

No synagogue can be all things to all people, nor will one excel in everything we want. So we have to figure out what's most important to us. If we want a synagogue with "all the trimmings," chances are it's going to be a large congregation, and that we're not going to get to know the rabbi as well. If we're interested in an intimate setting, or we want to be able to build a relationship with the rabbi that will afford us more of her or his time, we have to be willing to give up on something else. And as parents, we have to ask ourselves what our kids need.

When we bought our most recent house, my wife and I had to choose a new synagogue. There were lots of options, but for us, the choice was easy. One of the synagogues had a children's program that was infinitely better than anything else in town. It had no fewer than fifteen people working in it each Shabbat morning. This was no "managed chaos" scene. There were groups for each age group, an age-appropriate program, snacks for when they got hungry. Perhaps most tellingly, the program began not at 10:00 A.M. or 10:30 A.M., long into the adults' service, but at 8:45 A.M., exactly when the adult service began. The message was clear: "We'll cover the kids for you so you won't be distracted worrying if they are bored or fidgety."

The result? Our kids came to love going to synagogue on Shabbat morning. They were rarely in the main sanctuary with us, nor did they need to be. They were having fun, and at their young age, that's all we wanted. As they got older and moved into the older groups, there was real teaching. For pivotal times in the service, especially on holidays, they were brought in to watch and to see. And as they got to be closer to bar and bat mitzvah age, they were gradually mainstreamed into the adult service, because that's where that community thought they belonged.

For us, the kids' program was the most important element because we already felt comfortable in services. But had we not felt that way, we might have been more interested in a synagogue that had people to sit with newcomers and show them around, or an adult learner's service, or a class before services actually got started. Had we not already had friends in the community, we might have been interested in whether the synagogue had families who volunteered each week to invite newcomers home with them, so they could have a Shabbat dinner or lunch, and also meet some people in their newly adopted community.

The point is that we need to figure out what we want, what our kids need, and then find the best match. That might mean interviewing the rabbi. Or talking to the Hebrew school principal (more on that below). The rabbi doesn't have time to be interviewed? That should tell you something. Ask around in your neighborhood. Hang out during Hebrew school hours and see how things look, how the teachers speak to the kids, if the kids seem to be having a good time. Look at the synagogue's master calendar; how much is going on? Many synagogues have a Web site; check it out—what each synagogue chooses to put on its site can be very telling.

The basic point is simple: Unless we want to do this alone, we've got to get hooked up with a Jewish community. And synagogues are still the main address. Don't do this mechanically; decide what you want in a synagogue and then "shop around." You might even want to ignore denominational labels like Reform and Conservative. What you need to consider is which place offers the most of what you want.

THE CHAVURAH—SURROGATE FAMILY AND MUCH MORE

These days, synagogues are more than just places to pray. They're places to study, places to begin to plant the seeds of a Jewish community. One of the programs many shuls have begun to develop is the *chavurah* program. Based on the Hebrew word that means friendship, the *chavurah* is usually a small group of people who get together periodically (once every two weeks, once a month, or less often, perhaps just for holidays) to talk, to study, to celebrate holidays together. One of the earliest advocates of this program was Rabbi Harold Schulweis, whose Los Angeles congregation had almost two thousand families. Already in the 1970s, Rabbi Schulweis recognized that his congregation had simply gotten too big in some ways. Its large size made all sorts of exceptional facilities and programming possible, but it dramatically reduced the intimacy and warmth that people could reasonably expect. He decided that there had to be a way to "have his cake and eat it, too." The *chavurah* was the way he and a few other very creative rabbis responded.

Since then, the idea of *chavurot* (the plural of *chavurah*) has spread all over, and for many people, it has become a mainstay not only of their Jewish lives but of their social circle in general. In some congregations, the rabbi will visit those *chavurot* that are interested and teach; others will be self-taught. Some are more topic-oriented, like those composed mostly of parents with small kids who are interested in Jewish parenting issues. Still others work like a book club. And some are purely social.

For many people, especially those who have moved to a new city away from family, the *chavurah* becomes a surrogate family. They gather to celebrate holidays together, mark milestones and birthdays together, support each other if something serious or minor goes wrong. I've seen *chavurot* that have been together for twenty or more years.

As you look around for a shul, ask yourself if a *chavurah* is something you'd be interested in. If it is, do some asking. Is there a professional on the synagogue staff who is responsible for getting people assigned to *chavurot?* Does the synagogue routinely provide materials for the *chavurah,* or are the members on their own to figure out what they'd like to study. Does the rabbi *really* come to *chavurah* meetings if invited? Once in a blue moon, or regularly? And are there enough people like you (age, kids, interests, neighborhood) that you can feel relatively confident that you'll have a group that satisfies you?

The answer to the last question will depend very much on where you are going to live.

NEIGHBORHOODS AND CITIES

The mere idea that being Jewish parents will impact our decision about where to live might seem ludicrous. For many of us, it's probably the very last thing we'd think about when picking a city, or a neighborhood, or a street. But it's really not that far-fetched an idea.

If raising our kids in a "thick" Jewish environment (to help with immersion, community, and such) is important to us, then decisions about city and neighborhood should figure in our calculations. Here are some things we ought to ask ourselves:

• Is there a viable and interesting synagogue in town? Is there enough variety and choice among synagogues to foster a bit of healthy competition (to keep them as creative as possible) and to give us choice?

• What's happening to the overall Jewish population? Is it growing? Shrinking? Moving to the other side of town? Becoming more traditional? Less traditional?

• What's the school system like? (Not the public school system, but the Jewish school system.) If we were to decide that we would want a day school for our kids, is there one? Is it viable or just getting started and struggling? Is it over-enrolled with a long waiting list? Is it any good?

• Is there a Jewish high school in town? If our kids are young, we may have no idea whether we'd want that for them, but it's nice to have the option. And the presence of a Jewish high school will tell you something about the level of commitment to education in town, the numbers of Jews in the area, and more.

• What are the opportunities for adult Jewish education? Is it only through the synagogues (and if so, how good is that program), or are there other institutions of higher learning that would give us a place to keep learning?

• Is there a decent Jewish library? Is the Jewish population large enough that the local libraries get the best of what comes out on Jewish subjects?

• Is there a decent department of Jewish studies at the local university? If there is, do the faculty live in town? If they do, they're likely to enrich things tremendously. If they don't, ask yourself (or them) why they don't.

• Are there good Jewish youth groups? Which ones? Who runs them? How about Jewish day camps?

• Is there a JCC? Is it simply a Jewish health club, or does more go on there?

• Is there a Jewish Federation in town? How effective is it? How proactive and innovative is it? What's happened to the annual campaign in recent years? If it's rising, why? But more ominously, if it's in decline, what's that about? Does it tell you anything about the future of Jewish life in that town? Don't jump to conclusions; they may just be redirecting the money. See if you can find out.

• Are there any Jewish museums in town? Any other Jewish resources?

To be fair, there are very few cities that have all of these things— New York, Los Angeles, Boston, Chicago, and a few others are the most obvious ones. But that certainly doesn't mean that Jewish people should live only in those cities. As with anything else, your family should be very clear about what you want or need; smaller cities may have exactly what you're looking for. Nor will we necessarily have complete choice. Often, the city we live in is determined by a job, or family commitments. No matter what our situation, we have to ask ourselves both what we'd like in an ideal world and how we can make the most of the community in which we live.

It's also important to remember something else: Just as the concepts of "good Jew" and "bad Jew" are absurd, so, too, is the notion of a "good Jewish community." What makes a "Jewish community" good? The number of Jewish people in town? The sorts of institutions it has? The level of giving to the local Federation? Those things are measurable, but some important elements aren't so easily characterized. For example, is this a warm Jewish community? Do people look out for each other?

Not surprisingly, there is often an inverse relationship between the size of the community and its warmth. Larger communities will have more resources, but smaller Jewish communities tend to take especially good care of each other. In small, tightly knit communities, everyone matters a little more, and much less is taken for granted.

So there are no "right" communities and no "wrong" communities. Just as we have to decide which cities and neighborhoods are the safest, prettiest, and best investments, we also have to figure out which place is best for our style of Jewish parenting, which place will provide the support we'll need for raising our kids to care about Jewish life.

DAY SCHOOL OR HEBREW SCHOOL?

One of the most famous parts of the Passover Haggadah is the section called the "Four Sons." The Haggadah, the text that Jews recite during the seder, compares four different types of children. It tells of the wise child, the wicked child, the simple child, and the child who doesn't know how to ask. The wise child, according to the Haggadah, is the one who understands the tradition of Passover, feels honored to participate in it, and asks as thoughtful a question as he possibly can. The wicked child is the one who knows the tradition but is cynical, finds the whole enterprise of Passover oppressive, and asks "What is the point of all of this for you?" The simple child knows only enough to ask "What's this?," while the last child is the one who doesn't even know enough to ask anything at all.

Each generation of Jews has reinterpreted that section of the Haggadah, giving new meaning to what each of the children represents. One of my favorites comes from the Moss Haggadah, where David Moss, the artist who calligraphed this particular Haggadah, represented the four children as figures on playing cards. Why? He explained that in providing a different answer to each child, the Haggadah teaches us that having children is in some ways a bit like getting dealt a hand in a card game. We don't have any control over which cards we're dealt, but our responsibility is to do as much as we can with the cards we have. All our children will be different, Moss reminds us. The question isn't who's smart and who's not, but how can we best reach out and teach each one according to their individual styles and gifts. In the same way, decisions about schooling have to be made with the interests and nature of each child in mind.

There's an American interpretation of the four children that, though somewhat cynical, points even more directly to the importance of Jewish education. According to this reading, the wise son represents the generation of Jews who came from Europe, who knew the tradition and had reverence for it, and tried to raise their children to have the same values. But the next generation, the first generation of Jews born in America, resented being different. They knew the tradition, for they were sent to *cheder* (the Yiddish term for traditional Jewish school) but didn't enjoy it. These children, represented by the wicked child, found the teachers oppressive, the material irrelevant to their new lives in America, and the lifestyle a major hurdle to their becoming as American as possible. Like the wicked child of the Haggadah, they could ask sophisticated questions, for they knew a great deal about Jewish life, but they did so with cynicism, anger, and resentment. *Their* children, of course, didn't go to Hebrew school. The "wicked children," now all grown up, wanted to spare their own children the unpleasant experiences they'd had to endure, so they gave their own kids little or no Jewish education. This next generation of American kids is the simple child, the one who in the original simply asks "What's this." Exposed to their grandparents from time to time, these kids still saw some Jewish ritual, and could therefore ask. But everything they saw was strange to them, and they didn't even know enough to formulate a thoughtful question.

Finally, of course, the "child who doesn't know how to ask" is the generation that comes after the simple son. By this time, the original generation has died, the next generation resents the tradition, and the third knows virtually nothing about it. These kids, so removed from Jewish life, see virtually nothing and know absolutely nothing. They're the generation that can't even ask.

Like all stereotypical models, this analogy to the first generations of American Jewish life isn't entirely fair, but it's not without some basis in reality. There has been a dramatic decline in levels of Jewish knowledge, and part of the reason it's so hard to get our kids to care about being Jewish is that they know so little about it.

What we have to do is break that cycle in which each subsequent Jewish generation knows less than the one that came before. Somehow, we've got to intervene and provide our children with more than we were given, educational experiences that teach them more about Jewish life and make them feel more excited about participating in it. Our challenge, regardless of how we grew up, is to make sure our kids are educated Jews.

Now, it's not so easy to define what "an educated Jew" is. How much do our children really have to know, and what do we mean by "know"? If we say they ought to "know" Genesis, for example, do we mean they should be familiar with the stories? The classic commentaries on the stories? The original language? The potential meaning of the stories in contemporary Jewish life and discourse? Or something else?

What, for that matter, does it mean to be an educated American? Again, it's not so easy. But certain things we do know. We certainly want our kids to master the language of the culture (English), to be able to read and to write it well, to know the history of the country and to have seen many parts of it, to be familiar with major themes and tensions of American life, to have a sense for the subtleties of the culture, to know the major personalities and great works of literature, and to have read a bunch of the latter. A tall order? Perhaps, but most good high schools and colleges pull it off.

And there's the rub. Think about how many hours, day after day, year after year, our kids put in learning all that material (and much more). If we'd sent them to school for two afternoons a week and Sunday mornings, stopping when they were about fifteen years old, would we be happy with the product? Hardly.

So why should we expect anything different in Jewish life?

As American parents, we'd be devastated if our kids couldn't identify phrases like "fourscore and seven years ago," or "all we have to fear is fear itself," or "ask not what your country can do for you," or "I have a dream." As educated Americans, we all know who said each of those phrases, and knowing what we know reinforces our sense that we are thoroughly American. Will our kids be able to say the same thing about Jewish life, Jewish culture, Jewish literature? Producing literate Jewish kids takes a lot of work and a lot of time—much more than most of us have been willing to recognize over the past few decades.

Now comes the hard part. We can't do everything. If we want our kids to have the superb Jewish education that some cities now make possible, something will probably have to give. If we pick a day school (a school that has both secular studies and Jewish studies under one roof, where children learn both without having to go to a separate "Hebrew school" or "Sunday school"), we get the advantages of our children having Jewish experiences all day long (immersion, we've been calling it), lots more time in class in which educators can create a coherent and meaningful curriculum, and a focus of their life that's deeply and consistently Jewish. But there's also a give. Day schools cost a lot of money; with three kids in school, for example, parents can be looking at a bill of more than $25,000 ($30,000 once the kids hit high school) per year, before financial aid. If we're committed to the ideal of public education in America, there will be a tension. And most American cities now have phenomenal prep schools, at the very cutting edge of education, technology, the arts. As good as many day schools are, there are really only a few that can genuinely compete with the best of those private schools. We'll simply have to make a choice.

We can't have the best of everything when it comes to picking a school for our kids. Ultimately, we have to decide what's most important to us—and it has to be more than a gut feeling. Sure, we may have always thought Hebrew school was enough, but now that we're rethinking our agenda as Jewish parents, perhaps something more intensive is called for. Maybe we thought Hebrew was boring, so we don't want to make our kids go through it, but is it possible that someone in town is doing something more creative, more nurturing, more successful than what we had to suffer through? We ought to check around. Or—heresy of heresies—if we're "sure" that day schools are too expensive, is there anything we can do without? Do we really need to drive the kind of car we have? Do we really need a vacation home? A remodeled kitchen?

I'm being a bit extreme here because I don't believe that, as a Jewish community, we've asked ourselves enough questions about Jewish education. We anguish when we choose our kids' "regular" school; we get involved and vocal if we think they didn't get a good teacher this year; we ask what they're doing and complain if it's not academically aggressive enough. But how many of us anguish about the choice between day school or Hebrew school, or which Hebrew school? How many of us really know the differences between the Hebrew schools when we pick a synagogue or a school? Do we show the same interest in our kids' Jewish education that we do in their general schooling? The answers to those questions speak volumes, and they will most likely be critical in determining what kinds of Jewish commitments our kids grow up to have.

SUMMER CAMPS

A friend of mine, Elana, recently told me that the reason she sends her preteen daughter to a Jewish camp in the summer is so that when her daughter starts to experiment with sex, she'll be in an environment where everything is pretty safe, where the kids are nice, and where the whole environment is Jewish. "What's the worst she's gonna do?" she asked with a grin.

Elana is very smart, and she knows that bad things can happen to kids anywhere, even in Jewish camps, even with Jewish counselors. She wasn't being terribly serious when she told me her reasons, but neither was she being entirely untruthful. What she was saying was that she's glad to know her daughter spends the summer in an environment that stands for the same values that she and her husband try to communicate to their children, an environment where most of the kids and most of the counselors come from homes that more or less share the same values.

Many observers of American Jewish educational institutions believe that today's Jewish summer camps are by far the most effective ones we've built. After all, summer camps (especially overnight camps) offer immersion with almost no effort. They provide role models with whom our kids come to identify, whom they respect. Camps are the best place to make being Jewish into real fun. They're the place that being Jewish doesn't mean being different because they're communities that are Jewish to their cores. They're places where our kids develop friendships that will last a lifetime, where those initial romances are likely to blossom.

Indeed, the best of America's Jewish summer camps are unbelievably good. And in the event that we can't afford a Jewish school, or there isn't one in town, or we have our own reasons for not choosing one, summer camp is something to seriously consider. If we do have our kids in a Jewish school, summer camps are a great way to keep the immersion going while letting them have a summer filled with fun, a little learning, and friendships that will last a lifetime.

YOUTH GROUPS

If summer camps seem discretionary, then youth groups really don't matter all that much. After all, they're mostly social, and the quality of the programming varies dramatically from adviser to adviser, from year to year. Let's be serious, we might say to ourselves, how much does USY (United Synagogue Youth—the Conservative movement's youth program), BBYO (B'nai B'rith Youth Organization), or any of the others really matter?

Amazingly, recent studies of Jews in the United States show that they seem to matter quite a lot. I was astonished to read over the past few years that not only do youth groups actually have a big impact on kids' later Jewish involvement and identification, but it actually doesn't matter how good the groups are, whether they have excellent programs or mediocre ones or none at all. In retrospect, the reason is kind of obvious: Youth groups are important not so much for what the kids learn but because they give kids a social network that's Jewish, a set of Jewish friends with whom to grow up. What we've learned of late is that as important as formal education is, having very close Jewish friends when growing up is one of the most consistent predictors of later Jewish involvement and commitment.

It's something to think about. Regardless of whether there is a large choice or a small one, most communities have at least something to offer. Given what we've learned from sociologists lately, youth groups probably deserve at least a second look.

SMALLER JEWISH COMMUNITIES, VIRTUAL JEWISH COMMUNITIES

Not only is there no single ideal Jewish community, there are different models of what such a community should be. People in smaller Jewish communities tend to look at Jews in larger communities and wish they had all the resources cities like New York, Los Angeles, and Toronto provide. But smaller communities have distinct advantages the larger ones can't begin to approximate.

I did some work a few years ago on behalf of the United Jewish Appeal's "Un-Federated communities"—communities that were too small to have a Jewish Federation. As I met the Jews from these communities, in my case mostly from the South, I was moved by how well the members of the community knew each other, how they took care of each other, how deep were the roots that many of them had in their small towns. There was a sense of belonging, a feeling that they needed one another, and that each of them mattered. All the schools, museums, and other institutions of the larger cities can't begin to replicate that.

Every community has its benefits, but each also has disadvantages. What's important is that we enter with our eyes wide open, that we take advantage of what's good, and look to fill in what's missing.

Which brings us to "virtual Jewish communities," or the explosion of Jewish material on the Internet and the Web. Jews in very small communities, who for a long time have felt that there was no way to connect with other Jews, no way to benefit from their ideas, have discovered a virtual community through chat rooms, bulletin boards, Web sites, and e-mail that has, for many, become a lifeline to the "outside" Jewish world. Whether it's ideas for celebrating holidays, suggestions of the best Jewish software, meeting Jewish singles, they've discovered a new and important community.

I know several single people who have lived for years in Los Angeles, but who, in a community of almost three quarters of a million Jews, couldn't find anyone in whom they were interested. Then they joined AOL or some other service with a section allocated to Jewish conversations, and before long, they were engaged. Now they're married and have kids.

Computers are hardly the solution to all of humanity's problems, but used well and creatively, they're pretty amazing. A computer and a modem can connect you to Jews across the city, across the country, and across the globe. In these Jews you'll find people just like you or unbelievably different, but they'll be struggling with issues you've already thought about and whom you can help, and you'll find people who can help you. For adults, the Web and the Net provide instant introductions, and pretty rapid answers and guidance.

Our neighborhoods and our cities are critical, but the world's a rapidly changing place, and the boundaries of the Jewish community are changing with it. We need to see these shifting and expanding borders as a huge advantage, a major resource.

ISRAEL—WHERE OUR KIDS LEARN WHAT "HOME" REALLY IS

Having spoken a bit about the inner workings of local Jewish communities and "virtual" Jewish communities, we should pause for a second to remember that some of our most important resources are much farther away from home. Some, in fact, are in a place we rarely think of as "home": Israel.

No one can explain Israel's magic. There's just something about it that touches virtually everyone who visits. Something about Israel sends Jewish people back to their communities with a renewed sense that Jewish culture is alive, that the Jewish people are thriving, and that being Jewish means being part of something infinitely more meaningful than we ever imagined. What a great gift it would be if we could give that feeling to our kids.

What is that "something"? It's hard to pin down, but we do know some of the elements. One of the most important is that Israel is the only place in the world where Jews are not outsiders. Most of the people on the street are Jewish. The teller at the bank, the cashier at the supermarket, the ambulance driver, the orchestra, the docents at the museum, even most of the professional athletes are all Jewish. American Jews, kids definitely among them, get off the plane in Israel and suddenly feel something they've never felt before—they're part of the majority.

And as they leave the airport and begin to make their way into Israeli society, they see that the culture is also Jewish. The national holidays are the Jewish holidays. There's no decision to be made about whether to go to school on **Rosh Ha-Shannah**—there *is* no school to go to! In the supermarkets, the vast majority of the food has a kosher label. In many cities, as Friday afternoon comes to an end and Shabbat approaches, people can be seen hurrying home with flowers in their hands. Shabbat is Shabbat—not just for religious Jews but for almost everyone in some way. And a little later in the afternoon, in hundreds of neighborhoods across the country, as Shabbat actually begins, you can see dozens upon dozens of people making their way to a variety of different synagogues. In some cities and neighborhoods, an eerie quiet and peace descends. Shabbat isn't a private Jewish matter; the entire country changes pace.

And then there's Hebrew. In Israel, Hebrew is suddenly transformed from an archaic language into one that millions speak as a matter of course. As soon as we get off the plane, we are struck with how Hebrew is no longer the language of the prayer book, but the language of the street. Taxi drivers yell at each other in Hebrew, the waitresses at the restaurants speak Hebrew, most of the newspapers are in Hebrew, the billboards are in Hebrew, the graffiti is in Hebrew.

As recently as only seventy-five years ago, the *Encyclopaedia Britannica* wrote that Hebrew was a dead language, unlikely ever to be resurrected. But turn on the radio or TV in Israel, and you'll see how "dead wrong" the *Britannica* was.

Israel also makes it clear that there's no such thing as a "typical Jew." Lots of American Jewish kids grow up thinking there are "real" Jews, and then there are people like themselves. They don't think of themselves as authentic. But Israel belies that. In Israel, there are white Jews and black Jews. There are Jews whose native language is Hebrew, but also Jews who more naturally speak Russian, Amharic, Arabic, Farsi, French, Spanish, and, yes, English. There are Jews who dress in the traditional black garb of the Hassidim, and Jews who wear army uniforms. There are Jews who wear jeans and Jews with tattoos and nose rings, ear studs—the works. What does a Jew look like? You can't begin to answer that question once you've strolled the streets of Israel.

Somehow, all of this "conspires" to give us the feeling that we're home in a way we've never felt before. When our son Micha was five, I took a sabbatical from work and carted the family to Israel for a year. Micha didn't like it one little bit. He missed his friends, his house, his school. His new school spoke a language he really didn't know, it was hard to make friends with kids who didn't understand him, and he had to get used to living in an apartment instead of a house. In all, he was completely ready to go "home" to Los Angeles at the drop of a hat. And yet, in the midst of all his complaining, he seemed to figure out that something about Israel was different. As we were putting him to bed one night, tucking him in, he turned and suddenly asked, "If we're Jewish, why don't we live in Israel?" Out of the mouths of babes!

Most of us are not going to move to Israel. There are familial reasons, professional reasons, financial reasons, language reasons. But even if we decide that the United States or Canada or any other place is where we're going to live, it's worth showing our children that Israel is also their home. It's not just that every Jew automatically has the right to Israeli citizenship—by law. It's that once inside Israel, Jews suddenly feel they are home. That's an incredibly liberating feeling, and the earlier we give our children a chance to experience it, the more open they're likely to be to the other things we'll be doing as Jewish parents.

But amazingly, relatively few American Jews ever see Israel. Most statistics say that only somewhere around 25 percent of American Jews ever travel to Israel. That's tragic. It is important for our kids to see a Jewish community fully alive, fully responsible for the country it creates.

How do we do that? There are a variety of ways:

• Family trips to Israel during the summer. Getting to Israel costs a lot more than going to Yosemite or Disney World, but it's not nearly as expensive as it used to be. Find a time when the kids are old enough to appreciate it, and then take a few weeks in Israel. Start on an organized tour, but save a bit of time for just "living" there.

• A more extended trip? It's hard for most of us to get time off from work, but sometimes we can arrange a few months' leave. It's complicated to go to Israel for that amount of time (there are income issues, homes to rent, schooling to arrange, etc.), but it *is* doable. And Israeli public schools are basically free even to you, just because you're Jewish. Talk about being "home."

• A teen trip during the summer. More and more, American Jewish communities are trying to set up funds to make it possible for every Jewish teenager to participate in a group trip to Israel. But even though these funds are not fully operative, many kids still go. Most of the religious movements sponsor such trips, as do local Federations and Bureaus of Jewish Education. Ask the Federation, or check the Web; you'll find a list without too much difficulty.

• It's becoming more and more common for American teenagers to spend a year between high school and college on an Israel program. Most of these kids have already been accepted to college; they just defer their admission for a year. Some even get partial college credit for the experience—though it depends on which program they do and which college they'll be attending.

Will it matter if our kids graduate college a year later than their friends and peers? No, it won't. Furthermore, many parents find that their children actually get more out of college by virtue of having had a year to grow up, to get used to being away from home. They tend to arrive at college more aware of what interests them. And most important, they believe that this year shows their priorities. Getting seriously immersed in Jewish life as an adult, they say to their kids, is no less important than getting a college education—they're both critical.

- It's also common for American college students to travel during their third year of college. Some take only a semester, others do a whole year. Different arrangements are also possible. Israel has a number of excellent junior year programs—Hebrew University and Tel Aviv University are the biggest. A year studying in Israel creates a connection to the country and its people in a way almost nothing else can.

- Even after school's all over, there are opportunities. Israel has a variety of volunteer needs for all kinds of people, professionals and nonprofessionals alike. The Israeli consulate can give you more information.

No matter how we do it, getting our kids—and ourselves!—to Israel ought to be a serious consideration. There really are no words to describe exactly what will happen to them and how deeply they'll feel a connection to their people. Isn't that what we want?

THE WORLDWIDE JEWISH COMMUNITY

Aside from Israel, it is worth noting that there are Jewish communities all over the world. There are shuls in Hong Kong, Tokyo, Paris, Venice, Capetown, Buenos Aires, Moscow, and even Honolulu. When we go to these places, we don't usually seek out things Jewish; we're there to have fun, to get a sense of life in a very different place.

But at the same time, once we're going there, why not take the kids to see what there is of Jewish content. They might be struck by the submachine-gun-toting armed guards outside the synagogues in Rome, suddenly realizing how much they take for granted the safety and security of Jewish life in America. They may be moved by how empty the magnificent, large European synagogues are, understanding for the first time how much the Nazis destroyed. A synagogue in Venice? It adds a nuance to the memories of the gondolas and the waterways.

One of the things that make Jewish life so powerful is the sense that we belong, that we're part of something larger than our immediate congregations. It doesn't take much extra time, yet it can be a wonderful unexpected addition to the ways we give our children that sense of exactly who they are.

GRANDPARENTS: YOU MATTER—A LOT!

Jewish community doesn't only extend across continents, it also stretches across generations. If our children are moved by the fact that there are Jews today almost every place they go, imagine how touched they'd be by the stories their own family tells about what it was like to be Jewish only a few generations ago.

At the end of our family's Passover seder, late in the night, our kids are exhausted. At times it seems that no matter how hard they try, they aren't going to be able to stay awake. And then my mom starts to tell them what it was like growing up in *her* family, what she remembers about her grandmother and her parents' seder. And my kids' eyes open wide, mesmerized; it seems they could listen forever. And this shows truly how much grandparents who want to be involved have to offer.

In the years I've been teaching about Jewish life and reflecting on Jewish parenting with Jews of all ages, the one thing that has saddened me the most has been those people who, reflecting on how they raised their own kids, have concluded that they "blew it" and now it's too late. They wish their adult children shared their sense of how important Jewish life is, their love of the holidays or the magic and majesty of Israel. And they're often distraught about the minimal Jewish upbringing their grandchildren are getting.

My kids are still young and most of our raising them still lies in the future, but I can already begin to sense how we're going to feel if we look back and think, like many in the older generation, that we "blew" it. But then I realize it's inevitable that we'll feel that way. There are no perfect parents; we all make mistakes, including some big ones, about things Jewish or not. We're human, and while we're busy being parents we're also busy living our own lives, working on our marriages, building our careers, trying to live meaningful lives.

In that light, how could we not make mistakes? The first thing I want to tell grandparents is that there's no point in blaming themselves. The issue isn't who's at fault; we do the best we can as we go through the process. The second thing grandparents need to know is that their work isn't over when their children are grown; they have another chance to make a difference with their grandchildren. Grandparents who live full Jewish lives can be powerful models for their grandchildren, helping to create memories that will last a lifetime. Immersion is harder for grandparents to effect, unless they live close by; but even from far away, they can have an enormous impact. Kids adore their grandparents, and through them they learn about the past. Through them their link in the chain is strengthened.

~

Jewish life at its best is about making connections, establishing links. We want our kids to feel a tie to Jews of previous generations, but we also have to work to have them feel a connection to other Jews in their own community. Our challenge, as contemporary Jewish parents, is to decide what links will best serve our goals as parents, and then to search our communities to make the best use of whatever it has to offer. Our power to influence the chain, even two links down, is something we ought never overlook.

11

"DON'T KNOW MUCH ABOUT HISTORY"
Why Our Story Should Matter to Our Kids

Those of us who are teachers—elementary school, college, and as parents—have an obligation to explain to our students (or to our kids) why it's important for them to learn whatever it is we're teaching them. Throughout this book I have tried to explain why things we don't ordinarily consider as being significant in Jewish life might actually be important—whether it's about what a holiday means and how it fits into the larger picture of being Jewish, or why there are rules about what we can eat. And hopefully, when we're asked, we'll be able to answer any question thoughtfully. It's our responsibility to make it clear why something matters, either before we start or in the process of teaching.

Yet one thing we haven't spoken about is the Jewish tradition's emphasis on history. Whether in Hebrew school or day school, whether in elementary or high school, history pervades Jewish learning. Now, if your kids are history buffs, there'll be no problem. If they're not, they might loudly moan and groan and ask why they have to learn this. This chapter suggests some answers.

To put matters very simply, Jews study so much history because for us, knowing what happened in the past is our way of *continuing to live the past*. For Jews, history is not about recalling what happened, it's about taking part in what happened. It's about transporting ourselves back to a different place and time. Our goal is not to remember the events we study, but to actually *relive* them, to seek the experience over and over, to struggle with them anew, no matter how much time has passed.

We get hints of this in almost every nook and cranny of the Jewish tradition. Even in the Bible stories we learned as kids. When God sends Moses to Egypt to rescue the Israelites from slavery, Moses asks God what he should say if the people ask who sent him, and God responds, "This is what you shall say to the Children of Israel: 'The Lord, the God of your ancestors, the God of Abraham, the God of Isaac and the God of Jacob sent me to you.' This is My name forever, and My identity for eternity" (Exod. 3).

Notice that Moses is told to introduce God not as the Being who created the world, the God who fashioned all of nature, or the God who demands that human beings be just and caring, even though the tradition also believes those things. Rather, Moses is told to tell them about history. By mentioning Abraham, Isaac, and Jacob, Moses refers to God's commanding Abraham to leave his father's home and to go to a "Promised Land," the Binding of Isaac, God's rescue of the Patriarchs from hostile kinds—about history. That, says God, is "My name forever, and My identity for eternity."

In the story that we Jews tell about ourselves, history is critical. It's critical because it binds us to other Jews, who are also descendants of the participants of those dramatic events. To Jews, history is probably more important than such theological claims as "God created the heaven and the earth." In the Jewish world, history teaches us where we've come from, history teaches us who we are.

BEYOND MEMORY—LEARNING
TO "RELIVE" THE PAST

It was actually a billboard that made me realize how different the Jewish approach to history is from other approaches. One summer a few years ago, my wife and I packed the kids and a day's worth of junk food into the car for one of those typical family Sunday afternoon drives. We headed north toward the beach towns. Heading off the highway onto one of the smaller roads, I noticed a billboard.

It was the middle of June, and the billboard was inviting people to come to the town's main park on July 4 to join in a reenactment of the Civil War. If this reenactment was like many others that take place across the country, then all the people dressed up in the blue and gray uniforms of the Union and Confederate soldiers and acted out one of the battles. The theatrics, I assume, were followed by a July 4 barbecue.

I was struck by the difference between this tradition and the Jewish way of remembering history. While it's common in many cultures to reenact historical events, Jews simply don't do that. We would never think of it. The scars and pain are still too fresh. You can only reenact something when it's no longer painful.

In this California town, the Civil War was ancient history. There was no one around who remembered the battle, no one whose loss was so profound that the reenactment would be considered in poor taste. Thus, there was no reason not to have some July 4 theatrics.

But that's not the way Jews see things. Our lives are filled with constant reminders of ancient battles even though the survivors are long gone. It's not that we can't forget the past, but that much of Jewish life is devoted to keeping the memory alive.

You might think, OK, the battles of the modern State of Israel are much too recent to reenact—after all, there isn't one family that has not lost a son, a brother, a father. These wounds are incredibly fresh. But what about the destruction of the Temples in 586 B.C.E. and 70 C.E.? Or the Bar Kokhba Revolt against the Romans in 132 C.E.? Why don't Hebrew schools or Jewish camps reenact *those* events? Jewish kids learn about them, and they took place *thousands* of years ago.

Part of the answer is that those are mostly battles we lost, in which the victors were those who oppressed us. But it's also because we make a conscious effort to keep them fresh in our minds. To us, these events happened yesterday.

It's not as if we as Americans look upon the Civil War—or the Revolutionary War—without deep feelings. Especially in the South, the Civil War continues to evoke great passion. But the passion it evokes is different; it's no longer so painful. And that's partly a function of the passage of time.

That's why many Jews find it sobering that we're already at the point where the Shoah started half as long ago as the Civil War. Jewish memory is determined to keep the Shoah and the rest of our history fresh and critical no matter how much time may pass. The Civil War may be far enough away for Americans that it can be reenacted, but for Jews, the destruction of the Temple two thousand years ago is too close, still too painful.

That's part of what the holiday of **Tisha B'Av** (the Ninth of Av) is all about. We don't just read about the destruction of the two Temples (which tradition claims were both destroyed on the ninth day of the Jewish month of **Av**), we actually mourn them. In many synagogues I've attended, as we've sat on the floor in the dark, candles lit so we could read the pages of the book of **Lamentations,** I've seen grown men cry. Cry? Over the Temple? How could that be possible?

It's possible because for some, the destruction of the Temple and the world that it represented evokes memories of the Nazis only a few decades ago. Mourning a Jewish world destroyed by the Romans, they can't help but sob over the loss of their own Jewish world—their families, their homes, the lives they knew.

Yet there's also more to it. It's not only the elderly who shed tears over the Temple, it's often younger people as well. When the ritual works correctly, Jews observing Tisha B'Av actually experience the destruction of Jerusalem as if they were there. Through reading the vivid and pained poetry of Lamentations, sitting on the ground, fasting, being prohibited from washing or from wearing leather shoes, being urged to sleep on the floor, and even being forbidden to greet anyone on that day by asking how they are, we sense ourselves overwhelmed by grief, by loss, by a sense of violation. We all feel that way, even though we weren't there.

And that's the point. The power of the Jewish community comes from the fact that we "experienced" these losses together. The heartbreak was not that of our ancestors, it's ours. We try to relive the loss so as to feel that it happened to us. For if our memory gradually dissipates with time, one of the strongest bonds that hold our people together will be a thing of the past.

This approach to history can be hard for people to understand. It requires doing more than "observing" the tradition. "Observing" means watching, living outside. Our challenge is not to observe the holidays, but to live in them.

Once, late in the afternoon before the Ninth of Av, as I said good-bye to my secretary, I said, "So I'll see you tonight at services?" Fifteen years later I still remember her response. A woman with a great sense of humor, Sharon simply looked up from her desk and said, "Nope—my family didn't lose anyone when the Temple was destroyed!"

I remember her answer because it showed how, to her, this

wasn't her event, this wasn't her loss. In that regard, she's no different from many devoted Jews. But that's not how the tradition wants us to live. It wants us to remember that we *all* lost someone at the Temple; we were all affected, transformed, robbed of an entire era of Jewish history. The goal of Jewish life is to see ourselves as having been there.

WHY HISTORY? ANOTHER JEWISH PATH TOWARD IDENTITY

Even if we understand that Jewish life works this way, we still have to explain to our kids what the tradition is trying to accomplish. Why remember in order to relive? What's the point?

First and foremost is that this sort of collective memory (the French sociologist Émile Durkheim used the term "collective conscience") binds us together in a very powerful way. It is, in many ways, the glue that binds the Jewish world together. It's what gives Jews a sense of being linked, of having not only a shared past but a shared destiny.

Ask your kids to explain why religious college students in New York (among others) were the first to lobby on behalf of Soviet Jews. After all, Russian Jews were completely unlike them. They spoke a different language, lived a completely different experience, and most were not even committed to the religious principles at the very core of the lives of these American kids. So why the sense of urgency? Why the sense of responsibility?

Ask them to explain why Ashkenazi (European, Caucasian) Israeli air force pilots risked their lives to fly big, clunky passenger planes into a very tentative cease-fire in Ethiopia to evacuate as many Ethiopian Jews as they could. These people were of a different race, knew no Hebrew, and lived a form of Judaism that was completely foreign to most of the Jewish world. Most of them didn't know how to read, many had never seen an electric light switch or plumbing. So why risk everything to try to get them out? What was the connection?

What's at play in both examples is a sense of peoplehood, a sense that no matter how different we are from each other, we're part of the same entity. But where does that come from? What do I have in common with a Jew still living in Ethiopia? What did my wife and I share with the Russian refusniks we visited in Moscow, Kiev, and Odessa in 1981? We were completely different—we spoke different languages, shared few experiences; we were free, they were prisoners. So why this connection?

Jews understand that our links go much farther back than a generation or two. What those New York college kids understood was that they did have a link to the Soviet Jews. What the pilots understood was that the ancestors of those Ethiopian Jews may have become separated from the rest of the ancient Israelites when they fled the invading armies that destroyed Jerusalem more than two and a half millennia ago. While my family may have been in the United States for several generations, if we go back far enough, my ancestors may have been neighbors with those of the Jews we met in Kiev. What reliving our history is supposed to communicate to us is that way back when, we shared a history. And we *still* do. And because of that, we're part of the same people.

What we have to explain to our children, then, is that history isn't a *part* of what Judaism is; it *is* Judaism. There are Jews who live Jewish life with religion, and those who live without it. There are those for whom Hebrew is critical, and those who think it's totally unnecessary. But it would be hard to imagine an involved Jew for whom history, a sense of the past, was not central to his or her life.

Virtually every dimension of Jewish life has a historical twist. Clearly, many of the holidays do. Sukkot brings to mind the booths in which the Israelites resided as they made their way through the desert. **Hanukkah** and **Purim** remind us of battles Jews fought and won. **Passover** is not just a retelling of the story of the exodus; it's supposed to be a reliving of the story. The Haggadah instructs the reader, "in each and every generation, we are obligated to see ourselves as if we were liberated from Egypt." The seder is an opportunity not only to remember what was done for our ancestors, but to experience that past as ours, to see ourselves as the ones who were whisked out of Egypt.

The minor fasts all remind us of historical traumas. Even **Yom Kippur,** a holiday that would seem to have no historical overtones, actually "sneaks" in some history. In the *musaf* service on Yom Kippur day, in a section called the *Avodah,* the congregation actually "relives" the sacrifice ceremony the High Priest used to perform on Yom Kippur before the Temple was destroyed.

History colors other parts of Jewish life, too. At the end of the wedding ceremony, the breaking of the glass is supposed to remind us of the destruction of the Temple. When Israeli paratroopers get their "wings," they do so at a ceremony atop Masada, the mountaintop fortress the Romans conquered in 72 C.E. only after the defenders committed mass suicide. Standing on that site, the paratroopers say as part of their ceremony, "Masada will never fall again." History, nation, people, purpose—for us, they're all bound up together.

But there's more. It isn't just any old history that we learn and reflect on. It's a very specific kind of history: the history of a people. Compare Judaism's annual festivals with the holidays of the Christian calendar. In Christianity, you have Christmas, which celebrates the birth of a human being (a divine person in Christian theology), and Easter, which commemorates the resurrection of Jesus on the third day after his crucifixion—holidays that celebrate landmarks in the life of an individual. In Judaism, holidays revolve around events in the life of the nation. Where's the holiday for Moses' birth or death? Abraham's? King David's? The tradition might believe that it knows those dates, but there are no holidays to celebrate them.

The history that preoccupies the Jews, then, is the history of a people, the memory of a community, the experiences of a collective whole. The point of learning all this history, then, is that by learning about the past, and then reliving it, we come to see ourselves as part of the whole. This people's experience is not simply the experience of our ancestors; it's *our* experience, *our* story, *our* destiny, *our people*.

Part of what makes family ties so powerful is that over the course of time families share experiences, some easy and joyful, some difficult and challenging. And it is those hard times and tears that bring families together more than anything else. The same is true with friends and colleagues.

That's what our history as Jews is supposed to do. When we allow ourselves to live and relive it, we come to know and to feel that we're part of something much greater than ourselves. We'll know that whoever and wherever Jews may be, they are our people, our family, our responsibility.

DO UNTO OTHERS *BEFORE* THEY DO UNTO YOU?

As important as peoplehood is to Jews, though, it's not the only reason that history is so critical to how we think about ourselves. In addition to telling us where we've come from, history also gives us a sense of the kind of people we and our kids are supposed to be.

One of the many side effects of abuse in families is that the victims often become abusers themselves. The cycle of violence continues, generation after generation. Instead of the famous dictum of **Hillel,** "Do unto others as you would have them do unto you," these people seem to adopt a different approach—"Do unto others *before* they do unto you."

Such may well have become the natural response of Jews, too, given all the pain and suffering civilizations have dumped at our doorstep. Let's be honest; while we by no means have a monopoly on human suffering, we certainly do have a long record of being at the receiving end of cruelty. Yet our tradition does not foster an aggressive attitude. Rather, it wants us to relive our history and keep it fresh so that we understand how easy it is to cause pain, so we resolve never to do to anyone else what has been done to us, and to remind us that we are obligated to try to stop it whenever it occurs.

It might be helpful to show our children some of the many places our tradition specifically warns us against forgetting the past. For example, the Torah commands us, "You shall not despise the Egyptian, for you were a stranger in his land" (Deut. 23), "you shall love the stranger, because you were a stranger in the land of Egypt" (Deut. 10), or "when you gather the grapes of your vineyard, you shall not glean it afterward; it shall be for the stranger, for the orphan, and for the widow; and you shall remember that you were a slave in the land of Egypt; therefore I command you to do this thing" (Deut. 24). What we've been through is supposed to make us more sensitive and more responsive to the needs of people who are now as weak as we once were.

That's also the message some people find in Hanukkah. Tradition says we're supposed to place the Hanukkah candles in a window facing the street in order to "proclaim the miracle." But what exactly are we trying to proclaim, and to whom? According to at least one view, we're saying to the rest of the world, "We have been powerless in the past. We know what it's like to feel that there's no hope, no possibility." But, we continue, "look at these candles. Each night, we're going to light one more candle. One on the first night, two on the second, three on the third, and so on, all the way to eight. Each night our light will grow brighter, and we're here to say that just as we have survived as a people even in the face of adversity, we believe that you and others can, too." Hanukkah, in this reading, is a holiday in part about remembering that there are others who now suffer the way we did, and that we have an obligation to care, to encourage them, and, ultimately, to help them.

Another reminder as to why history matters: Take the alleged conflict between science and the biblical story of creation. A careful reading of the Torah's text reveals that there actually is no conflict. Science is interested in how we got here; the Torah is interested in why. The metaphors of the six days of creation aren't a scientific account—if they were, why are there two conflicting accounts, one in Genesis, Chapter One, and another in Genesis, Chapter Two? No, the Torah is not trying to explain how we got here; it's trying to show that human life is not an accident, and that part of being human is to have responsibility to history. Even the stories we tell about the "very first" human beings are designed to remind us that to be a Jew is to wonder about where we're headed, about what kind of person we feel we need to be.

Put this way, adjusted for our kids' ages and levels of knowledge, we begin to transform history from something that elicits a "why do we have to learn this?" to something that creates a sense of belonging, a sense of purpose.

ISRAEL—WHERE HISTORY COMES ALIVE

Having spent a bit of time explaining why history plays such a significant role in Jewish education, and why historical consciousness is something that is important for us to share with our kids, it should now be even clearer why connections to the State of Israel are so powerful.

Israel, quite simply, is where Jewish history comes alive. Israel gives us a completely different sense of what's old, what's new. Simply by being, Israel takes disconnected names, places, and events and breathes new life into them.

When my daughter was about ten years old, I had to make one of my regular work-related trips to Israel. I figured that she was old enough to get something out of the trip, so I took her along. Between work and meetings, we tried to see as much as we could, and one day I took her to the museum at the Tower of David in the Old City of Jerusalem. This museum traces the history of Jerusalem from its very earliest stages until the present; each phase of Jerusalem's history is marked by a stop along the tour. During the first dozen or so stops, as I explained to Tali what Jerusalem had been like, who had lived there and what had happened in those years, she would ask me, "What was happening in the United States at this time?" And each time, of course, the answer was the same: There was no United States.

Only when we got to the very end of the tour, the last two or three stops in the hours-long visit, was there something to say in response to her question about the United States. As we neared the end I began saying to her, "This is when George Washington was crossing the Delaware River in that famous picture you saw," or this was at about the same time as the Civil War. In her social studies class, George Washington and Abraham Lincoln had always seemed ancient. Now, viewed against the backdrop of Jerusalem's history, it seemed as if they had lived only yesterday. I don't think Tali ever thought of history in quite the same way again.

Israel is a country with a profound historical consciousness. The remains of the truck convoys that brought food to the stranded and besieged residents of Jerusalem during the 1948 War of Independence still dot the sides of the main highway from the airport. There are churches and mosques that are hundreds of years old. Recent excavations at the side of the Western Wall have unearthed, at the bottom of the wall, a street dating from the first century C.E. A street on which, quite possibly, Hillel or Rabbi Akiva or any one of the other famous scholars of that time may have walked. There's the Burnt House, a house that was apparently sacked and destroyed by the Romans on the very day they destroyed the Temple in 70 C.E. You can see the family's tableware, the remains of the walls of their home, some of their jewelry—all about *two thousand* years old.

Of course, as we take our kids to these places, we have to remember that each will understand and internalize things differently, depending largely on their ages. What a sixteen-year-old will get out of these experiences will be very different from what a nine-year-old will learn. But they all learn something.

This became apparent to me when, during the year our family was on sabbatical in Israel, I took our kids to see the King David Hotel, still the most prestigious hotel in Jerusalem, a part of which Jewish terrorists blew up during their campaign to force the British out of Palestine. Standing in the back of the hotel, Avi asked me which part of the hotel the Jews had blown up. I pointed to the wing of the hotel that's long since been rebuilt and told him the story of how early Jewish settlers had to fight to create the country we now take for granted. I assumed throughout all of this that Micha, our five-year-old, was basically getting nothing.

When we got home later that day, though, Micha suddenly asked about the King David. "Can you explain that to me one more time?" he asked. "Tell me again why the Maccabees blew up that hotel."

We had a good chuckle from his conflation of the Maccabees, who lived more than two thousand years ago, with Menachem

Begin, who later became Israel's prime minister. But at the same time, I realized that Micha wasn't as oblivious as I'd thought he'd been. Sure, he had gotten his history mixed up, but somehow, between what he'd heard at school about the Maccabees and what he heard with his siblings about the King David Hotel added up to one important message: Important stuff happened in this place; Jews have fought to have a spot to call their own. That message is probably the most important thing that he could have learned, all the details notwithstanding.

Nor is it only Jewish history that comes alive in Jerusalem. The Via Dolorosa, the path that Jesus walked on the way to his crucifixion, is still there, and anyone can walk it (check security conditions first, though, since it takes you through the Muslim quarter of the Old City). Remains of Roman construction and Crusader fortresses dot the Galilee. Near Caesaria there are still enormous sections of an aqueduct that the Romans built to carry water across a vast area. There are remnants of the Turkish occupation. The list goes on and on.

Even the lives of Israeli children are deeply colored by history. The way Israelis raise their kids reflects their sense of the bitter past that gave rise to their country, and the dangerous future these kids face. Look at what even a general guidebook to Israel says about what visitors should expect when they see Israeli kids:

> *Israel adores its children. Even more than in other countries they are indulged, undisciplined, ill-mannered and forgiven by everyone. Dare to mention that they might be a nuisance, and eyebrows are raised. . . . Even now, when Israelis look at their children, they are reminded of a dark past, and an uncertain future.*
>
> *Children seem to be everywhere. School groups, sometimes*

*in neat lines, but more usually like a horde of Tartars, are taken
to see every monument and memorial to Israel's creation. . . .
Overshadowing [this history] looms the Holocaust. Common
images of Holocaust victims are of adults. In reality, a quarter
of all Jews killed in the gas chambers were children. For Israelis
today, it is a joy to see Jewish children alive and enjoying their
liberty.*

Israel is a country virtually built out of history. Flip through a
typical guidebook to Israel, something like Fodor's *Exploring
Israel.* Page after page is filled with examples of what to see, and
more often than not, these things are older than anything that can
be seen in North America, older even than most of what can be
seen in Europe. That ancient quality, combined with the fact that
this is where many of the stories they have learned actually took
place, can make Jewish history come alive in ways we might not
have imagined possible.

The sooner we can figure out a way for our kids to experience
Israel and its richness, the sooner Jewish history and peoplehood
will take on meanings that no mere words can fully convey.

BACK TO PARENTING

All of this brings us back to the question of parenting and grandparenting. What can we do to infuse a sense of this history into
our kids' lives? How can we make it all come alive for them?

• The first step, of course, is to remember that they can't enjoy
what they don't know. This just brings us back to the importance
of asking hard questions about our kids' Jewish education. How
much do we want them to know? How much can they learn in

how many hours per week? What kind of investment are we willing to make so that they really know this stuff?

There are no easy answers to this. When we check out Jewish schools (day schools, Hebrew schools, religious schools) for our kids, we have got to be worried not only about how many hours it's going to take up per week, or how much driving it's going to entail, or how much it's going to cost. We have to ask how much are they going to learn? Do the kids coming out of this school know anything? Has the school done any assessment of how much they've learned about what? What do parents of kids currently in the school think about the education they're getting?

• Then there's the question of how it will be taught. Are our kids going to learn history as facts, "stuff they've gotta get right on a test," or as something magical, wondrous, a sense that this is who *they* are?

When my son Avi was around age five or six, he came home from school and asked how old his grandfather was when the biblical Abraham died! While I began to suspect that at five years of age he didn't yet have the makings of a world-class historian, I was actually thrilled with the question. For it meant that my son's teacher had told stories about the biblical Abraham so imaginatively that Abraham seemed as real to my son as did his own grandfather.

That's exactly the kind of education we want our kids to have, not only in Jewish life but in general. For that's where wonder and imagination come from, and that's where their Jewish "memory" and sense of belonging will come from. We picked our kids' schools largely because we wanted them to have those kinds of teachers. Obviously, since all school choices are compromises, we knew that to have such teachers meant we had to give up other things. But we knew we could accept that. We knew what was most important to us, and we tried to get as much of *that* as we could.

Admittedly, we were fortunate to be living in a large city with a substantial Jewish population and a variety of schools and teaching styles from which to choose. Not all communities have that. But the questions remain the same no matter where we live. What do we want for our children's educational experience? Are they getting it? And if they're not, to whom should we speak? How can we begin to make a difference in what they're getting?

- Remember, our kids live at home, not at school. No matter how good our kids' school may be, and even though they do spend the bulk of their waking hours there, no school can replace what our kids will learn and see at home.

And so we have got to ask ourselves again: What are we doing to make history come alive for our kids? Are we ourselves learning enough so that we can also teach them, infuse conversations with a bit of history here and there? Are there books in the house about Jewish history? Do we include "Jewish stops" on family trips to places like Philadelphia? New York? Ellis Island? There's quite a bit of Jewish history in those places. Or small synagogues in tiny communities in the South? Many of these shuls are still around, and often have exhibits about Jewish life in those areas. Our kids will be amazed at how committed those people were to keeping Jewish life going when it seemed almost impossible.

Or how about movies? Everything from the animated *Prince of Egypt* to *Exodus* to *Schindler's List*—kids learn from movies in a way that's different from how they learn in other settings. It's just as easy to rent one of these from Blockbuster as anything else.

• Travel! We all love it, and places like Israel and Europe are rich with Jewish history.

Kids learn a lot when they travel. My wife and I constantly marvel how each trip seems to bring out huge leaps of development in each of our children. They even seem to grow faster when we travel! Children are like sponges, eager to learn and to absorb everything they see. If we include even a drop of Jewish content or sight-seeing in all this, the impact will be much greater than we could probably imagine.

~

One of the goals of Jewish parenting, we've been saying, is to raise our kids so that a sense of Jewish belonging lies right at the very core of who they are. There are lots of ways of doing this, each of which contributes something special and unique. Now we know that history is another part of that "core." If we want our kids to sense the beauty and majesty of Jewish life, it's important that history be a part of it.

III

A JEWISH PARENT'S
REFERENCE GUIDE

12

HOW TO USE THE "REFERENCE GUIDE" SECTION

Don't know much about history, biology," or the Jewish holidays? Is the Jewish life cycle or the details of some of its celebrations more or less a blur? Confused about where the Jews were and when, and what happened at what point in Jewish history?

You're in good company. The purpose of this section is to give you a little introduction to these areas of Jewish life. In the first of these chapters, we look at the cycle of the holidays in general, and then to the holidays themselves. We'll cover the basics and leave you "armed" with lots of places to turn as you make learning about the holidays an ongoing, lifelong adventure. We're also going to offer preliminary introductions to all of the holidays, so Jewish parents of all backgrounds will have at least some basic information about each as well as the yearly calendar. Then we'll focus on several issues that face parents and children. Most important, we'll talk about interesting ways of thinking about the holidays so you can begin some meaningful conversations with your kids as the holidays approach or as you celebrate them. As part of this section, we'll offer ways to address the holiday based on each stage of your children's development, easy projects you can put together and resources to turn to for further information.

Even if you're pretty familiar with the Jewish holidays, don't assume that you should skip this chapter. We've been suggesting all along that Jewish parenting is largely about continuing and deepening one's own Jewish journey. With that in mind, I try to offer perspectives that are different, something new that you might be able to share with your older kids.

After the holidays, we'll turn to the Jewish life cycle, addressing it in a way that's similar to what we did with the holidays, but rather than covering all the specifics, we'll summarize the basics. We'll also suggest the broadest possible issues to think about as we approach each of these events. This chapter will be primarily about the "big ideas" to consider—by yourself or with your partner or even with your kids—at each stage. We'll look at the themes of each event: What is a bar mitzvah really all about? What's a defensible, intellectually sophisticated reason for circumcising Jewish boys?

We'll also go into what you can expect to see at life cycle events—at a *bris,* a girl's naming ceremony, a Jewish wedding, or a funeral. We'll cover what we as parents and grandparents can do to add Jewish content to other life events, such as the selection of a college or a child's moving into his or her first "grown-up" apartment. Want more information about a given subject? Don't worry! "Suggestions for Further Exploration" is filled with places to which you can turn.

Finally, this section concludes with a very brief overview of Jewish history. It will give you an idea of the basic stages of the Jewish people's experience, when they took place, what some of the events were, and who were some of the important personalities. And as is true of the other chapters of this section, the end of the book will give you a great deal of information on where to continue your exploration.

13

❧

THE JEWISH HOLIDAY CYCLE
A Parent's Perspective

Jewish parenting, as we've seen, has building blocks: memories, making times shared into Jewish time, the worlds of ritual and feelings, God and wonder. If that's the stuff of which good Jewish parenting is made, then what could be more powerful a tool for parents than the Jewish holidays? After all, the holidays help provide memories, they make regular, secular time into Jewish time, and when we allow their power and insight to truly touch us, we feel a connection—to God, to wonder, to feelings that we can't even articulate.

Sometimes it's hard to see how the holidays are such an important tool for Jewish parenting. Many of us grew up without the holidays being very central to our lives. Others observed some, but remember those times more as "command performances" when our presence was required but we didn't feel very much. Some of us have very painful memories of family dynamics associated with the Jewish holidays. We can't undo the experiences, but we can give our children more than we got. And if our childhood memories are happy ones, then we can try to give our kids even more of the same.

If we do it right, our children's memories of the holidays will be filled with joy, meaning, a sense of God and wonder, a feeling of belonging to something magical and mysterious—the very best that Jewish life has to offer. So, our job as parents is to learn enough about the holidays to make them into meaningful experiences for our kids. The question is "How?"

~

First things first. It's critically important that learning about the holidays become a lifelong adventure—for our kids *and* for the adults. One reason kids become adults who are not very interested in Jewish life is that growing up as Jews, or in a Jewish community, simply wasn't very interesting. And too often our own behavior sets up that situation. We send them off to Hebrew school in first or second grade, and they learn the basics about each of the Jewish holidays. Fine. But then we simply repeat the same story over and over, year after year, not even realizing how, in every other area of their lives, our children are becoming much more sophisticated and are being exposed to much more interesting material.

One question we need to keep in mind as we teach our kids about the holidays is: How does this level of information compare to what they're getting at school? When they're in nursery school or kindergarten, it's fine to explain to our children that Passover is about how the Jews were once slaves to Pharaoh, but now we're free. That is, after all, the basic story. But if that's still the level of discourse we give our kids when they're in high school, we create a terrible problem. High school kids are way beyond Passover as just about slaves going free. But if that's all they get, the result will be that they'll think that Judaism is stupid or, at the very minimum, so one-dimensional that it scarcely merits their attention.

Unless our kids can learn about the holidays and talk about them (even with us!) in a way that taxes their minds and touches the best of who they are, they will quickly decide that complexity, thoughtfulness, and meaning can be found in English literature but not in Jewish life. When they want to wonder about who they are as people, they'll turn to Camus and Sartre, not the insights of the scholars who helped compose the Rosh Ha-Shannah liturgy.

So we've got our work cut out for us. Very few of us know as much as we'd like to about the holidays. Chances are we, too, have thought about them in exactly the same way for a long time. So this is a great opportunity to learn along with our kids. We can be their partners in the search—which will impress on them that the holidays are not just "kids' stuff."

THE JEWISH CALENDAR AND ITS PECULIARITIES

Before we get to the holidays themselves, let's take a brief glance at the overall structure of the Jewish calendar. One of the things our kids may ask about centers around the fact that the Jewish calendar has a few "quirks." So let's start with a few introductory comments into the Jewish calendar and how it works.

Why Rosh Ha-Shannah Is Always Early or Late

At the end of the summer, as we gear up for a new year of work and school, Jews tend to look at the calendar to see when Rosh Ha-Shannah falls. Invariably, we always comment that it's early or it's late. Rosh Ha-Shannah never seems to fall at the same time each year!

This is because the Jewish calendar is different from the calendar on which the secular world is based. And most of us are a bit fuzzy on exactly what that difference is. When our kids ask, we feel clueless and silly. Why does Rosh Ha-Shannah fall on a different date each year? And what's with those strange Jewish months and their names? So we begin with the very basics.

The secular world's calendar (January, February, March, etc.) is what is called a solar calendar. The year is the amount of time it takes for the planet Earth to go around the sun—approximately 365 days.

Judaism's calendar is based on the moon; it's a lunar calendar.

That means the Jewish calendar is based on the rotation of the moon around Earth. Each time the moon goes around Earth, Jews begin a new month. Twelve of these cycles take *approximately* one secular year, but not quite. Usually, 12 Jewish months (29 or 30 days each, in most cases) adds up to about 352 days.

Since the lunar year is about twelve days shorter than the solar year, unless we did something to intervene, the Jewish calendar would get twelve days farther "behind" the solar calendar each year. Next year's Rosh Ha-Shannah would be twelve days earlier than this year's on the secular calendar, and in six years, it would be seventy-two days, or more than two months, earlier. Eventually, of course, Rosh Ha-Shannah could fall in the spring and Passover in the fall.

As strange as that might sound, that's *exactly* how the Muslim calendar works. Muslims also use a lunar calendar, and they follow its cycle precisely. That is why any given Muslim holiday, such as Ramadan, can and will eventually fall at virtually every time of the year.

But that won't work for Jews. For Passover is also called the Festival of Spring, and Hanukkah is typically seen as a time of creating light in the dead of winter's darkness (that doesn't quite work for Jews in South America or Australia, where the seasons are reversed). The creators of the Jewish calendar wanted to make sure that Rosh Ha-Shannah would always fall in the fall, that Hanukkah would consistently be a winter holiday, that Passover would always be in the spring. In order to do this, the Jewish calendar "plays around" with the lunar calendar a bit. Every now and then, an extra month (**Adar II**) is added to help the Jewish calendar "catch up" with the secular calendar. The mathematics of how often this is done are not simple, and they don't matter for us right now, but at least we now know enough to understand the basics of how this seemingly strange calendar works.

To help keep things straight, here are the months of the Jewish calendar, the approximate secular months in which they fall, and the holidays that fall in each of those Jewish months:

THE JEWISH CALENDAR

Hebrew Month	Approximate Secular Month	Holidays That Fall During This Month
Tishrei	September/October	Rosh Ha-Shannah The Fast of Gedaliah Yom Kippur Sukkot
Cheshvan	October/November	No holidays
Kislev	November/December	Hanukkah
Tevet	December/Januaury	Fast of the Tenth of Tevet
Shevat	January/February	Tu Bi-Shevat
Adar	February/March	Fast of Esther Purim
Nissan	March/April	Passover Yom Ha-Shoah (Shoah Remembrance Day)
Iyyar	April/May	Yom-Ha-Zikaron (Memorial Day for Fallen Israeli Soldiers) Yom-Ha-Atzma'ut (Israel Independence Day) Lag Ba Omer Yom Yerushalayim (Jerusalem Day)
Sivvan	May/June	Shavu'ot
Tammuz	June/July	Fast of the Seventeenth of Tammuz
Av	July/August	Tisha B'Av
Elul	August/September	No holidays but spiritual preparation for Rosh Ha-Shannah begins

Note, by the way, that these dates are not absolute. Certain holidays have to be adjusted a bit in one direction or the other so they don't fall on Shabbat. Some holidays can fall on Shabbat and others can't, but we won't go into those rules now—they can be a little complicated. Before you can be sure that a given holiday actually falls on a certain date, you pretty much need to check a calendar for that year.

There are lots of ways to check out the Jewish calendar and to get more information about it. Take a look at some of the suggestions at the end of this book for sources that explain this in detail. There's also lots of information available on the Internet, and great software about the Jewish calendar.

One final comment on the number of the year. We all know what 1998 is: It's a counting of the years since the birth of Jesus. (That's why many Jews won't use the abbreviation A.D., which stands for Anno Domini, Latin for "the year of Our Lord." When using secular dates, Jews tend to use C.E., which stands for "Common Era" or "Current Era.") But what's with the 5758 or similar numbers that we see around Jewish dates? That is also the number of the year, but in our case it is the number of years since the Creation of the world. Most of us know that the world was not created less than six thousand years ago. Only the most traditional Jews still take this number literally. But that system of counting, derived from accounts and discussions in the Bible itself, is still the accepted Jewish system for numbering years, even for those who view the stories of the Bible and their account of years metaphorically.

Why Do Jewish Holidays Have to Start at Sunset?

Another frequent question: Why do Jewish holidays start at night? The Passover seder comes the night *before* the first day of

Passover. Shabbat begins not on Saturday but on Friday night. We light the first Hanukkah candle on the night *before* the first day of the holiday. And that's true of every Jewish holiday and date; the Jewish day begins at sundown and ends at sundown the day after. Why?

The answer is fairly simple. You may recall that when describing creation, the Torah ends each day by saying "it was evening, and it was morning, Day One," or "it was evening, and it was morning, the second day." So the most common explanation says that this is why the Jewish day starts with evening and then proceeds to the following day. The next question might then be: Why does the Torah put it that way? Good question; and truth be told, no one really knows. Can we make allegorical explanations about beginning each day in darkness and moving to light as a metaphor for what we would like to do with the world, with our lives, with our children? Of course. But the "real," original reason is lost to time.

If your kids ask why the Jewish day begins at night, tell them the truth: That's how the days "were" when God created the world, and Jews have continued that ever since. If it still seems strange to them, show them how it's no more unusual than the "normal" system of starting a day at midnight. (Of course, they may then ask why the day starts at midnight, when no one is even awake— sometimes you just can't win.)

~

So much for the calendar as a whole; now it's time for brief reviews of the holidays, one by one. What follows is a *brief* introduction, a basic orientation as to what it's all about and some ways of making them meaningful for our kids. Please refer to the sources listed at the back of this book to continue the journey we're only beginning to map out here.

ROSH HA-SHANNAH

First things first! There's a difference between Rosh Ha-Shannah, which means "the Beginning of the Year," and the High Holy Days. And even though we commonly say Rosh Ha-Shannah and Yom Kippur in virtually the same breath, they shouldn't be confused or combined. Sure, you get one set of tickets for admission to both, but that's a function of synagogue efficiency, not Jewish theology! The two holidays are very different, and to explain the calendar well, we need to understand how.

Now, to be fair, it's not just modern American synagogues that have started grouping the two. Jewish tradition has a name for the two holidays together: **Yamim Nora'im,** which means "Days of Awe." But despite the tradition of grouping these holidays, we're better off keeping them separate so we can focus on what's unique to each.

Rosh Ha-Shannah Basics

Rosh Ha-Shannah is a two-day holiday, celebrated on the first two days of the year. Thus, its dates are always the first and second of the month of Tishrei. Rosh Ha-Shannah has a couple of very basic themes. The first, the one we're probably most familiar with, is the simple idea of a New Year. Jews typically wish each other a "shannah tovah," or a good year, and have a variety of rituals that express our hopes that the upcoming year will be sweet and wonderful.

But beyond the sweetness that we hope for, Rosh Ha-Shannah also asks us to reflect on the unpredictability of life. Tradition has it that at the beginning of each year, God examines each of us, causing each of us to come under God's gaze, just as a shepherd causes each of his sheep to pass under his staff. To use the metaphor of the liturgy, it is during this period (the ten days from the beginning of Rosh Ha-Shannah through Yom Kippur are also called **Asseret Yemei Teshuvah,** or the "Ten Days of Repentance") that God first writes our fate in the Book of Life and then seals that fate. Many of us remember the well-known line from the Rosh Ha-Shannah liturgy that says, "On Rosh Ha-Shannah [our fate] is written, and on Yom Kippur it is sealed."

In the Jewish calendar, Rosh Ha-Shannah is also the "birthday of the world." After we blow the **shofar** in synagogue during Rosh Ha-Shannah services, we recite a paragraph that actually says "Today is the birthday of the world." Related to the idea of the "birthday of the world" is the concept of God's supreme majesty over the world. Many people who go to synagogue on Rosh Ha-Shannah are either surprised (or bored) to see how often the idea of God as king or ruler appears in the **Machzor** (the Rosh Ha-Shannah and Yom Kippur prayer book). That is intentional; throughout history, Jews have been confronted by kings and rulers who were vicious and authoritarian. The Machzor was their way of saying that no matter what the rest of the world believed, we did not believe that this person was the ultimate ruler. Rosh Ha-Shannah became the day on which we proclaimed our faith that there is but one ultimate ruler, a ruler our tradition calls God.

Explaining Rosh Ha-Shannah to Our Children

As we said before, it's important that our discussions of the Jewish holidays change and grow as our children do. Rosh Ha-Shannah is no exception. When our children are very young, Rosh Ha-Shannah can be an opportunity to talk about new years, about sweet futures. Our youngest children will love dipping their apples in honey (see below for a discussion of the rituals of the holiday). As they get older, we can begin to talk about what we'd like the new year to bring, our hopes, our fears, our dreams. Do we as parents talk about this with our kids often enough? Did our parents do that with us enough? If not, Rosh Ha-Shannah is the time to begin.

As our kids grow up, we can teach them that Rosh Ha-Shannah is not only a holiday unto itself, but it begins the Ten Days of Repentance. Jewish tradition makes an interesting stipulation about the forgiveness we're granted on Yom Kippur (we'll come to Yom Kippur below); the tradition says that God can forgive us only for sins we've committed against God. For sins that we've committed against other people, we need to ask *them* for forgiveness before God can forgive us. Thus, Rosh Ha-Shannah is also when we begin approaching the people we love, and the people we may have hurt, and say something to them along the lines of the traditional petition, "If there is anything that I've done to hurt you or to cause you pain in the past year, I am sorry and I ask your forgiveness."

What our kids will learn is that it's not so easy to ask for forgiveness, particularly when we really want it. It's one thing to tell a brother that he has to say "sorry" to his sister after a fight; typically he mumbles something, letting her know that he's really *not* sorry, and then goes on! But on Rosh Ha-Shannah and the ensuing week, the stakes are higher—Yom Kippur is approaching, the day on which we're going to be forgiven if we're truly repentant—and we should teach our kids to begin to approach the people they really care about to ask for forgiveness. Kids can ask their siblings, their parents, their grandparents. As they get older, and feel more secure, they can approach their friends, especially those they trust the most.

As our children get older, we can teach them the Jewish phrase "*shannah tovah,*" which means not a "happy" new year, but a "good" new year. Jews wish each other not just a year filled with happiness, but a year filled with goodness, in which we do good, bring good to the world, and try to become good people.

Especially as they reach their teens, we can ask our kids to reflect on the difference between "goodness" and "happiness," and what "goodness" might mean to them at that stage.

They might even make up and send out their own Rosh Ha-Shannah card with a greeting that reflects their sense of what the year should bring. (With desktop publishing and color printers these days, it's not hard. They can even design an animated card and send it via e-mail!) Encourage them to make their own cards; if nothing else, it will invest in them the process of thinking at least a bit about what they really believe in, what's genuinely important to them. Teenagers are trying to figure this out anyway; why not make Jewish tradition one of the things they think about?

But let's not leave God out of the picture. If they're in synagogue much, our kids will see that the liturgy is filled with references to "the birthday of the world" and to God as king. What do they believe about the origins of the world? Even if they don't believe that the world is less than 5,800 years old, do they believe it was created with a purpose? By what? By whom? And if the phrase "God is king" sounds trite to them, what do *they* think is the power behind the universe? Is this all just one big accident or coincidence? How do they explain love? Conscience? The miracle of the birth of a baby? These are the things we can begin to talk with them about.

In addition to talking and explaining, though, there is more we can do to make Rosh Ha-Shannah festive and meaningful. That's where the ritual comes in.

Rosh Ha-Shannah Rituals

Rosh Ha-Shannah is not a holiday known for its rituals. On Passover, we have the seder. On Hanukkah, we light the *hanukkiah* (commonly, but incorrectly, called the "menorah").

But on Rosh Ha-Shannah, most of us think primarily of sitting passively in a synagogue, not about things we can do with our children. And while it's true that Rosh Ha-Shannah is not a holiday rich with home ritual, there are a few things we can do at home to make the holiday special.

The most common home ritual of Rosh Ha-Shannah is eating apples dipped in honey, as a symbol of the sweetness that we hope will be part of the year just beginning. Many families dip the challah eaten at Rosh Ha-Shannah meals into honey as well.

Other Rosh Ha-Shannah customs that use food are less well known but can also be lots of fun with kids. In many traditional prayer books, you can find a list of foods that are typically eaten at the Rosh Ha-Shannah table, and little sayings that are recited with each one. Each saying reflects a traditional Jewish wish for the new year. A few examples include:

> Pomegranate: "May it be Your will, our God and God of our ancestors, that our merits increase as [the seeds of] a pomegranate."
> Fish: "May it be Your will, our God and God of our ancestors, that [our People] be fruitful and multiply like fish."
> Fish head: "May it be Your will, our God and God of our ancestors, that we be as the head and not as the tail" (a prayer that the Jewish people not be attacked or made marginal by those around them).

Other foods are fenugreek, carrots, beets, and gourd. But there's no reason to limit yourself to the classically used foods (the pomegranate is the most common). Ask your kids to think about what they'd like the coming year to be or bring, and then have them figure out what sort of food might best symbolize it. If they're old enough, they can be responsible for buying the food, perhaps even writing a brief line that might be recited by everyone before eating it at the table. The only limit is their imagination!

Another custom that is common at Rosh Ha-Shannah is to eat a food on the second day (usually a fruit) that no one in the family has eaten in the past year. The origin of this custom had to do with giving us a reason to say the **Shehecheyanu** prayer, which thanks God for allowing us to reach this occasion on the second day of the holiday. The tradition is based on the idea that if we ate a new fruit on the second day, we *had* to say this particular blessing. It isn't really required for the holiday itself (because the second day is in many ways a "continuation" of the previous day), but by eating a *new* food, we would feel obligated to say this blessing.

It's a kind of Talmudic logic, but the upshot is that the new fruit can be interpreted as a symbol of all the newness of the year that is just beginning. The same can be said about clothing. There's a long-standing Jewish custom of wearing something new on Rosh Ha-Shannah. This need not be an expensive suit or outfit. In our family, we buy our boys a new white **kippah** each Rosh Ha-Shannah and our daughter picks out a new white blouse or sweater. Nothing very expensive, but each of them greets the new year with something special, clean, and new—all images that we have of the new year.

Another ritual associated with Rosh Ha-Shannah is worth mentioning, and that is the *tashlich,* which means "casting away." The custom of *tashlich* involves walking to a body of moving water and symbolically casting our sins into it so that they are "swept" away. Very often, we throw bread onto the water to symbolize those sins.

Since traditional Jews do not drive on holidays like Rosh Ha-Shannah, and many don't live within walking distance of a body of water, some people perform the ritual of *tashlich* at other times.

Some go the day after Rosh Ha-Shannah, or on Sunday if Rosh Ha-Shannah is followed by Shabbat. There's a very brief liturgy in traditional prayer books, but the essence is to be by the water, and to cast away something about ourselves. It's a ritual that's wonderful for kids.

Ask your kids what they're throwing away onto the water. What are they thinking about as they do it? What does it mean to them to be near this water as the new year begins? Why do they throw these sins onto the water and not into the wind? Their answers don't really matter. What's important to make the ritual exciting, fun, and meaningful, to give the kids a chance to express their own senses about how they'd like to be different as a new year begins to unfold.

And don't throw out those Rosh Ha-Shannah cards as they come in the mail. Many families display the cards they get during the holiday (in a window, on the mantelpiece, in the slats of a shuttered door) but throw them out right afterward. Don't! Save them; you can use them to decorate the *sukkah*—we'll talk about this when we get to the holiday of Sukkot.

So while Rosh Ha-Shannah is not really a "home" holiday, and the synagogue is still the main focus for what we'll do these two days, there is plenty that we can do with our children both to prepare for the holiday and during the holiday to make it fun and meaningful for them no matter what their ages.

THE FAST OF GEDALIAH

Just a few years ago, no book of this sort would have even considered mentioning the Fast of Gedaliah, which falls on the third day of Tishrei, or the day after Rosh Ha-Shannah. The Fast of Gedaliah, or **Tzom Gedaliah** as it's known in Hebrew, was by far the most obscure of all the fast days in the Jewish calendar. But ever since the tragic assassination of Israeli prime minister Yitzchak Rabin, this fast has taken on a new prominence. And it's very likely to become even more so as time goes on.

There are two different kinds of fast days in Jewish life. Some (Yom Kippur and the Ninth of Av) are sundown-to-sundown fasts, while others are sunrise to sundown. During all these fasts, traditional Jews abstain from eating, drinking, and washing. (The twenty-four-hour fasts have more restrictions, including, most importantly, the wearing of leather shoes and sexual activity—we'll discuss that when we get to Yom Kippur.) The Fast of Gedaliah is one of the "minor fasts," beginning at sunrise and ending at sundown.

A Brief History of Tzom Gedaliah

Why did this day become associated with the death of Yitzchak Rabin? It all has to do with the story of Gedaliah ben [son of] Achikam, as told in the book of Jeremiah, chapters forty through forty-three. Gedaliah, a ruler of the Jewish kingdom of Judea, had been appointed by the Babylonian conqueror Nebuchadnezzar. After Nebuchadnezzar conquered Judea, destroyed the Jews' Temple, and exiled much of the population, he appointed Gedaliah as his puppet. But a man named Ishmael ben [son of] Metanniah feared that the appointment of Gedaliah would mean that the throne would permanently pass from the legitimate line of monarchs, so he plotted to kill him. Gedaliah was informed of the plot but refused to believe that a fellow Jew would kill him. Indeed, he made a grand reception for Ishmael. But at the reception Ishmael killed not only Gedaliah but a large number of people who were with him.

Jews who abstain from eating on the Fast of Gedaliah, it is commonly said, fast not because Gedaliah was killed—many biblical kings were killed—but because he was killed by a Jew.

That, of course, is part of what was so tragic and horrifying about the murder of Yitzchak Rabin. I remember vividly the moment I heard the news. And minutes later, when my son saw how upset I was, he asked what was wrong. When I told him, he asked by whom. I said I did not know yet, but it was a Jew.

Avi's response was classic in its naïveté and innocence. He said, "But I thought Jewish people aren't supposed to kill." And that's precisely the point. We're not. Just one day after Rosh Ha-Shannah (the day that tradition says Gedaliah was murdered), many Jews have now begun taking the fast day more seriously to remind themselves and each other of how deeply embedded hatred can become. As the second phase of the Ten Days of Repentance gets started, many of us find it helpful to spend a day reflecting on how tragic the consequences of the things we hold dear—nationalism, political passion, religious convictions—can be. In this season of trying to bolster our religious passion, the Fast of Gedaliah is also a useful way to remind ourselves of the dangers of that passion.

Is This a Fast for Children?

Obviously, small children shouldn't fast, and there's probably no reason to talk about the day with them. But what about the older children, especially the teenagers? Parents who want to make Bible, Jewish history, and contemporary politics all flow together might want to try fasting with them on this day. Or just skip breakfast. Or breakfast and lunch. It's an opportunity for our children to be made to think not about the tragedies that others have brought on the Jews, but about the horrors that Jews have brought on themselves.

I happened to be in Tel Aviv on the third anniversary of Rabin's assassination, so I made a point of going to the spot where he was killed. There were a lot people milling about, a few lighting candles. Then, off to the side, I saw a man sitting on the ground in the lotus position, holding a sign. The sign, which is still clearly etched in my memory, said, "I'm fasting today, and I'm also not speaking. For even before the bullets were fired, the words had already started to kill."

What a powerful image to have in our minds in the middle of this period of repentance. As the new year begins and we pray to God for a year of good, of plenty, of health, and of joy, it's certainly worthwhile to ask our children to spend a day dwelling on the things that have gone wrong in our lives that we have brought on ourselves. How much is up to God? How much is up to us? Those questions, too, are part of repentance, part of growth.

YOM KIPPUR

As Yom Kippur is the holiest day of the year, one might expect that we would spend more time discussing it here than we would any other. But surprising as it may seem, though Yom Kippur is a critically important day, there's not much we do at home. Yom Kippur is a synagogue-centered day, the day when we repent our sins and pray for a "clean slate" with God and with other people; it's a day spent in meditation and prayer, ideally with community, usually in synagogue. There are precious few rituals that take place at home. The two most common are the *se'udah mafseket* (the meal before the fast) and the "break fast" meal after the holiday, but there are a couple of rituals we should show our kids. First, though, a brief explanation of the day.

A Brief Explanation of Yom Kippur

Yom Kippur falls on the tenth of Tishrei, or the week after Rosh Ha-Shannah. Though most people think of Yom Kippur as a sad day (probably because of the fast, which in most other holidays is a symbol of sadness), the **Mishnah** (a classic Jewish text from about 220 C.E.) tells us that Yom Kippur is actually one of the two most joy-filled days of the Jewish year. (The other is the fifteenth of Av, no longer celebrated in any noticeable manner.) It is a joyous day because it's the day on which we're guaranteed that if our repentance is sincere, and if we've asked for forgiveness from other human beings, we can truly enter the new year with a new start, "pure" in the eyes of God.

That idea of "purity" is expressed in one of the least-known rituals of Yom Kippur, of wearing white (white is even more central to Yom Kippur than it is to Rosh Ha-Shannah). In traditional communities, especially in Israel, women wear white dresses on Yom Kippur and men come to services in a traditional white robe called a *kittel*. When you stand in those synagogues, all you see is a sea of white, with black stripes on the *tallitot* that many of the men are wearing.

The symbolic purity of white is the reason that wedding gowns are traditionally white, why the Shabbat tablecloth is often decorated in white, why we wear white on Rosh Ha-Shannah and Yom Kippur. But also, Jews are buried in white shrouds that look a lot like the *kittel*. The idea behind wearing white on Yom Kippur is to remind us that our bodies, with which we're so often preoccupied, are going to die. Indeed, on Yom Kippur we are actually treating our bodies as if they were "dead." We don't feed them, give them drink, wash them, anoint them, dress them in leather shoes (a sign of luxury in ancient times), or allow sexual gratification. The whole emphasis is on that indescribable something that makes human beings human, that separates us from animals—Judaism calls it the soul.

Whatever we think of as the soul—conscience, memory, something that's eternal—it is the part of the person that Yom Kippur is all about, and that's probably the best way to begin to explain it to our children.

Explaining Yom Kippur to Children

Like all the holidays, Yom Kippur needs to be explained to different children in different ways. At the earliest stages, we can talk about saying "sorry" to people and to God, about what we're sorry about. Then we teach them the idea that God forgives us all on Yom Kippur.

As they get older, we can begin to present our kids with the ideas in the liturgy. (Here's an idea: If the liturgy seems to drag on—and it does for a lot of people—scan it for ideas you think are worth talking about with your child, and then take a walk—with your spouse, kids, significant other, whomever. Carve out the time we so rarely get and talk about what you just "discovered.") For example, the liturgy suggests that we're forgiven not because we merit forgiveness but because God loves us. (If that sounds Christian it's only because Jews have gotten uncomfortable talking about God.) We can then talk about God's love: What do our kids think God loves *about* them? How does God love us even when we don't live up to our potential? Do we love ourselves? What would we like to change for the next year?

One Jewish tradition not commonly discussed around Yom Kippur is very appropriate to the season, and that is the **ethical will**. It's like a "regular will" except that instead of telling our children "who gets what," an ethical will tells them what we hold dear, what we care about most, what we love about them, what our dreams for them are. Part of the Rosh Ha-Shannah and Yom Kippur celebrations is to remind us we're mortal, that at some point we're going to die—we've all heard the famous passage: "who shall live, who shall die, who by fire, who by water, who by thirst, who by hunger. . . ." We hope to live for a long time, and to watch our children grow up and become adults, but there's no guarantee. What the ethical will does is make sure that if the worst should happen, our children will have some record of what we were about, what we wanted for them.

That's why it's a wonderful idea to use the Ten Days of Repentance to write an ethical will, or use Yom Kippur to think about what you might write after the holiday. As our kids grow up, and particularly as they become teenagers, they, too, can write something that explains what their life is about. Have them do it *before* the holiday—it will give them a grounding in what the holiday is all about and make their day in synagogue more meaningful.

A warning about ethical wills: They are easy to begin but hard to finish. So force yourself—you know what happens to papers that are left undone: They sit around collecting dust until we just throw them out because they seem too stale. So if you're going to write an ethical will (and it doesn't have to be just to your children; you can write one to your parents, your siblings, your spouse or lover, your close friend), carve out some time and write it. It doesn't have to be perfect. Then put it in an envelope and file it in a place where you know it will be found if necessary. But finish it all in one sitting, or you won't finish it at all.

Our children will grow up and change, but the basic idea of Yom Kippur always stays the same. Our job is to model for them our heartfelt feelings for this day and to talk to them about what it means to us. That will teach them more than anything else.

SUKKOT—THE FEAST OF TABERNACLES

Because Sukkot—the Feast of Tabernacles—comes only five days after Yom Kippur, it seems to hit many Jewish families just when they feel they're completely "overdosed" on Jewish celebrations. That's understandable, but it's also too bad, because Sukkot is one of the most joyous and wondrous celebrations of the Jewish year. Sukkot is the first of the three "pilgrimage festivals"—festivals on which the ancient Israelites used to make a pilgrimage to Jerusalem (the other two are Passover and Shavu'ot), and its modern celebration tries to capture a bit of the joy and ecstasy our forebears must have felt as they entered the city they believed was the most sacred place on earth.

Before we go into the details of what Sukkot is and how we can make it special for our kids, we should review the structure of this holiday, since it can seem very complex. Here's how the days of the holiday unfold in the Diaspora and in Israel:

Day of the Holiday	Status of the Day Outside Israel	Status of the Day in Israel	Name of the Holiday
Day 1	Yom Tov (Sukkot)	Yom Tov (Sukkot)	Sukkot
Day 2	Yom Tov (Sukkot)	Chol Ha-Mo'ed	Sukkot
Day 3	Chol Ha-Mo'ed	Chol Ha-Mo'ed	Sukkot
Day 4	Chol Ha-Mo'ed	Chol Ha-Mo'ed	Sukkot
Day 5	Chol Ha-Mo'ed	Chol Ha-Mo'ed	Sukkot
Day 6	Chol Ha-Mo'ed	Chol Ha-Mo'ed	Sukkot
Day 7	Chol Ha-Mo'ed (Hoshannah Rabbah)	Chol Ha-Mo'ed (Hoshannah Rabbah)	Hoshannah Rabbah
Day 8	Yom Tov (Shemini Atzeret)	Yom Tov (Shemini Atzeret *and* Simchat Torah)	See names to left
Day 9	Yom Tov (Simchat Torah)	n/a	See names to left

Now, what are these holidays all about? For the basics, there are really two major holidays here: Sukkot and **Simchat Torah**. There are others—and for those, turn to "Suggestions for Further Exploration" for sources of information—but for most of our kids, these two will suffice.

Though we commonly say Sukkot is an eight-day festival, it's not really quite that simple. Sukkot outside of Israel is composed of several different parts: (a) the two first days, called **Yom Tov,** on which the celebration is similar to that of Shabbat; (b) then there are four days of **Chol Ha-Mo'ed,** the "workaday," or intermediate, portion of the holiday, on which most Jews go to work and behave more or less as they would on a regular weekday; (c) a fifth day of Chol Ha-Mo'ed, called **Hoshannah Rabbah;** and then (d) two more days of Yom Tov—also celebrated much like Shabbat—which are not technically part of Sukkot—the first of which is **Shemini Atzeret,** the second Simchat Torah.

The chart above shows how in Israel matters are just slightly different. Most holidays that are celebrated for two days in the Diaspora (outside of Israel) are celebrated for only one in Israel. (Rosh Ha-Shannah, which is celebrated for two days in both locales, is the only exception.) In Israel, there is one day of Yom Tov, followed by five days of Chol Ha-Mo'ed (of which the last is Hoshannah Rabbah), then *one* day of Yom Tov on which Shemini Atzeret and Simchat Torah are combined.

Some Basic Sukkot Themes

Sukkah is a Hebrew word that means "booth," or "tabernacle" as they're sometimes called in more formal translations. On Sukkot, our kids are likely to see two major ritual elements: the actual *sukkah,* and the "Four Species," commonly called the *lulav* and *etrog.*

According to Jewish tradition, the *sukkah* has to be a temporary structure with at least two and a half walls and a roof made of something that once grew from the ground but is no longer connected to it (palm fronds are common in California, cornstalks in Nebraska, and evergreen branches in the east). It's customary to decorate the *sukkah* with fruits hanging from the "roof," with drawings and posters on the wall, and often, with those Rosh Ha-Shannah cards that came a few weeks earlier that you had no idea what to do with.

As is true of all the holidays, Sukkot can be explained on many levels. With our youngest children, we probably want to use the classic explanation, given even in the Torah, that the purpose of living in the *sukkah* for a few days is to remember the *sukkah* that the Children of Israel (us, that is) used as their only shelter on their forty-year march from Egypt to the Promised Land. For little children, the waving of the *lulav* and *etrog* to all directions can be a simple way of acknowledging that God is everywhere—in front of us, in back, to the sides, up and down.

But if our explanation and appreciation of Sukkot goes only this far, our children will quickly tire of the holiday. As they get older, Sukkot has to take on issues that concern them as human beings. For many people in the modern Jewish community, Sukkot has become the consummate holiday about environmental issues. The fragility of the *sukkah* and the branches on the *lulav,* our exposure to the elements, and our willingness to step outside the "fortresses" of our homes makes this a great time to focus on issues regarding our obligation to protect and enhance the natural world we've inherited.

Beyond environmentalism, Sukkot can be a wonderful way of connecting with the idea that most of the things that really matter in life are not permanent. We spend a lot of time trying to accumulate things that seem permanent—cars, homes, the "stuff" that fills the house—but none of it really matters. Deep down we know the stuff that's really important is much more fragile: the love we have for the important people in our lives, our health and theirs, our dignity and character, the time we have while our kids are still young. These are issues we can talk with them about as they get older. Sukkot can be a time to see the difference between "need" and "want," between what really matters and what society and advertisers are trying to tell us.

One of the many explanations of Sukkot links it with the High Holidays that have just passed. Tradition has it that Yom Kippur is not the real end of the period of repentance; the "gates of repentance" are open, tradition says, through Hoshannah Rabbah, the final day of Chol Ha-Mo'ed. This means that Sukkot falls during the period of repentance. Why is that important, and what might it say to our kids?

The idea that Sukkot *needs* to fall during the period of repentance suggests that we must move outside our homes in order to repent. We're usually too guarded, too protective, too concerned with *things* to let ourselves experience the vulnerability that true repentance requires. We have to feel vulnerable to be able to truly open up. The openness and fragility of the *sukkah* is simply a way of reinforcing the Yom Kippur message that we may otherwise have been too busy or distracted to fully take in.

The Basic Rituals of Sukkot

What's the *sukkah* for? Eating and sleeping, living. Many Jews who build a *sukkah* try to eat as many meals as possible in it, often inviting friends and family for festive holiday meals. Very traditional Jews not only eat all their meals there, but they try to avoid eating anything at all when not in one. Some families try to spend as much time in the *sukkah* as possible, even when they're not eating. My cousin once brought a television into his *sukkah*—he needed a long extension cord—to both fulfill the tradition of "living" in the *sukkah* and also to watch a baseball playoff game he was determined not to miss!

In traditional communities, families sleep in the *sukkah* as a matter of principle. Sleeping with your kids on the *sukkah* floor with blankets or sleeping bags is a fantastic way to create wonderful memories of the joy of Jewish celebration. Tucking kids into "bed" outside, under the stars, and waking up with the sun, with their parents right next to them, gives children memories that they can treasure for a lifetime.

These days, it's not hard to build a *sukkah*. Gone are the days of schlepping to the lumberyard with the station wagon and dragging home a whole pile of two-by-fours. Today there are people in almost every major Jewish community who sell a variety of prefabricated *sukkot* (the plural form of *sukkah*). To find them call one of the major synagogues, look in the local Jewish newspapers in the weeks preceding Sukkot, or put a message out on the Web at one of the popular Jewish sites.

A prefabricated *sukkah* means that putting one up will not be an exercise in frustration. Put it away carefully each year, and your kids will look forward to the *sukkah* as an annual rite. Don't have the space to build a *sukkah*? Most synagogues have them, as do many Jewish community centers and hospitable families. Do a little asking; don't be bashful. Most people who build a *sukkah* like nothing better than to invite friends and strangers to celebrate the holiday with them.

Another major ritual item our kids will see and learn about on Sukkot is the *lulav* and *etrog*—also called the "Four Species." The *lulav* consists of a palm branch, two willow branches, and three myrtle branches. The *etrog* is a citron, a fruit that looks something like a large lemon. The commandment to gather these items is given in the Torah, and they are used in the daily services that take place on Sukkot during the first days of Yom Tov and the intermediate days of Chol Ha-Mo'ed. (The *lulav* and *etrog* are not used on the Shabbat of Sukkot, or on Shemini Atzeret or Simchat Torah; the latter two are a different holiday.) A blessing is recited each morning as we pick up the *lulav* and *etrog,* hold them together, and wave them in six directions (the four "classic" directions—east, south, west, and north—and up and down).

There's one additional custom on Sukkot, long ignored but now coming back into favor. It's an important one because it's a great way to involve our kids in the *sukkah* each and every night. Called **Ushpizin,** which is the Aramaic word for "guests," it is the custom of reciting a traditional paragraph in Aramaic that invites "guests" into the *sukkah* each night—but the guests that are invited are dead. We invite them to remind us of their gifts, their talents, and all they've given to the Jewish people. The guests traditionally invited (in this order, one per night) are Abraham, Isaac, Jacob, Moses, Aaron (the Priest, Moses' brother), Joseph, and (King) David.

The liturgy for "inviting" these guests can be found in any traditional prayer book. But what's nice about the Ushpizin for our kids is not just participating in this ancient ceremony but in making it exciting. Some ideas:

• Note that all the traditional guests are men. If you were to add women from the Bible or other texts of ancient Jewish life, whom would you add? Why?

• Instead of just inviting each guest in every night, talk about why your kids think that person might have been included. What did he or she do? What did that person accomplish for the Jewish people? What do our kids most admire about that person? What concerns them the most?

• Dress up like that person. Give a speech that the person might have given. Or allow the guests to be "present" cumulatively, so that each night, they can have "conversations" among themselves. What would they talk about?

• Who else would you add to the list? If you had to pick the seven greatest Jews of the modern period, whom would you pick? Why? What makes a Jew great? Is there a difference between being a great person and a great Jew?

Thus, unlike Rosh Ha-Shannah and Yom Kippur, which are rather bereft of home rituals, Sukkot is a virtual feast of opportunities. There are many more things you can do; those we've mentioned are a great place to start. From the preparations to the last day, this is a rich holiday with almost unlimited opportunities to create wonderful, cherished memories.

SHEMINI ATZERET AND SIMCHAT TORAH

In the minds of most American Jews, **Shemini Atzeret** and **Simchat Torah** are simple extensions of Sukkot. But they are, in fact, two completely different holidays (though celebrated in Israel on a single day). The confusion is understandable, as they immediately follow Sukkot without a break in between. Indeed, the Torah doesn't even assign a "theme" to Shemini Atzeret; though it later took on an agricultural aspect, most of those associations have been lost, and it's become a kind of "poor man's Sukkot." There's no *sukkah*, no *lulav*, no *etrog*, just a slightly different liturgy in the synagogue. And there are no home rituals, except for the kind of festive meal one eats on other holidays.

The next day, however, Simchat Torah, *is* a completely different day, a holiday that celebrates the joy of living a life rooted in Torah. (Note that this holiday is not about the joy of receiving the Torah—that's what **Shavu'ot**, or the Festival of Weeks, is about.)

Especially in traditional circles, Simchat Torah is a rather cathartic release of all the energy and intensity that's been building up since even before Rosh Ha-Shannah. These weeks are the most intensive period of celebration, petition, introspection, and observance of the entire Jewish year; nothing quite matches it. At the end of the month of Tishrei, having now observed a full month of repentance during Elul (preceding Rosh Ha-Shannah), Rosh Ha-Shannah itself, Yom Kippur, Sukkot, Hoshannah Rabbah, and Shemini Atzeret, Jews are tired. They've shown their devotion to a life of Torah, and hopefully, they've enjoyed it, but the intensity of this period can also wear us down. Jews who have invested in this process are now ready for something completely different.

That's what Simchat Torah provides. All of a sudden, after all the seriousness, Simchat Torah gives us the chance to explode in singing and dancing, first in the evening, and then all during the following day.

Simchat Torah is another synagogue holiday. Aside from festive meals, as on any other holiday, all its uniqueness is to be found in the synagogue, manifested in dancing, "sacred frivolity," and joy at the conclusion of the holiday season. There's not much to explain, and aside from finding a great place to dance with your kids, not much to do. But don't underestimate the importance of finding a good place to dance. People in general don't dance enough in life, and we certainly don't dance enough with our kids. This holiday is a time to let them know that, in addition to all the "serious stuff," Jewish life is about joy, about closeness, about celebration.

HALLOWEEN: IS IT A JEWISH ISSUE?

No sooner do the Jewish holidays end in the middle of Tishrei, usually sometime in October, than the secular calendar sends a holiday our way: Halloween. You might be surprised to find Halloween in a book on Jewish parenting, and ten or fifteen years ago you wouldn't have. But for some reason, perhaps because American Jews have become alarmed about assimilation, or because the more traditional elements of American Judaism have become somewhat more assertive, or because there is greater discussion of the Christian elements of Halloween than ever before, it has been suggested that Jews ought not celebrate it.

It sounds strange, at first, to think of Halloween as a Christian holiday, but there's some truth there. Halloween is the eve of All Saints' Day, which in some circles became All Hallows Eve. It's not too hard a stretch to see how All Hallows Eve eventually became Halloween. All Saints' Day apparently had its origins in 837, when Pope Gregory IV ordered the Church to celebrate a day in honor of all saints. Over the course of time, the holiday took on macabre elements, with a focus on witches, death, skeletons, and the like. Hence the costumes we're all familiar with.

So is Halloween a big deal for Jewish parents? It really depends on whom you ask. Each year, I watch as rabbis across the country and the world debate this issue through their writings. Some argue that the Christian roots of the holiday have long since been lost, so there's nothing wrong with it. Some suggest that even though we don't think of Halloween as a Christian holiday, that's what it is, and we should therefore keep our kids away from it. Others say that it doesn't matter. What should we do?

I think it depends—and frankly, I don't think it matters very much. My kids don't go trick-or-treating. Their (Jewish) schools encourage the parents not to participate, and in our neighborhood, lots of the Jewish kids don't. But I also don't believe for a second that allowing my kids to go out and collect candy would undermine their Jewish commitments. We happen not to do it, which helps us avoid questions of safety and which candies are kosher. But it's hard for me to get worked up about the issue.

So why raise it? First of all, because it may be an issue you will confront, so you should at least be aware that it's "out there" on some people's list of concerns. And second, because I strongly believe that there's one thing we should *not* say to our kids, and that is: We don't do Halloween because it is the gentile kids' holiday; our turn will come at Purim. I know lots of Jewish parents, including quite a few rabbis, who do say it, but I think it's a grave mistake. It only sets up a competition that we can only lose.

There's nothing wrong with telling Jewish kids that Halloween isn't their holiday. I have no problem with that. But to say that Purim will be their turn is to do two harmful things. First of all, it suggests that Purim is "just" a Jewish Halloween, which is certainly not true. (We'll see that Purim is actually a sophisticated holiday that we ought to take seriously.) And second, if Purim is "our" Halloween, we'll always come out in second place. The stores throughout the neighborhood don't get decorated for Purim. Costumes don't appear in all the markets. There aren't television specials, and not everyone in the neighborhood gets into it. If Purim is just our holiday, fine. But if it's our Halloween, it's bound to seem like second best. That is not a mistake we ought to make.

What should we do with Halloween? Each family needs to decide for itself. If not participating is going to make our kids resent being Jewish, it's probably not worth the battle. But then we ought to ask ourselves: If this subject can make our kids resent being Jewish, are we doing enough to fill their lives with positive Jewish moments, with a deep sense of identification, with supportive and loving Jewish community?

In the final analysis, what we do about Halloween may not be important. How we think about it, how we talk about it, and what our kids' reactions to the issue tell us about their identities—*those* are crucial issues about which we ought to think and speak very carefully.

HANUKKAH

If Halloween raises the question of what's Jewish and what's not, then it's December that is the "cruelest of months." For outside Israel, and especially in the commercialized West, there is no competition that is harder for Jewish parents than the tension between Christmas and Hanukkah, and so we need to take a careful look at it. If we can't speak to our kids meaningfully about Hanukkah, the word they'll most commonly associate with it will be "Christmas," and that will be a sad commentary on the Jewish lives we're providing them.

A Brief Introduction to Hanukkah's Rituals

If Rosh Hashannah, Yom Kippur, and Simchat Torah are the quintessential synagogue holidays, Hanukkah is one of the great home holidays. It falls on the twenty-fifth day of Kislev, usually sometime in mid- to late December. The basic theme of Hanukkah, which means "dedication," is a recollection of the rededication of the Temple in approximately 164 B.C.E. by the Maccabees (the sons of Mattathias and their followers) after it was desecrated by the Greeks. For the eight days, as soon as night falls on the evening before each day of the festival, we light candles in commemoration of the tradition that the Maccabees found only enough oil to keep the Temple's eternal light lit for one day, even though eight days would be needed to make more oil.

Thus, the most central ritual of Hanukkah is the lighting of the *hanukkiah,* also commonly called the "menorah." (Technically, the "menorah" is the seven-branched candelabrum that was found in the Temple, while it is the *hannukiah* that has eight candles for Hannukah.) The *hanukkiah* has space for eight candles, with a ninth space for the candle used to light the others. The ninth candle is called the **Shamash.**

Basically, the process of lighting the *hanukkiah* is simple. We use the Shamash to light the other candles in order to indicate that the eight major candles are used for no ulterior purpose. The first night, we recite three blessings, and then light.

- The first blessing is "Praised Are You, Lord our God, Ruler of the Universe, who has sanctified us with Your commandments, and commanded us to light the Hanukkah candles."
- The second blessing is "Praised Are You, Lord our God, Ruler of the Universe, who performed miracles for our ancestors in those days, at this season."
- The third blessing, the **Shehecheyanu,** reads, "Praised Are You, Lord our God, Ruler of the Universe, who has kept us alive, and sustained and enabled us to reach this occasion."
- On subsequent nights, only the first two blessings are recited. The third is omitted, as the Shehecheyanu blessing is typically recited only at the beginning of a festival.

How many candles do we light? Aside from the Shamash, which we light every night, we start with one candle on the first night, two on the second, increasing one each night until there are eight on the last night of Hanukkah. The candles are added from right to left, and we light the newest candle first, then move sequentially to the right.

There are a few paragraphs that are commonly recited after the candles are lit. The first is called **Ha-Nerot Halalu** (These Candles) and the second is the famous song **Ma'oz Tzur** ("Rock of Ages"). There are, of course, many other Hanukkah songs that can be found in books on the Jewish holidays, and many are available on tapes and CDs. There are computer programs for many of the Jewish holidays, but especially for Hanukkah. Make sure to look at Who Stole Hanukkah? (JeMM Software), which is a great educational tool and lots of fun.

The other tradition surrounding Hanukkah is the giving of presents. This practice originally started as **Hanukkah** *gelt,* Yiddish for Hanukkah money, which parents and grandparents gave to their kids to play with as they used the *dreidel* (a spinning "top" with four sides) for a game of chance. Over the years, Jews have been deeply impacted by the commercialization of Christmas, and today, the notion that a few coins might suffice as Hanukkah presents seems outlandish.

There are other traditions surrounding the holiday. Among them: potato pancakes fried in oil *(latkes),* because of the oil that was used for the eternal light in the Temple, and jelly-filled doughnuts (the most authentic are also fried, for the same reason) called *sufganiyot.* So, with the lighting of candles, decorating the house, singing of songs, special foods, and the exchange of gifts, there are plenty of ways to make this a very special time for our kids.

And don't be afraid to experiment. Let your kids build their own *hanukkiah* (nonflammable materials are highly preferable!). Teach them how to use an oil menorah rather than the usual candles. Give them a chance to try their hand at making *latkes* (lots of potato grating; it's a lot harder than it looks!). Especially as Hanukkah takes place in the dead of winter, when it gets dark early and kids aren't outside, this is a holiday that literally brings light to the dreariness of winter.

The Meaning of Hanukkah

But what is this holiday all about? Clearly, for the youngest children, we can explain that the Temple was captured by Greeks, who hated the Jews, and a group of very brave Jewish fighters (led by the Maccabee brothers) succeeded in recapturing the Temple. But when they got into the Temple, they found that there was only enough pure oil to light the Temple's eternal flame for one day; they wouldn't have any pure oil to keep the flame burning as the tradition required. But a miracle took place, and the oil that should have lasted only one day burned for eight. By then, of course, there had been time to prepare more pure oil.

But where do we go after that? As with other holidays, Hanukkah

soon becomes anemic and silly to sophisticated kids who are wondering why they are "left out" of the warmth and meaning of
Christmas. And as with all the other holidays we've discussed, there
are several ways of dealing with this. Let's focus on one particular
perspective.

What is Hanukkah? It is, in fact, a victory celebration. But as
our kids get older, particularly as they enter their teen years and
become somewhat more cynical, we should point out that it's a
very strange victory celebration. For even though Hanukkah originally celebrated a stunning military victory, the rabbis of the
Talmud were never entirely comfortable with the holiday's theme.

This discomfort with the celebration of military prowess was in
part a product of the rabbis' history. The Bar Kokhba revolt, which
had taken place several hundred years after the Maccabees, but
still before most of the rabbis lived, was an utter disaster. The
Greeks not only put down the revolt, they utterly destroyed the
Jewish communities who had begun it. The rabbis decided that a
holiday that might encourage Jews to take matters into their own
military hands again was a bad idea. And after that, as Jews lived
without a country of their own, and hence without an army, for
almost two thousand years, military might was utterly beyond
their reach. With time, Jews turned adversity into principle; much
of Jewish tradition became rather pacifist. In that light, Hanukkah
was slightly problematic, at least for the community's intellectual
leadership.

That historical twist gives us a chance to engage our kids in a
discussion of Hanukkah unlike anything they've done before.
Now that our kids are reading Shakespeare and good fiction, perhaps it's time to teach them to take Jewish texts seriously. Maybe
this would be a good time to point out that even in classic
Talmudic discussions of Hanukkah, this military celebration
avoids all mention of the Maccabees and their army. The Talmud
relates (B.T. Shabbat 21b):

What is [the reason for] Hanukkah? For our Rabbis taught: On the twenty-fifth of Kislev the eight days of Hanukkah [begin], on which . . . lamentation for the dead and fasting are forbidden. For when the Greeks entered the Temple, they defiled all the oils inside, and when the Hasmonean dynasty [the Maccabees] prevailed against them and defeated them, [the Hasmoneans] searched and found only one cruse of oil which lay with the seal of the High Priest, but which contained sufficient oil for one day's lighting only; yet a miracle occurred there and they lit [the lamp] with [that one cruse of oil] for eight days. The following year these [days] were appointed a Festival. . . .

In this version, Hanukkah has a more spiritual focus than in the earlier, more militaristic accounts with which we're familiar. While the Talmud certainly does not deny the Maccabees' role in the victory, the real hero for the Talmud is God. The Hasmonean victory over the Syrian king (though we commonly call Antiochus a Greek king, that is not entirely correct) is mentioned, but the more significant element in the Talmud is the miracle of the oil. By focusing on the oil, the heroic credit is given to God. The subtle implication is clear: Jews ought to wait for God to bring about their salvation and should not presume to bring that redemption about themselves. After all, the rabbis remind us, Jewish revolts against Rome and other occupying powers usually resulted in utter and devastating disaster.

Despite our rather common conception of Hanukkah as a holiday for children, it is really a time for serious reflection, for serious adult engagement with fundamental Jewish questions. For the rabbis, Hanukkah became a holiday about survival, about the spirit overpowering the sword, about goodness overcoming evil, and about the few—if their cause is just—ultimately vanquishing the many.

For our children, the message about Hanukkah ought to be just that: Judaism is partly about a voice that reminds the world of the power of the weak. It is our tradition's way of reminding us that we can rededicate ourselves to being the blessing of which God spoke to Abraham. "Just as we survived as a powerless minority," we cry out to the world, "so, too, can you." How many of our kids have thought about Hanukkah in that way? How many of our kids get sufficient reminders that part of what it means to be a Jew is to reach out and support powerless minorities with compassion and understanding?

Another thing to show our children, particularly because the rite of Hanukkah is so centrally based at home, is that the ritual is not just random; there's a reason behind what we do. Why not ask them to think about why we light one candle on the first night, and eight on the last.

For when we think about it carefully, this is actually a strange custom. After all, if the purpose of lighting the candles is to reenact the miracle of the oil in the Temple so many years ago, we appear to be lighting them in the wrong order. For when was there more oil—on the first day, or on the eighth? Logically, there was more oil on the first day, and it gradually diminished until there was none left. Would it not make more sense to begin Hanukkah by lighting eight candles and then letting the number of candles gradually decrease throughout the eight days?

Although the Talmud discusses this question, the most important explanation may lie not in complex Talmudic reasoning but in the simple visual and spiritual power of the ritual and its fire. Perhaps the tradition was trying to say something about the power of the weak, the perseverance of the oppressed. Maybe, as they increase in number each evening, the flames are meant to reassure people who worry that their own blazes will die out. The cumulative effect of a fire burning brighter and brighter, taking on ever more power, is a symbol of what we hope for when we think of them. The ritual responds by reassuring us that the power of our community, our people, our culture, and our tradition will not decrease, but will actually increase. The growing number of candles is the ritual's way of saying, "you will not dwindle, but rather, you will grow."

There's another side to this ceremony that's worth pointing out to our kids. It's something they see but may not notice. It's quite simple: As each evening of Hanukkah comes, Jews around their *hanukkiyot* (the plural of *hanukkiah*) are treated to a sort of ritual dance—a dance of flames and wicks. As the candles burn low, or as the oil gradually runs out, the fires do not simply disappear. For the last few moments of their burning they flicker, seemingly ready to be extinguished, when suddenly they leap back to life. One moment there is darkness, the next, light reborn and renewed. It is a quasi-desperate exhibition, a suggestion that the fire does not want to die; it struggles desperately to live. By lighting candles again the next evening, we are making our point that we will not allow the lights to go out.

And as our children grow older, let's raise with them the possibility that Hanukkah is not only about the flames of the candles. The downtrodden, the powerless, the dispossessed, and the all-but-vanquished are also flames. "We have survived, apparently against all odds," we say to the world. "You can, too."

That Jewish life brings a message of hope to the world also helps explain to our children the custom of placing the *hanukkiah* in a window facing the street. This isn't a private holiday; being Jewish is not a private thing.

Another discussion to have with our kids around Hanukkah begins with the questions we ask about Jewish history: Why do bad things always happen to the Jews? Where was God when . . . ? When understood in Hanukkah's light, the question becomes not why things happen to Jews but how Jews have responded.

One more point about Hanukkah: When the Maccabees finally succeeded in removing the Greeks from the Temple and found that there was only enough oil for one day, it might have made sense not even to try to relight the eternal light. They could have waited until they had prepared enough oil to keep the fire burning—after all, they hadn't put it out. The issue for our kids, here, may not be the miracle as much as the point that what we don't try will never work. Maybe the miracle was not so much the oil but the Maccabees' conviction, their fortitude, their commitment even in the face of a "reality" that should have told them that what they wanted simply wasn't possible.

If we can have even a few of these conversations, we'd transform Hanukkah from a "cute" holiday with candles and presents into something much more profound.

THE DECEMBER DILEMMA

Though we've alluded to it several times, it's important that we talk a bit about the "December dilemma," or what to say to our kids who are growing up in a distinctly Christian culture and a society in which Christmas is made so appealing and alluring.

In many ways, the December dilemma issue is much simpler than we commonly imagine. If we don't bring our kids up in a Jewish life that is warm, rich, full, and brimming with joy and meaning, then December is going to be very hard, and they will feel the sting of being "left out." Just saying "it's not our holiday" may be true, but it's not very satisfying.

Obviously, December 1 is a bit too late to address this! The most effective way to avoid the December dilemma is by our behavior throughout the year—as we put our kids to bed, as we decide which holidays to celebrate, as we pick Hebrew schools for them. If we have brought Judaism to life all year round, then December will not to be a problem.

But we should also be careful here. There's hardly anyone who doesn't feel a little left out at times. Christmas has invaded our culture; it's hard to avoid. Inevitably, our favorite radio stations play Christmas music for days, even weeks, before the holiday. Checkers at the grocery store, in trying to be friendly, wish us "Merry Christmas." Newspapers and televisions flood us with ads for "stuff" to buy, discounts to be had, "deals" to pursue. And much of the holiday *is* beautiful. Homes with lights adorning them, Christmas carols, the general sense of kindness that often pervades our neighborhoods and communities—much of it is really nice; why deny it?

In the end, part of what we as parents have to recognize is that raising our kids as Jews in a Christian culture is going to mean feeling left out at times. But that's true of life. When we get married, there are certain kinds of parties we ought not to attend. When we have children, there are certain kinds of vacations we can no longer take. If we're serious about race relations, then there are jokes we can't tell and shouldn't listen to. Yet none of this is really about exclusion—they're about standing for something.

Ultimately, our kids take their cues from us. If we're excited about being Jewish, interested in learning more, invested in Jewish causes, and proud of what Jews at their best have done, those sentiments will filter down. December may always be hard—it might even be hard for us—but it's a "dilemma" only if we're not sure what we're committed to.

TU BI-SHEVAT

After December, things get quiet for a while. January passes and winter ends. With spring just around the corner, a lovely Jewish holiday appears. It's called Tu Bi-Shevat, commonly translated as "Birthday of the Trees."

In truth, the words *tu bi-shevat* don't mean anything even

remotely like "birthday of the trees." Their literal meaning is simply "the fifteenth of Shevat," which is the day on which this holiday falls. And what is it? It's the new year for trees. If you're puzzled, here's a simple way of understanding this holiday.

In secular American life we have many different "years." We have a calendar year, which begins on January 1; an academic year, which starts around September 1; and many companies and schools have fiscal years that start some other time, often July 1. Each "year" has a day on which it begins. The same is true of Judaism.

The fifteenth of Shevat was the first day of the year for calculating the age of trees. According to Jewish tradition, the fruit of trees had to be tithed—a tenth had to be given to the Temple. But the tithe could be given only from fruit that had ripened that year. So there had to be some formal agreement as to when the year began and ended. The day that marked the new year for trees is Tu Bi-Shevat.

In modern times, of course, the Temple is no longer standing, and the tithing system has long since ended. But the holiday has not disappeared off Judaism's radar screen. Now, instead of dealing with tithing, it is cause for the celebration of trees. This is not a synagogue holiday, nor is it really a home holiday. It's an outside holiday. It's a time when people plant trees at home or in parks and children collect money for the planting of trees in Israel. It is a holiday that Jewish environmentalists have made into one of the zeniths of their year.

Recently, a new tradition called a Seder for Tu Bi-Shevat has also become popular. With the renewed interest in Jewish mysticism (commonly called **Kabbalah**), some ancient mystical traditions about fruit and Tu Bi-Shevat have come back into vogue. Just as the Passover seder is an opportunity to gather together in a home, to read a text, and to sample selected symbolic foods, so, too, with

the seder on Tu Bi-Shevat. People gather, read a variety of selections about the earth and our responsibility to protect it—written
by the group or "borrowed" from another source—sample
selected fruits, and make of a seemingly minor day a celebration of
the nature that we all too often take for granted.

Tu Bi-Shevat is one of those rare Jewish holidays that don't really
have any "laws" or "rules" associated with them. There's nothing
we're not supposed to do, nothing we have to do. It's simply a wonderful fun day for the celebration of something as common but as
wondrous as trees. For little kids, the idea of a birthday for trees is
fabulous. They can be very creative in imagining what kind of party
to have. Kids love to get dirty and dig holes, so let them plant
seedlings, water them, and watch them grow.

Of course, with older kids, we have to up the ante. We might join
with another family and write our own seder, asking each child to
contribute to it—a story, a poem, a riddle—and to create their
own rituals to celebrate the bounty of trees. For those more con-
templative, the mystical interpretations of Tu Bi-Shevat (see
"Suggestions for Further Exploration") may be interesting. In the
sixties and seventies, many young Jews seized on the fact that the
Torah forbids the destruction of fruit trees when besieging an
enemy city, and used Tu Bi-Shevat as a day of protesting war itself.
Simply put, there's no set ritual for Tu Bi-Shevat (a very unusual
phenomenon in Jewish life!), so it's up to our own creativity to
make the holiday as important and meaningful as we'd like. It's not
one of the most central Jewish holidays, but it can be a lot of fun.

PURIM

After Tu Bi-Shevat, we have about a month until Purim, which
falls on the fifteenth of Adar, the very next month. Purim, like
Hanukkah, is a Jewish holiday based on a historical event, and as

such, is not mentioned in the Torah. Like Hanukkah, Purim is commonly (and mistakenly) seen as a kids' holiday, something cute or fun, but not of much significance, which is simply not true. First, a bit of background.

The Background and Rituals of Purim

Purim is based on the story told in the biblical Book of Esther. It's a story of palace intrigue and plotting, in which Haman, the king's viceroy, plans to kill the Jews. He receives the king's permission to destroy them, but then Esther, who is one of the king's many wives (and who, unbeknownst to the king, is Jewish), figures out a way to intercede on behalf of her people. Ultimately, the Jews are given permission to destroy their enemies, and at the end of the book they kill Haman and his ten sons, as well as those who had sought to destroy them. (Here again, a Jewish holiday that celebrates our overcoming adversity through the use of violence—we'll talk about that very shortly.)

That's the simple story, the one we commonly teach young children. The observances of Purim are simple, and most are taken from the story itself. The Shabbat before Purim is called **Shabbat Zachor,** the Sabbath of remembrance. On that Shabbat, we read a section of the Torah that reiterates the command that Jews destroy **Amalek,** a tribe that had attacked the Jews in the desert, and of which it is believed Haman was a descendant. Then, on the day before Purim, Jews mark **Ta'anit Esther,** or the Fast of Esther. The Book of Esther tells that Esther fasted before going to see the king on behalf of her people. She was permitted to go to him only if summoned; to go to him otherwise was to take her life in her hands. So she fasted in supplication to God. To this day, traditional Jews fast on the day before Purim, from sunup to sundown.

Upon the conclusion of the Fast of Esther, Purim itself begins. The most important and noticeable observance of Purim is the reading of the **Megillah,** or the Book of Esther. In traditional communities, it's read from a parchment, without punctuation or vowels, just like the Torah is read in the synagogue. Liberal communities sometimes read it from a printed book. The Megillah (a Hebrew word that means "scroll") is read both at night and again the following morning. In addition to the reading of the Megillah, there are customs of giving alms to the poor (in Hebrew *matanot la-evyonim*) and sharing food with friends and family (usually distributed in baskets called *mishlo'ach manot,* or "the sending of foods"). One of the most common foods to send and eat are *hamentaschen,* a triangular pastry filled with jelly, chocolate, or poppy seeds.

As expression of our relief and joy at not being destroyed, there is also a Jewish tradition of getting so drunk that one can't tell the difference between Mordechai (Esther's uncle) and Haman (enemy of the Jews).

These customs aside, the tradition children are most familiar with is the custom of wearing masks and costumes. Not too long ago, the virtually universal custom was to dress up as one of the Purim story characters. Girls were often Queen Esther, boys were Mordechai, and the occasional contrarian dressed up as Haman. Today, those limitations are all gone, even in the most traditional of communities. Kids and adults alike dress up as everything from Teenage Mutant Ninja Turtles, Power Rangers, and Dilbert to animals of all sorts and political figures—almost anything goes. It's contemporary Judaism's masquerade ball, and it adds lots of fun to the festivities.

The Meaning of Purim

Purim, like Hanukkah, is one of those holidays commonly thought of as being for kids, but nothing could be farther from the truth. Purim is a perfect opportunity to both have fun with our little kids and to begin to impress upon the older ones that there's an enormous amount of sophistication to Jewish ritual and holiday life. How?

With little kids it's easy. They love the story of Purim; they love dressing up in costumes. As they get older, they can still do that, but they can also help deliver the *mishlo'ach manot* to neighbors and friends. They can help pick the charities the family will support on Purim day through the *matanot la-evyonim* (the tradition is that the money should go to people who need it on that day, so this is a chance to do some "hands on" work). They can help make the *hamentaschen* and decorate the house—there's almost no limit.

But Purim also has more substantive issues.

Let's go back to Shabbat Zachor, the Shabbat before Purim. On its surface, it's not particularly interesting. We read the passage about destroying Amalek, and then we go on.

But if you look carefully, things get more complicated. The tradition dictates that it is not enough just to read the passage; it is the responsibility of every adult Jew to *hear* each and every word of the reading. Normally, the reading of the Torah in the synagogue is a serious but not particularly tense time. In traditional settings, however, as this particular section is read, an absolute silence descends; children are reminded to be quiet, and the entire community strains to hear every word.

Here's what we have to help our kids understand: The passage that tradition selected for reading during Purim does more than review the historical record. It is about memory, with an important twist (Deut. 25:17ff):

Remember what Amalek did to you on your journey, after you left Egypt—how, unfettered by fear of God, he surprised you on the march, when you were famished and weary, and cut down all the stragglers in your rear. Therefore, when the Lord your

God grants you safety from all your enemies around you, in the land that the Lord your God is giving you as a hereditary portion, you shall blot out the memory of Amalek from under heaven. Do not forget!

There is something intentionally perplexing about this passage. Why does it command us to both "remember what Amalek did" and to "blot out the memory of Amalek"? How can we do both? The passage is probably trying to tell us that memory is complex, and that there are many things we ought to ask ourselves and our children as they grow: What are the things in life that are important to remember? Are we remembering enough? Are we passing it on? To our children? To theirs? To society?

Other questions emerge. How can we both "remember what Amalek did on the journey" and at the same time "blot out the memory of Amalek"? Does not the command to "blot out memory" preclude the performance of the command to "remember"? Perhaps the Torah has other questions in mind, something we could talk about with our kids: Is it important that the past be remembered? Are we better off destroying the memory of evil or preserving it? Why?

The more one examines the ritual of Shabbat Zachor, the more it becomes clear that this particular tradition also raises profound ethical questions, precisely the kind teenagers love to think about: Can the preservation of the past get in the way of forging a new future? Jewish tradition demands that Jews remember with indignation all that Amalek did to them. But at the same time, it also insists on a spirit of forgiveness and spiritual growth. In Exodus 23:9, the Torah warns, "You shall not oppress a stranger, for you know the feelings of the stranger, having been strangers in the land of Egypt." How should Jews balance the command to remember with the obligation to forgive?

In the aftermath of the Shoah, how should Jews honor the dying wishes of their fellow Jews who begged those who survived never to forget them, to remember to tell their story? Is it also important to make way for forgiveness? How will Jews and Judaism fairly perpetuate those memories in only a few years, when all those who were alive in 1945 have died?

Understandably, as our kids grow up, issues of memory, fairness, forgiveness, and identity become critical to them. Purim is a chance to show that what looks like child's play is actually very serious. There are other issues that can make Purim a serious and engaging holiday. Let's take just two more examples.

The heroes of the story, Mordechai and Esther, are in many ways not unlike the American Jews our kids live with. We know this in part from their names. At the time of the story, Mordechai and Esther were names of Babylonian gods—Mordechai from the Babylonian god Marduk; Esther from the goddess Ishtar.

That is no small point. To name Jewish children after a god or goddess of the prevalent culture is an astounding statement of assimilation. It would be like naming a Jewish child Chris or Christine. So Mordechai and Esther's names reveal something important about their parents' agenda. Like many American Jews today, they wanted to blend into the society around them; they did not want to be noticed.

We could make Purim very special by carefully reading the Megillah with our older kids. If we did, we'd notice that it explicitly states that when she was first brought to the king's harem, "Esther did not reveal her kindred or her people, for Mordechai instructed her that she not say" (Esther 2:20). Mordechai was aware that revealing her Jewishness might eliminate Esther from the competition. So he instructed her not to say anything about it. What we have in Esther, therefore, is not a story about people poised to become Jewish heroes. Esther and Mordechai start out as assimilated Jews, eager to keep their Jewishness private and their climb to power rapid.

Their tension is a profound one, a pull that has tugged on Jews for thousands of years, and it's one that our children feel all the time. How publicly Jewish should they be? Is it better to hide being Jewish so as not to make waves? There are very few American Jewish kids who don't wrestle with that question. It is our responsibility as Jewish parents to show them that the question doesn't make them "bad," that, in fact, the whole holiday of Purim is about that! So you see, Purim is much more than a Jewish version of Halloween. It is not a holiday about ghosts or goblins, nor is it simply devoted to the pure pleasure of dressing up and indulging. Purim is about identity and about the struggle of not knowing exactly who to be.

Now, add to the story the Megillah and the tradition of costumes and the custom of drunkenness, and you've got a holiday that affords respite and escape from the persistent tensions of who you are. Teenagers these days live in a culture in which alcohol and drugs are a way of dealing with the pressures of adolescence. Celebrating Purim won't make those pressures go away, but it can certainly make Judaism seem a lot more relevant.

One final point about Purim: The Book of Esther is essentially a book about ethnic Jews that is rather notorious in biblical literature for its omission of any mention of God. God plays no role in the lives of Mordechai and Esther, at least as far as the text is concerned. Indeed, when Mordechai implores Esther to intercede with the king to save the Jews, he doesn't even mention God. Why is this? Does he not believe God will help? Does he think that waiting for God breeds weakness? And more important, what do our kids think? What do we think? Are we talking about all that with our kids?

Purim is like much of the Jewish tradition. Experienced only in the most simplistic way, it has little to say to anyone other than the smallest of children. But if we give the holiday serious attention, if we let the texts and traditions of the holiday speak, Purim quickly raises questions that make it profound and provocative for all of us. Which it will be, depends on us.

PASSOVER

Just as Purim follows Tu Bi-Shevat by exactly a month, so Passover (the second of the three "pilgrimage festivals"—Sukkot is the first, and Shavu'ot is the third) follows Purim by almost exactly a month. There is probably no holiday in the Jewish calendar year that is richer, more complicated, and more profound than Passover, so our explanation should be seen only as a cursory overview. As we've been doing, let's start with a brief explanation of the holiday, its basic customs and traditions, and then talk about how we can make it a wonderful experience for kids.

Passover Basics

Like most Jewish holidays, Passover has its roots in a historical event. Hanukkah had the Maccabees, and Purim the victory over Haman; with Passover, we celebrate the Jews' redemption from Egyptian slavery. The stories of Moses, the Ten Commandments, the splitting of the Red Sea, and the drowning of the Egyptians are very familiar. If you want to set the tone for your kids before the holiday, you might want to watch Charlton Heston in *The Ten Commandments,* or the animated film about Moses, *The Prince of Egypt.* Either would be a good way of giving a bit of the background.

Of course, just as Hanukkah and Purim have taken on significance beyond any single historical event, so, too, is Passover no longer just about Egypt. It's about freedom, about Jewish freedom down through the ages, the question of what freedom means and how we safeguard that freedom for ourselves and for others. There is no Jewish book (except, perhaps, the Bible itself) that has been put out in more editions than the Haggadah. Collecting and reviewing different Haggadot (plural for Haggadah) is a great way to bring a lot of different perspectives into your family during Pesach.

Each year, we take our kids to one of the local Jewish bookstores and try to buy one or two versions of the Haggadah that we don't already have. (You don't have to buy many at a time to build a nice collection. Within a few years, it's not hard to accumulate dozens.) Then, in preparation for the seder, I review some of the new material in order to make the holiday new and fresh. Lately, some particularly wonderful material has appeared; there's the relatively new *Family Participation Haggadah,* the cartoonlike *Animated Haggadah* for kids, and even a CD-ROM Haggadah from JeMM software (for more information, see "Suggestions for Further Exploration").

Passover involves a lot more preparation than buying Haggadot and preparing for the seder. Indeed, the common joke among Jews who observe Passover in a traditional manner is that in case we'd forgotten what it was like to be slaves, the tradition requires so much work beforehand that we can't help but remember! That's an exaggeration, of course, but it is a lot of work.

The Structure of the Holiday

Before we get into the details of Passover, let's make sure we understand its structure. As you can see from the chart, Passover's structure is not all that different from Sukkot in some ways. As in Sukkot, the holiday begins and ends with days that are called Yom

Tov and bear most of the restrictions and appearances of a traditional Shabbat. The intermediate days, like those of Sukkot, are called Chol Ha-Mo'ed. And as was the case in Sukkot, when there are two days of Yom Tov in the Diaspora, there is only one in Israel. It's easy to get this information from any standard Jewish calendar, but when our children ask why it's set up this way, it's often helpful to draw the chart.

Day of the Holiday	Status of the Day Outside Israel	Status of the Day in Israel
Day 1	Yom Tov	Yom Tov
Day 2	Yom Tov	Chol Ha-Mo'ed
Day 3	Chol Ha-Mo'ed	Chol Ha-Mo'ed
Day 4	Chol Ha-Mo'ed	Chol Ha-Mo'ed
Day 5	Chol Ha-Mo'ed	Chol Ha-Mo'ed
Day 6	Chol Ha-Mo'ed	Chol Ha-Mo'ed
Day 7	Yom Tov	Yom Tov
Day 8	Yom Tov	

The Fanatical Search for Chametz

Most of the work before Passover centers on making the house "kosher for Passover." While Judaism has dietary laws aplenty for most days, the regulations for Passover are particularly strict. And these laws are so central to the observance of Passover that even many people who do not usually observe the traditions of *kashrut* (Jewish dietary laws) during the rest of the year still do so on Passover.

What's the general idea of the house being kosher for Passover? The tradition is that as the Jews were hurrying out of Egypt, they did not have time for their bread to rise, and they got a flat sort of food that we now call **matzah**. Not only do we eat matzah on Passover (and traditionally abstain from it for the four weeks between Purim and Passover—not much of an effort for most of us!!), but traditional Jews avoid all forms of leavened products. Exactly what can be eaten, and how and whether dishes or silverware can be made kosher for Passover, is a terribly complicated subject.

All those details aside, it's safe to say that in traditional households, *everything* gets cleaned out. Closets are cleaned and vacuumed, the kitchen is scrubbed, furniture is moved, and pillows pulled up to clean for crumbs. It's a huge amount of work, and it represents an almost fanatical desire to get rid of leavened products.

In addition to actually disposing of leavened products, we also "sell" those items that are too costly to throw out (liquor, for example). We use a traditional contract that "sells" these products to a non-Jewish person for the duration of Passover but ownership automatically reverts back to us at the end of the holiday. It can be very interesting to take the kids to the synagogue during the days before Passover when we appoint the rabbi as our representative to sell our *chametz,* or leavened products. Children are fascinated by a "sale" that doesn't involve money, that just involves pulling on a handkerchief in order to symbolize the transfer of ownership.

Finally, on the night before the seder, we actually "search" for *chametz.* We do this because tradition holds that we can sell only what we know we have. So crumbs and other pieces of *chametz* that we didn't sell have to be disposed of some other way; this two-part ritual (searching at night, and burning the next morning) is our way of "annulling" any *chametz* we didn't or couldn't sell.

The actual ritual of the search is simple. We put a few pieces of bread throughout the house, and then using a kit that consists of a candle (for seeing in the dark, for all the lights are turned off), a wooden spoon (for scooping the bread that we "find" into a paper bag), and a feather (for getting all the last crumbs into the bag), we "find" the pieces we've laid out and recite a brief blessing that's found at the very beginning of almost every Haggadah.

The search for *chametz* is a powerful experience. The whole family is gathered together, the house is dark and quiet (because we're not supposed to talk during the search), and together, we embark on the last stage of ridding ourselves of all leaven. In some households, everyone really knows where the bread is, and the search is more or less pro forma. But a way of making the ritual fun for children is to have them genuinely search for the bread. (Make sure you remember where you put it, and how many pieces you put out!)

The next morning, according to tradition, we're to burn the *chametz* that we found the night before. (Many people who still have their *lulav* from Sukkot burn it as well.) In many Jewish communities, synagogues or Jewish community centers set up huge cans for burning the *chametz*. Some communities even organize events with the local fire department, so that kids get the added bonus of being able to climb all over a fire truck when they're done!

Regardless of how strict or not strict you make the holiday, this is a wonderful, memorable, and fun way for kids to participate.

The Seder

Aside from preparing the house for Passover, the other major home ritual of the holiday is the seder. Outside Israel, most Jews conduct two seders (*sedarim* is the correct plural), one on each of the first two nights. Some liberal Jewish communities have moved to one seder only.

Though the details of the seder can be very complicated, the basic idea is simple enough. We gather together and read through the Haggadah as a means of reflecting on our freedom and its meaning. In the middle of the recitation of the Haggadah, we pause for a big meal. It's important to know, and really important to explain to our kids, that the essence of the seder ritual is the reading of the Haggadah, the eating of symbolic foods (salt water that represents tears, *charoset* that represents the mortar the enslaved Israelites used to make bricks for the pyramids, matzah that symbolizes the bread that didn't rise), and the discussion of freedom. Indeed, the Haggadah tells us that the more one discusses the story of Passover and its meaning that night, the more praiseworthy is that person. The seder is not supposed to be a rote experience; it's a guided—and hopefully very energized—conversation and reenactment that should engage our kids, teach them, and instill in them memories that will last forever.

Which leads us to the really big question about the seder: Is it for kids or adults? This is a critical question we have to decide before we can proceed with planning a seder. And while there is no one right way, there are, I think, a few definite "wrongs."

One of the obvious "wrongs" is to repeat what Jews did for generations, which was to ignore the children except for an occasional child's role like the asking of the Four Questions. It's important to let kids know that they are part of the seder, and that in fact children are in many ways the focus of the seder. So, if there are going to be children present, we have to factor them in, and we have to make sure that we've done things that will make it fun, interesting, and memorable for them.

But on the other hand, I also think it's a mistake to turn the seder into a kids' evening. Although that's become a very popular thing to do, there are a number of reasons why I think it's a bad idea. First of all, it's important to remember that we can't live our Jewish lives just for our kids. Adults also need spiritual sustenance and growth. A Passover solely for kids risks leaving the adults emptier than we'd like to be. The second, and related, reason is that as our kids get older, they can tell when we do things just for them and when we're doing something that matters to us. If our children are raised with the seder as an evening just for them, they'll eventually intuit that adults don't really need a seder—and the implications of that are the exact opposite of what we're trying to do.

So, how to proceed? There are many different roads. Some people truncate the seder a bit while their kids are young, but make sure that there's at least some time for adult discussion and reflection. Some people make a conscious effort to have the kids involved even in the adult sections, even if that means interrupting the conversation periodically so that children can speak. Others actually hire a baby-sitter to come to the house and play with the kids for parts of the evening. Still others do the whole thing, involve the kids as much as possible, and then, when the kids are tired, let them fall asleep, either on a couch or in their room, and continue with the seder and lots of adult conversation.

Again, there's no "right" way here, but I think it's important for kids to know (a) we're thrilled that they're part of this and we love teaching them, but also (b) the seder is something we do because we care about it; it's something Jewish people do regardless of whether there are children in the house.

There's almost no limit to what we can do to involve the kids in the seder, and since there are also numerous books on the subject (see "Suggestions for Further Exploration"), we'll offer only some beginning ideas.

Parts of the seder are specially designed for children. The Four Questions and Chad Gadya (a song at the end of the Hagaddah) are usually the favorites. Most kids in day school or Hebrew school learn the songs or stories of Passover, and we can easily find a place for them to tell their story, sing their song, act out their play. We can ask kids all sorts of questions as we go along: How do you think the slaves felt when . . . ? Why do you think God wanted the Israelites to be free? How do you think God felt when the Egyptians drowned in the sea? (The tradition says that God was distraught, for they, too, were God's children.) Kids can dress up like nomads and "wander" around the table (in some Sephardic communities, even the adults do this!). We can get special Haggadot for the kids—like the *Animated Haggadah.* If the kids have just seen *The Prince of Egypt,* we can ask them to tell stories from the movie (remember, though, that the story in the movie differs from the Biblical account in a number of significant ways!). There's really no limit. Just remember, it should be fun for them and they should see that we, too, are interested in learning more and experiencing the joy of Passover.

Back to the Question of Meaning

Our seder may be fun, but we still need to explain to our kids why any of this matters. Younger kids, of course, will be satisfied with stories about the Exodus, the idea that God wanted us to be free, and the like. For the older kids, we can start to reflect with them on what freedom really means. Is it about being free *from* something, or being free *to do* something?

Related to that, we can start our kids thinking about why we worked so hard to rid the house of leavened products. Aren't we toiling over rather minute details? Aren't we supposed to be celebrating freedom here?

The explanation is that our passionate devotion to the rigors of the Jewish tradition is our way of celebrating the freedom that enables us to live the religious lives we do. The Israelite slaves in Egypt didn't have that privilege. Neither did the Jews of the former Soviet Union. Nor do Jews in certain parts of the world to this very day. "Mere" freedom is no small thing. "Mere" freedom is a contradiction in terms; our freedom to be committed Jews is a treasure, and to demonstrate our enthusiastic acceptance of this freedom, we virtually throw ourselves into the details of celebrating this holiday and of ridding our homes of the leaven that has come to symbolize our enslavement in Egypt.

All of this can lead to a wonderful discussion about the concept that freedom is not an end in itself. The beauty of freedom is that it allows us to be part of something bigger (the Jewish people, a history) or to worship something (like God, instead of a king). Yes, the desire to get rid of leaven is "fanatical" in a way, but so is our desire to rid ourselves of enslavement.

Talk with your kids about the unbelievable things people have done to be free in the past. The Berlin Wall? Boat people? I remember the week our kids met a man in Jerusalem whose family had walked from their home in Iraq all the way to Israel shortly after the state was founded. For three years he and his parents and siblings and their two donkeys walked by night to Israel. That story had an unbelievable impact on my kids. This is the holiday to impress on children how unbelievably lucky they are that they were born into freedom.

And here, too, the more we learn, the more we'll be able to make the holiday come alive. Perhaps the older ones will resonate to the Hasidic idea that the leaven we're trying to remove from our lives is not just about the bread that didn't rise in Egypt but is also about the "puffiness" in each of us that we have to remove. Freedom is not just about freedom from tyranny but also about freedom from those parts of ourselves of which we're least proud. The Egypt that we're trying to leave is not just a physical place but a "place of narrowness"—the Hebrew word *tzar* ("narrow"), the Hasidim taught us, is in the middle of the Hebrew word *mitzrayim*

("Egypt"). What is it that our teenagers wish they had freedom from? What could they do to create that freedom? To earn it? To make it possible for others?

A full discussion of Passover would take volumes, but I hope I've given you a conception of where to begin. If you already celebrate Passover, perhaps I've given you some ideas to use in the future. That combined with the material suggested at the end of this book should have you well on your way to a meaningful, memorable, and joy-filled Passover the next time around.

COUNTING THE OMER

Believe it or not, even before Passover has ended, a new period of the Jewish year has begun—the Omer. It lasts seven weeks, begins on the second day of Passover, and continues through the day before the next and final "pilgrimage festival," Shavu'ot. (Since Passover is a holiday, and the Omer is a time period with virtually no ritual, there's no conflict between them. It's sort of like July 4 falling during baseball season!) The Omer had its origins in the agricultural life of the Jewish people and represented the period between the ripening of the barley crop (which was the first to ripen) and that of the wheat (which was the last). This meant that during these seven weeks, the welfare and well-being of the entire community hung in the balance. Later, the Omer was seen as the anniversary of a period of persecution under the Romans, and thus became our opportunity to commemorate a period of suffering. For that reason, as a sign of mourning, it's customary in traditional Jewish communities not to get married during the Omer. And perhaps as a way of trying to relive the tension that was part of being an agricultural community, in which an entire year's welfare depended upon the bounty of the crop, traditional Jews have a custom of counting each and every day of the Omer.

The Omer is a little-known custom, and as such, might seem like a surprising addition to a book on Jewish parenting. But we've added it to our discussion because it's another example of how what seems to be a rote (or even strange) ritual can convey profound meaning.

How does the Omer work? Each evening, traditional Jews recite a brief introductory paragraph, and then count the day. They include two critical elements in their counting: the first is a blessing, the second is a formula that enumerates the specific day:

Praised are You, Lord our God, ruler of the universe, who has sanctified us with Your commandments, and has commanded us to count the Omer. Today is the so-and-so day of the Omer, which is equivalent to so many weeks and so many days in the Omer.

So far, there is nothing particularly striking about this ritual. But there is something interesting here to show our children. Usually, in Jewish life, if a person accidentally forgets to perform a certain commandment, there is no perceptible punitive result. A person who forgets to pray in the morning can pray in the afternoon, and the next morning as well. A person who forgets to light Sabbath candles can certainly light them the following week. But things change with the Omer.

According to *halakhah* (traditional Jewish law), a person who misses two days in a row of counting the Omer may not recite the blessing on any subsequent days. Jewish law says, "If you forget more than one day in a row, you're out. You're excluded from the remainder of the ritual. So be very sure you don't forget!"

Why penalize someone who forgets to count for a few days? Ask your kids that question (maybe even at the seder), but be prepared with answers yourself! One possibility: By heightening our awareness of the importance of counting the Omer, the rabbis were trying to highlight the link between Passover, which celebrates freedom and survival, and Shavu'ot, which celebrates Torah and the giving of the law. By creating a "countdown" from Passover to Shavu'ot, Jewish tradition suggests that mere freedom is not enough.

What is Judaism's response to the challenge of taking survival and making it substantive? To move from Passover to Shavu'ot. To progress from freedom to law. For Jews, meaningful living requires law, and the law has to be real. It has to command. It has to govern our behavior. It has to limit our very instincts. It has to regulate what we can eat, wear, whom we marry. How do our kids feel about that? What do they think is the glue that holds a society or culture together?

For families who would like to observe the counting of the Omer, the liturgy (which takes about one minute to say in the evening) can be found in any traditional prayer book. The Omer can become almost a game. For my kids, the Omer is a chance to see how many nights they can "make it," what "tricks" they can come up with to remember to say the phrase every day for forty-nine days without missing. They set their watches to beep, they leave a prayer book under their pillow so their head will feel it before they go to sleep, they see my own sign, which I leave for myself on the mirror where I shave. It's kind of silly, but if immersion is what we're after, this is a fun way to inject a Jewish element of suspense into seven weeks of the year. With our younger children, we add the counting of the Omer to their "bedtime rituals," making the Omer part of the warmth and reassurance they feel just before drifting off to sleep.

For those families who choose not to make this a part of their lives, it might still be worthwhile to talk about it at the seder, when we count the Omer for the first time on the second night (toward the end of the seder). Or it might be a useful or interesting conversation as Shavu'ot grows closer. One way of making Shavu'ot seem relevant is to show its relationship to Passover, and the Omer is a great way to do it.

~

Before we get to Shavu'ot, there are a few other days that fall during the Omer that we need to mention. One is a classic holiday. The others have been added in modern times to reflect important events in recent Jewish history. We'll continue now with a brief discussion of Lag Ba-Omer, the traditional holiday in this group. We'll discuss the others, which are all modern Israeli holidays, at the end of the chapter.

LAG BA-OMER

Lag Ba-Omer falls on the thirty-third day of the Omer, or just about five weeks after Passover, on the eighteenth of Iyyar. (The word *lag* actually stands for "thirty-three.") There are a variety of explanations for the origin of the holiday. The most common one, though not necessarily the most correct, claims that a plague that devastated the students of the great sage Rabbi Akiva ended on that day.

In Israel, Lag Ba-Omer is celebrated with bonfires and picnics. Outside Israel, it is also a holiday, though not a very popular one. Many synagogues have some sort of outdoor program, as do youth groups. Lag Ba-Omer tends to be a holiday celebrated communally, and almost not at all at home. Indeed, people usually hear about Lag Ba-Omer because, in many traditional communities, weddings are not performed between Passover and Lag Ba-Omer, as the first thirty-three days of the Omer are considered a period of sadness and subdued joy (different communities have different limits regarding when during the Omer weddings are not performed).

SHAVU'OT

As we've mentioned, the Omer period lasts seven weeks, beginning with the second day of Passover and ending on the day before
Shavu'ot. The third of the three "pilgrimage festivals," Shavu'ot is
celebrated for two days outside Israel and one day in Israel.

Though Shavu'ot (the Festival of Weeks) clearly had agricul-
tural roots in the time of the Bible, the holiday has now come to
be called *zeman matan torateinu,* the time of the giving of the
Torah. Whereas Simchat Torah (celebrated about two weeks after
Rosh Ha-Shannah) celebrates the joy of *living* with Torah,
Shavu'ot celebrates the joy of our having *received* the Torah.

Unlike Passover and Sukkot, which have many well-known rituals, Shavu'ot is a holiday almost bereft of ritual. There is no seder,
no *lulav.* Aside from synagogue services, to which are added a few
special selections, the main rituals of Shavu'ot are the *tikkun leil
shavu'ot,* and the tradition (the origins of which are not really
known) of eating dairy foods on the first day of the holiday.

What is the *tikkun leil shavu'ot?* It's an "all-nighter" at the synagogue. To show our devotion to Torah and our appreciation for
having received it, Jews have developed a ritual of staying awake
all night, usually in small groups, studying Jewish texts and ideas.
(One contemporary Israeli historian has recently suggested, in all
seriousness, that this custom spread across the Jewish world as
communities began to have ready access to coffee!) Many synagogues have programs of study, lectures, or other presentations
that night. Until recently, only the most traditional synagogues
had programs that lasted all night; most others simply had a late-
evening program, after which people went home to sleep.

Recently, though, the custom of observing a *tikkun leil shavu'ot*
has begun to come back into vogue. There's something powerful
about the night, the dark, and the drive to push yourself to stay
awake even when your body is telling you it wants sleep. People

who attend and make it through the night feel that they've bonded in a powerful way with the rest of those who've made it. In traditional settings, the group that's made it conducts Shavu'ot morning services at first daylight, since they're really not in the mood for a long morning service. They want to *daven* (pray) and then go to sleep. But this tradition creates yet another powerful moment. Especially if you're in a synagogue with windows that face east, being part of this experience has you actually saying the liturgy that speaks of "God who creates light" as the sun is rising. The service began in pitch-dark night; by the time it's over, the sun has arisen and morning has started.

There's something very powerful about that. One of my favorite parts of Shavu'ot is walking home in the morning with my wife after we've been at a *tikkun* all night. There's a quiet magical quality to this time of the morning, with the entire city still asleep, and I find that as much as I enjoy the night of learning with my community, that walk home is really special.

The *tikkun* doesn't have to be for adults only. More and more youth groups are beginning to have all-night Shavu'ot programs for their teenaged members. They understand that the memories and bonding that come from being awake all night together is exactly what lots of young people are looking for. The closeness, sense of accomplishment, and fun that is part of this tradition is precisely the way to create the memories that are so crucial to our kids' Jewish development.

Making Shavu'ot a meaningful experience is therefore going to require that we do it with community. Unlike Passover, Shavu'ot doesn't give us a seder that the family can celebrate alone; unlike Sukkot, it doesn't call on us to build a *sukkah*. Shavu'ot makes the point that to really love Torah, to really experience the joy of the Jewish tradition, we've got to be part of something larger than ourselves.

Here are some things to try:

• See if you can find a synagogue in your area holding a *tikkun*, and attend for as long as you can.

• If your child is part of a youth group, find out if they're having a *tikkun*. If they're not, or if your child is not part of a youth group, call some of the larger synagogues and find out what's being planned.

• Can't find a *tikkun* in your area? Pick a Jewish topic (perhaps from some of the books listed in the back here) and study it with your family.

Shavu'ot is a day that leans more to community and older kids than to young children. If you're going to attend services, then, of course, younger children can participate, as with any holiday. But as important and meaningful as Shavu'ot can be, this is not the holiday that will excite the imaginations of our youngest kids. The magic and mystery of Shavu'ot will be theirs as they grow older, but only if we plant the seeds during the rest of the year.

THE "THREE WEEKS" AND THE MINOR FASTS

Beginning in the middle of the month of Tammuz, a sad period of the Jewish calendar begins. This period is called the Three Weeks, and it begins with the Fast of the Seventeenth of Tammuz (Shiva Asar Be-Tammuz) and ends with the Fast of the Ninth of Av (Tisha B'Av). During this period, observant Jews do not get married, attend musical performances, or do anything else that could be a sign of unusual joy. Many do not swim; some do not cut their hair. In the more liberal community, this period is only nominally marked; in some parts of the more traditional-liberal community, it is becoming more important as contemporary Jews seek more ways to fill their Jewish lives with ritual and meaning.

Mentioning the Three Weeks gives us a chance to mention the four minor fasts. Two of them (the Fast of Gedaliah, on the day after Rosh Ha-Shannah, and the Fast of Esther, on the day before Purim) we've already mentioned. The other two are the Tenth of Tevet, on which it is believed the Romans began their siege of Jerusalem, and the Seventeenth of Tammuz, on which they first breached the city's walls.

The minor fasts are different from the Yom Kippur and Tisha B'Av fasts in that they're sunup-to-sundown fasts, not sundown-to-sundown. Some of the specific rules about the fasts are also slightly different. Most Jewish communities do not mark these days. Increasingly, though, partially because the Fast of Gedaliah has taken on more meaning since the murder of Prime Minister Yitzhak Rabin, the minor fasts have begun to get a little more attention. In addition, as American Jews in particular begin to explore their tradition more deeply for ways to stem the tide of assimilation, some have made a deep commitment to remembering Jewish events of the past; for some, greater attention to these fasts has been a way to bring Jewish content to other days of the year.

TISHA B'AV

The last major date of the Jewish calendar year is Tisha B'Av. Like Yom Kippur, this is a "major" fast in that it lasts from sundown to sundown. Tisha B'Av, the ninth day of Av (usually sometime in late July or August), is the day on which—or so tradition has it—the two Temples in Jerusalem were destroyed, the first by the Babylonians in 586 B.C.E., and the second by the Romans in 70 C.E.

The Mishnah, one of the most important works of the rabbinic Jewish tradition, has a longer list of tragedies that took place on that date. It states that in addition to the destruction of the two

Temples, the Ninth of Av was also the date on which it was decreed that the ancient Israelites would not enter the Promised Land, that the Jewish community of Betar was captured, and the city of Jerusalem was plowed up.

Traditional Jews accept this list as a literal description of what happened on this day. Other Jews see the list as metaphorical, believing that the rabbis chose to group a variety of events onto a few days (some of the minor fasts also have a variety of calamities associated with them) so as to minimize the number of days of sadness in the Jewish calendar and to create intensive periods during the year when Jews would focus on the tragedies of the past. (For that reason, some people felt, and others still feel, that Holocaust Memorial Day should have been placed on a preexisting day of mourning such as Tisha B'Av.) But regardless of how many events actually took place on Tisha B'Av, this date has become the major date on the Jewish calendar for mourning the past.

Again, it's primarily in the traditional community that this date is commemorated. But many liberal congregations have programs even if most people there do not fast. One of the phenomena that have kept Tisha B'Av alive in the minds of many Jews is the fact that it typically falls in August, when many Jewish kids are in summer camp. Camp is the ideal place to explore the intensity of feeling associated with a day like Tisha B'Av, and many children find that day one of the most memorable of the summer

Outside of summer camps, however, Tisha B'Av is one of those holidays that really require a community, and usually a synagogue. Aside from not eating, showering, wearing leather shoes, or having sexual relations, there's no fixed ritual, and certainly nothing to do at home. This is a community observance, the central fixture of which is the public reading of the biblical book of Eichah (Lamentations)—a poetic reflection on the horror of

Jerusalem's fall. To make it meaningful, we've got to find a community that takes it seriously.

But don't assume that Tisha B'Av has to be boring or a completely depressing day. Our synagogue has many survivors of the Shoah as part of its community. For them, despite the existence of Shoah Remembrance Day, it is Tisha B'Av that really brings out their tears and their memories. For my children, watching these men—none of whom are young anymore, sit on the floor and weep as the story of the destruction of the Temple is told—has had a huge impact on them.

How many kids today have occasion to see firsthand a whole community of grown men weep? How many children in America today know someone who weeps for the village and family that ceased to exist half a century ago? This is the stuff of which powerful memories are made, and it is here that our children come to understand that they're part of something much larger than themselves. Tisha B'Av, like other parts of the Jewish calendar, has much to offer. The real question is how much we'll let this, and other holidays, become integral parts of the lives of our families.

FROM DESTRUCTION TO RENEWAL

There are seven weeks between Tisha B'Av and Rosh Ha-Shannah. This period is sometimes called the Seven Weeks of Comfort, because the prophetic reading for each Shabbat morning (the **Haftarah**) is one that consoles the Jewish people, assuring them that God's love for them is not lost. This is the perfect way to begin preparations for the High Holidays. We move from the depths of despair about all that we've lost to the beginning of hope and forgiveness once again. Four weeks before Rosh Ha-Shannah, at the beginning of the month of Elul, we'll actually begin to blow the shofar each morning (except for Shabbat) in the synagogue. We'll begin to "warm up" and move into Rosh Ha-Shannah mode weeks in advance, so that come the first of the High Holidays, we're already in the midst of the process of self-examination and repentance with which we began the year.

MODERN ISRAELI HOLIDAYS

Until the last few decades, a new Jewish holiday hadn't been introduced for about two thousand years. Why, then, have things changed? Why, after thousands of years of a virtually static calendar, are we seeing so much development? The answer is important, and it has to do with the nature of the times in which we're living. Whether we realize it or not, these are extraordinary times for the Jewish people, and the changes in our calendar reflect that.

Sometimes it's hard to appreciate how important an event really is when we're in the middle of it. Some items in the news that seem incredibly important at the time are almost completely forgotten a year later. And other items, those that start out as little events buried in the paper, have the capacity to change history. We are living in a time that has turned the Jewish world completely upside down, and as our kids get older, it's important to help them understand that. There's not a lot that we actually do for these new holidays, but if can bring them alive, we will add a rich layer to our kids' understanding of the times in which we're living.

Yom Ha-Shoah—Shoah Remembrance Day

Early in its history, the government of the State of Israel declared the twenty-seventh of Nissan (usually sometime in April) as a day to mark the destruction of European Jewry and the millions of victims of the Shoah. That is the day in which not only Israel but

Jewish communities throughout the world pause to remember the horrors that Nazi Germany and the rest of the world perpetrated during those dark years.

There's an ongoing debate about how early we should begin teaching our children about the Shoah. After a certain point, of course, it's not really up to us—they will learn about it in school and they will hear it discussed in the media as well as in a variety of other settings. I, for one, am one of those who believe that discussion of the Shoah ought to be put off for a while—until a child is nine or ten, I don't think that they need to know any more than they specifically ask. If the mere notion that human beings can be so horrible is upsetting to adults, why burden children with it? Gradually, we can tell them that there was a very bad man named Hitler who hated Jews and tried to kill all the Jews in the world.

When they are older, we can—and should—teach them about the complicity of the rest of the "civilized" world in the Shoah—much of Europe cooperated, and the Vatican knew but did nothing. We now also know that the Swiss, who long claimed to have been neutral, stole from the Jews after the war—refusing to honor insurance policies and denying them access to money deposited in Swiss bank accounts. The British kept Jews out of what was then Palestine, and FDR and the United States refused to raise the quota for immigration, preventing many Jews from finding safe haven. The list goes on.

What do we want our children to get out of this commemoration? Especially as they get older, let's try to get them to think about some of the following questions:

• How does an entire country, then a continent, then a world suddenly go so insane and evil that it can try to eradicate an entire people?

• Why have the Jews so often been on the receiving end of this sort of cruelty (though we should certainly make sure our children know that other peoples have also suffered terribly)?

• How will we perpetuate the memory of what happened when there are no longer any survivors?

• Can we—should we—ever forgive the Germans? Are we the ones to forgive, when we were not the ones who suffered? If we forgive, are we saying it's time to forget? And if we insist on remembering, do we perpetuate hatred?

How can we help our children see how critical the Shoah was to the destiny of the Jewish people? There is not a great deal of ritual associated with this observance, but here are some things we can do:

• Rent a movie for your children and *watch it with them.* You might rent *Shoah, Schindler's List,* or any one of a number of movies about that period.

• There are plenty of books for children about the Shoah. If your kids are teenagers and haven't read *The Diary of Anne Frank,* they should.

• Participate in some of the community-wide commemorations. Some of these, quite frankly, are a little boring for kids, and so shouldn't be the only thing the kids do. But it's probably still important for our children to commemorate this event in their home *and* as part of a larger community.

• If you can, take your children to a Holocaust memorial or museum (the best, by far, is the Holocaust Museum in Washington, D.C.) around this time of year.

• Participate in a new ritual being developed in some communities called a Yom Ha-Shoah seder. Like the Passover seder, this one tells a story (though here, the story is of the Shoah), uses special foods (raw potato peel that the Nazis served the inmates, eggs in salt, watery soup with dirt and rocks in it), and sings songs from that era.

• Light a *yahrzeit* candle and place it somewhere prominent so that we and our kids will see it continually for the twenty-four hours it burns. Let them know that this loss is also our loss.

• Find some way for your child to hear firsthand the story of a survivor, preferably "live," but if not, through video, the Internet, or some other means.

The last suggestion is clearly the most important. There will soon be no more survivors to tell the story, and an enormous opportunity will be lost. There is nothing as powerful for our children as hearing the story from someone who lived through it. When she was about nine, my daughter heard a member of our synagogue tell his story of survival. He tells it every year, but that was the first time she had heard it herself. This is a man she knows and cares for. She sees him in shul every Shabbat morning, knows his family. He's a very real person to her.

When he told his story, the details of which he recalls with agonizing clarity, she was transfixed. At the end, he told about when he and his closest boyhood friend were on a death march, being forced to march away from their camp so that the Allies would not find prisoners there. His friend collapsed from hunger and exhaustion, and a Nazi guard calmly shot him in the head. Our friend then told how he struggled to walk on, but after only a few yards decided that he simply could not go on any farther. He dropped into the snow and waited to be shot. The guard came over to him and muttered, "You're not even worth a bullet. I'll let you die slowly." The next thing he remembers he was waking up in the arms of an American GI.

My daughter will *never* forget that story, and the Shoah will never be abstract to her again. The idea that a man for whom she cares deeply wasn't "even worth a bullet" brought home for her the madness of that era. Eventually, she'll have to make sense of what it means for a full third of a people to be destroyed. She'll come to understand that European Jewry was unlike the Jewry of the rest of the world, and that almost all of them were killed. There's much she still needs to learn, but her openness to learning will forever be energized by the impact of this firsthand account from someone she knows. If all of us can make that possible for our children, we'll not only teach them a great deal but we'll be doing exactly what the victims wanted: taking steps to ensure that they are not forgotten.

And finally, those victims are not the only ones who shouldn't be forgotten. Half a century after the end of the Shoah, "ethnic cleansing" in Croatia and Serbia was back in the news, and again, for a long time, the world sat by and watched. What should our response as Jews be in these situations? Should Israel have a unique response? What does it mean to commemorate one genocide even as we watch others taking place? To have these conversations with our children is to give meaning and substance to a day that still very much merits our attention.

Yom Ha-Zikkaron—Israel Memorial Day

A few weeks later, on the fourth of Iyyar, is Yom Ha-Zikkaron. This is a day on which Israel commemorates the soldiers who have died defending the state. Unlike Memorial Day in the United States, which for most people is a day of department store sales, trips to the beach, and barbecues, Yom Ha-Zikkaron in Israel is serious business. There is scarcely a family in Israel who hasn't lost

someone in one of the wars. The ritual of the entire country coming to a complete halt for a moment of stillness and silence at the
sound of the sirens is the main observance in Israel.

There's not much that we do outside of Israel to mark the date.
Here, too, as on Yom Ha-Shoah, we can light a *yahrzeit* candle. But
whether you do or not, our kids should know that it is Yom Ha-
Zikkaron. The Israeli embassy and consulate can guide you to
whatever commemorations are taking place. And if you happen to
be in Israel that day (usually at the beginning of May), you'll experience a poignant and harrowing observance of respect, indebt-
edness, and loss.

Yom Ha-Atzma'ut—Israel Independence Day

The day after Israel Memorial Day is Israel Independence Day.
The change in mood could not be more dramatic. From a day of
commemoration, tears, visits to cemeteries, and the horrible pain
of loss that won't seem to go away, the entire country moves to celebrate a miracle: the very existence of the State of Israel. Israel
marks the occasion with celebrations in public parks, parades,
song festivals, and so on. Outside Israel, major Jewish communities usually have parades, assemblies, concerts, and the like.

Again, because Israel Independence Day is so new, there is not
yet consensus on how it should be celebrated. Some congregations
have special services that night and the next day. Others continue
with their regular services but add special prayers created for the
occasion. Still others do not recognize the day in any liturgical
way.

Regardless of whether we choose to attend a religious service,
it's really important that we help our kids come to understand
how dramatically Israel has changed the nature of Jewish life. This
is the first time in *two thousand years* that we have a sovereign state

to call our own. Little kids can celebrate Israel's birthday by making flags, dressing in blue and white, going to a concert, a parade, a festival. As our kids get older, though, they need to understand more, and there's a lot that we can do:

- Rent the movie *Exodus* so they can learn what the battle to make the country was all about.
- Kids who are readers (and we, their parents) can read any one of a number of books, including Martin Gilbert's *Israel: A History*, which is really excellent. Even if our kids aren't going to read it, we should—the book will give us plenty to discuss.
- We can give money to worthy causes in Israel.
- Make plans to visit Israel; talk with your kids about how you'll save for it, start using the Internet and the Israeli consulate to plan the trip, find out what groups from your community are going in the next few years.

Israel is one of those classic cases in which the magnitude of what has happened is so great that we just don't get it. For the first time in two millennia Jews have a place to call their own, a place where we determine the values of the culture. Israel changes everything for the Jewish world, and even if we live elsewhere, as Jews, Israel Independence Day is an important opportunity for us to bring some of these ideas home.

Yom Yerushalayim—Jerusalem Reunification Day

But we're not done yet. Just a few weeks later, on the twenty-fifth of Iyyar (about three weeks after Israel Independence Day), Israelis celebrate Yom Yerushalayim, or Jerusalem Reunification Day. This day is almost completely ignored outside of Israel; even in Israel, it's rather controversial (since the Six-Day War, which led to the reunification of Jerusalem, also led to the capture of the West Bank and many of Israel's controversial policies in administering that territory). There are no rituals associated with Jerusalem Reunification Day yet, but it's worth knowing about should your kids ask. Want to read a great book to make the story of Jerusalem come alive? Read *O Jerusalem* by Larry Collins and Dominique LaPierre. It's a gripping story of the battle for Jerusalem in 1948, but it's not a typical war story. Never again will you look at Jerusalem in quite the same way.

AND THE SEASONS, THEY GO ROUND AND ROUND

Yes, the seasons do go round and round. And our kids' childhoods quickly pass till one day we wake up and wonder where the time went. We can't, of course, stop time from passing, but we can give it meaning as it goes. And that's the purpose of the Jewish holiday cycle. Like life itself, it has periods of joy and phases of sadness. Like our psyches, it has times that are private and home-based and times that are public and communal. The Jewish year contains observances that are linked to history, and some that reflect our own spiritual and psychological need to feel part of something timeless and grander than any one individual.

So, you may be wondering, how much of this do I really have to do? After all, this sounds like a ton. I'm not used to anything even remotely like this, and I'm not sure I want to be! Where should I go from here?

It's important to remember that there's no one right way in this business. We can raise caring, thoughtful, committed, and knowledgeable Jewish children in a variety of ways. The only thing we have to do is to be honest with ourselves. In Jewish life, like in anything else, what we get out is a reflection of what we put in. Our children will quickly deduce that anything we do only sporadically can't be that important. The genius of the tradition is that by literally filling the year with observances, it communicates the sense that being Jewish, at its best, is a core part of who we are, something that touches us daily, weekly, monthly.

It's up to each of us to decide how much we're willing to invest in having that relationship come to life.

14

~

THE JEWISH LIFE CYCLE, AND THINGS TO THINK ABOUT AT EACH STAGE

If we were to name the two most important "cycles" that Jewish life addresses, they would undoubtedly be the calendar cycle—the holidays that punctuate and enrich the Jewish year—and the life cycle—the events that we mark as we, and our children, move from birth to adulthood.

As our children get older, we're almost certain to have occasion to take them to a *bris,* a **bat mitzvah,** a Jewish wedding, a Jewish funeral. How can we best prepare them? What should we know about these events so that we can answer their questions and make the experience more meaningful? And, remembering that Jewish parenting is also partly about being on our own Jewish journey, what should we think about and do for ourselves in this process?

Here, too, we start at the beginning, with the knowledge that we're going to have a child.

CELEBRATION OF PREGNANCY

It's surprising. Even though the Jewish tradition is literally filled to the brim with rituals, blessings, liturgies, and formulas for communal celebration, many contemporary Jews are struck by the fact that some of life's most wondrous moments come and go with no classic Jewish way of marking them. There are occasions that we want to treat as religious, transcendent moments, but Jewish life doesn't provide any guidance. The moment we learn we're going to have a baby is one of them.

Few couples *don't* remember how and when they found out that they were pregnant for the first time. Whether it was a phone call from the doctor's office, a visit to the office, a home pregnancy test, whatever—we remember the moment because somehow we knew everything was about to change. Given the rush of emotions that overwhelm us at that moment, why is it that Judaism doesn't have a ritual to mark it?

There are several reason for this. One, of course, is that it's only relatively recently that we've come to a single moment when we find out we're expecting a baby. In the past, in the absence of tests, this sort of information was only suspected at first; it took a while before we were absolutely certain. Thus, there was no ritual for the moment because there was no specific moment to mark.

Another reason is one I learned from my great-grandmother, albeit indirectly. When our daughter was born, my mom flew out to spend a week with us to help out. She got to our house when Talia was only a couple of days old and, of course, went right to the baby's room to see the new arrival. When she saw our daughter, so tiny and all swaddled in blankets, my mom told me that she remembered bringing me home from the hospital. And one of the things she distinctly remembered was that her grandmother (my great-grandmother) watched her "cooing" over me and grew concerned. "Don't love him too much, too early," my great-grandmother warned my mother.

At first, my mom was shocked. But then, she told me, she understood. My great-grandmother had given birth to a large number of children, and as was common in her day, many had not survived. She lived in a world in which birth was not automatically followed by raising and loving a child. It wasn't until somewhat later that families could be reasonably assured that their child would survive and be a permanent part of the family. This, I suspect, is another reason why our tradition has no specific way of celebrating the news that we're pregnant—too much was still undetermined.

But we live in a very different world today, and many of us want to mark the moment we know we're going to have a baby. Rituals and traditions are just beginning to develop.

• Some couples have written their own liturgies for this moment.
• Others go to the *mikvah.*

Most cities with major Jewish populations have *mikva'ot* (the plural of *mikvah*), though they're generally separate ones for men and women, which means that couples have to use them separately. The *mikvah* can be a very powerful moment. If you're going to the *mikvah* to mark the beginning of your pregnancy, take time beforehand to prepare. Relax. Some women (yes, even pregnant women) have a small glass of wine before they go. In the *mikvah,* take your time; don't be rushed. If people are waiting, they'll wait. Or make an arrangement to go at a time when people won't be waiting.

As you enter the water, remember that these waters, warm and nurturing, are our tradition's way of enveloping *us* in water, just as our new child is now going to grow and develop in different waters. Close your eyes. As you float, let your dreams, your hopes, your memories float with you. Alone in the water, unclothed, we're restored to the simplest and purest image of who we are, in much the same form as our child will be on the day he or she emerges into the world. If we can create even a few moments of feeling transported to a "place" where the absolute serenity of the *mikvah* approximates the serenity of the womb, we'll have marked this new period of our lives in a way we'll long remember.

For some people, though, the idea of the *mikvah* is an uncomfortable one. So know that there are other options.

• You might write an "ethical will" (see the section on Yom Kippur).

Knowing that your baby is on the way, but knowing nothing about who this person will be, keep a diary of your hopes and dreams, your fears and worries. At some point in your child's life, you might even give it to him or her to keep.

• Other couples find the news that they're going to be parents is an opportunity to begin to set aside time for studying and thinking about Jewish issues.

Many couples find that after they mark the moment themselves, they like to be part of a larger group as they prepare for the baby's arrival. One of the more popular ways to do this is as a member of a Jewish Lamaze class, or some other birth preparation class with a Jewish component. These classes cover the same basic material on labor, delivery, and postnatal care as other classes do, but they typically add material on birth ceremonies for boys and girls, picking a Jewish name, and related issues. The classes vary dramatically from place to place and instructor to instructor, so ask around and get some recommendations.

• Another way to add an element of Jewish content, even if it's not just at the moment that we learn we're expecting, is to take seriously the process of picking a name.

Ask yourself some basic questions: Do you want your kids to have classically American names but with a Hebrew name that they'll use in Jewish settings? Or would you prefer a name that sounds perfectly common except that it has clear Jewish or biblical roots (David, Rachel, Hannah)? Or, given the fact that a name is critical to who a person is, do you want to use your child's name as a way of reminding her or him (and everyone else, as well) that this person is Jewish? Israeli names, Hebrew names, and other easily identifiable Jewish names are becoming increasingly popular among some circles of American Jews. These people *want* to make a statement about who their child is.

Again, there is no right or wrong way to go about this. But as you make these decisions, know that what you decide will say a great deal about who you want your child to be.

MISCARRIAGE

Jewish tradition does not have an ancient, universally used ritual for miscarriage. There's no commonly recognized liturgy, no universal ceremony. There are probably a number of reasons for this. In ancient times, women didn't know with certainty that they were pregnant before they miscarried, and miscarriages were common. Also, rituals in Jewish life are somewhat public (even going to the *mivkah* is not entirely private, as there is always an attendant as well as other women in the waiting room), but miscarriage is something many couples wish to mourn privately. Finally, some feminist thinkers argue that tradition simply didn't consider the loss women experience, and hence created no ritual. Ultimately, we don't know why there is no ritual; we just know there isn't one.

Losing a pregnancy is a deeply personal issue, but this is one of those areas where women can look to other women for rituals that

294 A JEWISH PARENT'S REFERENCE GUIDE

will help with closure. There's a world out there filled with spiritually sensitive, deeply learned Jewish women who have begun to create new rituals and to write about them; a list of some of the best places to start can be found at the back of this book.

THE MOMENT OF BIRTH

There are also no major ceremonies for the actual moment of birth. Part of that is due, of course, to the fact that in ancient times the husband may not have been present, and the woman was far too exhausted to participate in a ritual. The Talmud does discuss what blessings a women might say upon the birth of a boy and a girl (both are blessings of thanksgiving; interestingly, they're not the same blessing), and contemporary Jewish feminists have begun collecting inspirational prayer and poetry written by women for women as labor begins and even at the moment of birth. Many of these compositions are lovely; we've listed a few sources for these in "Suggestions for Further Exploration."

BIRTH RITUALS FOR BOYS

If the beginning of pregnancy and the loss of pregnancy have been ignored by tradition, the same certainly cannot be said of the birth of a boy. After all, there's probably no ceremony more commonly associated with Jewish life than the *bris* (a shortened form of the full Hebrew term most commonly used for the circumcision and naming ceremony, namely, *berit milah)*, but there's also probably no ritual that is more misunderstood. Believe it or not, it's ultimately not about circumcision. The circumcision is simply the way we express the larger theme of the *berit milah,* which is the formal bringing of the child into the covenant of the Jewish people.

The *Berit Milah* Ceremony Itself

As confusing as it sometimes seems, the *berit milah* is actually not a terribly complicated ceremony. It consists basically of two parts: the ritual circumcision, and giving the boy his name. Note, by the way, that neither part of the ceremony makes the boy Jewish. In traditional Jewish communities, a child is Jewish if he or she is born to a Jewish woman; some Reform rabbis are following a policy of "patrilineality"—that is, recognizing the child as Jewish as long as one of his or her parents is Jewish and he or she receives a Jewish education and upbringing. This ceremony is about formally recognizing a boy child as part of the covenant, not about "converting" him.

The Torah explicitly commands that this ceremony take place on the eighth day of the boy's life; thus, except in cases of medical impossibility, that is by far the pervasive custom. Later Jewish tradition also added a stipulation that the ceremony take place during daylight hours, not at night. In the first part of the ceremony, the baby is brought into the room, often by a grandmother. Everyone rises and greets the baby with *barukh ha-bah,* Hebrew for "welcome!" Basically, the baby is placed on the knees of an honored guest, and the *mohel,* the person performing the circumcision, recites a paragraph we'll discuss below, receives the father's explicit permission to circumcise the child on the father's behalf, recites a blessing, gives the father a specific blessing to recite, and performs the circumcision. With an experienced *mohel,* the actual surgical procedure takes only seconds.

After the circumcision, another two blessings are recited, the first over the wine, and the second acknowledging that God instructed Jews to make this the way in which they formally demonstrate their acceptance of the covenant. Amazingly enough, that's all there is to it.

The second half of the ceremony involves giving the baby his name. There is a traditional formula that is read, in the middle of which the *mohel* will ask the father or mother for the boy's name and then recite it. Next comes a blessing for the child's welfare, and in many communities, also a prayer for the full recovery of the mother from her delivery. Finally, as with weddings and other celebrations, a festive meal follows.

While there is much more that could be said about the ceremony, those are the basic elements. The question that we have to ask ourselves, and that we'll probably want to discuss with our own kids when they're old enough to attend a *berit milah* and to ask, is "What is this all about?"

The Meaning of the *Berit Milah*

In order to understand the power of the *berit milah*, the first thing we have to acknowledge is that the whole idea makes people very uncomfortable, which is why people so often make silly comments before a *berit milah* and why the *mohel* opens with a joke. There's a palpable tension in the room. The baby is so small, so vulnerable, so innocent. How can we explain the tradition's stipulation that we circumcise him? Now? In this way?

Let's admit it. While most Jewish parents have a *berit milah* for their newborn sons, it would be an exaggeration to say that they want to. I remember the *brise*s of my own sons vividly, but even more than that, I remember the aftermath. I remember that in the first week of my first son's life, I was an active diaper changer. My wife, after all, had just given birth, was getting up in the middle of the night to nurse, and was understandably exhausted. I was also part of that generation that wanted to be completely involved in everything, so I dove right in and rapidly became an expert diaper changer.

Then came the *bris*. Though I'd been to hundreds of them, this was *my* son's *berit milah,* and I didn't know what was coming. The *mohel* gave us an instruction sheet about how to care for him in the days after the procedure, but he didn't warn us that it's perfectly normal for the wound to be red and swollen for a number of days. The first time I changed Avi's diaper after the *berit milah,* I was too upset to finish. I called my wife, who instinctively understood, and I walked away. I waited days, maybe a week, before I could change his diaper again.

When our next son was born, I knew what to expect, and so did my wife. We used more or less the same pattern; until the *berit milah* I was definitely on diaper duty. But afterward, and for the next few days, I was granted a reprieve.

I'm telling this story because it brought home to me how conflicted we as parents are about the *berit milah.* But in the end my discomfort got me thinking, and it taught me a great deal. I began to wonder why our tradition would have us begin our son's life with a ceremony about which we are so conflicted. On one level, of course, the answer is simple: We don't know why the Torah commanded this, but it does, and for generations and centuries we've responded.

Still, there must be something else, it seemed to me. I looked again at the ceremony, especially at the first words the *mohel* recites, taken from Numbers 25:

The Lord spoke to Moses, saying, "Phinehas, son of Eleazar son of Aaron the priest, has turned back My wrath from the Israelites by displaying among them his passion for Me, so that I did not wipe out the Israelite people in My passion. Say, therefore, 'I grant him My pact of peace.'"

What a strange way to begin the *berit milah!* Why begin such an important ceremony with such a strange introduction? What's that passage really all about?

It's actually a reference to a story about the Israelites in the desert on their way from Egypt to the Promised Land; some of the men became involved with Moabite women, and began sacrificing to Moabite gods. God commanded Moses to kill those who had done this, but just as Moses was gathering the people, one of the Israelites purposely brought in his Midianite "companion" (today, we'd probably call her his "significant other"). When Phinehas, son of Eleazar, saw this, he took a spear in his hand, followed the Israelite into the chamber, and killed both the Israelite and the Moabite woman.

Now, why in the world would the *berit milah* start with a story like that? Try to think about this creatively, and treat the liturgy of the *berit milah* as a kind of literature that needs to be understood on its own terms.

Maybe this passage is part of the ritual because the *berit milah* is trying to raise a variety of critical questions to the parents as they formally bring their son into the covenant. The *berit milah* essentially understands the tension and anxiety that we feel at that moment, and asks (with Phinehas in mind): "What in life is so sacred that we would risk all for it?" Are there any causes which are so important to us that we would let no one stand in their way? If there are none, what do we ultimately stand for?

I hope we'll never have to kill for something we believe in. But it's not a bad idea to ask ourselves: "What would we kill for?" Is there anything that matters that much to us? Is there anything about the *Jewish world* that matters that much to us? And could Judaism have been around this long if there weren't always some who were willing to give all to keep the enterprise going?

Those are tough questions, and they have no clear answers. Maybe what the *berit milah* is saying to us as new parents is that we have to decide what message and what values we want to transmit. Could this ceremony be our tradition's way of getting us to think about these things?

Another possibility: Maybe we are *supposed* to feel uncomfortable; perhaps that's the whole point of the ceremony. We don't perform the *berit milah* because it's what we want to do; in fact, we really *don't*. We do it because it is demanded of us. It's tradition's way of saying "This isn't just *your* child."

True, we conceived him, and we're responsible for raising him and for taking care of him. But he's not ours. In some strange but palpable way, he belongs to the Jewish people. He's being "drafted" at the *berit milah*. The Jewish tradition is saying: "We haven't been around for two thousand years because we've *chosen* to be part of this tradition." And we have an obligation to continue what's lasted for so long. Publicly entering your son into the covenant is your way of showing that you will raise him for a lifetime of commitment to the Jewish people, to our way of life, to the values that have helped us endure for more than two thousand years.

It's serious language, and it's a serious demand. But Jewish life, the tradition occasionally tells us, is serious business. Don't let the *mohel* make a joke. Tell him that you want this to mean something, and that tension is healthy, productive. Make the most of it.

Other Ceremonies

There are other ceremonies that surround the birth of a baby boy. Since we're concentrating here on only the main events of the life cycle, we'll mention them only briefly.

In traditional communities, it's customary to have a **Shalom Zachar** (Welcome, Son!) reception on the Friday night after the birth. Typically, the people who attend this "open house" share words of Torah and do a great deal of singing. There's even a tradition that you're comforting the baby during his first Shabbat outside the security of the womb. But regardless of where the tra- dition started or what it was originally intended for, it's a won- derful feeling to have a house filled with people, sharing thoughts and song to welcome a new baby to his first Shabbat. Unfor- tunately, this custom is not particularly common in most parts of the Jewish community anymore. But it's certainly not a hard one to reintroduce.

Then there's the **Pidyon Ha-Ben** ("Redemption of the First Born"), which I actually heard one person refer to seriously as "Pig in the Pen." It's a ceremony that takes place on the thirty-first day of the boy's life. In this ceremony, the parents essentially "redeem" him from the service he would have served as an assistant to the priest in the Temple (this tradition began long before there were rabbis; until the rabbinic period, priests were the religious leaders of the community). Since only boys were expected to perform this service, only boys are redeemed; there is no parallel ceremony for girls.

The parents give five **shekels** (not the modern Israeli kind, but an ancient valuation) to a priest, and thus figuratively "buy back" their son. This ceremony fits well, of course, with our second description of the *berit milah;* it's a reminder that we know the child isn't really ours, but that he's our responsibility. In some powerful way, he is owned by the Jewish people.

Because the child is being redeemed from service to the priest, the ritual requires that a real "priest" (a Jewish man who is a Kohen, a man whose lineage could theoretically be traced back to the priests of old) be present. For that same reason, a child of a Kohen or Levi (people whose lineage could theoretically be traced back to the Levites of the biblical period) doesn't have to be redeemed. (If you're not sure whether your family are priests, Levites, or Israelites, you need to ask previous generations. If you have wedding documents from parents or grandparents, your rabbi can probably help you figure out your status.) Furthermore, because of a technicality in the way Jewish law understands the passage in Numbers 18, only boys who are their mother's first pregnancy and who are delivered vaginally must be redeemed. If the mother had had a miscarriage prior to this pregnancy, or if she'd had a girl first, or if this child was delivered by C section, the Pidyon Ha-Ben isn't done.

There's a formula and a brief ritual for the redemption that can be found in most prayer books. If you don't have it, your rabbi does. Since ancient shekel coins no longer exist, the custom has developed of using five silver dollars. Some organizations, including the Israeli government, have minted coins for this purpose; they're completely symbolic and add a wonderful dimension to a ceremony that's too little appreciated.

BIRTH RITUALS FOR GIRLS

Unlike the situation with boys, there is actually no specific ceremony for girls. Until recent times, girls would be named in the synagogue on a Shabbat morning or a morning on which the Torah was read. The girl's father would get an *aliyah* to the Torah, after which the rabbi would read a paragraph blessing the mother and the newborn daughter, formally giving the daughter her Hebrew name.

This naming ritual is a lovely ceremony, but it's rather low key, and in comparison with what is typically done for boys, strikes many contemporary Jews as inadequate. In response to that, a new genre of rituals for girls has developed. The genre is typically called either a *berit bat* ("the girl's covenant") or a *simhat bat* ("the celebration of a daughter").

Despite the general consensus about the name for the ceremony, there's almost no agreement on what the ceremony should be. It's become very popular for couples to write their own ceremonies, taking readings from other Jewish sources, writing some of their own, and involving other members of the family in writing and reading the ceremony. Many families choose to use wine in the ceremony while others use candles and Jewish symbols of femininity and womanhood. Many of these ceremonies speak of women in the Jewish tradition who have stood for important ideals or who have accomplished great things. Very commonly, family members will also reflect on the name that's been chosen, the values the name represents, and the hopes and dreams they have for their child.

There are lots of resources for finding previous examples of *simhat bat* ceremonies; some of the classic books and anthologies are listed in "Suggestions for Further Exploration." Many local rabbis keep sets of sample ceremonies that they're happy to share, or they can direct you to people who've done such ceremonies and who would probably be willing to make you a photocopy of what they did.

The fact that these *simhat bat* ceremonies are all so different means that if you're going to bring your own child to one, there's not a lot you'll be able to tell them beforehand. You can explain that this is the family's way of giving the baby a name, and that the family will probably also explain why they chose the name. But beyond that, you won't know much about what's going to happen. Yet that uncertainty can also make the ceremony fun and exciting. You and your kids can try to imagine what *might* be used in the ceremony (cups of wine, candles, etc.) and then see if you were right.

One word of caution, especially if you're creating a *simhat bat* ceremony for your own child. Try as we might, it's very hard to create a ceremony that has the same deep emotional power of the *berit milah.* There are several reasons for this. First and most obviously, since we're not actually doing anything surgical to the girl's body, the tension and anxiety that is provoked by the surgical part of the *berit milah* ceremony does not arise here. Second, because the *simhat bat* is relatively new, and because there are still so many variations of it, the people in attendance tend to be keenly curious. While that's wonderful, it also means that the predictability that often makes ritual so powerful isn't easily achieved.

When we're at a wedding, part of what allows us to feel so deeply moved is that we have a basic sense of what's going to happen next. There's a pretty standard formula for all weddings—Jewish, Protestant, Catholic, and so on. While each has specific deviations, the order of things is more or less predictable. This means that while we're sitting at the wedding, we're not as focused on the structure of the ritual itself; we're somewhat freer to allow our feelings and our emotions to get the better of us.

We're not there yet with the *simhat bat.* Because the ritual is so new, we tend to be a bit more self-conscious about it, and that takes away from the ability simply to feel. With time, as the ceremony becomes more standard, and one basic formula begins to emerge, these issues will become less important. In the meantime, we should just be prepared for this.

Another problem with the *simhat bat* is that, because it's new, people don't tend to think it's as important as a *berit milah* is—especially the older generation. For example, my grandparents in New York didn't come out to Los Angeles for my daughter's *simhat bat.* My grandfather was a well-known rabbi and one of my most important teachers; having both of my grandparents present at their first great-grandchild's *simhat bat* would have meant a great deal to me, and I was hurt they didn't come. They said the trip was a long one, which was true, but I knew that if we'd been having a *bris,* they would have been there.

The only way to make progress on this front is to tell our friends and our family that to us this is a serious ceremony and that we'd like people to view it as absolutely critical as a *bris*. If we believe that ritual is a universal human way of expressing feelings that words can never capture, then the birth of a daughter needs a ritual no less than the birth of a son.

STARTING SCHOOL

When we talked about community, we addressed the importance of schools, including how carefully we need to think through the choice of Hebrew school versus day school, which school of each genre to choose, and so on. Now it's time to focus on getting our children excited about school. More to the point, can we help make the beginning of school—whether it's public or Jewish—a meaningful Jewish moment?

One way of making school a Jewish moment is, of course, to put our kids in a Jewish school. Many families are understandably conflicted about day school (a full day's program in a Jewish setting, obviating the need for Hebrew school and giving kids a rich Jewish environment during the day). Some people are committed in principle to the idea of public education, while others have concerns about the potentially high cost of day school tuition. For many families, though, a Jewish preschool proves to be a comfortable way to start. It gives children a warm and Jewish environment in which to start school, and it serves as a way for parents to meet other Jewish families. As many Jewish preschools are connected to or actually run by synagogues, the choice of a preschool is often tied to the choice of a synagogue community.

As important as preschool is, by the time kids are in fourth or fifth grade, preschool is but a faint memory—even for the parents. It's the long-term school experience that will have an impact on our kids' Jewish self-image. Our challenge is to make those years meaningfully Jewish. We can do that through choice of school, the materials we choose to teach them ourselves, and through ritual.

And there's a ritual that Jewish communities have used for centuries to mark the beginning of a child's schooling. On the first day of school, it was customary for the *melamed,* the Hebrew name used for the teacher, to open the Bible to the first page that the children would actually study and to drip some honey onto it. The child would then bend over the book and lick the honey off the page. The point of this was to teach the child from the very beginning that learning Torah is sweet, wonderful, and filling. The memory of that first day of school, a memory which many of us still have in some way, was to be colored forever by a sense of sweetness and a sense of an intimate love for the world of books.

Unfortunately, this ritual has fallen into disuse in many communities. But there's nothing to stop you from reviving it! Why not suggest to your children's teacher that this would be a wonderful way to begin? And if you're not comfortable with that, or if they're not open to it, why not do it yourself at home? Gather the whole family together and present your child with the gift of some book on the occasion of beginning school; then have the kid lick honey off the page. Wouldn't a child remember this for a lifetime? (When we did this with our kids, we happened to use a very expensive book, so we covered the page with cellophane!) We discussed, at the very beginning of this book, the importance of creating Jewish memories for our kids. Why not add the beginning of school to the other Jewish memories we try to create?

As beautiful as this ritual can be, though, it's obviously not enough. Marking the beginning of school is a wonderful thing to do, but we also have to transform the experience of being in school to one that has Jewish associations, if not actual content.

The mere idea that the beginning of "regular" school ought to be transformed into a Jewish moment might seem silly, but it's not. Our children will spend more time in school than they will at almost anything else for the next decade and a half (at least!) of their lives. If being Jewish has nothing to say about that part of their day, then being Jewish is relegated to a minor place in their lives.

The challenge is to figure out how to add Jewish moments to our kids' secular lives. One way is to create opportunities for them to think about Jewish parallels to things they're learning at school. If they're learning about "community," for example (police officers, doctors, firefighters, postal carriers, etc.), then why not have discussions about the people who make up the *Jewish* community? If they're learning about famous Americans, we can find and talk about *Jewish* personalities who stood for ideals and had the courage to act on them. If school is covering Martin Luther King, Jr., how about Moses? Or Abraham Joshua Heschel, the rabbi who marched with King in Alabama? Or if it's George Washington, then how about David Ben Gurion, the creator and the first prime minister of the State of Israel? Or Haym Salomon, the American patriot who was a financier of the American Revolution and a founder of one of Philadelphia's first synagogues?

You get the point. If immersion is what we're after, then we have to create connections between what happens in school and the world of Jewish life. One of the great advantages of day schools is that they'll do much of that "work" for us; one of the things that distinguish the best day schools is their ability to create links between general studies and Jewish studies. In these schools' finest moments, the boundaries between the two begin to disappear. If you choose a day school, you'll have that advantage. But if you feel some other path is better for your children and your family, don't give up on the idea of the links; you'll just have to work a bit harder to create them yourself. That "work," which can actually be fun, is part of the journey that being a Jewish parent is all about.

THEY CALL IT *HEBREW* SCHOOL

One of the great ironies of Hebrew school these days is that our kids don't learn Hebrew. In the worst cases, of course, our kids will end up saying they didn't learn very much about anything, but if we choose our kids' school with care, we won't have that problem. When our kids get to the age of learning to read and write, we should ask ourselves: What languages do we want them to learn? More specifically, we need to ask ourselves how important it is to us that they learn Hebrew. Whatever we decide, this is the time in their lives to begin to play it out.

When we're not thinking about Judaism or about Hebrew, we take languages very seriously. We expect our children to learn at least one additional language (in high schools it's usually French or Spanish, and in the exceptional high schools, it's often also Greek or Latin), and we have no doubt that they're capable of it. Why do we want them to learn these languages? Not only because it's great for getting into college, but because we know that each language they learn opens an entire world for them. And education, of course, is in part about opening up worlds.

So what about the Jewish world? Chaim Nachman Bialik (1873–1934), perhaps the greatest Hebrew poet of the modern era, is credited with having said that to encounter the Jewish tradition, its rituals, and its texts through any language other than Hebrew is like "kissing the bride through the veil." It's a kiss, Bialik seemed to be saying, but it's hardly the stuff of which dreams are made. Intimacy gets lost; distance is created. To "know" the Jewish tradition through a language other than Hebrew, Bialik claimed, is not to know its power, its beauty, or its magic.

So, if we want our kids to see and to feel the mystery and the wonder of Jewish life, they have to experience its power, beauty, and magic. Hebrew can be an important part of that.

It is time to ask ourselves how much of a commitment we are

going to make to this. Are we going to pick a school with this in mind? Are we also going to learn Hebrew so as to infuse the house with the sounds and lilt of the language? Are we going to try to get our kids to Israel so they can learn the language through immersion?

Again, there are no right or wrong answers, but as responsible parents, we need to think through the implications of whatever we decide. If we choose to make Hebrew a priority, it's going to take time, money, and a lot of effort. If we choose not to make it a priority, we're setting our kids up to feel like outsiders not only when they go to Israel but also every time they visit a synagogue, attend a seder, or meander through the Jewish section of a library.

It's one thing not to know a language; it's quite another not to know your own language. I don't know Arabic or Russian. I'd like to, because they are languages spoken by quite a few people in Israel, where I spend a lot of time, and because I'm fascinated by those cultures. But not knowing them is not a barrier between me and my culture. Nothing about not knowing Arabic or Russian suggests to me that part of my soul is somehow off-limits.

But I think that if my parents hadn't seen to it that my brothers and I learned Hebrew at an early age, I'd be cut off from things that today are important to me. I'd see all these Hebrew words and letters in the synagogue, and I wouldn't know what they said. And deep down, I'd intuit that this "Jewish stuff" had nothing to do with me. I'd go to services on Rosh Ha-Shannah, perhaps; I'd read the English, but regardless of how good the translation, it couldn't begin to express the majesty of the original Hebrew. And I think I'd be left out, cut off, blocked by a "veil" from an intimate encounter with the tradition that is mine.

There are many explanations for why American Jews have given up on Hebrew, learning other languages with relative ease but not giving Hebrew a serious attempt. Some have to do with not wanting to appear as outsiders in America, while others pertain to discomfort with Israel—whatever. And, of course, learning a language takes many hours of hard work, and in the past decades, we've radically diminished the number of hours per week that our kids attend Hebrew school. It doesn't really matter why the majority has shifted; the important issue is what we'd like for our kids.

Do we want our kids to learn Hebrew? When should they start? When they're young and it's easier, or when they're older and they can decide for themselves? Are we going to look at day schools because of this? Time in Israel? Have an Israeli student live with us for a while? Supplement whatever's going on in school with Israeli videos, movies, and kids' TV programming? Will we get one of the easier Hebrew newspapers delivered to the house and try to work through that?

Important questions. Language is an important part of who we are; it may also be an important part of the kind of Jew our kids become. Which means we have even more thinking to do!

BAR/BAT MITZVAH

The world of bar and bat mitzvah is a complex one, for they are celebrated at a difficult point of childhood. When children are entering adolescence, they desperately want our trust and our connection to them, but they are also "individuating"—making it clear to them and to us that they are their own people. These are tough years for lots of kids, and planning a ceremony that's meaningful is going to take a lot of communication.

Perhaps the most important thing you need to do is to figure out what you want the celebration to mean. What do you want to say with it? Are there messages you want to convey to your child? Messages you want to avoid?

If Philip Roth read the following newspaper article from late 1998, he would probably have been distressed that he'd long since finished and published *Goodbye, Columbus,* for it would have been exactly the kind of material he loves to use for his ongoing satirical treatment of American Jewish life:

PITTSBURGH (AP)—A 13-year-old girl "obsessed" with Titanic *got the bat mitzvah of her dreams when a hotel ballroom was transformed into the luxury liner, with 12-foot steaming smokestacks at the buffet table, phosphorescent artificial icebergs and a "steerage" section for the children.*

The Pittsburgh Post-Gazette *reported that the celebration . . . cost as much as a half-million dollars. Her father . . . would not confirm the price tag, but [the event coordinator], who spent a year planning the gala, said "it was nowhere near that."*

The piece de resistance was a gigantic photo, 10 feet above the floor, featuring [the girl's] face superimposed over actress Kate Winslet's body in a famous "Titanic" scene on the prow of the ocean liner. [The bat mitzvah girl] appeared to have teen heartthrob Leonardo DiCaprio smiling over her shoulder.

The movie played over and over again on a 12-foot screen above a balcony at the Westin William Penn, one of Pittsburgh's fanciest hotels. . . . Arriving guests were greeted at the hotel entrance by a turn-of-the-century carriage loaded with hatboxes and vintage suitcases. Inside, reflective aqua-tinted lighting along the walls and the phosphorescent blue and green icebergs made it appear as if the ballroom was under water. Children sat in the "steerage" section with barrels and trunks, while adult tables featured roses, crystal candelabras and replicas of the heart-shaped blue diamond necklace from the movie. The dance floor was hand-painted.

The bat mitzvah—or bar mitzvah, for boys—is a religious celebration marking a Jewish child's 13th birthday. It is the point when the child passes into religious adulthood. . . . "This was a very unique religious ceremony and a party second," [the girl's father] said.

This story, admittedly rather unique, offers the perfect opportunity to reflect on how we should think about the institution of bar or bat mitzvah in our children's lives. Is this the sort of party we want for our kids (even if we couldn't possibly afford it)? What should be the religious dimension of the whole celebration? For that matter, what do we mean by "religious"? What do we mean by "religious adulthood"?

When that article first appeared in the press, it was widely discussed. Many people were troubled by what they saw as the extravagance of the affair; others actually thought that even if they couldn't personally afford something like that, it was a wonderful idea. "People should take time out of life simply to celebrate and have fun," they basically said. "That girl must have felt very loved that night, and the passage into adulthood is a perfect time for parents to show their kids how deeply they love them."

So it's really not all that simple. What is the bar or bat mitzvah really all about? That's what this story and the many reactions to it give us an opportunity to ask. If we put aside the party for a second, what are the basic elements we'd like to have our child's celebration include? Here are some issues we should probably consider:

• What do we want out of that experience? Do we want our child to learn something for that particular day, or do we want to push harder and have our child learn a variety of different skills that she or he could then use for a lifetime?

Thus, if they're going to read a portion from the Torah, do we want them to learn their part from a tape, or by learning how to read the notes? Do we want them to use transliteration, or do we want to make sure they're genuinely comfortable with reading Hebrew?

• Most bar and bat mitzvah celebrations have some public "performance" element to them. Is that enough for us? Is there something else we'd like them to experience in preparation or on that day? Are we doing enough to make sure that they actually have that experience?

• What do we mean by adulthood? At thirteen (or twelve, which is the traditional age for girls to become bat mitzvah), our kids are clearly not adults. But everyone uses that word on these occasions. What do we mean when we use it? What message do we want our kids to walk away with?

• "Bar mitzvah" and "bat mitzvah" are Hebrew phrases that actually mean "subject to the commandments." Is our preparation for and celebration of the bat or bar mitzvah really giving our kids an opportunity to think about what "commandedness" means in Jewish life, and how they might reflect it in their behavior from this moment on? As they look at us, will they see any reflection of the idea of "commandedness" in us?

• Where is God in all this? What would we consider a genuinely religious ceremony? Do we want God to be a central part of our children's experience, and what will we have to do to make that happen?

• And money. It's become natural in North American Jewish life for bar and bat mitzvah ceremonies to be rather costly, to say the least. On the basis of what principles do we want to decide how much to spend? What are we communicating to our kids when we decide what to spend? Are we including them in those discussions? Have we discussed with them the idea of giving away a portion of the money they might receive as a *tzedakah* to a worthy charitable cause?

There is no end to the possibilities that are available to us when we celebrate this important transformation in the lives of our children. Some people take the family to Israel and avoid the entire American "scene." Some do both. Some have rather standard celebrations but work closely with the child to find some additional project that will be genuinely meaningful.

It's for that reason that there are many books filled with ideas about bar and bat mitzvah, many of which are listed in "Suggestions for Further Exploration." For our purposes here, the issue is what message we want to convey to our kids as they approach this milestone. What are the elements we want in the celebration? Social? Ethnic? Learning? Spiritual? God? Growth? Fun? Israel? Why is each important to us?

If we take the time to work on those issues before we actually start planning the day, we'll probably find that we can transform what has too often become a rote party into a celebration that is as much fun as we'd like but also reflective of the values that we're most intent on passing on to our kids.

DOES BAR MITZVAH MEAN GRADUATION?

Another part of planning for the bat or bar mitzvah is to begin to think clearly about "the Sunday after." The issue, of course, isn't the "Sunday," but the next couple of years. What are our plans for our child's continuing Jewish education? To continue? To stop? To leave it up to him or her?

At this point, it should come as no surprise to you that, for me, twelve or thirteen is not the time to stop. The reason is very simple. Throughout our discussion of Jewish life, we have been stressing that what most commonly turns young adults off from Jewish life is their sense that Judaism has nothing to offer them, that it's not sufficiently sophisticated or nuanced to merit their attention, that it's just "the same old stories," time and again.

So now we have to ask ourselves: How are we going to combat that? Imagine that your children didn't work on their reading skills past the seventh grade. Would they become avid readers, the kind of people who go into bookstores and suddenly wish they had more time to read? If we never took them to a museum after they turned twelve or thirteen, would they grow up to be interested in art? Music? Natural history? As much as our kids are growing up around bar and bat mitzvah time, they're not adults. They are kids who are just beginning to learn how to think critically and to address really interesting issues. This is not the time to stop teaching them.

It's tragic that, in order to hold on to as many members as possible, many (if not most) American synagogues have had to institute a several-year Hebrew school requirement (waived if the child is in day school) prior to the bar and bat mitzvah in order for the child to be eligible. What this does, of course, is get parents to join the synagogue for several years before the event, boosting the synagogue's membership rolls. What it also suggests, even if unintentionally, is that synagogue membership and Jewish education are things American Jews will do if they're forced to by the rules of the institution; but given an option, they'd prefer not to do it.

The synagogues may very well be right in this assessment, but it's a sad one. It's sad not only because it reflects the enormous distance that many Jews feel from their tradition and their community's institutions, but also because it reinforces our sense that "as soon as the event is over, we can get out."

The question isn't whether we *can* get out; the question is whether we *should*.

The options available to us for post–bar and bat mitzvah Jewish education vary enormously from community to community. So we need to evaluate our choices clearly:

• If there are resources available, and we're committed to our children not having a seventh-grade view of Jewish life (any more than we'd want them to have a seventh-grade view of literature for the rest of their lives), we need to check them out and determine what we think would be best for them.

• If there are no formal resources available, we have to be creative. Is there anyone in town whom we can hire on a private basis to be a tutor to our kids? Are there any other kids whose parents might be interested in joining us? Can a local rabbi suggest someone? Would the rabbi be willing to do it (and is the rabbi the right person)?

• How much of this do we want to be part of ourselves? Do we want to pick something and set up a very fixed time during the week when we'll study something with our own kids? How about spending an afternoon or evening studying together and then going out for ice cream or dinner with the child alone?

• Do we want to subscribe to Jewish periodicals for our kids as they reach this age? If they're avid readers of *Sports Illustrated*, *PC Magazine*, or *Time*, do we want to add the *Jerusalem Report* or *Moment Magazine* (or, if they're particularly good readers, *Lillith* or *Tikkun*) to the list, just to keep them abreast of what's going on in the larger community?

The most difficult issue in all of this usually isn't the resources that are available. Rather, it's a matter of what our children will want to do. And this is no small issue. If most of their friends are not continuing in some formal type of Jewish education after the "big bash," it's likely that our kids aren't going to want to either.

That has implications for where we live, what kind of school we send our kids to, whether they should attend a youth group—all of which will have bearing on who their friends are. But it may also speak to something else: the undeniable fact that when they are twelve or thirteen (or even fifteen or sixteen), we don't let our kids make their own decisions.

We decide how late they can stay out, *we* have something to say about the balance between watching TV and reading, or about being at home versus being away, or about how much energy they're going to invest in school. Bottom line: Most of us would never consider letting them drop out of school after ninth grade because they don't like it or because it's boring; we have a sense of what they need to know, and we don't leave the decision up to them about whether they're going to learn it. If we don't let them make that choice but we do let them decide about Jewish education, what message are we communicating about our priorities? About our sense of Judaism's importance? And what implications will all that have when, four years down the road, we want to suggest that they take a course on something Jewish during their freshman or sophomore year?

Here, too, there are many ways to proceed. We simply have to ask ourselves what outcome we want, and what route is most likely to lead to it.

PUBERTY AND ADOLESCENCE

Let's be honest. Puberty is not something most kids want to talk to their parents about. As much as we might think we dread it, it's much more uncomfortable for them. So we'll raise it; we'll eventually talk to them about sexuality, the development of their bodies, and the need, no matter what else, to remember that these days unprotected sex can be life-threatening. Mothers often prepare their daughters for the onset of menstruation, and depending on the child, there will probably be other issues we'll either want to or feel a need to talk to them about.

Beyond that, it's going to be difficult. It's the rare family where kids feel comfortable talking to their parents about their initial sexual explorations, their disappointments, their hurts. But even if that's natural and understandable, it's still unfortunate, because we live in a culture that treats sex as an issue of power, guilt, or manipulation—rarely as an expression of love or personal commitment.

That makes sexuality, particularly as children enter puberty and adolescence, something we simply have to talk about. If (a) in their teenage years they are going to be so preoccupied by their bodies, their sense of their own sexuality, their first forays into the world of serious relationships, and if (b) we want Judaism to be a central part of their lives during this critical phase, it's probably important that (b) say something about (a). So it's important that we raise at least a few issues with our kids:

- Jewish tradition doesn't think sex is bad, dirty, or only for procreation. Indeed, one of the three things a husband promises his wife in the traditional marriage document is her sexual gratification, and unwillingness to have sex for an extended period of time is actually grounds for divorce in Judaism. Becoming a sexual person does not mean having to distance oneself from Jewish life.

- Judaism also takes people and their feelings seriously. The tradition obviously sees marriage and sexuality as going hand in hand, but that reality has changed—even in much of the traditional community. What matters is that we ask ourselves ques-

tions about our use of sex: Are we comfortable enough with ourselves and with the other person to be relatively sure that neither
of us is likely to get hurt? Are we sure we're not using the other
person? That they're not using us?

• Or to put matters in theological terms: The Jewish tradition
says that each and every person is created in God's image, that
there's something divine and sacred about each of us. In sexual
encounters, we are more vulnerable and emotionally exposed
than at almost any other time. Is our sense that our sexual
encounters take the sanctity of the other person (as well as our
own divinity) seriously?

• A more controversial question: American civilization's
notion that "our bodies" are our own business notwithstanding,
what do we want to make of Judaism's claim that all human activity, including sex, has to be made sacred? The tradition of *kashrut,*
for example, is about making the consumption of food sacred.
The point of Shabbat is partially the sanctification of time. And
Judaism tries to do the same thing with sexuality.

Traditional Jewish married couples abstain from sexual contact
for about twelve days each month, from the beginning of the
woman's period until a week after the end of her period. In traditional Jewish communities, the Hebrew word *tum'ah* (somewhat
incorrectly translated as "unclean" or "impure," it actually means
something like "in a different spiritual category"—there really is
no accurate English equivalent) was used to describe women who
were menstruating. Lately, women who are both traditional Jews
and feminists have sought other language to explain what the tradition means when it uses *tum'ah* with regard to menstruating
women (see "Suggestions for Further Exploration).

Especially with our daughters, this is an issue we should discuss
so they'll know what's going on if someone should mention this

tradition to them. Ultimately, however, for most of us, the issue with our kids is not to advocate the Jewish abstention from sexuality during this period of time or to disparage it; the important point is to ask them to think about sexuality in general. Our task is to get them to muse on whether sexuality can or should be sanctified, and whether Judaism's notion that we achieve sanctity through limitation makes any sense. If being Jewish gets them to think seriously about issues that might not have crossed their minds before, whether they may agree or disagree with it, they're likely to respect it.

• More than anything, Judaism places a premium on life. So our message to our kids needs to be clear. No matter what else we may urge or suggest, they have to be careful. It's true that (for complicated reasons we won't go into) the Jewish tradition does not typically approve of condoms as a means of birth control, but that ruling was issued long before AIDS, long before sex could kill. Whatever else our kids are going to do or not do, we need to make it clear to them that it's a Jewish value to be careful, and to live healthfully.

Are these going to be comfortable or ongoing conversations? Probably not. But we can make a very big point to our kids if we just point out that sex and Judaism aren't different worlds, that there are a variety of different and often conflicting attitudes to premarital sexuality in the committed Jewish community. Sex does mean thinking about right and wrong, of course, but not in the mechanical, stereotypical way we commonly think religion requires.

Sexuality is not the only issue that makes adolescence a trying time for parents. A good deal of ink has been spilled on the subject of dealing with adolescents, and many tears shed. We're not going to cover that same ground here, except to make a couple of brief points.

• The first point is that no matter how well we're doing as Jewish parents before our kids hit these turbulent years, these years are going to be tough. Period. That's probably good, by the way, because it means our children are growing up and becoming individuals just the way they're supposed to. But as our kids begin to resist the Jewish "stuff," the most important thing is to stay the course. We might have to be a bit flexible at times, but the general principle we've talked about matters even more: The things that are important to us have standards, limits, requirements. This is the point at which our kids are testing to see what's genuinely important to us. Our message has to be clear and consistent.

Peers, by the way, will be the most important element here. If our kids are in a school with lots of involved Jewish kids, or in a youth group, or involved in Jewish summer camps or summer trips to Israel, then their search for a "base" that's not their parents' home has the potential to still be one where Jewish issues and Jewish causes are primary. We probably don't want all their issues to be Jewish ones, but to the extent that we want this culture and tradition to be part of their lives at this formative stage, peers are critical.

This is also where the "big ideas" we've been discussing about Jewish life really begin to matter. Our kids are incredibly sophisticated when they're teenagers. They're not as grown up as they think they are, but their thinking has usually become much more subtle and complex. It's now, more than ever before, that they're wondering whether this Jewish stuff has anything to say to them. They may be assuming that it doesn't.

This is why we have to be prepared. If they want to know why

we care that they're home for Hanukkah candle lighting, we'd better have something pretty meaningful to say about Hanukkah and how it relates to stuff that really matters. If we want our kids home for Shabbat, and we know that's going to mean that there are social events they might miss out on, we need to be able to explain why Shabbat matters. Family time is part of it, to be sure, as is the simple value of "tradition." But Shabbat, as we saw, is much more.

Our answers need to be challenging and thoughtful; if they are, we at least have a chance! If we've got good and sophisticated things to say, and we've learned how to create Jewish moments at home that are filled with joy, comfort, and a sense of being accepted for who we are, there's a reasonable chance that our kids will experience Jewish moments as a haven from the turbulent and competitive world they normally occupy.

• Adolescent kids also sense hypocrisy like a shark smells blood. They're on the lookout all the time, and we need to be prepared to change our own patterns to show them that we're not asking anything of them we wouldn't ask of ourselves.

Adolescent kids are simply not going to be willing to accommodate themselves to our sense of what's important in Jewish life if we don't have a coherent way of explaining how we've chosen what we do and what we don't do. For if it's all a matter of our personal taste and choice, their natural (and justified) question is going to be, "Fine! That's *your* choice! Why can't *my* choice be different?"

At a certain point, of course, we all make choices, and they'll come to understand that. But in the meantime it's important for us to ask ourselves what is the foundation for our own choices. We need to be able to explain that to our kids. We need to be willing to examine it and have its flaws and inconsistencies exposed, and

we need to be able to show them that our seriousness about our principles colors our life and sets limitations on our behavior no less than it does theirs.

Adolescence is the time when kids begin to think broadly about principles in life. They're interested in existentialism, in the experiment of socialism. They're concerned about gender roles in society, race relations, the environment. In some ways, many of them are more principled at this point in their lives than most of them will ever be again. They're keenly aware of what strikes them as inequality or inconsistency. They'll look for the flaws in Jewish life, too, and in our form of Jewish life in particular. The time to prepare for this, of course, is long before the storm hits, but if we're found to be "wanting" in some way, it's important that we be willing to acknowledge that and be open to making the changes and fixing the flaws our kids have pointed out.

• Parents are also people. This means that even as we're working hard to be good parents, we're also living our own lives. As our kids are growing up, perhaps even reaching adolescence, we're also going through our own struggles. We're trying to reinvent our marriages to fit our forties and fifties rather than our twenties and thirties, we're wondering whether we want to stay in the same career, and often, when our kids are older and out of the house more and more, we find that we're ready for a more serious Jewish search than we'd ever had time for.

There's nothing wrong with undergoing this Jewish search. But often, parents of preteen or teenage kids suddenly decide that they want to make profound changes not only in their own Jewish lives, but in their kids' Jewish lives as well.

In some cases, we as parents go through this transformation because something about the way our kids are growing up tells us

that we haven't been doing enough. Perhaps we've never given much thought to Jewish issues altogether, and now want to make this part of our family's life. Or maybe we've always had certain values and fundamental commitments that we were certain would rub off on our kids, but suddenly we realize that it hasn't happened. So now we want to "ratchet things up" a bit, move a little closer to what we've been calling immersion or identity formation.

Or it might have nothing to do with our children at all. We might be going on our own spiritual journey, and it just happens to be taking place when our kids are in their teens. We have got to be very careful here. Making this transformation with kids who are older is not as simple as we might think. It would be rather absurd to suddenly tell a fourteen-year-old who has never had a Jewish moment in his or her life that at bedtime we're going to start singing the Shema with them. If Shabbat has never been a serious part of your family's life, deciding to start just when the kids are into dating on Friday night is going to cause an explosion. This is a minefield, and we've got to tread carefully.

But at the same time, that doesn't mean that all hope is lost for bringing some of these traditions into their lives. The older our kids become, the more conscious they are of their searches for a sense of meaning, a feeling of belonging in their lives. They may not talk about it openly, especially with us, but they're searching—they're trying to figure out who they are and how the world makes sense. If they see us engaging in that same search, they may not say so explicitly, but they'll notice. They'll see that their struggles are not radically different from the issues people like their parents face. Will they be willing to be home for Shabbat dinner? Maybe yes, maybe no. But knowing that their parents are "into being Jewish" in a new and profound way will register, whether they admit it or not. Our search can plant the seeds for their openness to Jewish life, even if we don't actually see it for years.

~

Regardless of the situation in our own family, having teenage kids is tough. Yet if we're thoughtful and honest, searching and consistent, understanding yet principled, our kids will ultimately come to see that there's substance here, that being Jewish and taking Judaism seriously actually matters to people they love and respect. With a lot of hard work, and a bit of luck, adolescence can be the time when we bring our kids to a new level of Jewish commitment and appreciation.

DATING

Dating is serious business. It's the time during which our kids begin to figure out the mechanics, politics, and meaning of relationships. It's important to us because we want them to grow up to have healthy, committed, loving relationships, and we want their first forays into that complex world to be safe, fun, and real growth experiences. But here, too, our "strategy" is simple. As we discussed in the chapter on rules, our rules about dating have to be the culmination of our years of showing our kids what matters to us. If we've been successful at that, we have a chance. If we weren't, it's going to be an uphill—and probably losing—battle.

Now, our kids will tell us, if they haven't already, that whom they date is none of our business. That's both true and not true, depending on the issue and their age. If they're still home, and we think they're seeing someone who's dangerous, then it's our business. If we think they are being mistreated—not the occasional hurt of teenage relationships, but something more profound— then it's our business. If we just happen to like one of their friends more than another, that's *not* our business. But if it's important to us that our kids marry someone Jewish, then we have to make it clear that the religion of the people they date *is* our business, especially while they're still living at home.

So let's assume that we have communicated those values to them, and that we do care that they marry a Jewish person. Does it really matter whom they date in high school?

Statistics say yes. Ever since the 1990 National Jewish Population Study suggested that 52 percent of Jews intermarry, sociologists have been looking hard at dating patterns, intermarriage patterns, and the like. And though there's still much more that we have to learn, one recent study has suggested something very interesting: *Kids who date only Jewish kids in high school are more likely to marry Jews regardless of whom they date in college.* Similarly, kids who date non-Jews in high school are statistically more likely to marry non-Jews, even if they predominantly date Jews while in college.

There are many potential explanations for this finding, including the possibility that kids who date only Jewish kids in high school do so because their parents insist on it, and those parents are also people who probably infused a lot more Jewish life into their kids' upbringing. The study also suggests that the social patterns we establish in high school have much more influence than we've realized in the past, and that the messages we convey to our children at this stage about what is and is not acceptable to us actually continue to resonate for many years hence.

We have virtually no say in what our kids do in college. Yet if we plot a careful course when they're in high school, we can do a great deal to achieve the end we have in mind.

Which leads us to one more question: Why does it matter whom our kids marry? Aren't there lots of Jewish people who marry non-Jews and live vibrant, exciting, and committed Jewish lives?

The answer is yes, it can happen, but it's not likely to. To be sure, there are people who manage to pull this off. But they're the great exception to the rule. As we've seen throughout this book, a meaningful and thoughtful Jewish life tends to be a life where Judaism colors much of what we do. And as we've been told a million times in Hebrew school, Judaism isn't just a religion, it's a culture, a people, a history.

So living that way doesn't leave much that isn't touched by Jewish values, sentiments, commitments. It's certainly not that every waking moment of one's life has to be a Jewish moment, but it is the case that it's hard to live a Jewish life; it's even that much harder for someone who has never been exposed to it. These things may not matter to our kids while they are in their early twenties, but it is very likely to become important when they have their own children. Jewish affiliation and commitment are then often high on the list. What we don't want them to discover when they have children is that their choice of a life partner now makes Jewish life impossible.

It's terribly difficult to convey all of this. Love is a pretty powerful thing, for them no less than it was for us when we were their age. Their passion at this moment is likely to overshadow anything we might say. So we have to make the point much earlier. That's why we ought to be clear when they're in high school whom they may and may not date. That's why, long before they're in high school, we have to set things up so that it's clear to them that we care about this. And most important, that's why we have to raise them in a home in which being Jewish is core to who they are. If we do that, then they are not likely to be particularly interested in someone who doesn't speak that spiritual language.

Of course, there are no guarantees here, only best efforts. But like lots of things in life, the best efforts often work.

PICKING A COLLEGE

Picking a college isn't something we typically think of as a Jewish endeavor. After all, there are lots of other issues to consider—what city, cost, large research university or intimate undergraduate setting, the size and reputation of the faculty, the kind of community available, and much more. Why and how can Jewish issues even begin to be a part of this?

The "why" is simple. College is the time that young people, more than ever, settle upon the social patterns, intellectual interests, and spiritual directions that will guide them for the rest of their lives. The friends we make, the interests we pursue, and the "self" that we begin to define in college are very much a part of the person we are many years later.

But at the same time, college has become a great wasteland for much of American Jewry. Freed at last from their parents' ability to direct their Jewish involvement, many American Jewish college students use these years as an opportunity to drop the whole thing. For many, it's the college years that mark the period in which Judaism went from being a small "blip on the screen" to being absent altogether.

To a certain extent, there's not much we can do about this. By this point we've taught them a great deal about who we are and what we care about. Our Jewish commitments were part of that message, and that's what they're going to take with them. The programming has already been done.

College is a time of searching, of wondering, of asking questions they might not have been ready to ask earlier. And it's not unusual for a college student who had earlier shown no interest at all in "spiritual" issues to suddenly be searching. It's common for kids who shunned Jewish involvement when their parents were forcing it on them to suddenly inquire a bit into their tradition. Even students who come from traditional homes, and who basically assume that they'll maintain that pattern of Jewish life, now have the opportunity to build their own Jewish community, to test a few limits, and to decide for themselves what really matters to them.

For all of these people, the resources that are available at a college can make a big difference. Thus, when checking out potential colleges or visiting them, there are a variety of things you ought to investigate:

- What's the size of the Jewish community on campus? How active is it? What are the Jewish organizations on campus?
- If there's a Hillel or the equivalent of a Hillel, check it out. Where is the building? In the middle of campus or someplace on the periphery? Does it look occupied? Can you get a sense of what sort of student hangs out there?
- Is there a Jewish studies faculty, and what is its size? Are any of them involved in the Hillel? Do they have any other connection to the Jewish community on campus? What sort of Jewish studies courses are offered?
- Does the university library have a decent Jewish collection? Talk to the librarian. Find out how extensive the collection is. What about Jewish periodicals, both popular and scholarly?
- Check out the bookstore. Is there anything in the general reading section on Jewish life? That will be some indication of who's on campus and what they're thinking about.
- Who are the Jewish community professionals on campus? What's the size and nature of the Hillel staff? Are they kids themselves, barely out of college (some of whom, by the way, are excellent), or seasoned professionals? Is there a Hillel rabbi? Can you meet him or her? What's your son's or daughter's impression?
- Since the High Holidays often fall right after the beginning

of the fall semester, it can be tough for students to leave and to come home for the holidays. Are there services on campus? How many people go? Are there options? Do local synagogues welcome students?

• Check out those local synagogues.

• And what happens on Shabbat on campus? Is there a Friday night service? A Shabbat morning service? A Shabbat meal? Is there a variety of alternative services to choose from, or only one?

• If your family is traditional, and that's the sort of community you'd like your daughter or son to have, find out what's available. Is there kosher food on campus? Does getting the kosher food mean the students have to eat separately from other students, or can they get kosher food in one of the main dining halls? Perhaps most important, are there a reasonable number of other students who live this way; will your son or daughter have a community?

Contrary to what we may remember from our own college days, American university campuses today are religious environments. To be sure, not everyone on these campus is involved in religious life, but the percentages are much higher than they used to be. Whatever we may think our son's or daughter's interests are now, the likelihood is that they will have some inclination to give religion a try during those years. Being away from home, dealing with the stress and pressure of college's academic and social life, figuring out who they are as they enter adulthood—these are all reasons why they are likely to cross paths with religious life at some point during their undergraduate years.

They may do their exploring in a large lecture course that affords them anonymity, or in a more intimate prayer or Bible study group that provides the personal connection lots of college kids are looking for. There are dozens of other avenues they might explore. But the bottom line is that they *are* likely to explore.

We don't know if or when that moment will come, or whether they'll head off to the Hillel or a Jewish studies course when it does. But if it's there they might. If it's not, then by default the searching they do will be in a culture or community other than Judaism.

GOING TO COLLEGE

The decision about which college having been made, it might seem that there's little else to do but get through the last precollege summer, pack, and head off to campus. But here, too, it's worth thinking about whether there's anything one might do to make even this a Jewish moment. At this point, there are no special rituals or liturgies. And even if there were, our kids probably wouldn't want them. They're nervous, self-conscious, anxious to get going. So the trick is to find some Jewish way to mark the occasion. Here are some of the common ones:

• In addition to all the other books and resources that we're sending our kids off with, is there something Jewish that can be added to the stash? A prayer book so that when the spiritual urge hits they at least have a Jewish address right there? Or a book on Jewish life that we think might give basic answers?

The easiest way is to grab something we already have on the shelf, but that's not necessarily the best way. The last thing our kids are going to want in college is to "dabble" in yet another thing in which they don't feel competent. So if the books already on the shelf don't overcome that, it's probably time to get some recommendations and buy a new one or two.

The likelihood is that some course—on religion, literature, history—will list part of the Bible as required reading. That's a good enough reason to send kids off with a Bible that offers a decent, modern, thoughtful Jewish perspective. The King James Version (or some variant on it) is likely to be the translation sold in the bookstore on campus. And a Christian reading of the text is likely to be the default one. There's obviously not much we can do about that, but we might at least want to make sure that when questions come up, we've sent our child off to college with a reference that offers a Jewish alternative.

And don't forget books in general. College should be the time when our kids learn to love books, reading, ideas. Toss a contemporary, thoughtful book on Judaism in with the rest of the pack. They might not think they need it or that they'll use it, and it may sit on the shelf for a year and a half, but it's not likely to sit there forever. If it's a decent book, chances are it will address some of their questions. Ultimately, they might just read the whole thing!

• Computer stuff has become a pivotal part of the stash. Laptop computers, printers, Zip drives—these seem as basic today as the jeans and sweatshirts of yesteryear. Fine. Make the whole computer enterprise a Jewish one, as well.

Along with the dictionary, encyclopedia, and games CD-ROMs, there are a number of decent Jewish titles. The entire *Encyclopedia Judaica*—the most widely used English-language encyclopedia on Judaism—is available on CD-ROM. There are also a number of Internet sites that are great for seeing what's available at any given moment (see the list included in "Suggestions for Further Exploration").

And speaking of the Internet, it's become a necessary part of every student's life. Why not include a book that describes the depth of Jewish material that's available on the Internet? Sure, lots of these URLs could be found just by doing a search, but some are hard to find. The good books of this sort contain hundreds upon hundreds of sites, and they don't cost very much.

• Ritual objects are an important part of Jewish life. Our kids may have grown up in a home in which a Kiddush cup was a regular part of the Friday night table, or a *mezuzah* was a "natural" part of the door. There's no reason to end this when the kids go off to college. Indeed, this is precisely the time to give them an opportunity to build this into their own adult life.

If your children receive a Kiddush cup on the occasion of their bar or bat mitzvah, send it off to college with them. There's no point keeping it at home, and even if it doesn't get used at school, it will make the point that Jews take their "Jewish stuff" with them as they move from place to place. Moving to college is in all likelihood the first of many moves that our kids will make in the next few years. The message we communicate about what's worth taking with them will resonate for years.

Or what about a *mezuzah,* the ritual container that holds the Shema that Jews attach to their doorposts? It's the *mezuzah,* more than anything else, that defines a Jewish home. Can we raise the possibility of putting one up on the dorm door? Or might a *mezuzah* be appropriate when they rent that first off-campus apartment?

And finally, holidays. Take Hanukkah as only one example. If Hanukkah is important at home, it should also be important at school. Particularly when the campus begins to overflow with symbols of winter and Christmas, it's nice for our kids to have something tangible to add a Jewish dimension to all of it. Do you want to send them to campus in the fall with a *hanukkiah?* Or would it be better to mail the *hanukkiah* and the candles to them a week or two before the beginning of the holiday? That doesn't matter much, but the rituals do.

• There are also things that can be done from afar to fill life on campus with Jewish content. Synagogues and magazine subscriptions can also help.

Some synagogues encourage parents to submit their son's or daughter's address so the synagogue can send them its bulletin or newsletter. The better ones also send out appropriate reading materials before the High Holidays, *hanukkiah* and candles around Hanukkah time, matzah and a Haggadah before Passover, and so on. These gestures are a nice way of keeping the synagogue a part of their lives while they're in college; occasionally, some of the reading materials are also good.

Find out if your synagogue has such a program. If they do, sign up. If they don't, it's probably just because no one's thought of it.

Finally, don't forget that the U.S. mail delivers even to university campuses! Subscriptions to magazines like the *Jerusalem Report, Moment Magazine, Tikkun,* and others are an inexpensive and easy way to keep the Jewish content flowing. Put it on your charge card once, and the issues keep coming all year long.

Whatever steps you decide to take, it's the theory that's important. If college is the time when Jewish allegiances are tested, this is not the time to allow the connection to break. Find out what's available on campus, figure out what you can do that your daughter or son might appreciate. It doesn't have to be brilliant, creative, or ingenious—the mere fact that you do something will make the most important impact.

THAT FIRST APARTMENT

Just a brief note about "that first apartment," or the few abodes that follow. Once our kids—and it's kind of hard to call them "kids" at this point, even though they'll always be our kids—move into their own postcollege apartments, all the trappings of "kid-hood" are gone, and they're undeniably adults, but . . .

This is the time for subtlety. I've watched lots of parents try to pressure their "kids" into continuing the Jewish practices they had grown up with, to no avail. If they're not doing it by now, parental pressure is simply not going to make it happen. That doesn't mean, by the way, that it's not going to happen in the future; it just means that grown children are not receptive to their parents' input anymore.

But that doesn't mean we should throw in the towel. Ever so gently, we can still find ways of both validating and acknowledging this new stage in their lives while at the same time continuing to infuse Jewish consciousness. Upon their renting the apartment, a *mezuzah* is the perfect gift. Other gifts—housewarming, hostess, birthday—can be small (or not so small) things that will give the home a Jewish feel: a cookbook here, there a Kiddush cup; an "illu-minated" Haggadah, a *havdalah* set, a *tzedakah* box. There's an incredible amount of contemporary Jewish art being produced these days, from styles that imitate time-honored traditions of Jewish craftsmanship to new, contemporary looks.

The idea is to respect our grown-up children's identity as adults while still recognizing that they're often more open to subtle reminders and suggestions than they might think.

MARRIAGE AND WEDDINGS

Bookstores today are filled with books about Jewish weddings. Those are mostly for couples planning weddings or for the par-ents of the bride and groom. There is a lot of work and a lot to consider. This section can't possibly cover even a fraction of that material, so we're going to take a different approach. Instead, we'll focus on what our younger kids are going to see at a wedding, so that when they attend their first one, you'll be able to explain what's going on.

Before the Ceremony

In traditional Jewish weddings, a number of important and interesting steps take place before the couple actually stands together and is married by the rabbi. Very often, especially in weddings in the more traditional community, the festivities begin with a *tisch,* the Yiddish word for "table." Often, this is called the **chassan's tisch,** or the "groom's table." At the *tisch* (which takes place about an hour or so before the ceremony, and which is open sometimes to men and women, and sometimes only to men—it depends on the community) the groom tries to give a speech, usually on a Jewish subject, during which he is constantly interrupted by his friends. Typically, people are sitting around a long table, good Scotch is flowing freely, and each time the groom mentions a word or a theme that reminds someone in the group of a song, that person begins to sing the song and everyone joins in. The point, obviously, is not to hear the speech, which frequently never gets finished, but to give people an opportunity to drink a bit, sing a lot, and generally celebrate with the groom in these last minutes before the actual ceremony.

The bride is not usually present at the *tisch,* because in traditional communities, the bride and groom don't see each other on the day of the wedding. In some cases, especially in today's more egalitarian communities, the bride has her own *tisch,* with the same attempted speech, singing, and so on. (The consumption of Scotch, I am told, is substantially less at a woman's *tisch!*). If there is no women's *tisch,* the bride is seated on a large chair that looks like a throne of sorts, and is greeted by her friends, who wish her well and share "last minute" thoughts with her.

This quiet moment is then interrupted by the sound of the men's group leaving the room in which the groom's *tisch* took place and entering the room where the bride is seated. The men "dance" around the groom in concentric circles and sing and dance as they make their way to the bride. At this point the bride and the groom see each other for the first time that day. In some weddings, this can get a bit wild and loud, but if the kids know what's coming, they'll be able to appreciate the celebration without being frightened.

The next major step in the wedding process is the signing of the *ketubbah,* or the traditional marriage document. (In states where the civil marriage license also has to be signed, it's typically signed at this point.) The *ketubbah* is an ancient document, usually written in Aramaic, that essentially enumerates the groom's responsibility to the bride in the case that their marriage ends in divorce. To many moderns it seems rather counterproductive to interrupt wedding festivities to sign a document about the demise of the marriage.

But it's important to recognize that the point of the *ketubbah* is different. In an era in which men who tired of their wives would simply dispose of them without regard to their well-being, the *ketubbah,* which stipulated the husband's financial obligations to the wife in such an event, was actually a revolutionary document. In its own way, the *ketubbah* was a radical feminist step forward: It acknowledged that the woman had rights and that the husband had obligations to her, something the ancient world did not usually assume. Understood that way, especially if we also remember that many couples today sign prenuptial agreements, the *ketubbah* ceremony can be much less troublesome to modern sensibilities than it may seem at the outset.

During the *ketubbah* signing, the groom indicates his acceptance of the terms of the document by grasping one end of a handkerchief that the officiating rabbi extends to him. Then two witnesses (men in the traditional community, either gender in more liberal communities) sign the *ketubbah* indicating that they witnessed the groom accepting the terms listed there.

After the completion of the *ketubbah* signing, the groom veils the bride, or, if the bride is already veiled, the groom lifts the veil to make sure that he is marrying the right woman! This tradition is based on the biblical story of Jacob, who labored for seven years to marry Rachel only to find after the wedding that her father had substituted her sister Leah. (He then worked for another seven years to earn the right to marry the daughter he loved. You can find the story in Genesis 29.) Obviously, we're not particularly worried these days that the groom will marry the wrong person (especially since today's veils are hardly the veils of yesteryear), but the ceremony is a quaint one, giving everyone a chance to remember that Jews have been marrying each other in more or less the same way for thousands of years.

In many communities, the occasion of the veiling of the bride is an opportunity for the bride's father to bless her. Sometimes he reads a traditional biblical passage that tradition has chosen for this moment, and in other cases he does that and follows it with words of his own. Some rabbis actually use this moment (which in some weddings is open only to family and very close friends) as an opportunity for those assembled to say anything they'd like to the couple as they get ready to proceed to the actual wedding ceremony.

The Ceremony Itself

The ceremony begins with the processional. Though most wedding parties give great thought to the processional, the truth is that Jewish tradition doesn't stipulate very much. What matters is

338 A JEWISH PARENT'S REFERENCE GUIDE

that the bride and groom have to somehow get to the **chuppah,** the canopy under which they'll be married. The most common arrangement is that family (grandparents, siblings, etc.) go down the aisle first. When they are all in position, the groom is accompanied all the way down the aisle by his parents. Then, in some communities, the groom puts a *kittel* on over his suit or tuxedo.

The *kittel,* which is a white robe, symbolizes purity, as does the white of the bride's wedding gown. The *kittel* also resembles Jewish burial shrouds, and as such reminds the couple and those assembled that the bride and groom will be together for the remainder of their lives.

After the groom puts on the *kittel,* he turns and faces the back of the room, in the direction from which he just came. At this point, the bride's parents walk her about two-thirds of the way down the aisle, kiss her, and then walk the rest of the way as she waits. When the bride's parents have reached their destination (usually, but not always, under the *chuppah),* the groom walks to where she is standing, and together they approach the *chuppah,* symbolically entering their new home as a couple.

At this point, it's common for the bride to circle the groom seven times. This was probably a way to express the idea that the bride's life would revolve around the groom's, and for that reason many modern couples skip this tradition altogether. Others have the bride circle the groom three times, after which he circles her three times. Still others reinterpret the traditional ceremony in a variety of ways. One of the common interpretations is that when we have something in our lives that we love and care about, we take pains to guard and protect it. What the bride is doing when she walks around the groom, this new interpretation suggests, is figuratively constructing her protective wall of love around the man she is marrying.

At this point the actual ceremony begins. The basic outline of the ceremony is as follows: the rabbi (or the cantor, if there is one) sings an opening welcome to the bride and groom. Then, holding the first of the two cups of wine, the rabbi chants the blessing of the wine and then the *birkat erusin,* or the "betrothal blessing." In ancient times, this "betrothal" was actually the first half of the wedding ceremony, in which the couple were in many ways married but did not live together until the second half of the ceremony had been completed about a year later. Today, the two halves are collapsed into one, but both ancient ceremonies remain. After the rabbi chants these two opening blessings, the groom and bride both take a sip of wine from the cup.

The next stage of the wedding is the ring ceremony, which is the actual moment of marriage. In some cases, you will hear the rabbi ask two witnesses—chosen in advance—to come forward and watch the exchange of rings. Then, in very traditional Jewish weddings, the groom places a ring on the bride's finger. The bride does not place a ring on the groom's finger because traditional Jewish law stipulates that a man can betroth a woman, but not vice versa. In slightly more modern ceremonies, the bride *does* place a ring on the groom's finger but doesn't say anything at that moment. Some communities have the bride place a ring on the groom's finger and recite a biblical verse instead of the traditional wedding formula. In the most liberal communities, she recites virtually the same formula he does.

After the "ring ceremony" comes the reading of the *ketubbah.* It is read here in part to serve as a clear divide between the two ceremony halves: the *erusin* (betrothal) ceremony and the *nissu'in* (nuptial, or marriage) ceremony. The officiating rabbi (or someone else given this honor) typically reads at least major portions of the document in the original Aramaic, and then a quasi-translation in English. In more traditional settings, the entire document is read in the original and there is seldom a translation.

After the reading of the *ketubbah* it's common for the rabbi to speak to the couple. This is the end of the *erusin* ceremony. Typically, the service then continues with the *nissu'in* ceremony, which is basically composed of the **Sheva Berakhot** ("The Seven Blessings"). The blessings begin by speaking of God as the creator of humankind, then continues with the theme of humanity in the perfection of the Garden of Eden, and finally, about love and joy. After these blessings, during which the rabbi holds the second cup of wine, the groom and bride each sip the wine again.

Perhaps the most famous traditional element of the wedding ceremony is the breaking of the glass, traditionally done by the groom. A small glass is wrapped in a handkerchief or cloth napkin, and after the conclusion of all the rabbi's remarks, the groom steps on the glass, shattering it. The traditional explanation of this suggests that even in our most joyous hour we pause to recall the destruction of Jerusalem and the similar tragedies that have befallen the Jewish people. Other explanations include one that says that just as the glass has now been entered into a new state, with the pieces irretrievably intermixed, so, too, will the lives of the couple be forever intermixed. Others have said that the couple should have as many happy years together as there are pieces of broken glass. Either way, the custom of breaking the glass is synonymous with Jewish weddings, and if we take our children to even a very modern ceremony, they're more than likely to see it.

In almost all cases, a festive meal (with lots of dancing) follows the ceremony. In traditional communities, the bride and groom go to *yichud,* a special room where they spend their first moments together as husband and wife. Shortly after *yichud,* especially in traditional communities, it's likely that the photographer will need a few more minutes with the bride and groom, since they couldn't be photographed together (as they didn't see each other) before the ceremony.

During *yichud,* everyone else begins the celebration, with food, drink, and dancing. When the couple rejoins the "party," the celebration takes off in earnest—the more traditional the community, the more energetic the dancing tends to be.

One of the things that can be very impressive to our kids is how ancient the Jewish wedding ceremony is. If they're old enough to have even a semblance of a historical sense, they'll probably be amazed to think that certain elements of the ceremony (the *ketubbah,* the ring, the traditional formula) have been used for close to two thousand years, perhaps a bit more. If we explain that that was long before there was a United States, long before there was electricity or cars, that it goes all the way back to the ancient Greeks and Romans, they might be awed not only by the energy of the experience but by its historicity as well.

Many couples, especially those who are having a wedding more traditional than those their friends and family are used to, distribute an explanation of the various stages of the wedding. If you review the material we've presented here and go over with your child whatever explanations the couple provides before the ceremony begins, you can make going to a wedding an experience that is filled with joy, awe, comfort, and understanding.

DIVORCE

To say that divorce is profoundly traumatic for everyone involved is an understatement. When kids first learn that their friends' parents are getting divorced, they start asking questions: What is divorce? Why do people get divorced? How do you get divorced? What they are really asking is: Are my parents going to get divorced?

Hopefully, the answer is no. And if that's the case, by all means, we ought to tell our kids. A completely truthful answer might well be "No, we're not planning on it, but you never know." But it's the wrong answer. The right answer is one that creates comfort and predictability for our kids, and assures them that their world is secure.

Why Does Jewish Tradition Permit Divorce?

It might be helpful to know, when explaining divorce, that there's a beautiful tradition about why Jewish life permits divorce. This *midrash* (a kind of rabbinic folktale) has it that when each of us is born, there is another "half" to our soul "out there" waiting for us. Sometimes we think we've found that other half and we marry that person. But then we learn that the souls don't really match. Divorce, says this tale, is the first step to going out again to find the missing half of our soul.

Now, obviously, this *midrash* needs to be taken with a grain of salt, especially with older kids. For it doesn't explain how a person could have more than one deeply satisfying marriage, nor does it account for the hurtful things people in troubled relationships do to each other. But especially when our kids are young, when they are looking for a way to understand what's happening to their family, this approach can be helpful. There are also many books on the market to help kids through divorce. Many of them are very well done, and if the need arises, it's worth consulting them. If you're fortunate enough to have a caring, thoughtful rabbi, he or she can also be very helpful.

Divorce is generally a very private matter (though the fact that it's happening usually becomes public very quickly), and as such, there's not a tremendous amount that we need to share with our kids (depending, of course, on how old they are) about the technicalities of the process. It's helpful, though, to have some idea of how a Jewish divorce proceeds so we can explain it to them, and to reflect at least briefly on how to make sure our divorce doesn't get in the way of the kids' still being part of a Jewish community.

The Divorce Ceremony

The actual divorce ceremony in Judaism is restrained, private, and quick. Typically, there are six people present: the husband, the wife, two witnesses, the *sofer* (scribe, who will write the *get,* or the traditional divorce document), and often the couple's rabbi. Technically, the rabbi doesn't need to be present; at times, the rabbi is also trained to be a *sofer,* but that is becoming rarer in our day. Today, a rabbi is almost always present at a divorce ceremony; however, if a rabbi were not present, the rabbi's role in the description that follows would be filled by the *sofer.*

The process of writing the *get* takes between ten minutes and half an hour, depending on the *sofer.* There is a "scripted" conversation between the rabbi, the *sofer,* the witnesses, and the couple in which it is ascertained that the witnesses are acceptable witnesses, that the *get* was written specifically for this couple, and that the husband is not giving the *get* to his wife in any way against his will.

After the scripted conversation, the wife removes all the jewelry from her hands and holds her hands outward, palms up, in order to receive the *get.* The *sofer* folds the *get* in a specific way, and hands it to the rabbi. The rabbi then gives the *get* to the husband (where the *sofer* acts as rabbi as well, he gives it directly to the husband), who in turn gently lets it fall into the palms of his wife. He then recites the following phrase: "This is your *get,* and with it you are divorced from me from this moment forth, and you may now be married to any [other] man." Indicating her acceptance of the *get,* the wife lifts up her hands and walks a few steps; she then returns the *get* to the rabbi. After a few more arrangements on the part of the *sofer* and the rabbi, the husband and wife are each given a small document called a *petor* ("release"), indicating that their divorce was duly executed under Jewish law.

Jewish Life After Divorce

Even if the execution of the actual ceremony is simple, making Jewish life meaningful for our kids after divorce is not. When one of the parents is Jewish and the other is not, it's very common for the postdivorce syndrome to involve some interreligious competition for the kids' loyalties. Even if the civil settlement stipulates certain arrangements in this regard (and it often does, as Jewish parents frequently want some agreement that the child will be raised as a Jew), making that work and overcoming the (quite understandable) tendency of the non-Jewish parent to resist becomes quite difficult. There are no easy solutions, except to say that the couple needs to think through very carefully what they want before the actual divorce, and needs to communicate about the ongoing process afterward. If they fundamentally disagree, no court or outside authority is going to make things work; it's going to be tough all the way through, and the children are likely to view religion as the battleground of their parents, not a place they can go to find the security they need.

Even if both parents are Jewish, matters are not simple. If a child ends up splitting time between two homes that are not particularly near each other, it's quite possible that they may also split their time between two congregations. Or they may be at only one congregation but much less frequently than before. Either way, the child loses out. For it's precisely when parents split up and family structures have to be reconfigured that children need peer groups, a sense of stability, and in many cases, a spiritual outlet for their hope, their wonder, their need for comfort. Parents too often steal that from their kids by making religion and Jewish life one of the "turf" battles they choose to fight. If we take our kids' spiritual needs seriously, we'll have to recognize that the issue of how to keep them deeply and happily involved in Jewish life is a critical one. I've lost count of the number of people I've taught in their twenties and thirties, people desperately searching for a spiritual home, who've told me that their parents' divorce was the beginning of the end of their involvement in Jewish life.

Another dimension of the world of Jewish divorce must be mentioned. It's called the problem of the *agunah.* In Hebrew, *agunah* means "anchored," and it refers to a woman who cannot convince her husband to give her a *get.* According to traditional Jewish law, only the husband can initiate divorce proceedings. Thus, until he decides to give his wife a *get,* she cannot remarry even if the civil divorce has long since been settled. (He can't either, of course, but he's not being controlled by her.)

Why would a husband not give his wife a *get?* Because he's angry, hurt, holding out for a better deal in the civil settlement, or because there is someone the ex-wife wants to marry. There are an infinite number of reasons, but none of them are good. The problem of the *agunah* is one of the most harrowing moral problems of the Jewish world today, and virtually every Jewish community is struggling with how to address it. The Reform community no longer requires a *get.* Parts of the Conservative community have developed a system of marriage annulment that can occasionally be done without the husband's approval (though not everyone in the Conservative rabbinate is in favor of this policy). In the Orthodox community, a few maverick rabbis have also resorted to annulment, while others are exploring ways of exerting public pressure on the husband.

Our interest here is what we communicate to our own kids if we are party to making our wives *agunahs.* To be sure, a completely amicable divorce is rare, and even those are often tense. We are probably angry and hurt and in emotional pain. But we still must ask ourselves what we want our children to hear, to see, and to learn about what it means to be Jewish. If we use Jewish tradition to punish, extort, or cause pain, they'll learn that lesson well, and their feelings about being Jewish will reflect that lesson for decades to come.

Divorce is never fun or easy, but it can be done reasonably well. Jewish tradition would say that having had the blessing of being given these children, we now have the obligation of doing at least that.

DEATH, BURIAL, AND MOURNING

At some point children begin to confront the world of death and mourning. It's not easy, or pleasant, but it's a part of life. Our job as parents is to make that introduction as comforting and meaningful as possible.

If our children are fortunate enough not to lose anyone very close to them too early in life, we have the advantage of being able to expose them to this world slowly, carefully, gradually. We need to explain, to let them ask questions, and to be honest with them in letting them know that there are certain parts of this that we, too, simply don't understand.

Jewish funerals are intentionally stark. Traditionally, they do not involve flowers, and they end with those assembled actually shoveling earth onto the casket. It's a harrowing sound, and it's meant to be. And when the occasion finally arrives, we have to ask ourselves if our children are ready for it. We have to know our kids, and do what's good for *them,* not for anyone else.

Explaining death to children is a delicate and subtle process, and there are some excellent materials listed at the conclusion of this book that offer a complete discussion of the various approaches. Your rabbi or friends may have others to suggest as well. But what's most important to remember is that when kids ask us about death, they're asking about something that we ourselves don't fully understand. And while we're not necessarily afraid of our own deaths, we're certainly afraid of losing the people who are important to us. That makes it all the more difficult to clearly think through how we ought to explain death to our children.

Here, though, it's important to return to an issue we discussed toward the beginning of this book: our job as parents to foster our kids' faith, not to undermine it. It's at moments like this that children's desire to believe that the world is protected by a caring and loving God is particularly strong. We may be feeling something quite different at this moment, so our needs and our kids' needs may not be the same.

At the same time, we have to be careful not to make God so central to what has happened as to make God responsible for the death itself. The answers that many parents give—that God "wanted Grandpa up in Heaven with Him"—may sound lovely, but it can also leave a child to wonder why God, who has everything, couldn't wait just a little longer to take Grandpa away. So let's not make God the enemy in this no matter what we might personally be feeling. As we construct the explanations we give our children, it's important to concentrate not only on what we're saying but on how they are going to hear what we say.

There is no good explanation as to why people die young, why innocent children get sick. And that concept may be something that's OK to share with our kids. But saying just that is not enough; couple it with a sense that there's something eternal about us, that we have a soul, a special part of us that continues to live forever. How do we know there's a soul? We may not be able to see it, but like love, when we feel it, we know it's real. We just know.

Our job is simple at moments like these: to show how Jewish life and Jewish community make it possible to go on, to know that we're loved, and to keep alive the memory of the person we miss so deeply.

The Funeral

Traditional Jewish funerals are simple and plain, but it's worth reviewing the basic elements so that if we take our children to one, we can prepare them in advance for what they're going to see.

Before the funeral itself, there is a tremendous amount of attention given to the body. It is washed and clothed in burial shrouds called *tachrichin.* The deceased person is then placed in the coffin and watched ("guarded"); the deceased person is never left alone until the funeral itself.

Jewish tradition mandates that the coffin be a plain, pine box, so as not to distinguish between rich and poor at the time of burial, and in order to ensure that the coffin is made of materials that will decompose and return to their natural elements. As a symbol of respect for the deceased person and a desire to bring them to their "final resting place" as quickly as possible, the tradition requires that the burial take place as quickly as possible after death, usually the next day or the day after. Jewish tradition also mandates that the coffin be closed. Depending on the circumstances of death, and whether family members were present before the deceased was placed in the coffin, civil law may require that an immediate family member view the body to confirm the person's identity. Occasionally, a very close family member may wish to have the coffin opened momentarily. "Viewing" the body is not a Jewish tradition.

If our kids want to know why, the answer is simple. When we're alive, we can usually determine how we look before other people see us. When we wake up in the morning, there are a variety of things we do before we let anyone else (especially outside our family) see us. It matters to us how we appear, and usually we have some control over that. But when we're dead, we no longer have any say in how we look. The tradition says, therefore, that in deference to the person's possible wish to be remembered as a vital human being, our last glimpse of them ought not to be after they've died.

Shortly before the actual service begins, the rabbi may perform the *keriyah* (Hebrew for "tearing") ceremony with the family. In traditional communities, when a person's parent, sibling, spouse, or child has died, he or she actually tears his or her clothing. In many communities, though, that practice has been replaced with the cutting of a small black ribbon that is pinned to the mourner's shirt or blouse. The ribbon (or the real garment, if that was torn) is worn for the entire *shiva* period.

Lately, many families from all walks of Jewish life have begun to consider returning to the tradition of ripping an actual garment, knowing that the custom of the ribbon began only because people didn't want to rip their clothes. People are asking themselves: Is our grief over the loss of our parent not worth the cost of a shirt? What are we telling ourselves when we use the ribbon? What are we telling our kids? These are important questions; each family will determine what speaks most powerfully to them and what seems appropriate, but the question is worth asking. If we know that someone close to us is mortally ill and is going to die soon, we ought to consider in advance whether we want to use the ribbon or actually rip our clothes at the moment of death. Either way, we have an opportunity here to create a very powerful memory for our children; we should give it some very careful thought.

A Jewish funeral does not have many elements. Sometimes family members will speak, or read something they or the deceased wrote. Close friends may reminisce. Some communities allow music, and occasionally play a recording of something that meant a lot to the person who died. Typically, a rabbi offers a eulogy that summarizes the person's life and helps shape the way we ought to remember him or her. A cantor or the rabbi may chant Psalm 23 or the El Maleh Rahamim, a prayer that speaks of God as merciful and asks God to care for the soul of the deceased person in the "eternal resting place." Sometimes the Kaddish, the memorial prayer, is recited at this point. In some communities, though, it is recited only at graveside.

After the conclusion of this part of the ceremony, the congregation makes its way to the grave site. In communities like New York, where cemeteries are often a long drive from the chapel, it is acceptable that people not go to the actual burial; family and very close friends, of course, do. In other communities, such as Los Angeles, where the funeral chapel is often on the cemetery grounds, it is common for everyone to go. Different rabbis and different communities have different standards for the order of the procession from the chapel to the grave. You'll be given instructions at that point, but it's very common (and traditional) for the coffin to be carried from the front of the chapel to the rear as the entire congregation stands in respect.

At the actual grave, the service is brief. Some rabbis cut the *keriyah* at this point. Some have done it already; others assume that the mourners have torn their own clothing. The coffin is lowered into the ground, and then those assembled take turns moving three shovelsful of earth into the grave. In traditional communities, no one leaves until the entire casket is covered or until the entire grave is filled. The act of filling in the grave is called a *chesed shel emet*— a wholly altruistic act. Tradition says that while a person is alive, anything we do for them might be done with the expectation that we'll get something in return. At this moment, however, when they are unable to do anything for us, we fill in the grave as a symbol of escorting them to their final "home," knowing full well that we get nothing back.

After the grave is filled, a prayer called Tzidduk Ha-din ("The Justification of God's Judgment") is recited in traditional communities. A special Kaddish is recited, and then those assembled form two lines facing each other. The mourning family walks between these lines to their cars, and the funeral is over.

After the Funeral—The Period of Mourning

After the funeral, a rather complex series of mourning periods begin. The first period is the week of *shiva*, a Hebrew word that means "seven" and which refers to the seven days of mourning that commence with the funeral. A second period, which also begins at the burial, is *sheloshim*, which means "thirty" and refers to a thirty-day period of somewhat lessened mourning restrictions. The final period, which is counted from the day of death, is the eleven-month mourning period a child observes for a parent. The precise customs for these periods are very complex. What we cover here is what your child might actually see immediately after the funeral and during the week of *shiva*.

As you leave the cemetery, you may see people filling a large cup with water and then pouring it over their hands. This is a way of spiritually "purifying" themselves, moving from the spiritual space of death at the cemetery to the realm of life and vitality. Often, some sort of arrangement is set up outside the home of the chief mourner, so that those who come to visit immediately after the burial can wash there.

There is usually an abundance of food at the mourner's home, most of it provided and arranged for by friends. This is actually a traditional custom called the "meal of healing," a time to fortify the body after the exhausting hours or days that have passed before the funeral. This meal, which doesn't usually have an official beginning or end, also marks the beginning of the *shiva* period.

When people refer to this first week after the funeral, they commonly say that the family is "sitting *shiva*." What they mean is that the family is following the Jewish tradition of "sitting" in their home for seven days after the funeral (Shabbat is excepted; one can leave the house to go to synagogue services on Shabbat). And your child should know what to expect if you bring her or him with you to pay a "*shiva* call."

The people who "sit *shiva*" are the siblings, children, parents, and spouse of the deceased. Other family members may certainly participate in these rituals, but the obligation to do so rests only with these people. As a sign of mourning, traditional families sit on very low hard chairs or stools. The mirrors in the house will be covered, and the family will often not wear leather shoes—both considered signs of luxury, almost self-indulgence. When visiting a family that is sitting *shiva*, the tradition is to offer expressions of sympathy and to talk about the person who has died.

You might think that the most appropriate thing would be to get the mourner's mind off their loss and on to something else, but Jewish tradition disagrees. The tradition essentially believes that mourning is a process that has stages, and that for the progression of stages to move forward, we first need to confront the reality of what has happened. That is one of the explanations for the absence of flowers at a Jewish funeral. To the extent flowers "beautify" something that needs to be seen as very stark, the tradition felt they get in the way of that process.

This desire to confront the painful reality head-on is also one of the reasons we shovel earth into the grave, and it's one of the reasons we make a point of speaking about the person who has died when we sit *shiva* or visit a family sitting *shiva*. We don't want to forget the person who has died.

The other element that is often present at the *shiva* home is a service. Some mourners invite people to visit them all day long, while others find they need time to themselves, and thus set up "visiting" hours in the morning and in the evening. Some have people visit only in the evening. Either way, in traditional communities, visits in the morning are usually accompanied by the recitation of **Sacharit,** the morning service, while evening visits open with **Ma'ariv,** the evening service.

≈

Should children visit families sitting *shiva?* There's no right answer to that. It depends on the situation, on the child, on the relationship the child had to the person or to the family. Ultimately, though, visiting a family sitting *shiva* is a wonderful way to introduce children to the Jewish world of death and mourning as a world of caring, of offering comfort. This is a part of life they will have to confront eventually, and there's nothing macabre about a *shiva* house. People look just like they always do; their interactions are "normal" and the visits are often quite pleasant.

These visits are a way of showing our kids that Judaism has the capacity to make even life's tragic phases more comfortable, and that a large part of what being Jewish is about is offering comfort and friendship to people who need it. Very often, these visits are memorable ones for our children. If we can make them into positive experiences, we've started them on the process of learning that being Jewish is about community and caring, two things we hope they'll value no matter how they choose to live their Jewish lives.

A FINAL THOUGHT

Many of our children's most powerful early memories will be of life cycle events. They'll always remember the birth of younger siblings, the first weddings they attended, funerals that touched them deeply. Most of us still recall the day we went off to college, and some of us remember the first day of first grade. These events shape us and touch us. Our challenge as Jewish parents is to use these events as opportunities to teach our kids about Jewish life, to portray Jewish life as profound, sensible, and meaningful. These events are peppered throughout our lives; used wisely, they become another tool in our continuing effort to immerse our kids in a world of Jewish meaning.

Being Jewish is about being part of something larger than we are, something timeless, something that creates community in which we can live, sanctify, mourn, laugh, and love. It's time to show our kids how lucky they are to be part of this.

IV

CONCLUSION

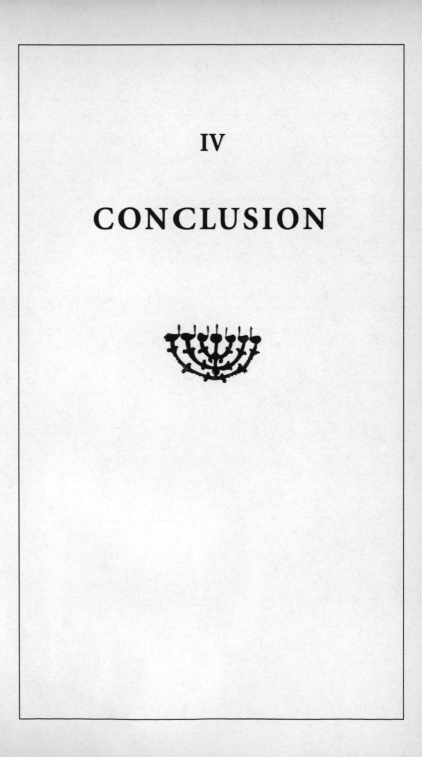

15

OF MODELS, MERMAIDS, AND MUSIC

Models, mermaids, and music might seem like very strange topics for the conclusion of a book on Jewish parenting. But our goal is to use these three *M*'s as a way to round out our thinking about Jewish parenting. Simply put, these three *M*'s are a useful way to focus on what might be the three most important things to remember as we leave this book and begin the journey in earnest. The first is the critical and primary importance of parents and of homes in forging our kids' Jewish identities; the second is our willingness to let our kids do their own exploring; and the third is our understanding that ultimately our kids are individuals whose religious sensitivities and instincts that we can influence but that we can't ultimately shape or control.

DOES YOUR MAILBOX KNOW YOU'RE JEWISH?

We've spent a considerable part of this book exploring resources outside our homes that can help us in providing a rich and exciting Jewish upbringing for our children. Synagogues, museums, JCCs, libraries, college campuses, Israel, communal celebrations, and life cycle events can all add depth and content to the foundation that we provide at home. But that's the key: All of these elements are valuable only if they build on a foundation that *we* provide, that *we* model.

Ultimately, more than any rabbi, any teacher, any trip to Eastern Europe or Israel, it is the parents who are going to shape their children's feelings about being Jewish. What *we* do, what *we* learn, what *we* read, what *we* talk about, what *we* attend—that's the stuff of which their Jewish identities will ultimately be built.

To be a thoughtful and successful Jewish parent, then, is really to be a thoughtful and involved Jewish person.

The Private Detective Test

Imagine that someone hired a private investigator to follow us around from Monday morning through Thursday night, asking the P.I. to write down everything we did that had anything to do with Judaism. What would the detective come back with? Would the file be virtually empty, or would it have a long list of "hints" suggesting that Jewishness pervades our lives?

That's where the mailbox comes in. What comes in the mailbox? Are there Jewish magazines, Jewish newspapers, pieces of mail from the various Jewish organizations we're involved with? What reading material is stacked up on our nightstand? What lectures, concerts, movies are on the family calendar? What Web sites are bookmarked? Would a review of our checkbooks reveal a list of Jewish organizations that we try to support? What sorts of books line the bookshelves in the house? What lies around on the coffee tables? If we've got art in the house, is any of it Jewish? Are there physical indications that this is a Jewish home?

No matter what else we do, our actions and our loves will speak louder than anything else. This is the sort of stuff we simply can't outsource, nor should we expect anyone else will do the job for us. We wouldn't leave our kids' moral or intellectual development exclusively in the hands of someone else; our children's religious, spiritual, and Jewish development is no different. We're their models; what we do and who we are speaks to them more clearly than anything else.

JUDAISM CAN'T BE JUST FOR KIDS

Earlier we spoke about the importance of having standards and rules for our kids in order to communicate to them the importance that we attach to being Jewish. But modeling is an important issue here, as well. Our kids will hear loudly and clearly the messages that we communicate (partially) through the rules we set for them, but they'll also be watching closely to see if we follow the rules ourselves. If the rules are for them but not for us, they'll see the hypocrisy, and we'll do a tremendous amount of damage.

If we insist that our kids go to synagogue services with their Hebrew school class, but they notice that we never go, they'll quickly conclude that adults don't *have* to go to services, that we're just making them go because they're kids. This virtually guarantees that they'll stop going as soon as they can. If we insist that they go to day school or Hebrew school to learn about being Jewish, but they never see us going to a class, reading a Jewish book, or investing in Jewish learning, they'll quickly conclude that Judaism is about double standards, and that it's certainly not for adults.

One summer one of my students at a summer program for Jewish college and postcollege students came up to me on the very first day and said, "I just want you to know, I don't want to be here. My parents made me come; they said that if I didn't come to this, they wouldn't pay for my trip to Europe later in the summer. But don't waste your time on me. They just want me here because they're freaked out that I've got a non-Jewish boyfriend. They figure you're gonna get me to break up with him. Forget it. I'll put in my four weeks, but I'm not interested."

OK, I thought to myself, this is going to be interesting. So I asked her to tell me about the home in which she grew up. Did they do a lot of Jewish things? Were her parents invested in Jewish life? What did they love about it? Did she have any idea why it was important to them that she marry a Jewish man?

The response to each question was a blank stare. The family didn't do anything, she told me. She went to a couple of years of Hebrew school as a kid, but that was it. No family holiday celebrations. Her parents weren't into it, she said. The more she told me, the more it sounded like they weren't into anything Jewish. And as for why she should marry somebody Jewish: "They just go ballistic at the thought that I might do anything else."

So I had my opening. I said to her, "Do me a favor. Go to the public phone next to the dining hall and call your parents. Tell them that you've already spoken to the rabbi here, and tell them that he told you that whom you marry is none of their business. Tell them that he said you should do whatever you want."

She looked at me like I was nuts. So I explained to her: "Parents have a right to have values, and to hope that their kids will share those values. But they can't ask their children—and especially their adult children—to commit to a value they don't personally express. The reason most parents don't want their kids to marry a non-Jew—unless they're just racists, in which case there's no logical argument to be had—is that they want their kids and grandkids to live an intensive, exciting Jewish life. But your parents didn't do that. Everything they did showed that being Jewish didn't matter much to them. So if it didn't matter much, and they did nothing all these years to get you to love it and to know it, why should they tell you whom to marry?"

Because she was angry, and because she wasn't entirely sure I was serious, she actually went to the phone. And she actually made the call. And she actually told them what I'd said. (I never heard from them!) And after the call, she said, "So now what?"

I told her: "I hope you don't marry a non-Jewish guy. I hope that if this guy is for you, that he'll convert. And if he's not for you, I hope you'll find a Jewish person to spend your life with. But I want you to do that because being Jewish excites you, moves you, speaks to you, touches you. If it does that, you won't want to share your life with someone who's not a part of it. My job over the next four weeks is to show you why I love it, to try to get you to love it, and to try to help you find your way in. Then you have to decide how you want to spend your life."

What was interesting to me was that she responded. She stuck it out, got invested in the process, and left at the end of the experience much more open to Jewish life than she had been when she first arrived. It wasn't hard. All we had to do was to acknowledge how unfair her parents were being in setting a standard for her that was in no way reflective of the values they themselves seemed to live.

In some way or another, too many of us make her parents' mistake. We avoid rules all throughout our kids' early years, then suddenly have rules about whom they can date and marry. What kind of sense does that make? They go to college, and we look through the course listing with them, suggesting a Jewish course here or there, but they never saw *us* study anything Jewish. They're often stunned by the hypocrisy.

We tell them how wonderful Jewish life is and how important it is that they learn about it, but nothing we actually do ourselves suggests it means anything to us. This double standard simply won't work. If we're serious about Jewish life, we should let our kids know that—by the standards we set for them and by the standards we set for ourselves. If we want them home on Friday night, *we* have to be home on Friday night. If we want them to study, *we* have to study. If we want them to respect Jewish leaders, we have to model the same respect (we radically underestimate the damage we do when our kids hear us ragging on the rabbi, the cantor, the synagogue). They will take seriously what we show them we take seriously. There's a much better chance they'll love Jewish life if we show them that *we* love Jewish life.

As important as rules are for our kids, they're just as important for us. As I've said throughout this book, being a Jewish parent is also about reimagining our own Jewish journey.

THE COMMITMENT NOT TO UNDERMINE EACH OTHER

When we use the phrase "our Jewish journey," we sidestep one crucial fact: No couple is made up of two identical people. No two parents are completely alike, and very few couples are made up of two people who think about Jewish life and Jewish commitment in precisely the same way. This means that as much as it's going to be critical that we communicate clearly with our kids about what matters to us, it's no less important that we talk to each other about what matters to us, about our visions for our children's Jewish lives.

There are certain times that it's virtually impossible for us not to address this issue. Choices about schools, or summer camps, are an example. But even when thinking about which school to choose for our kids, many of us mask the real issues behind details like location, cost, and quality of secular education. These issues are important, some even crucial, but so is the kind of Jew we want our kids to be, the kind of Jewish life we're prepared to live in order to lead them in that direction. Ultimately, these conversations are not really about our kids but rather about us—about what we want, about our spiritual needs, about our willingness to think about Jewish life in a way that's different from what we might first have expected when we met or decided to start having children.

If one parent wants to embark on a serious and passionate Jewish journey and the other is simply uninterested, it's almost impossible for the interested parent to succeed.

I've seen this on dozens of occasions: The father wants to bless his children at the Shabbat table but the mother thinks he's nuts. So she always finds something else to do during those moments—fiddling with something in the kitchen, chatting aimlessly with someone else at the table, whatever. What she is communicating to her kids is that as far as she's concerned, this really is kind of ridiculous. The convoluted and confusing message to the kids—and the not so subtle battlelike background noise—makes it almost impossible for that moment to be one of transcendence, intimacy, and unbounded love.

I once talked with a couple about how they put their kids to bed at night. The mom desperately wanted to sing the Shema, but her husband refused. "It's just not us," he said. "It's too Jewish." He had no objection to *her* saying the Shema, but he wanted her to know that he wasn't going to do it. She felt he was thereby undermining her even on nights when she put the kids to bed by herself. She felt that her kids would come to see this as "mom's thing," not a universal moment in which they were tied to Jewish people throughout the world, a moment in which their family simply allowed God's presence to come into the room. And she was right. The mixed practice yielded a mixed message and subverted the possibility of making that moment powerful and compelling.

The year we moved to Israel for a year's sabbatical our son Micha was five years old. We were anxious for all our kids to learn Hebrew that year, and had actually anticipated that Micha would have the easiest time since he was the youngest. Much to our surprise, though, he was the one who resisted the most. When I picked him up from school one day his kindergarten teacher told me that she had tried to teach him a certain word in Hebrew, but he refused to repeat it or to learn it. When she pressed, he looked at her and said, "I don't have to learn Hebrew; I'm going back to America at the end of the year."

I was pretty horrified, since it was both impolite and completely contrary to what we wanted him to get from that year. As we walked home, I asked him if he'd really said that. He admitted that he had. I asked him where he got the idea that he didn't have to learn Hebrew. After a lot of stammering, he told me that he had heard a girl in his class say exactly the same thing.

We knew this little girl's family. And we knew that it was her father who had long wanted to come on sabbatical to Israel while her mom had been pretty opposed. Her mom was less than uninterested; she flat out hadn't wanted to come. She didn't want to live in an apartment much smaller than the house she was used to; she didn't want to give up the conveniences, luxuries, and sense of comfort that life in the States provided her. She knew she'd miss her friends, and she didn't relish the idea of being a "foreigner" for an entire year.

Over the course of time, when we found a moment to subtly raise this incident with those parents, it became clear that the mom had never told her child that she didn't need to learn Hebrew because she was going back to America. But this girl had picked it up; she saw that her mom was not invested in the whole experience, was slightly resistant and a bit put out. That's all it took to convince this child that this whole experience wasn't that important and that Hebrew didn't matter.

For our discussion, of course, the issue isn't whether or not our kids will learn to speak Hebrew. The issue for us is to recognize that a united front is critical if this "journey" is going to be an emotionally powerful one for our kids. When they see both parents invested in the process, kids sense that the life their family leads is part of the natural order of things; it makes them feel secure, comfortable, and confident.

But when our kids sense that these issues are actually a battleground between parents, no matter how subtle, we steal all the power of the moment from them. Most kids hate when their parents fight. Even if they know that their parents aren't going to get divorced or even stay mad for very long, they just can't stand it.

They'll tiptoe away from anything they think might trigger a conflict. If Jewish life, religious life, spiritual life—call it what you will—is an area where our kids sense even tacit disagreement, they'll come to experience it as a place from which they're better off staying away.

The idea of a "united front" doesn't mean we have to agree about absolutely everything Jewish, even in front of the kids. It's fine for the kids to see that we each have passionate commitments to various things, and it's even healthy for them to see that people who care about each other can figure out a way to live together when there are strong difference about things.

When December comes to Los Angeles, I always enjoy taking our kids out in the van at night to show them the lights decorating all the houses. Especially in neighborhoods like Beverly Hills, there are incredibly beautiful homes that are decorated so dramatically that it's breathtaking. While my wife always comes along, she basically doesn't like the idea. She doesn't think it's healthy to make Christmas seem so alluring when we go to such lengths to remind them that Christmas is not our holiday. My sense, on the other hand, is that our message about the "big issues" is very clear, and one night of touring Beverly Hills won't undermine that. What they're seeing is pretty lights, something they're going to notice either way, whether we show it to them or not.

I mention this minor disagreement because we've never tried to hide it from our kids. They know how we each feel. But there is simply no way in the world that they could interpret either of us as not being committed to Jewish life. When they know that we both love Shabbat, that we both care about our synagogue community, that we both love to study Jewish texts, that we both read lots of Jewish stuff (in addition to lots of non-Jewish stuff), this disagreement can't possibly suggest to them that one of us doesn't care or is opposed to Jewish life. The issue is how much of a commitment to Jewish content and values the parents share. If it's a substantial amount, it's probably even healthy for them to see that we're not monolithic.

Regardless of how much dissension we choose to let our kids see, the important thing to remember is that we're their models. Individually and as a couple, we'll be the ones who communicate to them what's important and what we care about. Given that the cultures in which we live don't make a commitment to Jewish life a natural choice or even an easy one, a united, coherent, and clear message about our own lives and our own loves becomes more important than almost anything else.

TOO JEWISH—OVERCOMING THAT NAGGING FEAR

There's a kind of dark little secret about Jewish life in America, and it has a lot to do with being a Jewish parent or grandparent. The secret is that many of us want our kids to like being Jewish, even to love being Jewish, but we don't want them to be *too* Jewish.

The phrase "too Jewish" is one that comes up all the time. I can't begin to count how many parents have expressed some pride in whatever Jewish interests their kids had, but then added that they hoped they didn't become "too Jewish." I've never really understood that comment. Each time I hear it, I feel like asking, "Well, what's the maximum percent Jewish you'd like them to be?"

Asked that way, of course, most people would eventually realize that they don't necessarily mean so Jewish that they wouldn't read general literature or that they wouldn't have non-Jewish friends or that they would lose touch with the rest of the world; relatively few Jewish parents have that to worry about. No, what they really mean when they say "too Jewish" is that they don't want their kids to be too *noticeably* Jewish. Particularly in previous generations, when there was a great fear of latent anti-Semitism in

America (it's still there, of course, hidden but alive), this notion of "too Jewish" might have stemmed from parents' fear that their children might "stick out in the crowd," become victims, or jeopardize the family's perceived place in society. Today, with such hostility much less common, "too Jewish" usually reflects the parents' hopes that their kids won't become more religious, observant, or committed than they are. Often, of course, the two concerns are really intertwined.

I remember one harrowing episode: A mother called me at my office to tell me that her daughter had gotten involved in a cult, and that she had been told I could help get her daughter out. The truth was that I didn't know very much about cults, but I did know someone who was considered an expert in this business. So I put her in touch with this man, confident things would then proceed smoothly.

A week or so later, the cult expert called to tell me that the mother had been very grateful for his help, and they decided to meet. As soon as they met, he said, the mother's demeanor changed. She simply said that she didn't need any assistance and got up and left.

He was stymied, and asked me to find out what had happened. I called the mother, who told me that she didn't realize the guy I was sending her to was an Orthodox rabbi. "What difference does that make?" I asked her. To which she responded, "I don't want my daughter in the cult, but I also certainly don't want her to be *that* Jewish. I'd rather leave things alone."

I explained that even though this man was an Orthodox rabbi, his agenda wasn't to get Jews into Orthodoxy; it was simply to get them out of cults, and into some form of Jewish life. My argument was to no avail; once she saw his beard and his *kippah*, she didn't want to work with him. As far as she was concerned, he was even more dangerous than the cult.

Lest we imagine for even a brief moment that the idea of "too Jewish" is not very common or often spoken about, we should know that "Too Jewish" was the name of a 1997 exhibit at the Armand Hammer Museum of Art in Los Angeles and at the Jewish Museum in New York. The exhibit was fascinating; what most of the pieces had in common was that they were explorations of the various artists' misgivings about and discomfort with being Jewish. With everything from chocolate busts called "Venus Pareve" to pieces of matzah with bow ties on them, the exhibit illustrated that the struggle for Jewish comfort in a secular world is a pretty universal one.

Isn't that pretty much what that dad was telling me when he said he didn't want to sing the Shema with his kids at night? Wasn't he saying that having grown up in America, he'd always imagined putting his kids to bed in exactly the same way he perceived everyone else did? (Of course, he probably also underestimates the number of Christian children who utter a prayer before going to sleep at night!)

We can understand his struggle. He wanted his kids to be "good Jews" but not to be "too Jewish"—not to have to give up any piece of being part of the rest of the world. It's understandable, but it's not so easy to pull off. The problem is that we live in a culture that tries to convince us that it *is* easy; our culture, though, deceives us.

Jews have been dealing with this for a long time. Remember our discussion of Purim, and our suggestion that one of the themes that Purim addresses is that of identity, pride, the desire to hide, the question of how noticeable we want to be? If there's a Jewish holiday almost two thousand years old that addresses this issue, it can't be that new or that uncommon.

But the problem has become more acute lately. And strangely, America is the source of our struggle. Most of us have been raised in a culture that suggests that we can be both Jewish and American, and that there's no tension whatsoever between them. We can be anything, many things, all things. We know this from lots of places, but especially from the movies we make for kids.

Remember *The Little Mermaid*? In Hans Christian Andersen's original version of the fairy tale, a young mermaid makes her first trip to the surface of the sea and falls in love with a world completely unlike her own. It sparkles and shimmers. It's gorgeous. Suddenly, her own sea-world seems drab in comparison. She dreams of joining the human world, of gaining a soul, of marrying the prince. Now her fish tail, which had always seemed natural to her, is an impediment, and she wants nothing more than to trade it for human legs.

Enter the wicked sea-witch, who offers to create a brew that will dissolve the mermaid's tail and replace it with legs—but for a terrible price. Though the former mermaid's legs will be beautiful, they will also be painful; every step she takes will feel as though she is stepping on sharp knives. Even worse, if the Prince doesn't marry her, she won't get a soul, and then, warns the sea-witch, the mermaid will dissolve into the foam on the sea.

As if that's not enough, the witch reveals an even higher price. In exchange for the magic brew, she also demands the mermaid's voice, renowned throughout the mer-kingdom for its sweetness and beauty. The mermaid can become human, but only at tremendous and horrifying sacrifice.

Yet her love for the Prince and her enchantment with his world is so deep that the mermaid decides to accept the offer and drinks the brew, leaving the only world she's ever known. But, we quickly learn the human world can never be hers, for she cannot speak. She is beautiful, but an oddity. The Prince loves her, but because they can't converse, it never occurs to him to marry her. Ultimately, he marries a Princess from another kingdom, and as the witch had warned, the mermaid does not get the soul she so desires. She senses her death approaching, and soon, she turns into the foam upon the sea and disappears forever.

What a sad story! But sad stories like that don't sell lunch boxes and pajamas and lots of stuffed animals. So Disney had to make a few changes. In the 1990s version of *The Little Mermaid,* things had to work out differently. Ariel (the mermaid's name in the movie version) gets human legs, but suffers no pain. She loses her voice, but gets it back when Prince Eric kills the sea-witch. Because the mermaid-turned-human can speak, the Prince does marry her. She and the Prince sail into the horizon and presumably live happily ever after.

What Disney is telling us is that the classic American myth is true, that you can live comfortably in more than one world. You can marry the Prince, but you don't have to leave your family behind.

But is that really true? It is certainly more true in contemporary North America than it's ever been for Jews. And more than ever before, we can live in more than one world at the same time—but not completely, and that's where Disney's got it all wrong. Something does have to give. We can't go out on Friday night *and* be home for Shabbat. We can't bring in KFC takeout *and* have a kosher kitchen. Sandy Koufax taught us that you can't both pitch in the World Series *and* observe Yom Kippur. There are choices that have to be made. The mermaid does not have to give up anything that matters to her in the end, but life in the real world is not quite that simple. Choices have to be made, and none of the choices is perfect or completely comfortable.

Once we know that, we'll be able to understand that our kids may make choices different from those we made. Given the tenuous balance between participation in the widest possible swath of American culture and a passionate "journey" into Jewish life, they may decide that their generation, or their campus, or their friends, or their personality requires a balance different from what worked for us. They may choose to be less noticeably Jewish; they may also choose to be more.

It's always hard when our kids choose something different from what we chose. It can feel like an implicit rejection of some of the choices we made—for ourselves and for them. Sometimes our kids' decisions are rejections of what we've done. And as uncomfortable as that is, it's normal, inevitable, and actually healthy.

In the end, of course, it all comes down to "why?"

Why be Jewish? That's like asking "Why fall in love?" or "Why love music?" Can anyone really explain why one piece of music moves them? That no matter how many times they hear a particular song it brings back memories and tears to their eyes or smiles to their faces, or why certain symphonies simply transport them to places indescribable?

But if the answer to "why be Jewish?" is ultimately about the music of Jewish life, we need to recognize that we can't be sure what sort of music our kids will love. No one can guarantee that their kids will love Mozart or Stravinsky, any more than we can be sure that our kids will like Joni Mitchell more than Madonna. It's not just "different strokes for different folks"; it's deeper than that.

Everybody is different. Different sounds and rhythms speak to us, move us, make us cry, give us hope. Each of us has a favorite music that can drill right to the center of our hearts, our souls, our hope and dreams, fears and worries. There's no explaining exactly why one sound is more powerful and compelling than another.

And that's how the music of Jewish life works. Our challenge as parents is to make sure our kids are exposed to the music of Jewish life at its very best, its most powerful, its greatest majesty.

We have no guarantees that when our kids grow up they will play the music we do. But as long as they *play* the music, as long as they love it, as long as something about it calls to them in a way no words can describe, we will have succeeded.

The journey of Jewish parenting is exciting, exhilarating, challenging, and occasionally a little crazy-making. But like any journey, it's the kind of experience that almost inevitably alters and impacts everyone who goes along. It will change us, forever. It will shape our children, profoundly.

So we end where we started, with Hillel the sage. After he told the prospective convert that being Jewish was about treating the other as we'd want to be treated ourselves, he said *"zil gemor"*—"go out and learn." The same is true for us. We know how beautiful the music can be, we know the elements that give it its beauty. That's the beginning. Now it's time to go and learn, to get out and have fun, to explore, to celebrate, and to grow. The rest will follow.

APPENDIX

A QUICK BIRD'S-EYE VIEW OF JEWISH HISTORY

Throughout this book I have made reference to people and events in Jewish history. Yet for many of us, Jewish history is a bit of a "blur"; we're not quite sure what happened when, or who came before whom. In "Suggestions for Further Exploration," we've provided a variety of sources on Jewish history so you can get a much fuller picture.

As you read through the following, remember that especially in the earliest periods, dates are very approximate and hotly disputed in some circles. In this chart, facts and trends are stated as if there's absolutely no controversy about them, but that's obviously not the case. Historians are still deciphering events in every single phase of Jewish history; this is a bird's-eye view that, by definition, takes a rather "popular" approach, leaving the more technical debates and issues to the books that can best describe them.

This road map should be a helpful place to get started as you learn how we got from Abraham to where we are today.

THE BIBLICAL PERIOD
(2000–538 B.C.E.)

Approximate Dates	What Happened and Where	Important Personalities, Major Trends and Ideas
2000–1500 B.C.E.	The period of the patriarchs and matriarchs, in which tradition asserts that Abraham was told by God to leave Mesopotamia and to make his way to what we now what we now call Israel. This nomadic family establishes	Abraham, Isaac, Jacob, Sarah, Rebecca, Rachel, and the other figures we read about in the book of Genesis. This is the story of a family that will eventually become a nation during and after

THE BIBLICAL PERIOD (*Cont.*)
(2000–538 B.C.E.)

Approximate Dates	What Happened and Where	Important Personalities, Major Trends and Ideas
2000–1500 B.C.E. (*Cont.*)	itself in this new land and eventually, migrates to Egypt, where they are enslaved.	the period of slavery in Egypt.
1280 B.C.E.	Exodus from Egypt. After the Ten Plagues, Pharaoh finally agrees to allow the Israelites to leave. He changes his mind, of course, and is drowned as the sea that had split to let the Israelites cross closes in on him and his army. The Israelites then wander in the desert for forty years on their way to the Promised Land. On the way, they stop at Mount Sinai, where they are given the Ten Commandments and the other laws that become the basis of Jewish tradition.	This is the material covered in the beginning of the book of Exodus, in which Moses is the primary Jewish figure. If the book of Genesis told the story of a family, the "Israelites" now constitute a "people," numbering many hundreds of thousands, perhaps even a few million.
1250–1200 B.C.E.	When they finally reach the Promised Land, what we would call the east bank of the Jordan River today, the Israelites begin the process of conquering the Land of Canaan, and of dividing it up into parcels for each tribe.	Joshua is the key figure in the conquest. After the conquest, the Israelites are ruled by a series of leaders called "Judges," among whom are Deborah and Samuel. This is also the occasion of the famous conquest of Jericho.
1020–928 B.C.E.	The Israelites decide that they need to be ruled by a king. The period of the Judges thus comes to an end and the era of the	The three monarchs who rule over the entire people are Saul, then David, and finally, Solomon. The First

THE BIBLICAL PERIOD (*Cont.*)
(2000–538 B.C.E.)

Approximate Dates	What Happened and Where	Important Personalities, Major Trends and Ideas
1020–928 B.C.E. (*Cont.*)	monarchy begins. Especially later in this period, the borders of the "Jewish" empire expand dramatically, and during certain periods, the kingdom possesses great military power and enjoys great financial wealth.	Temple is built, and the religious center of of Israelite religion is clearly established in Jerusalem. Priests are the religious functionaries; there are no rabbis yet. The main form of religious worship is sacrifice.
928–586 B.C.E.	After Solomon's reign, the kingdom splits into two: a northern kingdom called "Israel," and a southern kingdom called "Judea." The causes of the split were complex but certainly included differences of religious culture between the regions, as well as financial and political considerations. The northern kingdom falls in approximately 720 B.C.E., while Judea falls in 586 B.C.E., at which time the First Temple is destroyed.	The first king of the north is Jeroboam, and the first king of the south is Rehoboam. During this period the prophets also become an important part of Israelite culture; people like Isaiah, Jeremiah, Hosea, and Micha offer their social critiques of the establishment during this time. These prophetic critiques become the basis of much of Judaism's tradition of "social responsibility."
586–538 B.C.E.	During this period, the elite and much of the Judean population is exiled to Babylonia. Eventually, Cyrus allows the Jews to return to Judea. The second Temple is eventually built, beginning what is called the "Second Commonwealth." As these are the latest events described in the Hebrew Bible, this concludes the biblical period.	This is the first major period of exile and the beginning of a Diaspora community. From this point on, there is never a point in Jewish history in which there is not a major center of Jews outside the Land of Israel. The Bible credits Ezra and Nehemiah with the leadership of the Jewish during this period.

THE SECOND TEMPLE PERIOD
538 B.C.E.–72 C.E.

Approximate Dates	What Happened and Where	Important Personalities, Major Trends and Ideas
445–332 B.C.E.	After the construction of the second Temple, the Israelites restore a way of life somewhat comparable to what they had prior to the first destruction.	Even though life seems to return to normal, the seeds of change have already been sown; the people now recognize that as long as their religious life depends on a place and a building, when that building can be destroyed and they can can be removed from that place, they are vulnerable.
332–167 B.C.E.	Alexander the Great conquers the area and the Jews now live under the Greeks. Though benevolent at first, Greek rule becomes harsh and repressive, culminating with Antiochus IV, who desecrates the Temple and tries to outlaw the practice of Judaism in Judea.	Greek culture becomes the pervasive culture of that part of the world, and as is true today, Jews have to wrestle with what should be the appropriate boundaries between their own culture and the culture that surrounds them.
167–164 B.C.E.	The Maccabean rebellion, which we celebrate during Hanukkah, initially defeats the Greeks and recaptures the Temple. Judah Maccabee and his fellow Hasmoneans rededicate the Temple (Hanukkah actually means "dedication"). While the uprising is initially successful, the Maccabees are eventually defeated by the Greeks, and do not achieve their goal of completely ridding the country of Greek influence and domination.	The rebellion had political and religious elements, to be sure, but it was also a cultural battle. Jews disagreed strongly among themselves over how open they should be to foreign cultures, a debate that continues to this day. Mattathias and Judah Maccabee are the most famous leaders of the uprising. They become the symbols of bravery and of Jewish resistance to foreign oppression.

THE SECOND TEMPLE PERIOD (*Cont.*)
538 B.C.E.–72 C.E.

Approximate Dates	What Happened and Where	Important Personalities, Major Trends and Ideas
164–40 B.C.E.	The Hasmonean dynasty, led by a variety of Jewish figures, is closely controlled by the Greeks and then the Romans. Eventually, after a very complex series of events, Judea loses independence and become completely subservient to Rome.	With time, the Hasmonean dynasty becomes corrupt and infused with the very Greek values they had tried to fight. Infighting becomes a major issue, as does collusion with "the enemy."
40 B.C.E.–72 C.E.	This is the period of post–Hasmonean Roman rule over the Jews. The period ends with the revolt of the Jews against the Romans in 67 C.E. The Romans are ultimately victorious. They destroy the Temple in 70 C.E., and Masada, the last stronghold of the Jews, falls in 72 C.E. with the mass suicide of its defenders.	The destruction of the second Temple brings with it the end of sacrifice as a possibility, and the need for a new form of religious practice. In truth, alternate forms of religious expression had already begun to develop. Even before the Jewish life was filled with sectarian disagreements. Groups disagreed about theological issues such as the afterlife and human authority to make new laws, and took very different positions as to how Roman power and influence ought to be combated.

THE RABBINIC PERIOD
72–600 C.E.

Approximate Dates	What Happened and Where	Important Personalities, Major Trends and Ideas
±200 B.C.E.–72 C.E.	Even while the second Temple stood, the early seeds of what later became known as rabbinic Judaism were already sown. Legal disputes later recorded in the Mishnah took place during this period.	Some of the best-known "sages" of this period were Hillel and Shammai. Shammai, incidentally, appears to have died in the same year as Jesus.
72–220 C.E.	This is what is commonly called the period of the Mishnah. Though its beginning date is difficult to determine, the closing date is clear, because that is the year in which Rabbi Judah the Patriarch organizes many generations of oral tradition into a fixed form that becomes known as the Mishnah.	By this point, religious leadership of the community is no longer in the hands of the priests, as there is no Temple. The power of the rabbis begins to be more dominant. This is the period of Rabbi Akiva and many of the other sages mentioned, for example, in the Passover Haggadah. The development of the Mishnah is a critical development because it establishes a tradition that can now be studied anywhere, making the creation of long-term Diaspora communities more likely.
220–±500 C.E. and meanwhile . . .	In the land of Israel, the "Palestinian" Talmud develops. Jewish institutions of religious leadership and political quasi-independence continue, though with less independence as time goes on.	The Palestinian Talmud is a less developed work than the Babylonian Talmud, which developed over a longer period of time, and which is still the fundamental text studied in the yeshivah world of traditional Judaism.

THE RABBINIC PERIOD (*Cont.*)
72–600 C.E.

Approximate Dates	What Happened and Where	Important Personalities, Major Trends and Ideas
220–±600 C.E.	A major Jewish community develops in Babylonia, and two major academies of study are established. Babylonia becomes the major center for Jewish scholarship, and perhaps for the first time, "center stage" of Jewish life shifts away from Judea to a Diaspora community.	Rabbis are now the undisputed religious leaders of the community, while others serve as the political leaders. Rav and Samuel are the first religious leaders of this community. With time, a large group of sages develops, and the Judaism that we now commonly think of as "normative" and natural becomes more fully and developed.
meanwhile . . .		
±500 B.C.E.–600 C.E.	A Jewish community is developing in Arabia and parts of Africa as well. Some of the earliest members of these communities may have been those who fled south when Babylonia attacked from the north in 586 B.C.E.; some people believe that the Ethiopian Jewish community had its origins here. Later, and throughout this period, a Jewish culture continues to develop in North Africa, and will eventually become the Sephardic tradition.	The Sephardic tradition is commonly overlooked as we gaze at Jewish history. Because most of Jewish history is told by academics who are of European (or Ashkenazic descent, and because many of the most visible events happened in happened in Europe, we tend to forget that a vital and vibrant culture of Sephardic Jews developed throughout that period. This myopia continues to bedevil Israeli attempts to create harmony in a society composed of both groups.

THE MEDIEVAL PERIOD—HIGHLIGHTS
600–1500 C.E.

With the beginning of the medieval period, Jewish history becomes even more difficult to track in a tabular format than it was prior to this. Jewish life begins to thrive in a large number of areas—from "Israel," to northern Africa, to Spain, and then eastward into central and eastern Europe, and still, back in Babylonia, too. All we can do for this period is to point to some of the highlights of the period, knowing full well that this is an extremely cursory treatment.

Approximate Dates	What Happened and Where	Important Personalities, Major Trends and Ideas
638	Jerusalem is conquered by the Arabs.	Islam had been developing for about fifteen years at this point, and had quickly grown and overtaken this part of the world. Jewish-Muslim relations were occasionally good, often difficult, a tension that continues to this day.
589–1038	The Geonic period is the first major post-Talmudic period in Jewish scholarship and religious life. The Geonim were the leaders of the Babylonian Jewish community during this time.	The period ends with the death of one of the greatest scholars of this period, Rav Hai Gaon. The Geonim continued the learning of the Talmudic period, and laid the foundations for much of the scholarship that would later follow. The earliest Jewish legal codes are produced during this period.
±1000	Christian Europe begins to take on the anti-Jewish sentiments that many Jews commonly associate with Europe. Jews are expelled	The Crusaders take over not only much of central Europe but "Israel" as well. Thus, in addition to difficulties with the

THE MEDIEVAL PERIOD—
HIGHLIGHTS *(Cont.)*
600–1500 C.E.

Approximate Dates	What Happened and Where	Important Personalities, Major Trends and Ideas
±1000 *(Cont.)*	from Mainz in 1012, and shortly thereafter the Crusader period starts.	Muslims in North Africa and the Arabian peninsula, Jews now also confront an antagonistic Christian world.
±1050	Jews under Muslim sovereignty suffer greatly but also produce phenomenally important works of legal scholarship, poetry, and philosophy. This is one of the richest intellectual periods of Jewish life, despite the often harsh outward circumstances.	The most famous personality of this group is Maimonides, who died in 1204. One of the greatest Jewish minds ever, Maimonides wrote *The Guide for the Perplexed*, a very important philosophic work, as well as the Mishnah Torah, a legal code that remains critically important.
±1000	Jewish life in France thrives—again despite often difficult circumstances. Much of the continuation of Talmudic study takes place here.	Rashi, the famous commentator on the Bible and the Talmud, lives during this period. He dies in 1105.
1492	The Inquisition and the expulsion from Spain. Even as Columbus was discovering America, Spanish Jewry was being forced to choose between conversion and execution.	This period gave rise to the phenomenon of the Marranos, those Jews who claimed to have converted to Christianity but who tried to preserve Jewish life in the secrecy of their own homes.

THE EARLY MODERN PERIOD—
A BRIEF SUMMARY
1500–1800

By this point, Jews have spread to virtually every corner of the Western world.

A Sephardic world continues to exist in **Spain** and **Portugal,** though the Inquisition also spreads to Portugal. By the end of the 1500s, the heyday of the Jewish communities of Spain and Portugal has basically passed.

Moving to the east, Rashi's community in **France** continues to be a major center of scholarship and even commerce, though Christian restrictions on Jewish participation in the guilds and much of the agricultural world forces some Jews into moneylending, a profession for which they will later be assailed.

Farther east still, Jewish communities exist in **Italy,** central Europe (**Germany** and **Austria**) as well as eastern Europe (**Poland** and **Lithuania**). For the most part, Jewish communities face continuous mistreatment from the surrounding culture. European Christianity has become profoundly anti-Semitic; some scholars argue that the anti-Semitism that saw expression in the Crusades and the Inquisition finally exploded with its ultimate venom in the Shoah under Hitler. Jews are not particularly involved in the arts; with few exceptions, the culture in which they lived made that impossible. But while the "list of events" of this period looks like a long series of massacres, expulsions, and restrictive edicts, the intellectual world of the Jews continued to thrive. The fifteenth, sixteenth, and seventeenth centuries were periods of tremendous intellectual growth for the Jews, in the best sense of that term.

In the late 1500s, Kabbalah begins to develop more rapidly in Safed, in the north of **Palestine**. Judaism had long had a mystical tradition as one of its many streams, but the late sixteenth century saw a great flowering of this tradition. Jewish life in **Palestine** in general, however, was not flourishing at this point. There was a noticeable Jewish population living there, but it was small and continuously vulnerable.

In 1654, Jews begin to arrive in New Amsterdam, later called New York, and the Jewish communities of North America have their earliest beginnings.

THE BEGINNING OF NATIONALISM AND THE EMANCIPATION

1800–1930

Though it's always dangerous to say that there was such a thing as *the* major trend of a period, it is probably the case that after the difficult but still productive period of the Middle Ages and the early modern period, the single most important development that would affect the Jews was the rise of nationalism. Coming first to western Europe, the emancipation of the Jews that came along with nationalism was wrapped in controversy. French and German citizens disagreed bitterly about how to handle and to treat their Jewish populations.

Jews, too, wondered about this new era. Nationalism was accompanied by the political emancipation of the Jews (in 1848 in Germany, for example), which understandably undermined the authority of the traditional rabbinate. While many celebrated their emancipation for obvious reasons, others saw cause for concern. They recognized that access to society at large would mean that the rabbinate would lose its hold over Jewish individuals and families. If the inaccessibility of secular life had previously meant that Jews would have to accommodate themselves to the rulings and standards of religious authority, the emancipation spelled the end of that authority's power.

Along with the end of rabbinic hegemony came the flowering of new forms of religious expression. Reform Judaism, now one of the two largest movements in American Jewish life, had its beginnings in Germany during this period. Positive-historical Judaism, which later became the Conservative Judaism of the United States, also traces its intellectual roots to this period. It would be incorrect to assert that Judaism had been monolithic since what we now call rabbinic Judaism triumphed in the period of the Mishnah and Talmud. Judaism has never been monolithic. Nonetheless, it *is* fair to say that the emancipation of the Jews (along with many of the philosophic and intellectual currents of the times) brought about forms of Jewish religious expression that would probably have seemed unthinkable only a few decades earlier.

Finally, Jews began to develop their own form of nationalism, which they called Zionism. Though the religious Jewish world had expressed a desire to return to Zion ever since the fall of the second Temple, it was Theodore Herzl, the founder of the political Zionist movement, who actually began the process that would lead to the creation of the State of Israel.

THE SHOAH
1933–1945

The tremendous potential that many Jews believe now existed in Europe came to a sudden and devastating end with the rise of Nazism and the destruction of European Jewry. Jews commonly say that the Nazis killed one-third of the world's Jews. While that is technically true, it misses the larger point that over 90 percent of European Jewry was decimated. An entire Jewish world, one that had taken virtually a thousand years to build, was destroyed almost overnight while the world either colluded with the Nazis or simply watched. The devastation of that period still casts a dark shadow over Jewish life. In Europe, life has scarcely begun to return to Jewish communities in Eastern Europe. American Jewry, traumatized by what it saw happen in Europe (and its conclusions about what being "different" can cause), but also conflicted by its own apathy and inaction during the Shoah, exhibits a tendency toward "blending in" that makes passionate Jewish life difficult. Israel, surrounded by hostile nations, is also composed of many people who barely escaped the Nazi gas chambers, creating a very complex emotional climate. While some of the Jews lost in the 1940s may have begun to be replaced, the Jewish world that was destroyed will never return.

THE STATE OF ISRAEL

As we've discussed in this book, the creation of the modern State of Israel is of such vast significance that it's difficult to appreciate what it really represents. Israel marks a return to the sovereignty that was lost with the fall of Jerusalem in 70 C.E., and brings with it the possibility of escaping the anti-Semitism that has characterized much of the world since then. Perhaps even more important, Israel is now a stage on which Judaism can create for itself its own vision of a just and caring society, a society in which Judaism doesn't simply exist but rather defines the values of the society.

How well is Israel doing? Not perfectly, to be sure, but then again, how well was the United States doing after *it* had existed for fifty years? Created in the shadow of the Shoah, at war for most of its history, struggling to absorb millions of immigrants, Israel can still be said to be a modern miracle. It may well be that the degree to which its potential will be realized depends on Jews around the globe and the ways in which they will join this enterprise.

THE FUTURE

What is the future of the Jewish people? In certain ways, things have never been better. American Jewry enjoys a level of prosperity and security that is probably unprecedented in all of Jewish life. Jews are at the center of politics, the arts, the humanities, science, and more. Tolerance isn't even the issue anymore; Jews are accepted in ways that were unthinkable only decades ago.

The State of Israel is the realization of a two-thousand-year dream. It has been recognized by countries throughout the world, has a thriving economy, has absorbed millions of immigrants, and will in only a few short years be the dwelling place of more than half of the world's Jews.

But at the same time, important questions remain. American Jewry is assimilating at rates that many consider to be profoundly frightening. American Judaism is both the most creative and the least successful at holding on to its population. Israel, at the same time, faces the crisis of rampant secularization and hostility to religion on the part of large segments of its culture, and the challenge of conducting affairs of state with decency and morality. The economic gap in Israel is one of the world's widest, and deep social divides between religious and secular, Ashekanzi and Sephardi, hawks and doves, predominate.

Could it be the "best of times and the worst of times"? However one characterizes it, there is no doubt that our children's generation will see profound shifts in the nature of Judaism across the globe. Our task, if we're willing to undertake it, is to prepare them to take active, passionate, and thoughtful roles in the tumultuous changes that undoubtedly lie ahead.

GLOSSARY OF TERMS
AND NAMES

The following is a list of names and terms that appear throughout this book. The definitions that follow are popular ones, designed only to assist the reader in understanding the book and the subjects it discusses. In the text of the book, these terms are noted by being in **bold** type. Similarly, if a definition here refers to another term that is explained in this Glossary, that term is also in **bold** type.

AARON: Moses' older brother and the first Jewish priest. He helped Moses in his leadership of the Jewish people after their Exodus from Egypt and through the desert.

ABRAHAM: The first of the three Jewish patriarchs and, by tradition, the first monotheist and the founder of the Jewish religion. Historians date the period of Abraham at approximately 2000–1500 B.C.E., or about 3,500 to 4,000 years ago.

ADAR/ADAR II: The sixth month of the Hebrew calendar, Adar generally falls in February or March. When the Hebrew calendar requires a leap year, a second month of Adar—Adar II, or Adar Bet—is added after the first. The holidays celebrated in Adar are the Fast of Esther and **Purim**.

AGUNAH: The Hebrew word that means literally "anchored." It commonly refers to women whose husbands will not grant them a *get,* a traditional Jewish divorce, which thus prevents these women from remarrying.

ALIYAH: A Hebrew word that means "going up"; it refers both to the ceremony of being called "up" to the Torah to recite blessings before and after a portion is read, as well as to moving to the Land of Israel.

AMALEK: An ancient people mentioned in the **Torah**. Amalek attacked the Israelites on their journey from Egypt to the Promised Land. The Torah commands that the Jews blot out the memory of Amalek.

AMIDAH: One of the two central elements of the Jewish prayer service. The weekday version (as opposed to the versions for Shabbat and holidays) is also known as the Shemoneh Esrei, or the "Eighteen Benedictions." In much of rabbinic literature, the Amidah is also called Ha-Tefillah, or "The Prayer."

ANNO DOMINI: Latin for "the Year of Our Lord"; used in Western culture to count the year in terms of the time elapsed since the birth of Jesus. Jews typically do not use this phrase.

ARAMAIC: A language that uses the same alphabet as Hebrew, and some of the same roots, but that is nonetheless a different language. The two Talmuds are written in Aramaic, as are some portions of the Bible and the *siddur.* Aramaic was the spoken language of the Jews of Babylonia, a community that grew rapidly after the destruction of the second Temple.

ASHER YATZAR: The name of a blessing in the *siddur* that thanks God for creating the body with openings and valves that allow it to function properly. Traditional Jews also recite this prayer after using the bathroom.

ASSERET YEMEI TESHUVAH: A Hebrew phrase meaning the "Ten Days of Repentance," referring to the period that begins with **Rosh Ha-Shannah** and concludes with **Yom Kippur** ten days later. It is a period during which Jews are encouraged to repent their sins of the past year.

AV: The eleventh month of the Jewish calendar; it usually falls in July or August. The fast of the **Ninth of Av** commemorates the destruction of the two Temples and, according to tradition, a variety of other calamities as well.

AVODAH: A Hebrew word that means "worship" or "sacrificial cult," it often refers to the service on **Yom Kippur** afternoon by that name, a service that "relives" the details of the sacrificial rite performed by the High Priest on the ancient Temple on Yom Kippur.

BA-MEH MADLIKIN: The name of the second chapter of the Tractate Shabbat in the **Mishnah;** it deals with the laws on the lighting of the Shabbat candles, portions of which are recited in the Friday evening service.

BAR MITZVAH: Literally "subject to the commandments," this phrase refers to the point at which a boy becomes an adult and, according to tradition, is obligated to fulfill the requirements of Jewish law. For boys, the age is thirteen. The phrase also refers to the ceremony at which the child is formally called up to the **Torah** for the first time.

BAT MITZVAH: Literally "subject to the commandments," this phrase refers to the point at which a girl becomes an adult and, according to tradition, is obligated to fulfill the requirements of Jewish law. For girls, the age is twelve, but some communities have changed it to thirteen. The phrase also refers to the ceremony used to celebrate the girl's reaching Jewish adulthood. The content of the ceremony varies from community to community.

BEKHOR: The Hebrew term meaning "firstborn male."

BERIT BAT: The "covenant of a daughter"—the phrase actually refers to the modern naming ceremonies being created for girls. The ceremony is also sometimes called a **Simchat Bat.**

BIRKAT ERUSIN: A Hebrew phrase that means "the marriage blessing"; it is a reference to the second blessing of the wedding ceremony. The first blessing is the one over wine.

BOOK OF ESTHER: See **Megillah.**

BRIS: The colloquial term for the Hebrew phrase *berit milah,* or ritual circumcision, typically performed on the eighth day of a Jewish boy's life as the fulfillment of the explicit command in the Torah that all Jewish boys be circumcised on the eighth day.

CHAD GADYA: An Aramaic phrase that means "one kid goat," it is the name of a song that appears at the conclusion of the **Haggadah.** In parable form, the song tells the story of the Jewish people who are oppressed by various people but finally redeemed by God.

CHALLAH: A braided egg bread eaten as part of the Sabbath and festival meals.

CHAMETZ: A Hebrew term that means "leavened products." It refers to such items as breads, cakes, and pasta made out of certain grains that have come into contact with water and that tradition therefore prohibits on **Passover.**

CHANUKKIAH/CHANUKKIYOT: The Hebrew word for the candelabrum that is lit on the holiday of **Hannukah.** *Chanukkiah* is the singular; *chanukkiyot* is the plural.

CHAROSET: A food mixture of apples, walnuts, cinnamon, and other fruits or nuts that is used during the **seder** to represent the mortar used by the Hebrew slaves when they were enslaved in Egypt.

CHASSAN'S TISCH: A Yiddish phrase that means, literally, "the groom's table." It refers to the preliminary stage of the wedding ceremony in which the groom's (male) friends constantly interrupt a "speech" he is trying to give by drinking and singing songs.

CHAVURAH: From the Hebrew word "chaver," or "friend," this word is commonly used to refer to a group of people who meet on a regular basis to study and to celebrate life cycle events or Jewish holidays. Today, many such groups are organized by synagogues.

CHEDER: The Hebrew word for "room." It usually refers to the small Hebrew schools (often consisting of one room) where small children would get their first formal Jewish education.

CHESHVAN: The second month of the Jewish calendar; usually falls in October. There are no holidays celebrated during this month.

CHOL HA-MO'ED: The Hebrew name for the intermediate days of a holiday (**Sukkot** and **Passover**) during which work is permitted.

CHUPPAH: Hebrew for canopy, almost always referring to the canopy under which the bride and groom stand during their wedding ceremony.

DAVEN/DAVENNING: A Yiddish word meaning "prayer" or "to pray."

DAYS OF AWE: See **High Holidays.**

DEBORAH: A prophetess and judge in Israel a century or so after the Israelite conquest of Canaan.

DEUTERONOMY: The English name of the Hebrew book Devarim. This is the fifth and last of the Five Books of Moses. Most of the book is devoted to Moses' farewell address to the Israelites before his death, an address that in many ways summarizes much of what is in the earlier books of the **Torah.**

DIASPORA: The term used for Jewish communities outside the Land of Israel.

DREIDEL: Similar to a spinning top with four sides, the *dreidel* is used for a game played during **Hanukkah.** On each side of the *dreidel* is a Hebrew letter: *nun, gimmel, heh, shin,* which stand for the phrase *nes gadol hayah sham*—"a great miracle happened there." In Israel the *dreidel* is modified so that the letters stand for the phrase "a great miracle happened here."

EICHAH: The Hebrew name for the book of Lamentations, a poetic description of the horrors of the destruction of Jerusalem in 586 B.C.E. that is recited in the synagogue on **Tisha B'Av.**

EISHET CHAYIL: "A Woman of Valor"—this is a poem taken from the thirty-first chapter of the biblical Book of Proverbs. In traditional homes, it is recited by husbands to their wives at the beginning of the Friday evening Shabbat meal.

ELUL: The twelfth month of the Jewish calendar; it usually falls sometime in August or September. The month before the holiday of Rosh Ha-Shannah, it is a month characterized by the recitation of penitential prayers and the blowing of the **shofar** in the morning.

ERUSIN: A Jewish status roughly equivalent to something between our notions of "engagement" and "marriage" that used to last for a year prior to the actual completion of the marriage. Today, the process of *erusin* and *nissu'in* (the second half of the process) are combined into one wedding ceremony.

ESTHER: The main female hero of the Book of Esther. Esther won a "beauty contest" run by the king and became one of his many wives. She later used her position to intercede on behalf of the Jews when it became clear that Haman was about to destroy her people.

ETHICAL WILL: A document written as a "last testament" for one's children or other loved ones, but instead of dividing up the property in the estate, this document articulates the values and ideals that the person feels are most important, and that she or he would like to pass on to others. There is no special format for this document; it is basically a letter that tells those who read it what values were critical to the person's sense of who he or she wanted to be.

ETHICS OF THE FATHERS: Pirkei Avot in Hebrew, this is a tract of the **Mishnah** that contains the sayings and religious-ethical teachings of the rabbis from the last centuries before the common era and the first few centuries of the common era.

ETROG: The Hebrew word for "citron," a lemonlike fruit that is one of the **Four Species** used with the *lulav* on the holiday of **Sukkot.**

EXODUS: The English name of the Hebrew book Shemot. This is the second of the Five Books of Moses, which traces the history of the Jews from their enslavement in Egypt, through the Exodus, to Mount Sinai, and into the desert.

FOUR SPECIES: The four agricultural products that are combined to make a complete *lulav* and *etrog* set for use on **Sukkot.** They are the palm branch, willow, myrtle, and citron.

GENESIS: The English name of the Hebrew book Bereshit. This is the first of the Five Books of Moses, composed primarily of stories of the creation of the world, the flood, and the history of the patriarchs and matriarchs.

GET: The classic Hebrew word that refers to the document of Jewish divorce.

HAFTARAH: A reading from one of the prophetic books of the Bible, recited on Shabbat in the synagogue after the completion of the reading of the weekly portion from the **Torah.** Usually, though not always, the selection from the prophets bears some thematic connection to the Torah portion read directly before it.

HAGGADAH: The text that Jewish people recite during the **Passover** seder. The Haggadah is essentially a retelling of the story of the Exodus from Egypt.

HALAKHAH: A Hebrew term that is used to refer to "Jewish law" but is actually derived from the root that means "to go." Thus, *halakhah* essentially means "the way we are to go."

HAMAN: The villain of the **Purim** story, recounted in the biblical Book of Esther. According to the tradition, Haman plotted to have the Jewish community of Persia murdered, but instead, he and his ten sons were hanged from the very gallows he'd built for the Jews.

HAMENTASCHEN: From the Yiddish words that mean "Haman's pockets," these are small cakes of baked dough filled with poppyseed, apricot, prune, or other fillings that are eaten during the holiday of **Purim.**

HA-NEROT HALALU: "These Candles," a liturgical paragraph recited immediately after the lighting of the **Hanukkah** candles. The paragraph reminds us that the candles are holy, to be used only for proclaiming the miracle of Hanukkah, and not for any other profane purpose.

HANUKKAH: An eight-day winter holiday celebrating the rededication of the Temple in Jerusalem after it was recaptured from the Greeks by the Hasmoneans. Hanukkah falls on the twenty-fifth day of the Hebrew

month of **Kislev,** usually sometime in December. Its most well known ritual is the lighting of the *hanukkiah,* commonly (though a bit incorrectly)
called the "menorah."

HANUKKAH *GELT:* Literally "Hanukkah money." In traditional Jewish
communities, Jewish children would receive a small number of coins on
Hanukkah with which they could "gamble" while playing *dreidel* games.

HASMONEAN: Refers to the family of Jewish revolutionaries who battled
the Greeks during the second century B.C.E., regaining control of the
Temple in Jerusalem from Greek rulers in 167 B.C.E. The holiday of
Hanukkah celebrates their victory and the miracle of the oil that burned
much longer than expected.

HASIDIM/HASIDIC: A term that means belonging to or stemming from
the Jewish community that had its roots in the pietistic movement started
by Israel Ba'al Shem Tov (1699–1761). Today there are many different
branches of Hasidim, most with their own charismatic leaders and their
own religious emphases.

HAVDALAH: A Hebrew word meaning "separation." It usually refers to the
ceremony that concludes **Shabbat.** The ceremony uses wine, spices (to
allow the scent of Shabbat to linger), and fire (symbolizing the return to
a period of time in which the use of fire is permitted).

HECHSHER: Based on the Hebrew word "kosher," it is a term that usually
refers to some symbol or other printed indication that a food item was
prepared under rabbinic supervision and is kosher.

HIGH HOLY DAYS: A translation of the Hebrew phrase *yamim nora'im,* it
refers to the holidays of **Rosh Ha-Shannah** and **Yom Kippur.**

HILLEL: A sage of the period of the **Mishnah,** he lived from the second half
of the first century B.C.E. until the first quarter of the first century C.E.
Hillel was perhaps the greatest scholar of his time, known not only for his
knowledge but for his humility as well.

HOSHANNAH RABBAH: The last day of **Chol Ha-Mo'ed** during the
holiday of **Sukkot.** According to tradition, this is the day on which the
Gates of Repentance close at the conclusion of the High Holiday season.

INQUISITION: A campaign in Spain, which began in 1481 and reached its
peak in 1492, in which Jews and other non-Christian believers were forced
to choose between coerced conversion or emigration from Spain.

ISAAC: The second of the three Jewish patriarchs, the son of **Abraham.**

IYYAR: The eighth month of the Jewish calendar; it usually falls sometime
in April or May. The eighteenth of Iyyar is **Lag Ba-Omer,** a holiday that
coincides with the thirty-third day of the counting of the Omer.

JACOB: The grandson of **Abraham,** the son of **Isaac** and the third of the
three patriarchs. Jacob received the name "Israel" after he wrestled with
the angel of God. Jacob's twelve sons became the twelve tribes of Israel.

JOSEPH: The eleventh of Jacob's twelve sons, he was his father's favorite and was sold by his brothers into Egyptian slavery. Later, he rose to become the second-highest official in the Egyptian government and was reunited with his family when they came to Egypt due to famine in their native land.

KABBALAH: A term that refers to one of Judaism's mystical traditions.

KABBALISTS: Jews who are part of communities that practice **Kabbalah,** a form of Jewish mysticism.

KADDISH: An Aramaic prayer that appears in several different forms in the Jewish liturgy. Although the prayer is used for a variety of purposes, the most well known is the "mourner's Kaddish," recited by family members both at the funeral and then for a specified period of mourning thereafter.

KASHRUT: A Hebrew term that refers to the body of Jewish dietary laws.

KERIYAH: The Hebrew word that means "tearing." It refers to the custom of tearing one's garment upon learning of the death of a relative (sibling, parent, child, or spouse). Today some people cut a black ribbon at the time of the funeral instead of actually rending their clothing.

KETUBBAH: The traditional Jewish marriage document. It guarantees women, among other things, a financial settlement in case of divorce. In the ancient Near East, this was a radical change from the typical treatment of women.

KIDDUSH: A Hebrew word meaning "sanctification." It generally refers to a prayer recited on Friday evenings and Saturday mornings that sanctifies the Sabbath day. It is also recited on festivals, and is usually recited over a goblet of wine.

KING DAVID: Considered the most important king of Israel, David established Jerusalem as the capital of the Jewish people. Tradition claims that he was also the author of the biblical Book of Psalms.

KIPPAH/KIPPOT: The Hebrew term for the skullcap worn by Jewish men (and, in a few communities, some women) to cover their heads as a sign of humility before God. Some Jews wear this head covering at all times, while others wear it only when eating or when in the synagogue. In some liberal communities, the *kippah* is no longer worn. *Kippah* is the singular, *kippot* the plural.

KISLEV: The third month of the Jewish calendar, corresponding to November or December. The twenty-fifth of Kislev marks the beginning of the eight-day winter festival of **Hanukkah.**

KITTEL: A white kimono-like robe traditionally worn by Jewish men on Yom Kippur and their wedding day. The white of the robe symbolizes purity, and the style of the garment is meant to remind us of the burial shrouds in which we will one day be placed.

KLEZMER: A gypsylike form of Jewish music that some people believe began in the mid-1600s. Typically played with a violin, clarinet, and other instruments, klezmer has recently come back into great popularity.

KOHEN: A Jewish man descended from the "priestly" chain who could theoretically trace his lineage back to the biblical Aaron. The role of the Kohen today is mostly honorific; he receives the first *aliyah* in many traditional synagogues, and is the person from whom the parents of a baby son "redeem" their son (see **Pidyon Ha-Ben**). Aside from Kohen, the other two possible categories for Jewish males (women are not included in these categories) are Levite and Israelite.

LAG BA-OMER: The thirty-third day of the **Omer,** the day on which many of the prohibitions of the Omer (the prohibitions on cutting hair, the ban on marriages, etc.) are lifted in many traditional communities.

LAMENTATIONS: See Eichah.

LATKES: Pancakes made of potatoes and onions and fried in oil; eaten during **Hanukkah.**

LEAH: The fourth of the matriarchs, one of the wives of **Jacob.**

LEVI: Descendants of the tribe of Levi, one of the twelve tribes of ancient Israel.

LEVITICUS: The English name of the Hebrew book Va-Yikra. This is the third of the Five Books of Moses, which is composed mainly of priestly regulations of sacrifice and other elements of priestly work.

LULAV: The palm branch used during the holiday of **Sukkot,** waved in six directions (east, south, west, north, up, down) to symbolize God's presence everywhere. Technically, the *lulav* is only one of the four species, the palm branch itself, but the term is often used to refer to the entire set of **Four Species.**

MA'ARIV: The Hebrew name for the evening service, one of the three services that traditional Jews recite daily.

MACCABEES: The Jewish "freedom fighters" who battled the Greek occupiers of ancient Judea during the second century B.C.E. Their successful battle for Jerusalem led to the rededication of the Temple and to the subsequent creation of the holiday of **Hannukah** to celebrate this event.

MACHZOR: The special prayer book used specifically on the **High Holidays.** Technically, the phrase also refers to the special prayer books available for **Sukkot, Passover,** and **Shavu'ot** as well, but the most common usage is for the High Holidays.

MA'OZ TZUR: "Rock of Ages," a song sung on **Hanukkah** after the lighting of the candles, summarizing the many victories of the Jews when their own destruction seemed inevitable. Today, many families sing only the first of the stanzas.

MASADA: A mountain fortress on the west side of the Dead Sea, atop which Jewish zealots fighting the Romans were besieged in 72 C.E. at the end of the revolt against Rome. Realizing that they had lost the war and faced either death or enslavement, all the inhabitants of the mountain committed suicide before the Romans overtook the mountain.

MASORTI JUDAISM: The Hebrew name for the Israeli counterpart to the Conservative movement. The Hebrew word *masorti* means "traditional."

MATANOT LA-EVYONIM: Hebrew phrase meaning "gifts to the poor." Taken from the Book of Esther, it now refers to the custom of giving to the poor on the day of **Purim.**

MATRIARCHS: Sarah, Rebecca, Rachel, and Leah—the four female personalities critical to the earliest stages of Jewish life. Sarah was married to **Abraham,** Rebecca to **Isaac,** and Rachel and Leah to Jacob.

MATZAH: The unleavened "bread" that Jews eat during the holiday of **Passover,** based on the tradition that when they fled Egypt, there was not enough time to wait for the bread to rise.

MECHITZAH: A Hebrew word that means "separator" or "separation," a divider between the men's and women's sections of Orthodox synagogues.

MEGILLAH: A Hebrew word meaning "scroll." Technically, there are five scrolls in the Hebrew Bible (Esther, Ruth, Lamentations, Ecclesiastes, and the Song of Songs), but when one says "the Megillah," one is referring to the Book of Esther, which is read in the synagogue on **Purim.**

MELAMED: Hebrew word for "teacher," usually of young children at their earliest stages of Jewish learning.

MENORAH: A Hebrew word for the seven-branched candelabrum that was found in the Temples in Jerusalem. In popular (but technically incorrect!) usage, the word is also used to refer to the candelabrum used on **Hannukah.**

MEZUZAH: A small ritual object that is affixed to the doorposts and contains sacred texts. The command to affix these to the doorpost is found in the **Torah** and recited as part of the **Shema.**

MIDIANITE: From the tribe of Midian, one of the nomadic tribes of the ancient Middle East. Midian was often at war with the Israelites, though Moses' father-in-law, Jethro, was also a priest of Midian.

MIDRASH: A Hebrew term that means "exploration" or "investigation." It generally refers to rabbinic narratives or homilies that explore scriptural sources for additional insight and meaning.

MIKVAH: The Hebrew term for a ritual bath. Typically, the *mikvah* is used by women before marriage and after their menstrual periods (before resuming sexual relations with their partners), and by men in some communities before the Sabbath and festivals.

MISHLO'ACH MANOT: A Hebrew phrase meaning "sending of food," taken from the Book of Esther. Today the phrase refers to the custom of giving gifts of a few food items to friends on the day of **Purim**.

MISHNAH: The earliest major document of rabbinic Judaism, it was compiled by Rabbi Judah the Patriarch in approximately 220 C.E.

MIZRACHI: A Hebrew word that means "eastern," it is often translated as "Oriental," referring to Jews from Arab countries such as Syria, Morocco, and Iraq.

MOABITE: A person who comes from the tribe of Moab. For much of Jewish history, the Moabites were enemies of the Jewish people, descendants of Lot's incestuous relationship with his eldest daughter. However, Ruth—one of the great female heroes of the Bible—was a Moabite.

MODEH ANI: The name of a prayer thanking God for restoring our souls to us in the morning, after we've slept all night. It appears at the beginning of many prayer books, and is traditionally the first phrase uttered upon waking in the morning.

MOHEL: A Hebrew word that refers to the person who performs a *berit milah,* or a ritual circumcision.

MORDECHAI: The main Jewish male character in the Book of Esther. Mordechai was Esther's uncle; it was he who encouraged her to become a member of the king's harem and later encouraged her to use her position of power to save the Jewish people.

MOSES: The leader of the Jewish people during their forty-year trek through the desert on their way from Egypt to the Promised Land. According to tradition, Moses received the Ten Commandments from God atop **Mount Sinai** and then taught them and the rest of the Torah to the Jewish people.

MOUNT SINAI: The mountain that tradition says was the place upon which the Jewish people received the Torah several months after they left Egypt.

MUSAF: A Hebrew word that means "additional," this is the name of the additional service recited on Sabbaths and Festivals, corresponding to the additional sacrifice that was offered on these days when the Temple in Jerusalem still stood.

NINTH OF AV: See **Tisha B'Av**.

NISSAN: The seventh month of the Jewish calendar; it usually falls sometime in March or April. The holiday of **Passover** begins on the fifteenth of this month and continues for eight days. **Yom Ha-Shoah**—Shoah Remembrance Day—is commemorated on the twenty-seventh of Nissan.

NISSU'IN: A Hebrew word that means "marriage"; it is also used to refer to the second half of the wedding ceremony.

NUMBERS: The English name of the Hebrew book Ba-Midbar. This is the fourth of the Five Books of Moses, which summarizes the experience of the Israelites in the desert on their way from Egypt to the Promised Land.

OMER: Literally, the first sheaf cut during the barley harvest. The ritual of the "counting of the Omer" takes place during the forty-nine days between **Passover** and the holiday of **Shavu'ot**.

PALESTINIAN TALMUD: One of the two Talmuds, this was the one completed in the Land of Israel in approximately the year 400 C.E. Less elaborate than the Babylonian **Talmud**, this is also the lesser studied of the two.

PASSOVER: The eight-day springtime festival in which Jews celebrate their redemption from Egyptian slavery. During the holiday, traditional Jews abstain from eating all leavened foods and products. The Hebrew name for the holiday is Pesach.

PATRIARCHS: Abraham, Isaac, and **Jacob**—the three "founding fathers" of Judaism.

PESACH: The Hebrew word for Passover; see **Passover**.

PETOR: A Hebrew word that means "release," often referring to the document that a couple receives after a Jewish divorce. This document indicates that the divorce was completed according to Jewish law and that each individual is therefore free to marry someone else.

PIDYON HA-BEN: The "redemption of the firstborn son" on the thirty-first day after his birth. The firstborn son is redeemed by his parents from service to the priests by making a ceremonial payment to a **Kohen**.

"PILGRIMAGE FESTIVALS": A term referring to the holidays of **Sukkot, Passover,** and **Shavu'ot**. They are called the "pilgrimage festivals" because it was at this times that ancient Israelites were called upon to make a pilgrimage to Jerusalem in order to offer sacrifices there.

PURIM: The festival that falls on the fourteenth or fifteenth of the Hebrew month of **Adar** and commemorates the victory and survival of the Jews of Persia during the time of **Mordechai** and **Esther**. It generally falls in February or March.

RACHEL: The third of the matriarchs, one of the wives of **Jacob**.

REBECCA: The second of the matriarchs, the wife of **Isaac**.

REFUSNIKS: The term used for Russian Jews who were refused permission to leave the Soviet Union. They often lived under very difficult circumstances from the time they applied to leave until they were finally granted exit visas.

ROSH CHODESH: The beginning of the Jewish month, tied to the lunar cycle. Rosh Chodesh is celebrated as either a one- or two-day holiday. When it is a one-day holiday, it coincides with the first day of the new

month. When celebrated for two days, it coincides with the last day of
the previous month and the first day of the new month.

ROSH HA-SHANNAH: The Jewish holiday that commemorates the
beginning of the Jewish New Year, celebrated on the first day of the
Hebrew month of Tishrei. Rosh Ha-Shannah typically falls in September
or very early October.

SARAH: The first of the matriarchs, the wife of Abraham.

SEDER/SEDARIM: The Hebrew word for "order" (seder is the singular,
sedarim the plural). It often refers to the meal and recitation of the
Haggadah on the first two nights of Passover. In Israel, only one seder is
conducted, on the first night of the holiday.

SE'UDAH MAFSEKET: A Hebrew phrase that literally means the "ending
meal" and refers to the last meal eaten before the Fast of Yom Kippur.

SEVENTEENTH OF TAMMUZ: See Shiva Asar Be-Tammuz.

SHABBAT: The Hebrew word for "Sabbath." The seventh day of the week,
a "day of rest," which begins at sundown on Friday evening and ends at
nightfall on Saturday night.

SHABBAT ZAKHOR: The "Shabbat of Remembrance," the Sabbath immediately prior to the holiday of Purim. On this day, Jews read a special section from the Torah about the tribe of Amalek, who attacked the Jews on
their way from Egypt to the Promised Land.

SHACHARIT: The Hebrew name for the morning service, one of the three
services that traditional Jews recite daily.

SHALOM ZACHAR: A ceremony that takes place on the first Friday night
of a Jewish boy's life, in which he is welcomed to the community with
song and discussions of Torah.

SHAMASH: The name of the "ninth" candle of the hanukkiah. Since tradition says that the Hanukkah candles must be used only for proclaiming the miracle and not for any practical purpose, we're not permitted to
use any of the eight for the purpose of lighting the other candles.
Therefore, this candle is added as a "servant" to the others.

SHANNAH TOVAH: A Hebrew phrase meaning a "good year"; it is the
greeting Jews exchange around the time of Rosh Ha-Shannah. Unlike
Western cultures, in which people wish each other a "happy" New Year,
the Jewish emphasis is on the "goodness" of the year.

SHAVU'OT: The Festival of Weeks—a holiday that falls seven weeks and one
day after Passover and celebrates the giving of the Torah at Mount Sinai.

SHEHECHEYANU: A blessing that thanks God for having allowed us to
reach a particular occasion or season of our lives. In English it reads,
"Praised are You, Lord our God, who has kept us alive, sustained us and
allowed us to reach this occasion."

SHEKEL: The currency of the modern Israeli state, as well as name of a currency that was used in biblical times.

SHELOSHIM: A Hebrew word that means "thirty." It often refers to the thirty-day period of mourning for a relative (sibling, parent, child, or spouse) that begins on the day of the burial. Special customs and restrictions that traditional Jews observe during this period are lifted after the thirtieth day.

SHEMA: A Hebrew word that means "listen," it is also the name of a central element of Jewish liturgy, portions of which are included in the *mezuzah* attached to doorposts. This liturgy is a major element of both the morning and evening services.

SHEMINI ATZERET: A Hebrew phrase that roughly translates to "the Eighth Day of Assembly." It is the name of the festival that follows immediately after **Hoshannah Rabbah,** which is the last day of **Sukkot.** For all intents and purposes, Shemini Atzeret is seen as one of the concluding days of Sukkot.

SHEVA BERAKHOT: A Hebrew phrase that means "seven blessings." It refers to the blessings that are recited at the conclusion of the wedding ceremony, and in traditional communities, at the conclusion of the festive meal that follows the ceremony.

SHEVAT: The fifth month of the Jewish calendar; it usually falls sometime in January or February. The fifteenth of Shevat is **Tu Bi-Shevat,** celebrated as the New Year of the Trees.

SHIVA: A Hebrew word that means "seven"; it refers to the seven days of mourning for a relative (sibling, parent, child, or spouse) that begin on the day of the burial. During this time, traditional Jews remain in their houses, cover mirrors, sit on hard low chairs, and observe a variety of other mourning-related restrictions.

SHIVA ASAR BE-TAMMUZ: The seventeenth day of the Hebrew month of **Tammuz,** marked as a minor fast day commemorating the day in 70 C.E. on which the Romans breached the walls of Jerusalem.

SHOAH: A Hebrew word meaning "calamity" or "devastation." It is the term many Jews use for the Nazi Holocaust.

SHOFAR: The ram's horn that is sounded in the synagogue on the two days of **Rosh Ha-Shannah** and at the conclusion of **Yom Kippur** services. In traditional communities it is also sounded throughout the month of **Elul.**

SHUL: A Yiddish word, related to the word for "school," that means synagogue.

SHULCHAN ARUKH: A Hebrew phrase that literally means "a set table," it is also the name of Judaism's classic code of Jewish law, edited by Rabbi Joseph Karo and published in 1565.

SIDDUR: A Hebrew word meaning "order," it is also the term for the Jewish prayer book, containing the daily and Sabbath liturgies.

SIMCHAT BAT: The "celebration of a daughter"—the phrase refers to the modern naming ceremonies that are being created to celebrate the birth of a girl. Also referred to as a **berit bat.**

SIMCHAT TORAH: The holiday that celebrates the Jewish people's study of Torah. The annual cycle of reading the Torah is completed on this day, and a new cycle is begun. Simchat Torah follows **Shemini Atzeret** in the Diaspora; in Israel, it is celebrated on the same day as Shemini Atzeret.

SIVVAN: The ninth month of the Jewish calendar; it usually falls sometime in May or June. **Shavu'ot,** the holiday celebrating the receiving of the Torah at **Mount Sinai,** is celebrated during this month.

SOFER: A Hebrew word that means "scribe," referring to the person who writes a **Torah** scroll, a *mezuzah,* or a *get* (a Jewish document of divorce).

SUFGANIYOT: Jelly-filled doughnuts eaten during **Hanukkah.**

SUKKAH: A temporary boothlike structure built after **Yom Kippur** for use during the holiday of **Sukkot.** The *sukkah* symbolizes the booths in which the Israelites lived during their forty years in the desert.

TA'ANIT ESTHER: A Hebrew phrase meaning "the Fast of Esther." This fast falls on the day preceding **Purim.** The fast commemorates Queen Esther's having asked the Jews of Persia to fast on her behalf when she went to inform the king of Haman's plan to kill the Jews.

TACHRICHIN: The Hebrew word for the white burial shrouds in which Jews are traditionally laid to rest.

TALLIS/TALLIT/TALLITOT: A prayer shawl, which has *tzitzit* attached to its four corners. In many traditional communities, only married men wear a *tallit.* In more liberal communities, all men (and even some women) wear them. *Tallis* is the common European pronunciation. *Tallit* is the Israeli pronunciation, and *tallitot* is the plural.

TALMUD: A Hebrew word meaning "teaching" that is generally used to refer to the Babylonian Talmud, Judaism's greatest compendium of legal and ethical teachings, compiled between approximately the second and sixth centuries C.E. Another Talmud, the **Palestinian Talmud,** was produced by the rabbis of Palestine between the second and fifth centuries. When the word "Talmud" is used alone, however, the reference is almost always to the Babylonian Talmud.

TAMMUZ: The tenth month of the Jewish calendar, which usually falls sometime in June or July. The fast of the seventeenth of Tammuz commemorates the day the Romans breached the walls of Jerusalem in 70 C.E.

TASHLICH: A Hebrew word taken from the verb "to cast out," it refers to a ceremony during **Rosh Ha-Shannah** in which Jews go to a natural body of moving water and symbolically cast their sins onto the water.

TEFILLIN: An Aramaic word used to refer to phylacteries, the black leather boxes and straps that contain biblical passages inscribed on parchment that are worn on the forehead and arm during morning prayer.

TEVET: The fourth month of the Jewish calendar, corresponding to the month of December or January. The fast of the Tenth of Tevet falls during this month.

TISCH: See Chassan's Tisch.

TISHA B'AV: The Ninth of Av—a day of fasting that commemorates the destruction of the two Temples in Jerusalem as well as a few other tragedies that befell the Jewish people.

TISHREI: The first month of the Jewish calendar; it usually falls in September. The holidays celebrated in Tishrei are **Rosh Ha-Shannah,** the Fast of Gedaliah, **Yom Kippur, Sukkot,** and **Simchat Torah.**

TORAH: A Hebrew word that means "teaching," it commonly refers to the Five Books of Moses, or the Pentateuch. These are the first five books of the Hebrew Bible.

TU BI-SHEVAT: "The fifteenth of Shevat," celebrated as the New Year of the Trees. Tu Bi-Shevat usually falls in mid-January.

TZEDAKAH: A Hebrew word that means "righteousness" or "justice." It is the term commonly used for the giving of charity.

TZITZIT: The specially knotted fringes worn on the four corners of the *tallit* in fulfillment of the biblical command in Numbers 15:39. This term also refers to the undergarment worn by traditional Jewish men that has the same knots attached.

TZOM GEDALIAH: The "Fast of Gedaliah"—it usually takes place the day after **Rosh Ha-Shannah.** It commemorates the assassination of a ruler named Gedaliah by a fellow Jew. Because of its historical relevance, some contemporary Jews use the day to memorialize Yitzhak Rabin, the Israeli prime minister who was murdered by a Jew.

USHPIZIN: An Aramaic word that means "guests." It often refers to the custom on the holiday of **Sukkot** to invite "personalities" from Jewish history to join the meal in the *sukkah.* One guest is invited each night. The traditional order is Abraham, Isaac, Jacob, Moses, Aaron, Joseph, and King David.

YAHRZEIT: The Yiddish term that refers to the anniversary of someone's death, observed according to the Hebrew calendar.

YAMIM NORA'IM: See High Holidays.

YARMULKE: See *kippah.*

YICHUD: A Hebrew word that means "alone," referring to the time immediately after the Jewish wedding ceremony in which the couple is alone together before greeting all their guests.

YOM HA-ATZMA'UT: Israel Independence Day, commemorating the dec-

GLOSSARY OF TERMS AND NAMES

laration of the State of Israel on May 14, 1948, corresponding to the fifth of Iyyar in the Jewish calendar.

YOM HA-SHOAH: Shoah Remembrance Day, observed on the twenty-seventh day of Nissan. It usually falls between mid-April and early May.

YOM HA-ZIKKARON: Day of Remembrance, a day set aside to recall Israeli soldiers killed in the line of duty since the formation of the State. Yom Ha-Zikkaron falls on the day before Yom Ha-Atzma'ut.

YOM KIPPUR: A Hebrew phrase that means "Day of Atonement." It refers to the Jewish holiday that falls the week after Rosh Ha-Shannah and is commonly considered the holiest day of the year. On this day, Jews repent their sins and seek the strength to live better lives during the coming year.

YOM TOV: A Hebrew phrase that literally means "good day" but that now refers to a holiday. Yom Tov is the portion of the holiday in which work is not permitted; the laws of Yom Tov are very similar to the laws of Shabbat, though not identical.

YOM YERUSHALAYIM: "Jerusalem Day," declared as a holiday after the Six-Day War in 1967, as a celebration of the reunification of Jerusalem. It falls on the twenty-fifth of Iyyar, about three weeks after Israel Independence Day.

ZEMIROT: A Hebrew word meaning "songs" that refers to the special songs written primarily for Shabbat, commonly sung at Friday night dinner and Shabbat afternoon lunch at the table.

ZIONIST: A supporter of the Jewish national movement that advocated the formation of the Jewish state. Today the term is used loosely to mean a lover or supporter of Israel.

SUGGESTIONS FOR FURTHER EXPLORATION

Throughout this book we've been suggesting that an important part of being a thoughtful, passionate, and creative Jewish parent is to be on our own Jewish journey. Our passion for Jewish life, expressed in our own study, our own exploration, and our own curiosity will teach our children a great deal, perhaps more than words will.

This book has touched on a wide variety of topics and issues in Jewish life, all of which can be explored much more fully than space here allowed. Below, organized by chapter, you'll find suggestions of books, software, Web sites, and more designed to help you learn more about many of the topics we've touched on throughout these pages.

Chapter 1: Yes, You Can Do This!

Chapter 2: How to Use This Book

Here are some general books on Jewish life and Jewish parenting to get you started. Most of these are classics; you should be able to find them in almost any Jewish library, and you may want to add them to your own.

Cowan, Paul, *An Orphan in History: Retrieving a Jewish Legacy* (Garden City, N.Y.: Doubleday, 1982). An account of Cowan's odyssey as he rediscovers his Jewish roots and finds new religious meaning and energy in a Judaism he had never taken seriously. An eminently readable and deeply compelling personal statement.

Donin, Hayim Halevy, *To Raise a Jewish Child: A Guide for Parents* (New York: Basic Books, Inc., 1977). This is one of the best-known parenting books on the market. A bit dated (it's over twenty years old), it still has a wealth of good advice.

Steinberg, Milton, *Basic Judaism* (New York: Harcourt, Brace, Jovanovich, 1947). Probably the finest statement on the essence of Judaism, this very brief and readable volume has an excellent section on God.

Strassfeld, Michael, and Sharon Strassfeld, *The Jewish Catalogue: Volumes I, II and III* (Philadelphia: Jewish Publication Society, 1973, 1976, and 1980).

Products of the 1960s revival in Jewish spirituality, these paperback volumes have become classics. They contain excellent introductions to countless Jewish rituals, combining humor, wisdom, and much practical advice. Though slightly dated stylistically, they remain excellent both for reference and for getting started in Jewish ritual life. These are classics that transformed the world of Jewish books. Take a look!

www.jewishparenting.com Check out this excellent Web site. It's one of the very best around, getting better all the time. It's got columns and feature just like a regular magazine, a personals section, and more. You can also subscribe; you'll find the place to do that on the bottom of the home page.

Chapter 3: "Jewish Parenting 101"—Immersion, Memories, and Identity

Chapter 4: Using Jewish Life and Holidays to Create a Rhythm for Time
Becker, Ernst, *The Denial of Death* (New York: Free Press, 1977). This is not a book about parenting, or about Judaism. But it won a Pulitzer Prize and deals with the question of how our knowing that we're going to die affects us. In that regard, it's related to much of what we've talked about in this chapter. It's not easy reading, but it's a classic, and has fascinating insights peppered throughout.

Complete Artscroll Siddur, The (New York: Mesorah Publications, 1984). A prayer book produced by the Orthodox community, this edition contains the full text of almost all major Jewish rituals, and a very literal translation for those who wish to study the text in detail. If you want to see the other publications available through Artscroll, check out their Web site at *www.artscroll.com.*

Hammer, Reuven, *Entering Jewish Prayer* (New York: Schocken Books, 1994). The newest full-volume introduction to the structure of the service and its spiritual content. A very thoughtful and sensitive introduction to the world of Jewish prayer, one that you might want to look at as you rethink the world of prayer and the role it can play in your family's life.

Gordis, Daniel, *God Was Not in the Fire: The Search for a Spiritual Judaism* (New York: Scribner, 1995). A discussion of the ways in which Jewish life gives expression to our spiritual and most personal yearnings. It examines Judaism's impact on our inner lives and spiritual selves, and has sections that address the role of Jewish life and holidays in sanctifying time.

www.jewishmusic.com/dfr.htm This is the Debbie Friedman home page. It's got all her works for sale and a phone number to find out about scheduling and appearance information.

www.tara.com: This Web site bills itself as the "very best in Jewish music," and it is, in fact, *very* comprehensive. If you've got a Real Audio player, you can actually listen to segments of many of the CDs they sell. They also sell videos and tapes, and have a good search engine for finding what you're looking for.

Chapter 5: The Space We Make for Feelings

Carter, Stephen L., *The Culture of Disbelief: How American Law and Politics Trivialize Religious Devotion* (New York: Anchor Books, 1994). This book is about neither parenting nor Judaism, but it's a fascinating—and pretty readable—discussion of how American culture is basically unreceptive to religious commitment. If you want to read something that will get you thinking about what we're "up against," this book is definitely a worthwhile read.

Gordis, Daniel, *God Was Not in the Fire: The Search for a Spiritual Judaism* (New York: Scribner, 1995). Some of the ideas we've discussed here about ritual and feeling are explored in much greater detail in this book.

Greenberg, Blu, *How to Run a Traditional Jewish Household* (Northvale, N.J.: Jason Aaronson, Inc., 1993). Greenberg writes both as a feminist and as an Orthodox Jew. This is one of the finest introductions to the many rituals that are part of Jewish home life, written with sensitivity, wisdom, and an inviting style. For an introduction to Jewish ritual, it's excellent.

Strassfeld, Michael, and Sharon Strassfeld, *The Jewish Catalogue: Volumes I, II and III* (Philadelphia: Jewish Publication Society, 1973, 1976, and 1980). There's really nothing better for an inviting and warm introduction to many of the rituals that make up Jewish life.

Chapter 6: Making Space for God

Donin, Hayim Halevy, *To Pray as a Jew: A Guide to the Prayerbook and the Synagogue Service* (New York: Basic Books, 1980). An excellent introduction to the structure and customs of Jewish prayer from a mainstream Orthodox perspective. Part of a series that includes *To Live as a Jew* and *To Raise a Jewish Child*.

Dorff, Elliot, *Knowing God* (Northvale, N.J.: Jason Aronson, Inc., 1992). A personal statement by one of Conservative Judaism's most important personalities, this volume is very accessible to the lay reader and does an excellent job of introducing the reader to Judaism's most important and enduring theological arguments.

Gordis, Robert, *A Faith for Moderns* (New York: Bloch Publishing Company, 1971). Somewhat dated, this volume remains one of the finest modern rationalist arguments for God and Judaism. For committed rationalists, the section on God will be very helpful.

Heschel, Abraham Joshua, *Man Is Not Alone: A Philosophy of Religion* (Philadelphia: Jewish Publication Society of America, 1951). Heschel was one of the most important Jewish thinkers of the twentieth century, and by far the most poetic. This book is not merely about spirituality; reading it is a spiritual experience.

Kushner, Harold, *When Bad Things Happen to Good People* (New York: Schocken Books, 1991). This is a classic, the book that first put Rabbi Kushner on the map. It's a best-seller among both Jewish and non-Jewish audiences, and offers a wonderfully warm and embracing view of God. Even if the theology of a God who's not all-powerful doesn't always speak to you, the book will.

————, *When Children Ask About God: A Guide for Parents Who Don't Always Have All the Answers* (New York: Schocken, 1985). Rabbi Kushner has been called "America's rabbi" with good reason. His books are marvelous, insightful, and entertaining. This is an important addition, particularly good for parents trying to figure out how to talk to their kids about God.

Miles, Jack, *God: A Biography* (New York: Vintage Books, 1996). It sounds strange that anyone would write a biography of God, but that's what Jack Miles did. He won the Pulitzer for it, so you know it's pretty creative. In fact, it's better than that. Work your way through it, and you'll never see the Bible in quite the same way again.

Wolpe, David, *The Healer of Shattered Hearts* (New York: Penguin Books, 1991). If Jewish parenting is also about beginning our own journey into the world of Judaism and spirituality, there's no better place to start. Wolpe's focus may be the way God "heals shattered hearts," but the book is really about more than that. It will introduce you to a whole new way of thinking about God and Jewish life, one that you can then to transmit to your kids.

————, *Teaching Your Children About God: A Modern Jewish Approach* (New York: Harper Perennial, 1995). Wolpe is one of contemporary America's most moving Jewish writers; all of his books are well worth reading. This one is specifically about our topic.

Chapter 7: The Wonder of Shabbat

Gordis, Daniel, *God Was Not in the Fire: The Search for a Spiritual Judaism* (New York: Scribner, 1995). A discussion of the ways in which Jewish life gives expression to our spiritual and most personal yearnings. It examines Judaism's impact on our inner lives and spiritual selves.

Greenberg, Blu, *How to Run a Traditional Jewish Household* (Northvale, N.J.: Jason Aaronson, Inc., 1993). Greenberg writes both as a feminist and as an Orthodox Jew. The introduction to Shabbat in this book is a great hands-on way to get started.

Greenberg, Irving, *The Jewish Way: Living the Holidays* (New York: Simon and Schuster, 1988). While there are quite a number of "how to" books about the Jewish holidays, none comes close to this one in explaining in thoughtful and sophisticated language the meaning behind them and the spiritual beauty of the Jewish calendar year.

Heschel, Abraham Joshua, *The Sabbath: Its Meaning for Modern Man* (New York: Farrar, Straus and Giroux, Inc., 1951). A classic, this brief book is the most poetic statement about the meaning of Shabbat written in the modern period. The beauty of its imagery consistently moves both newcomers to Jewish ritual and those who have long participated in it.

Ives, Robert, *Shabbat and Festival Shiron* (Beverly Hills, Calif.: Robert Ives, 1992). This small book contains the full text—in Hebrew, English, and transliterations—of the prayers and songs for the Shabbat table. Its brief explanations are also very helpful, especially for newcomers to the Shabbat traditions.

Wolfson, Ronald, *The Art of Jewish Living: The Shabbat Seder* (Woodstock, Vt.: Jewish Lights Publishing, 1996). Wolfson's books are the best of the "how-to" genre on those holidays and life cycle events he has covered. They are highly readable, accurate, and provide an excellent introduction for people interested in learning how to participate in these various rituals. Wolfson also has produced a companion guide to the *Shabbat Seder,* describing the blessings, giving transliterations, etc.

Chapter 8: "Why Do We Have To?"

Feldman, David M., *Birth Control in Jewish Law: Marital Relations, Contraception and Abortion as Set Forth in the Classic Texts of Jewish Law* (New York: New York University Press, 1968). If you're wondering what a book on birth control is doing in this section, that's understandable! But the reason is that the Introduction to this book is an excellent general discussion of how Jewish law works. For a bit of history and an idea of what the Jewish legal process is all about, this is a great place to start.

Gordis, Daniel, *God Was Not in the Fire: The Search for a Spiritual Judaism* (New York: Scribner, 1995). This book is mentioned again because it has a section on the importance of *halakhah,* or Jewish law and standards, as a key to the Jewish spiritual experience.

———, *Does the World Need the Jews?* (New York: Scribner, 1997). A discussion of whether the Jews should still be seen as the "chosen people," this book has a chapter on the centrality of laws and rules for the Jews' uniqueness today.

Chapter 9: Rosh Chodesh and the "Jewish Moon"

We've included a longer list than usual for this section, because there are so many different perspectives to present and discuss. Yet even this list is far from exhaustive. Check out a good Jewish library, or one of the on-line bookstores, or a good bookstore in town, and you'll find much that isn't here. All of these are well known and well worth knowing about.

Adelman, Penina V., *Miriam's Well: Rituals for Jewish Women Around the Year* (Fresh Meadows, N.Y.: Biblio Press, 1986). A creative and fresh look at women's rituals for New Year, Rosh Chodesh, pregnancy and birth, menopause, menstruation, fertility and infertility—all organized around the yearly cycle of months.

Adler, Rachel, *Engendering Judaism: An Inclusive Theology and Ethics* (Philadelphia: Jewish Publication Society, 1998). Adler's career has been a fascinating one to watch. She wrote a much-discussed article in the first of the *Jewish Catalogues* defending the traditional use of the *mikvah,* and gradually became more disenchanted with the tradition. This book is her finest work yet—a major challenge to men and women to take seriously the ways in which the tradition still needs to make room for women.

Berkovits, Eliezer, *Jewish Women in Time and Torah* (Hoboken, N.J.: Ktav Publishing House, Inc., 1990). Berkovits was an Orthodox rabbi, but radical in many ways. In the early part of the book, he basically intimates that the tradition does not even treat women as Jews! A provocative and informative book, though on the serious side.

Biale, Rachel, *Women and Jewish Law: An Exploration of Women's Issues in Halakhic Sources* (New York: Schocken Books, 1984). For readers interested in a discussion of Judaism and feminism, this is an important volume. Biale is very critical of some of Judaism's traditional stances. Even those who disagree will find her discussion thoughtful and her collections of original sources extremely useful.

Fishman, Sylvia Barack, *A Breath of Life: Feminism in the American Jewish Community* (New York: The Free Press, 1993). Offers a picture of the changing lives of Jewish women in the last decade of the twentieth century. Discusses feminism, marriage, parenthood, sexual and gender roles, prayer, education, and the tension between Judaism and feminism.

Greenberg, Blu, *On Women and Judaism: A View from Tradition* (Philadelphia: Jewish Publication Society, 1983). A wonderful book on feminism and Judaism written from the perspective of the Orthodox community. Readers may be surprised to see how committed to feminism a noted Orthodox figure like Blu Greenberg can be.

Heschel, Susanna, *On Being a Jewish Feminist* (New York: Schocken Books, 1983). The daughter of the famed philosopher Abraham Joshua Heschel, Susanna Heschel is an accomplished scholar in her own right. This collection of essays, a wonderful introduction to many of the basic issues that Jewish feminists confront, is now a classic.

Koltun, Elizabeth, ed., *The Jewish Woman: New Perspectives* (New York: Schocken Books, 1976). Written by men and women, this book deals with life cycle and new rituals, women in Jewish law, models from our past, Jewish women in modern society, and women in Jewish literature.

Ochs, Vanessa L., *Words on Fire: One Woman's Journey into the Sacred* (San Diego: Harcourt, Brace, Jovanovich, Inc., 1990). An insightful and self-aware account of an American woman's first serious encounter with the study of Jewish text in Jerusalem. Of interest not only to women concerned with a uniquely female approach to these texts, but to anyone curious about the power the traditional world of "learning" has for its adherents.

Orenstein, Debra, *Life Cycles: Jewish Women on Life Passages and Personal Milestones* (Woodstock, Vt.: Jewish Lights Publishing, 1994). Orenstein is a Conservative rabbi, but has edited a book that reflects the views of women from all sectors of the Jewish community. The book contains sections on pregnancy, childbirth, infertility, naming, adolescence, being single, coming out for lesbians, marriage, divorce, intermarriage, conversion, parenting, menopause, aging, death, and mourning; personal narratives, prayers, rituals.

Plaskow, Judith, *Standing Again at Sinai: Judaism from a Feminist Perspective* (San Francisco: HarperSanFrancisco, 1991). A classic feminist critique of the Jewish tradition, Plaskow really ought to be read by men and women. The basic sections of her book are those on Torah, Community, God, sexuality, and the repair of the world.

Schneider, Susan Weidman, *Jewish and Female: A Guide and Sourcebook for Today's Jewish Woman* (New York: Simon and Schuster, 1984). Written by the editor of *Lillith*, an important women's magazine, this volume explores issues such as the calendar, access to Jewish study, sexuality and reproduction, family relationships, marriage, divorce, and power structures in the Jewish community.

Umansky, Ellen M., and Dianne Ashton, ed., *Four Centuries of Jewish Women's Spirituality: A Sourcebook* (Boston: Beacon Press, 1992). An interesting approach in that it deals not only with the current issues that women face; this chronological treatment deals with all the issues of infertility, marriage, mourning, menopause, etc. It presents the works of various writers, also of varying quality, but makes for a very interesting collection.

Weiss, Avraham, *Women at Prayer* (Hoboken, N.J.: Ktav Publishing House, Inc., 1990). A great way to see a liberally inclined Orthodox rabbi discuss the roles of women in Orthodoxy. Weiss offers excellent explanations of the reasons behind the limitations on women's roles and explores possible expansions of those roles within the Orthodox community.

Wolowelsky, Joel B., *Women, Jewish Law and Modernity: New Opportunities in a Post Feminist Age* (Hoboken, N.J.: Ktav Publishing House, Inc., 1997). This book is written from a traditional Orthodox perspective, and implicitly argues that some of the women's movement was a "tempest in a teapot." Many readers may or may not agree, but Wolowelsky's is an adept attempt to preserve Orthodox Jewish tradition while taking the needs and claims of contemporary women seriously.

Chapter 10: "Don't Try This Alone"
As our discussion of the "Jewish global village" has touched on virtually every dimension of Jewish life, it's obvious that we can give only a few suggestions for all those many topics. Many of the issues in this chapter are covered in readings suggested elsewhere in this list. What follow here are some of the wonderful resources that might not have made it into other parts of the list.

Donin, Hayim Halevy, *To Raise a Jewish Child: A Guide for Parents* (New York: Basic Books, Inc., 1977). We mentioned this book above, but we do so again because of its excellent section on picking a school. Donin's advice on how to go about this should be taken very seriously.

Halkin, Hillel, *Letters to an American Jewish Friend: A Zionist's Polemic* (Philadelphia: Jewish Publication Society of America, 1977). Halkin is certainly correct when he calls his book a "polemic," but it is also a classic polemic. A series of "letters" from a hypothetical American-turned-Israeli to a friend still in America, it reflects the classic arguments about why Jewish life in Israel is the only real authentic option for Jews. The last twenty years have complicated the issue, and Halkin's book does not address many of the responses that American Jews might make today. Still, its passion is compelling. This is a wonderful place to begin for readers interested in thinking more about the place of Israel in Jewish life.

Hartman, David, *Conflicting Visions: Spiritual Possibilities of Modern Israel* (New York: Schocken Books, 1990). It took the tragic assassination of Yitzchak Rabin to bring many of the tensions of Israeli life to the attention of American Jews. But Hartman, one of Israel's most interesting philosophers, wrote this work long before Rabin was murdered. Hartman, a committed Zionist, is also a moderate, and in this book he explores Israel's condition and some of its spiritual implications.

Levin, Michael, *The Guide to the Jewish Internet* (San Francisco: No Starch Press, 1996). The Jewish Internet has become more complex than you might imagine. There are literally hundreds, if not thousands, of Jewish sites on the Web. Take a special look at this volume, which includes sections on such topics as archaeology, chat rooms, colleges and universities, various movements and denominations, on-line encyclopedias, Israel, gays and lesbians, music, software, video and film, etc. Note that these sites may change; a good search tool will help you find them anyhow.

Protexsia Plus+, a "concierge" for making arrangements for trips to Israel. Regular tours can be booked through travel agents, of course, but if you're interested in something a little more tailored to your family or your trip, it's very helpful to have someone on the inside who knows about setting these trips up. A number of people do this, but we've had a great experience with this group, which can be reached at *protexsia@netmedia.net.il.* Their Web site is *www.virtual.co.il/travel/protexsia/index.htm.* Phone number in Israel is (from the United States) 011-972-2-993-8120.

For a listing of software related to Jewish life, there are two places in particular to look. One is Davka software, which produces a wide variety of both scholarly and child-oriented software. Their Web site is *www.davka.com,* and it conveniently lists the many different programs they sell. Many of the kids' programs are cute and inexpensive. Another great site for Jewish software is Torah Educational Software, which can be found at *www .jewishsoftware.com* (800-925-6853). They market a wide variety of products with some overlap. You can purchase products directly from their Web site, via a secure server. For those who own the now very popular Palm Pilot by 3COM, check out *www.penticon.com,* which makes a Hebrew keyboard for the Pilot, as well as a wonderful calendar program that gives you Hebrew dates, Jewish holidays, Torah reading portions, and much more right on the screen. They also have a great program called "Omer" for counting the Omer on your Palm Pilot. Another great spot is the Jewish Communications Network, at *www.jcn18.com/,* which is also worth checking out. See additional items listed in the holiday section below.

We also mentioned that some synagogues have Web sites. A few are really terrific and give you a great idea of what that congregation is all about. If you're interested in seeing one of the best of these Web sites, take a look at *http://bethelsudbury.org/.* It's a wonderful Reform congregation, and will give you a sense of how much you can learn from a great synagogue Web site (of a great synagogue, by the way!). For a Web site that lists all the Reform congregations in the United States and provides a lot of information on Reform Judaism, see *http://www.uahc.org/* (Union of American Hebrew Congregations). For information on Reconstructionist synagogues, see *http://www.shamash.org/jrf/.* Conservative synagogues and information can be found at *www.uscj.org* (United Synagogue of Conservative Judaism). Orthodox congregations are listed under *www.ou.org* (the Orthodox Union).

One title that deserves special mention is the CD-ROM version of the *Encyclopedia Judaica,* produced by Judaica Multimedia. In addition to the full text of the printed version (though not the very popular calendar of the Index volume), the CD-ROM version adds sound, video clips, and more. It's the standard home Jewish reference, now improved in this new format. Unlike the printed version, this one is fully text searchable, which makes it even more useful than the print. This is great for families of all backgrounds, and a perfect "going to college" gift. It's available from Davka, Torah Education Software, and many other places. Their Web site is *www.ejudaica.com.*

Kids' software is also available from JeMM Productions, at *www.jemm.co.il.* Their U.S. ordering number is 800-871-0694. In addition to holiday titles, which we mention in the holiday chapter, they produce *Portrait of Israel,* a wonderful collection of photographs, sound clips and narration, a multimedia magazine called *JeMM Mutimedia Magazine,* and an excellent new program for college students that is available through their partners in this project, "Lights in Action." This new program tackles serious and compelling contemporary issues of interest to college students with a serious and knowledgeable Jewish angle. The Lights in Action Web site is at *www.lia.org.*

Want to check out Israeli society through its chat rooms? Hebrew obviously helps here, and you can find a Hebrew chat room at *http://walla.co.il.* If you don't have the Hebrew fonts to read some of the screen, there are links to sites from which you can download and then install the fonts.

Chapter 11: "Don't Know Much About History"

Cahill, Thomas, *The Gifts of the Jews* (New York: Doubleday, 1988). Cahill is not Jewish, but that only makes his book more fascinating. The question he looks at is what have the Jews contributed to civilization that the world would otherwise not have. A very engaging and interesting read.

Collins, Larry, and Dominique LaPierre, *O Jerusalem* (New York: Touchstone Books, 1998). A gripping and moving account of the battle for Jerusalem in 1948. Reading this book will give you a better sense than anything else of why Jerusalem ranks so high in Israeli's consciousness, and how a people can have a love affair with a city.

Funkenstein, Amos, *Perceptions of Jewish History* (Berkeley: University of California Press, 1993). Funkenstein's book is an implicit rebuttal of Yerushalmi's book (listed below). Both Funkenstein and Yerushalmi, giants in the field of Jewish history, are interested in the power of Jewish memory. This is an academic book, but is well worth reading despite the occasionally difficult sections.

Gilbert, Martin, *Israel: A History* (New York: William Morrow and Company, 1998). A wonderful, not too difficult, and incredibly complete history of the State of Israel. Gilbert is the preeminent historian of Israel these days;

his books of maps have made him very famous. This book is a terrific way to understand how Israel got to be the way it is.

Gordis, Daniel, *Does the World Need the Jews? Rethinking Chosenness and American Jewish Identity* (New York: Scribner, 1997). An argument that in order to become passionate about the Jewish future, we have to have a conception of what makes the Jews not only important but critical to the world. But at the same time, how do we argue that we're critical to the world without suggesting that we're better? This book is an argument that it can be done.

Hertzberg, Arthur, *Jews: The Essence and Character of a People* (San Francisco, HarperSanFrancisco, 1998). Similar to Cahill in its orientation, Hertzberg's book tries to answer the big questions, such as: What are the Jews all about? What makes the Jews genuinely different? A fascinating book from an intellectual giant.

Johnson, Paul, *A History of the Jews* (New York: Harper and Row, 1987). Though there are many one-volume histories of the Jews, this is among the most accessible. It is rather recent, and its non-Jewish author has a palpable awe for the accomplishments of Jews throughout history. For readers interested in a broad sense of who the Jews have been and what they have accomplished throughout their history, this is the place to begin.

Yerushalmi, Yosef Hayim, *Zakhor: Jewish History and Jewish Memory* (New York: Schocken Books, 1982). A scholarly but approachable analysis of how memory works in Jewish life. Very stimulating, though a little difficult. A classic for those interested in pursuing the issues of nostalgia and memory raised in this chapter.

Chapter 13: The Jewish Holiday Cycle

Collins, Larry, and Dominique LaPierre, *O Jerusalem* (New York: Touchstone Books, 1998). A gripping and moving account of the battle for Jerusalem in 1948. We mentioned this book above, but list it here again as a great way to give some meaning to Yom Yerushalayim, Jerusalem Reunification Day. Read this book that week, and your day will be transformed.

Goodman, Phillip, *The Rosh Ha-Shannah Anthology, The Yom Kippur Anthology, The Hanukkah Anthology, The Passover Anthology, The Purim Anthology, The Shavuot Anthology,* and *The Sukkot/Simhat Torah Anthology* (Philadelphia: Jewish Publication Society, 1980s and 1990s). These books are a tad dated by now, but they have a wealth of information, background, customs, rituals, songs, etc. They're classics in the literature on the Jewish holidays.

Greenberg, Irving, *The Jewish Way: Living the Holidays* (New York: Simon and Schuster, 1988). While there are quite a number of "how to" books about the Jewish holidays, none comes close to this one in explaining in thoughtful and sophisticated language the meaning behind them and the spiritual beauty of the Jewish calendar year.

Hammer, Reuven, *Entering the High Holy Days: A Guide to the Origins, Themes, and Prayers* (Philadelphia: Jewish Publication Society, 1998). A new and thoughtful introduction to the High Holiday liturgy, this is a great way to get prepared if you've always found those days off-putting or impenetrable.

Moss, David, *The Moss Haggadah* (Jerusalem: Bet Alpha Editions, 1990). This is not inexpensive (it lists for about $185), but if you're interested in beginning to collect beautiful editions of the Haggadah, this is *absolutely* the place to begin. Moss's explanations are powerful, his calligraphy stunning, and his creativity will leave you breathless. You probably won't want to use this at the table, but you will want to own it if you can. It's astounding.

Strassfeld, Michael, *The Jewish Holidays: A Guide & Commentary* (New York: HarperCollins, 1985). A wonderfully informative, educational, and open-minded introduction to the holidays, their rituals, and their meaning. If you're looking for one introductory volume that's good for people of all levels, this might well be the book to get.

Waskow, Arthur, *Seasons of Our Joy: A Celebration of Modern Jewish Renewal* (New York: Bantam Books, 1982). Self-described as a new-age guide to the Jewish holidays, this volume will give readers a sense of the many different ent ways the Jewish holidays can be interpreted. This is a more creative, "new age–like" interpretation of the holidays than that offered in some of the other books listed here. If that's your bent, then this is a book you'll cherish.

Wolfson, Ronald, *The Passover Seder* (1988) and *Hanukah* (1990) (New York: The Federation of Jewish Men's Clubs and the University of Judaism). Wolfson's books are the best of the "how-to" genre on those holidays and life cycle events he has covered. They are highly readable, accurate, and provide and are an excellent for people interested in learning how to participate in these various rituals.

Zion, Noam, and David Dishon, *A Different Night: The Family Participation Haggadah* (Jerusalem: Shalom Hartman Institute, 1997). If you're going to buy only one Haggadah, this is the one! It's a perfect way to transform your seder from a rote, boring experience to one that is invested with Jewish knowledge, exciting conversation, and deep sensitivity. With interesting content for adults and children alike, this is a wonderful addition to any library.

For a great software package with a perpetual Jewish calendar, you can log onto *http://users.aol.com/calmaven/* and check out "Hebrew calendar." It's an excellent program, very moderately priced.

The Artscroll series of prayer books and other explanatory texts is excellent. These are Orthodox prayer books, but have become very popular in all walks of Jewish life for their clear and informative explanations, instructions, and print. You can take a look at their entire line of publications at *www.artscroll.com.*

We already mentioned the JeMM CD-ROMs. Their holiday titles are fantastic, and kids love them. My kids play them for hours on end. Check out *The Interactive Haggadah, Who Stole Hanukkah,* and an upcoming title on Purim. Their Web site is *www.jemm.co.il.*

Chapter 14: The Jewish Life Cycle
There are literally dozens, probably hundreds, of contemporary books that address topics in the Jewish life cycle. When you add in the birth books, wedding books, and such, there's too much to include here in any meaningful way. We've tried to include some of the standard classics, as well as some titles off the beaten track that you might not have come across. But for most things, there's nothing as valuable as scanning the shelves in a good library, or browsing on-line in one of the larger on-line booksellers. For now, here are some starters:

Bulka, Reuven P., *Jewish Divorce Ethics: The Right Way to Say Goodbye* (Ogdensburg, N.Y.: Ivy League Press, 1992). Traditional. Mixture of psychology and Jewish law.
————, *Jewish Marriage: A Halakhic Ethic* (Hoboken, N.J.: Ktav Publishing House, Inc., 1986). Traditional; discusses love, sexuality, etc.
Cardin, Nina Beth, *Out of the Depths I Call to You: A Book of Prayers for the Married Jewish Woman* (New York: Jason Aronson, 1995). Originally written in Italian, these prayers have been translated and commented upon by Cardin, a feminist and Conservative rabbi.
————, *Tears of Sorrow, Seeds of Hope; A Spiritual Companion for Dealing with Infertility and Pregnancy Loss* (Woodstock, Vt.: Jewish Lights Publishers, 1999). Cardin is a capable writer and editor, a committed feminist, and a deeply knowledgeable Jew. Her book was not available when this list was compiled, but if her previous work is any indication, this will be well worth looking at, particularly for people going through these traumas.
Feldman, David M., *Birth Control in Jewish Law: Marital Relations, Contraception and Abortion as Set Forth in the Classic Texts of Jewish Law* (New York: New York University Press, 1968). For issues related to the tradition's take on sexuality and birth control, this is the classic academic book. Not easy reading, by any means, but perfect for those interested in the development of Jewish law on the subject.

Orenstein, Debra, *Life Cycles: Jewish Women on Life Passages and Personal Milestones* (Woodstock, Vt.: Jewish Lights Publishing, 1994). We mentioned this book in the section on women's issues, but repeat it here because so many of the chapters are related to life cycle events. One additional volume has been published, and a third is planned.

Geffen, Rella, *Celebration and Renewal: Rites of Passage in Judaism* (Philadelphia: Jewish Publication Society, 1993). An edited collection with articles on birth, marriage, divorce, etc. A nice introduction to the life cycle events and their meaning in Jewish life.

Gordis, Daniel, *Does the World Need the Jews? Rethinking Chosenness and American Jewish Identity* (New York: Scribner, 1997). We mentioned this volume earlier, but mention it again as a place to read a new "twist" on the meaning of the *mezuzah* in Jewish life, at times of inaugurating our own new Jewish homes, or those of our kids.

Kolatch, Alfred J., *The Complete Dictionary of English and Hebrew First Names* (New York: Jonathan David Publishers, 1984). The classic baby name book, though there are also others on the market. You might want to check out *A Dictionary of Jewish Names and Their History* by Benzion C. Kaganoff (New York: Jason Aronson, 1996). You can log onto *www.amazon.com* and look for keywords like "Jewish" and "name" and see the list of things that turns up.

Kushner, Harold, *When Children Ask About God: A Guide for Parents Who Don't Always Have All the Answers* (New York: Schocken Books, 1985). A wonderful book particularly if tragedy should strike and parents need to figure out how to talk about this with their children.

Salkin, Jeffrey, *Putting God Back on the Guest List: How to Reclaim the Meaning of Your Child's Bar or Bat Mitzvah* (Jewish Lights, 1996). A wonderful book about making the Bar and Bat Mitzvah genuinely religious and spiritual. Salkin also wrote a companion volume for kids.

Silverstein, Alan, *It All Begins with a Date: Jewish Concerns on Intermarriage* and *Preserving Jewishness in Your Family—After an Intermarriage Has Occurred* (New York: Jason Aronson, 1995). Silverstein is a conservative rabbi; these books reflect a sensitive and thoughtful balance of the demands of Jewish tradition and the realities of contemporary American Jewish Life.

Wolfson, Ronald, *A Time to Mourn, A Time to Comfort* (Woodstock, Vt.: Jewish Lights Publishing, 1996). Wolfson's books are the best of the "how-to" genre on those holidays and life cycle events he has covered. They are highly readable, accurate, and provide an excellent introduction for people interested in learning how to participate in these various rituals.

For information on specific rituals, some of the best sources are the *Artscroll Siddur* (mentioned elsewhere in this chapter, and see *www.artscroll.com*),

Isaac Klein's *A Guide to Jewish Religious Practice* (New York: Jewish Publication Society, 1979), and Michael and Sharon Strassfeld's *Jewish Catalogues* (also mentioned earlier).

Chapter 15: Of Models, Mermaids, and Music

Artson, Bradley Shavit, *It's a Mitzvah: Step by Step to Jewish Living* (New York: Behrman House and the Rabbinical Assembly, 1995). After finishing this book, readers may want to know how to begin to make Jewish tradition and commitments a greater part of their life. Artson's book is the latest contribution to this genre. It is a superb, highly accessible book, with creative ideas and more suggestions of where to turn for further learning.

Prager, Dennis, and Joseph Telushkin, *Nine Questions People Ask About Judaism* (New York: Simon and Schuster, 1981). There is no one more committed to the premise that Jews have a message to the world than Dennis Prager. Central to Prager's and Telushkin's argument is Judaism's introduction to the world of ethnical monotheism.

Telushkin, Joseph, *Jewish Literacy* (New York: William Morrow and Company, Inc., 1991). This book contains 346 very brief chapters that trace Jewish history and ideas from the very beginning to the present. People interested in building a solid Jewish knowledge base appreciate the brevity of the chapters, allowing the reader to work through several pages each day without stopping in the middle of a chapter. The superb index also allows the book to serve as a mini-encyclopedia of Jewish life.

Wolpe, David, *Why Be Jewish?* (New York: Holt, 1995). In an exceedingly brief and readable essay, Wolpe manages to make a very poetic and thoughtful case for Jewish belonging. Wolpe's characteristic poetic style is no less evident here than in his other wonderful books.

For some other great Web sites, check out the *Jerusalem Post* Internet edition at *www.jpost.co.il*, or the English version of the Israeli daily *Ha-Aretz* at *http://www3.haaretz.co.il/eng/htmls.1 1.htm*. You can see the Web site for the once Yiddish and now English paper, *The Forward*, at *www.forward .com*. You can't really see the text of the paper here, but it will tell you a bit about the paper, and give you some subscription information.

At the beginning of this book we mentioned *www.jewishparenting.com*, but it's worth mentioning again—it's a great site. To start building a great Jewish library, check out the offerings of the Jewish Publication Society, which is still the premier publisher of Judaica in the United States.

Chapter 16: A Quick Bird's-Eye View of Jewish History

Gribetz, Judah, Edward L. Greenstein, and Regina Stein, *The Timetables of Jewish History: A Chronology of the Most Important People and Events in Jewish History* (New York: Simon and Schuster, 1993). A wonderful book.

Kind of a "coffee-table book" in style, it's a tabular look at Jewish history throughout the ages. Makes for hours upon hours of fascinating reading and page turning. It's technically out of print, but you can find it at various places. Don't forget that you can search for used and hard-to-find books on the Web, as well. Try *http://www.acses.com/i2b.htm* and *www.bibliofind.com*—two great places to start searching.

Encyclopedia Judaica, CD-ROM version. We mentioned this above, but it deserves special mention here, as well, because of its "TimeLine" feature. There's a chronological bar from 2000 B.C.E. through 2000 C.E., and you simply drag the pointer across the bar to see events in three different categories: Jewish Culture, Jewish History, and General History. You can also enter any term or person into a search bar, and the timeline will move to the period in which that event took place or that person lived. It's a wonderful tool that will fascinate kids as well as adults for hours on end.

INDEX

ABOUT THE AUTHOR

DANIEL GORDIS teaches and lectures widely across the United States and beyond. A rabbi and professor, he is the author of two previous books, *God Was Not in the Fire: The Search for a Spiritual Judaism* and *Does the World Need the Jews?: Rethinking Chosenness and American Jewish Identity.* He and his wife are raising a daughter and two sons.